ARS UNA: SPECIES MILLE
GENERAL HISTORY OF ART

ART IN FRANCE

BY

LOUIS HOURTICQ

AGRÉGÉ DE L'UNIVERSITÉ

INSPECTOR OF FINE ARTS IN THE CITY OF PARIS

NEW YORK

CHARLES SCRIBNER'S SONS

PREFACE

CERTAIN kindly disposed *confrères* who have taken an interest in the following work have asked me now and then whether I intended to deal with French Art in fifty volumes or fifty pages. I have written a good deal less and a good deal more—too much or too little, it may be objected. Compared with works which exhaust the material and those which condense it into a few drops of elixir, this little book has but one merit—that of existing. For the art of our country has never been treated as a whole, save in treatises on universal art, where the French chapters appear in their due order, or in general histories of France, where the names of artists defile at the end of a volume, like baggage at the rear of a convoy. Why has it not been thought necessary to co-ordinate these different chapters, as has been done so efficiently and so frequently in the history of our politics and our literature?

It may be that the very variety of French Art invites to special studies rather than to general appreciations. It does not present that unity of character which is so striking in most other countries. In England, in Germany, in Italy, in Holland, in Spain, art reveals itself as the work of a single race, and even in some cases of a single century. In France, artistic continuity embraces very different styles, all equally original and sincere. No one would hesitate to say which has been the golden age of Greece, Italy, Spain, England or Flanders. In France, it is impossible to pronounce without scruple; each century, from Philip Augustus to our own day, has partisans.

The individuality of France is very ancient. It has been continually, and sometimes violently modified, but has very rarely shown signs of exhaustion. Art is distributed throughout its history, and has always been well adapted to its vicissitudes. It has not, as in other countries, expanded with that momentary exuberance which manifests the full vitality of the human plant and exhausts it. It reveals rather the changing forms of society than a fixed ethnical type. If there has not always been a French School, or in other words, a great family of artists and a sort of material kinship founded upon community of methods, there has always been a French Style, that is to say, a moral resemblance between works inspired by the same collective taste.

Art has known periods of magnificent expansion, the bloom and fruition of a race; but these have been for the most part brief and intermittent. France has had such periods; the years of the past are full of the work of a society which has always been able to fashion an adornment to suit its taste; our active civilization has never failed to supplement the repose of nature by its industry. Hence it is very difficult to include the art of France in a statical definition; the best that can be given is the very law of its development: its essence is that suppleness and fidelity with which it has always adapted itself to a society in perpetual process of reconstruction.

Above these minor variations, two great phases are easily discerned: the Christian, feudal, and communal France of the Middle Ages created Gothic Art as its form of expression; the rationalistic and strongly centralised France of modern times adopted the language of Classic Art. These opposite styles express the successive aspects of the same soul with equal sincerity. Yet they would seem mutually exclusive; the Classicists despise the Middle Ages, and the modern restorers of Gothic taste have not yet forgiven those who superseded it. A trustworthy book on French Art is only possible if its writer abandons these exclusive predilections; they are natural in artists who must either believe in the superiority of their ideal, or fall short of it; they are inexcusable in the historian, who misses his function altogether if he does not make the past more intelligible. Our sympathies should follow French taste in its successive tendencies. To sacrifice Notre Dame to Versailles, or Poussin to the Master of Moulins is to renounce one half of the French soul; our art, by its wealth and variety, invites its historian to show a supple intelligence and a catholic taste.

Is this French peculiarity enough to explain the lack of a general history of French Art? It should have also embarrassed the historians of French literature, but in that field there is no lack of general histories because literature is on our university programmes. On the other hand, there exists no history, good or bad, of our art because art with us is not a subject of official instruction. The universities do not love the plastic arts. They have never known anything but books. The walls of our ancient colleges have only heard the names of momuments and of artists, when Cicero or Quintilian happened to refer to Greek Art. To-day, when public instruction deals with everything, it continues from habit to ignore the fine arts —or not only from habit, but from deliberate purpose, for the Areopagi have decided that these subjects must not be allowed among the disciplinary courses adapted to forming the minds of young functionaries. Ignorance of art, which was only fostered by the force of tradition, has, since their decision, attained the dignity of a principle. Does academic austerity suspect in it some frivolous amusement and must we recognise in its defiance or its disdain a weakened form, placid, and as it were pedagogical, of the old theocratic hatred for images? Or, indeed, is it simply impossible to explain to people that a thing which they have never made use of can be useful? However this may be, time alone, as the generations succeed each other, can change the opinion of the university. Let us wait for the moment when the curiosity about art grows great enough to force its way over the walls of our schools.

Let us be just, however. The history of art is already established in the higher education. Doubtless it will spread from those summits down through all the schools, and we might indulge the fairest hopes if we did not have to fear a serious misunderstanding. Our higher education very naturally applies to the study of monuments of art the methods of learning and of criticism which are so satisfactory elsewhere. A late comer in the numerous family of historical sciences, the history of art wears the apparel of its older sisters. We could wish that it had garments made after its own measure, though not more comfortable. Nothing can be more legitimate than profound inquiry in order to acquire all possible certainty and exactitude. The biography of a sculptor, the history of a church, demand many and difficult researches. There is nothing more creditable than a thesis on painting full of sound learning, even if the author has never seen a picture. The outer phenomena of art are amply sufficient to occupy for centuries armies of scholars, and we must after all admire ascetics who are detained by scruples of accuracy in the libraries and the repositories of archives where science is created, far from the museums and the monuments, where there is always risk of surrender to sentiment. But is it really the history of art which should be taught? Should art furnish here material for special historical methods? Or, rather, should it not be accepted for itself, for the meaning embodied in the language of form and which our eyes must discover? In literature, the biographies of the authors will never cause their writings to be forgotten, for the reading and comment on good books are among the excellent traditions of our educational system. But in the plastic arts the corresponding habit is yet to be born. The day when the history of art should penetrate into our schools would not necessarily be that on which art began to be taught. The history of a book is one thing, the reading of it is another. That distinction does not interest our universities. There, learning is not utilitarian and would not be inconsolable if it gained no end at all.

But the confusion would be deplorable in our schools, where young minds should be nourished and not given stones for bread.

If intellectual education has for its object to put us in touch with the best thought of our ancestors, why neglect this easy way of introducing young Frenchmen to the France of olden times? How much reading and thinking is needed in order to evoke one of those impressions which are like the brief summary of a whole generation or society! The masterpieces of art arouse them at the first contact. Those silent tongues have a marvellous power of illuminating in a flash the obscure and profound regions which words describe without always revealing. Even when they have lost their religious or social usefulness, these ancient monuments hold a thousand reminders and an atmosphere of antiquity breathes from them. Life in leaving them has left them its fragrance.

But, above all, these works undoubtedly preserve the best that was in the past. In turning over our archives Michelet heard the confused wail of the generations. Political and social history practically tell only of human struggles. What else should they talk of? The nations that have a history are the ones who struggle to unmake and remake themselves. How can we help concluding that every period is only a difficult transition to a happier time? To any one who looks back, the road to the present appears cluttered with débris and the ruins which were really hearths and altars seem to us to have been merely obstacles along the route. Why not acknowledge that when it is not rendered tame by the idyllic spirit or pedagogic teaching, history too often rouses our pity or our indignation to leave us unalloyed sympathy with the past? Truth is strong food and we understand how to frail organisms it is almost poisonous. All these "dead who speak" enlist us in their struggle, or rather they reinforce our own quarrels with the hatred accumulated for centuries. Let us add to all the hate and sorrow which echo from the archives of the police, intrigue, the acid literature of memoirs or merely from the diary of official gossip, the luminous history which the plastic arts tell in their own way. These alone give us reasons for sympathising with the past and can put our spirits in harmony with it. Made from the best of humanity, these works unite all generations in the admiration which they arouse. We receive, if we merely bend affectionately over them, a little of the serene exaltation which they radiate.

Let us teach the way to know France through the monuments of her art. Let us listen to these witnesses: They are truthful ones and they make us know the past better because they make us love it; they give us a more profound knowledge of the centuries because they awaken our powers of love and of admiration, and they illuminate our annals by the reflection of their charm. Let us work with all our heart in order that the children of France may one day journey through the history of their country by that highway of beauty.

The function of handbooks such as these, which cannot pursue the phenomena of the artistic spirit into all its objective ramifications, must be to trace and explain those innate subjective characteristics which no fashion in external forms can wholly disguise. As we follow its evolution, we shall realise that the underlying character of French Art is no less persistent and apparent than that of other nations, and, in spite of those superficial variations which are so obvious, we shall recognise its essential unity.

LOUIS HOURTICQ.

Paris, 1911.

BIBLIOGRAPHICAL NOTICE

A survey of the bibliographical history of French Art would suffice in itself to show us what has been the special conception of art formed by successive generations. In the Middle Ages, when Art was exclusively the handmaid of Religion, texts contain only passing allusions to its monuments. After the Renaissance, it becomes more independent, and a special literature is devoted to it. Finally, in the nineteenth century, the century of history, not only contemporary art, but all its manifestations in the past, interested amateurs and scholars.

The most instructive of these works on French Art have been quoted at the end of each chapter to which they refer, arranged in the following order: original documents, general works, works on architecture, sculpture, painting, and the minor arts. Some, by reason of their extensive range, could not be connected with any special chapter. Such are:—

GENERAL WORKS

S. Reinach, *Apollo*, new edit., Paris, 1910; American ed., 1907.—C. Bayet, *Précis d'Histoire de l'Art*, new edit., Paris, 1908.—K. Woermann, *Geschichte der Kunst alle Zeiten und Völkern*, Leipzig, 1900-1905, 2 vols. have appeared.—X. Kraus, *Geschichte der christlichen Kunst*, Freiburg, 1896, 1897, 2 vols.—L. Courajod, *Leçons professées à l'école du Louvre*, Paris, 1899-1903, 3 vols.—A. Michel, *Histoire de l'Art*, published under the direction of A. Michel, Paris, 1905, 6 vols. have appeared.—The chapters by S. Rocheblave, in the *l'Histoire de la Littérature française*, published under the direction of Petit de Julleville and by A. Michel, in *l'Histoire de France*, published under the direction of Lavisse and Rambaud.—The chapters relating to Art in the History of France, published by Lavisse.—The works of S. Reinach, K. Woermann, and A. Michel quoted above contain important bibliographies.

DICTIONARIES.—REVIEWS.—BIBLIOGRAPHICAL INVENTORIES

Mémoires inédits sur la vie et les ouvrages des Membres de l'Académie, Paris, 1854, 2 vols.—P.-J. Mariette, *Abecedario*, Paris, 1851 et seq., 6 vols.—A. Jal, *Dictionnaire critique de biographie et d'histoire*, Paris, 1872.—L. Dussieux, *Les Artistes français à l'Etranger*, Paris, 3rd edit., 1876.—E. Bellier de la Chavignerie, *Dictionnaire général des Artistes de l'Ecole française*, Paris, 1882, 2 vols.

The principal periodicals to consult for French Art history are: *Les Annales archéologiques* of Didron, which no longer appear.—*La Revue archéologique*.—La *Gazette archéologique*.—Le *Bulletin monumental*.—La *Collection des Congrès archéologiques de France*.—La *Revue de l'Art chrétien*.—*Le Moyen Age*.—*Les Archives de l'art français* and *Nouvelles Archives de l'Art français* (an analytical Table is inserted in vol. xii. of the *Nouvelles Archives*).—Les *Réunions des Sociétés de Beaux-Arts des Départements*.—Les *Mémoires de la Société des Antiquaires*.—*Repertorium für Kunstwissenschaft.—Zeitschrift für christliche Kunst.—R.* de Lasteyrie and E. Lefèvre-Pontalis have undertaken: *Bibliographie général des travaux historiques et archéologiques publiés par les Sociétés savantes de France*, Paris, 1888.

La Revue universelle des Arts no longer appears, but the *Gazette des Beaux-Arts*, with its supplement: *la Chronique des Arts et de la Curiosité*, and the *Revue de l'Art ancien et moderne*, with its supplement: le *Bulletin de l'Art ancien et moderne*, succeed in interesting the general public in archæological research and art-history.

BIBLIOGRAPHICAL NOTICE

L'*Inventaire* (unfinished) *des richesses d'art de la France* and l'*Inventaire des richesses d'art de la Ville de Paris* contain catalogues of the works of art in civil and religious buildings.

The titles of publications which have been very frequently quoted have been abbreviated as follows: R. A. = *Revue archéologique*; B. M. = *Bulletin monumental*; A. A. F. = *Archives de l'Art français*; R. S. B. A. D. = *Réunion des Sociétés des Beaux-Arts des Départements*; G. B. A. = *Gazette des Beaux-Arts*; R. A. A. M. = *Revue de l'Art ancien et moderne*.

GENERAL WORKS ON THE HISTORY OF ARCHITECTURE

Viollet-le-Duc, *Dictionnaire de l'Architecture française*, 10 vols., Paris, 1854-1869.—Viollet-le-Duc, *Entretiens sur l'Architecture*, 2 vols., Paris, 1858-1872.—Planat, *Encyclopédie d'Architecture*, Paris.—W. Lübke, *Geschichte der Architektur*, Leipzig, 1886.—A. Choisy, *Histoire de l'Architecture*, Vol. II, Paris, 1900.—Lance, *Dictionnaire des Architectes de l'Ecole française*, 2 vols., Paris, 1872.—Ch. Bauchal, *Nouveau Dictionnaire des Architectes français*, Paris, 1887.—*Archives de la Commission des Monuments historiques*, Paris, 1855-1872, 4 vols.—*Archives de la Commission des Monuments historiques*, published by A. de Baudot and A. Perrault-Dabot, Paris, 1899 (in course of publication).

GENERAL WORKS ON THE HISTORY OF SCULPTURE

E. David, *Histoire de la Sculpture française*, Paris, 1853.—W. Lübke, *Geschichte der Plastik*, Paris, 1884.—L. Gonse, *La Sculpture française*, Paris, 1895.—St.-Lami, *Dictionnaire des Sculpteurs de l'Ecole française jusqu'à Louis XIV*, Paris, 1898.—L. Gonse, *Les Chefs-d'Œuvre des Musées de France: La Sculpture*, Paris, 1904.

GENERAL WORKS ON PAINTING

A. Siret, *Dictionnaire historique et raisonné des Peintres*, Paris, 1883, 2 vols.—Emeric David, *Histoire de la Peinture au Moyen Age*, Paris, 1863.—A. Champeaux, *Histoire de la Peinture décorative*, Paris, 1890.—Woltmann and Woermann, *Geschichte der Malerei*, 1879 et seq.—Ch. Blanc, *Histoire des Peintres, Ecole française*, Paris, 1862, 3 vols.—Paul Mantz, Luc-Olivier Merson, Henry Marcel, *La Peinture en France*, Paris (*Bibl. de l'Enseignement des Beaux-Arts*, 3 vols.).—L. Gonse, *Les Chefs-d'Œuvre des Musées de France, La Peinture*, Paris, 1900.—L. Hourticq, *Le Peinture des Origines au XVIe siècle*, Paris, 1908.

GENERAL WORKS ON THE MINOR ARTS

A. Dumesnil, *Le Peintre graveur française*, Paris, 1835-1871, 11 vols.—C. Duplessis, *Histoire de la Gravure en France*, Paris, 1861.—H. Delaborde, *La Gravure*, Paris, n.d.—L. Rosenthal, *La Gravure*, Paris, 1909.—Le *Musée des Arts décoratifs*, published under the direction of L. Metman; 2 Albums engraved on wood and 1 on metal have been published.—Viollet-le-Duc, *Dictionnaire du Mobilier français*, 4 vols., Paris, 1855-1873.—Labarte, *Histoire des Arts industriels*, Paris, 1872-1875.—E. Molinier, *L'Emaillerie*, Paris, 1891.—E. Molinier, *Histoire générale des Arts appliqués à l'industrie du Ve à la fin du XIIIe siècle*, Paris, 1896.—E. Molinier, *L'Orfèvrerie religieuse du Ve à la fin du XVe siècle*, Paris, n.d.—H. Havard, *Histoire de l'Orfèvrerie française*, Paris, 1896.—E. Babelon, *Histoire de la Gravure sur gemmes en France*, Paris, 1902.—J. Guiffrey, *La Tapisserie, son histoire depuis le Moyen Age jusqu'à nos jours*, Tours, 1885.—G. Migeon, *Les Arts du Tissu*, Paris, 1909.—H. Havard, *Dictionnaire de l'Ameublement et de la Décoration*, Paris, n.d., 4 vols.—J. Quicherat, *Histoire du Costume en France*, Paris, 1876.

CONTENTS

PART I
CHRISTIAN ART

CHAPTER I

CHAPTER II

CHAPTER III

CHAPTER IV

PART II
CLASSICAL ART

CHAPTER I

CHAPTER II

xiii

CONTENTS

ART IN FRANCE

FIG. I.—ROMAN BRIDGE ON THE VIDOURLE, NEAR LUNEL. (*Photo. Gouzy.*)

PART I

CHRISTIAN ART

CHAPTER I

ROMAN, BARBARIAN, AND CHRISTIAN ORIGINS

Roman Gaul: Roads, Towns and Buildings.— Remains of Roman Civilisation in Barbarian Gaul. — Christian Gaul. — The Great Sanctuaries. — Oriental Influences. — Barbaric Elements.

GAUL, as a whole, began to participate in antique civilisation under the Roman rule. A highly centralised administration united the provinces which extended from the Rhine to the Pyrenees, from the ocean to the Alps, imposing a common existence and a common culture upon them. When one travels along a Roman road it is very easy to understand how the dwellers in these regions were sensible of a distant solidarity. Their roads, even when disused, are not obliterated; they still indicate the ancient route across fields. Stretching in purposeful rigidity from point to point, regardless of mountains and valleys, they bore the legions to the frontier, and carried the will of Rome into the interior. Every

1

halting-place along them was the nucleus of a future city of France
At the cross-roads we shall find the active centres of Roman art.

FIG. 2.—ROMAN THEATRE, ARLES.

A network of more natural and less geometrical highways, corresponding to the local geology, was related to this vast system of main roads. And yet the extremities, from Arles to Cologne, from Lyons to Saintes, felt that they were members of one body. Thus the solid causeways, built for eternity, were the channels of human intercourse during the Middle Ages; they transported pilgrims and merchants to sanctuaries and fairs respectively. From Burgundy to Provence, from Tours to Roncevaux, they maintained uninterrupted communication, even when these provinces were no longer united by Roman centralisation.

The conquerors brought their Latin habits with them; buildings akin to those of Italy rose in the cities where they established themselves; an official art, easily imposed on a country innocent of architecture, and immune from all local influence, manifested its identity at Narbonne, Bordeaux, and Reims: it was an urban and utilitarian art, created for the enjoyment of great cities. After the decay of Marseilles, Narbonne and Fréjus rose to importance, and close at hand, Orange and Nîmes, whose ancient monuments are among the finest in the world. Arles, the Rome of Gaul, began her glorious existence as a capital, a city of luxury, art, and pleasure. But this municipal civilisation soon outgrew Provence. Municipalities raised triumphal arches dedicated to emperors; Trèves, Reims, Besançon, Langres and Saintes have preserved these proud

FIG. 3.—TRIUMPHAL ARCH OF SAINT-RÉMY.

structures. Towns of second and third rate importance had their amphitheatres; the more wealthy among them boasted thermæ.

Temples were no doubt numerous; they disappeared to furnish columns for the new basilicas of youthful Christianity. Around the great cities rose the rich villas of the Gallic aristocracy, and beyond these a vague population, the *Pagani*, long re-calcitrant to Latinism and subsequently to Christianity. Roman culture had pene-trated only into the towns; but monkish hosts ploughed the fallows of the country-side; after the municipal art of the Gallo-Romans came the rural art of the Roman-esque epoch.

The Gallo-Roman monuments were of imperishable strength. The walls and vaults of the Romans were built with a cement so solid that the whole structure became homogeneous as a single rock; the heavy rubble-walls were encased in small dressed stones, form-ing enormous masses, to which courses of flat bricks or freestone gave sharp contours, salient angles and projecting cornices; upon this robust masonry pilasters and pediments were applied as façades, the whole casing reproducing the elegant forms of Greek architecture. But to raise buildings of this nature, it was necessary that a powerful authority should exist, able to discipline

FIG. 4.—MAUSOLEUM OF SAINT-REMY.

armies, to exact forced la-bour, to subject thousands of arms to a common enter-prise. The downfall of the Empire arrested the great works of the Gallo-Roman municipalities. Such of their buildings as survived the cataclysms of the Mid-dle Ages seemed the more imposing from the ruins heaped around them.

FIG. 5.—BRIDGE OF SAINT-CHAMAS.   (*Photo. Gouzy.*)

When in the third cen-tury the dykes were first broken down on the frontier by the tide of barbarian invasion, the Gallo-Romans entrenched themselves hastily in their towns, and destroyed many a building in order to throw up ramparts. Among the masonry of these hurriedly constructed defences, columns, capitals and statues have been found. But

after the fourth century, resistance died down and no obstacles were opposed to the invaders. The towns were pillaged, and it was long before they recovered the prosperity of the Pax Romana. The ancient cities which had been so active and so opulent during the first centuries of Christianity, shrank and shrivelled in their over-spacious boundaries.

FIG. 6.—ARCH OF MARIUS, AT ORANGE.
(*Photo. Neurdein.*)

Long, empty centuries succeeded; yet they played their part in the development of French art. It was during this period that antique civilisation, decomposing, combined with new elements. It will be well to enumerate what these were before they united to form Romanesque art.

The dominant feature in this slow and confused genesis, was the tradition of the Empire; antique buildings still subsisted amongst the general decomposition. Those who strove to preserve some little intellectual culture remained Gallo-Romans among the barbarians; and when some one among the new chiefs, a Clovis or a Charlemagne, desired to consecrate his power, he donned the purple and took the title of Consul or of Augustus.

FIG. 7.—GATE OF MARS, AT REIMS.
(*Photo. V. Courleux.*)

The barbarian anarchy was dominated by the majesty of such memories; the great works left upon French soil by the conquerors still form the setting of human activities. In the regions where the antique civilisation was most deeply imprinted, there are towns where the houses are huddled in the forsaken thermæ and amphitheatres; certain quarters of Nîmes and Bordeaux are enclosed by the boundaries of the arenas. Men destroyed the temples, but they used their entablatures for the adornment of basilicas. Gallo-Roman centres became the birthplaces of Romanesque art: Toulouse, Auvergne, Poitou, Burgundy, and, above all, Provence and the Rhine valley. In Provence, the transition from antique life to that of the Middle Ages was so insensible that the Christians occasionally worshipped in the old temples after adopting the new religion. The Romanesque

FIG. 8.—RUINS OF THE PALACE OF GALLIENUS, AT BORDEAUX.

art of these regions is not always readily distinguished from late Roman art; on the banks of the Rhine, again, there was a tardy but vigorous florescence of the seed sown by the legions. This fringe of the Empire was more profoundly Romanised than the interior; Latin civilisation had flourished more densely here, in order to oppose a barrier to the advance of Germanism; the foundations of the dyke were not obliterated by the barbarian flood.

Meanwhile, Christianity made its way among the Gallic populations. For centuries, painters and architects worked solely for the Church. Christianity inaugurated the artistic geography of France. Her first monuments are no more. The Merovingian

FIG. 9.—AQUEDUCT KNOWN AS THE PONT DU GARD.

basilicas, so lovingly described by Fortunatus and Gregory of Tours, have entirely disappeared; but traditions, more durable than buildings, have survived. The conversion of Gaul had begun in the second century. Certain famous martyrs associated the idea of evangelisation with that of martyrdom; the popular imagination saw torture and blood in the beginnings of Christianity. The remains of these martyrs fixed a religion of transcendent dogma and strange rites on French soil, and caused the close relation between the art of the Middle Ages and the worship of relics. It was at this period that holy places began to attract the veneration of crowds, and to become the goals of pilgrimages. The tradition had already taken form in the time of Gregory of Tours. "In the reign of Decius," he writes, "seven men, after being ordained bishops of Rome, were sent to preach the faith in Gaul: Gatianus, at Tours; Trophimus, at Arles; Paul, at Narbonne; Saturninus, at Toulouse; Denis, at Paris; Austremonius, in Auvergne; and Martial at Limoges." The addition of a few more names—St. Eutropius of Saintes, St. Julian of Brioude, St. Benignus of Dijon, St. Germain of Paris, and, above all, St. Martin of Tours —would make this list of evangelists synonymous with that of the principal sanctuaries of Gaul, and incidentally, with that of the principal monuments of Romanesque art.

FIG. 10.—EX-VOTO, STONE.
(Museum of Saint-Germain.)
(Excavations of Comte Espérandieu at Mont Auxois.)

FIG. 11.—FIBULA OF CLOISONNÉ GLASS.
(Cluny Museum, Paris.)

FIG. 12.—GATE OF SAINT-ANDRÉ, AT AUTUN.
(*Photo. Neurdein.*)

The question of Oriental influences in western art remains very obscure. Antique art in its Byzantine form had wilted, but it had at least survived, together with the political organisation, whereas in the West it had succumbed with the rest of the Empire. When it came to life again among the Gallo-Franks, at first artificially, at the will of Charlemagne, and then enduringly in the Romanesque period, it manifested an undeniable affinity with Byzantine works. Gaul had known a Greek culture before her Latin civilisation. Hellenist navigators had settled in Provence long before the Roman legions had marched from Italy. After, as before the conquest, it was her Mediterranean face that Gaul turned towards the common civilisation, and on that face that she received some rays of Oriental light. Marseilles was a Greek

FIG. 13.—HYGEIA OR DEMETER.
(Museum of Saint-Germain.)
(Excavations of Comte Espérandieu at Mont Auxois.)

colony; Nîmes retains in her coat of arms the palm-tree and the crocodile which recall her Græco-Egyptian origin. Christianity was but one of the treasures that Syria and Greece deposited on the Gallic shores. Among the earliest texts of our Christian records is an address from the communities of Lyons and Vienne to "their brethren of Asia and Phrygia." The first Gallic martyrs, the Bishop Pothinus, Attalus of Pergamus, Alexander of Phrygia the physician, came from Asia; at a much later period, the time of Gregory of Tours,

FIG. 14.—THE BAPTISTERY OF SAINT-JEAN, AT POITIERS.

Syrians were numerous in many cities in the heart of Gaul. But, above all, pilgrims began to wend their way to the holy regions where the new God had risen on the world. As it gradually converted mankind, so, too, Christianity turned men's souls to Greece and to Asia. The plastic arts were thus but a consequence of the establishment of the faith; the religious conquest brought Byzantine images in its wake.

FIG. 15.—STATUETTE OF CHARLEMAGNE FROM THE CATHEDRAL OF METZ.
(Carnavalet Museum, Paris.)

The part played by the barbarian populations is more difficult to define, and those who cling to preconceived ideas may exaggerate or minimise it at will, for material evidences are lacking. In the buildings that were raised, Roman or Byzantine traditions were at first predominant; nevertheless, a strange and fantastic decoration makes its appearance here and there, a decoration analogous to that of barbaric jewels, to certain northern woodcarvings, and to the miniatures of Saxon manuscripts. Monsters entwined among interlacing ornament like wild beasts caught in nets, roll, writhe, and bite each other, and these violent forms are found in Romanesque sculpture, perfectly distinct from Byzantine fancies, which were conventionalised with greater science and severity.

The barbarians were skilful smiths, and excellent goldsmiths; they were expert in the use of fire and metal. They set uncut gems in gold; they not only forged swords and lances but they also, it seems, brought with them the art of decorating crosses, chalices, reliquaries, and book-covers with large cabochons. The goldsmiths' work of the Merovingian period was renowned throughout the Middle Ages; inventories make frequent mention of "the work of St. Eloi (Eligius)." St. Eloi became the patron saint of goldsmiths, and his native place, Limousin, the centre of the enamel industry. But the barbarians, coming from thickly wooded regions, were rather wood-

FIG. 16.—CROWN OF KING RECESWINTHE.
(Cluny Museum, Paris.)

men and carpenters than masons or architects. They built wooden churches, castles and towns, no vestiges of which remain. If these structures made way for Gallo-Roman masonry, the magnificent timber framework of the lofty roofs survived throughout the Middle Ages. The high towers, the spires, all those pointed forms which soared heavenwards in the mediæval town, were reared by daring carpenters on the massive structures of Roman architecture.

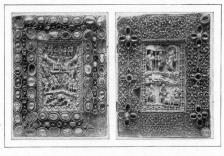

FIG. 17.— COVER OF A PSALTER OF CHARLES THE BALD, IN THE BIBLIOTHÈQUE NATIONALE. (*Photo. Berthaud.*)

Houses with pointed roofs and houses with flat roofs distinguish the France of the north and the France of the south respectively. After the Renaissance, the French roof gradually became less lofty; nevertheless, even in the seventeenth century, what most surprised an Italian after he had crossed the Alps was the height of the roofs.

FIG. 18. — CAROLINGIAN PILLAR IN THE CHURCH OF CRAVANT.
(*Photo. Mts. Historiques.*)

But on the whole, the barbarians probably constructed less than they destroyed. The rare buildings of the confused Merovingian civilisation which survive show how the Christian spirit adapted itself to ancient customs. The Baptistery of St. Jean at Poitiers, the Chapel of St. Laurent at Grenoble, are antique structures adapted to the use of the new religion. The oldest parts of the "Temple St. Jean" show the small dressed stones of the Roman builders, among which freestone and brick supply the modest decoration; the delicate cornices and the pediments preserve the ancient forms, which Poitevin architects were not to forget. The first converts baptised in this building might have fancied themselves in the hall of some Roman thermæ; after the tenth century it became a little church decorated in the Romanesque style. In St. Laurent of

Grenoble, the capitals surmounted by heavy impost blocks recall the art of Ravenna and Constantinople. The Carolingian buildings of Germigny and Aix-la-Chapelle are also Byzantine. Nothing durable save the Roman monuments has survived from these periods in which art was almost non-existent; the antique civilisation, as it decomposed, evolved in a Latin, and then in a Byzantine form. The founders of mediæval art were to work upon the basis of a Roman building.

BIBLIOGRAPHY

S. Reinach, *Description raisonnée du Musée de Saint-Germain*, Paris, 1894 ; *Les Gaulois dans l'Art antique*, Paris, 1889.—E. Espérandieu, *Recueil général des bas-reliefs de la Gaule romaine* (Collection of unpublished Documents), Paris, 1907, 2 vols. have appeared.—C. Barrière Flavy, *Les Arts industriels de la Gaule du Ve au VIIe siècle*, 3 vols., Toulouse, 1901. — Léon Joulin, *Les Etablissements gallo-romains de la plaine de Martres Tolosanes*, Paris, 1901.—C. Jullian, *Routes romaines et routes de France* (*Rev. de Paris*, 1900).—J. Quicherat, *Mélanges d'Archéologie et d'Histoire*, Paris, 1886.—R. de Lasteyrie, *La Basilique de Saint-Martin de Tours*, Paris, 1892.— Marcel Reymond, *La Chapelle Saint-Laurent de Grenoble*, Paris, 1896.—A. Marignan, *Un Historien de l'Art Français : Louis Courajod, les Temps francs*, Paris, 1889.—L. Bréhier, *Les Colonies d'Orientaux en Occident au commencement du Moyen Age* (*Byzantinische Zeitschrift*, 1903).

FIG. 19.—CLOISTERS OF MOISSAC.

CHAPTER II

MONASTIC OR ROMANESQUE ART

Monastic Life: the Benedictines of Cluny and Citeaux.—The Propagation of Art by means of Pilgrimages.—The Origin of Romanesque Architecture.—Regional Types: Auvergne-Languedoc, Burgundy-Provence, Poitou-Saintonge, Northern France.—The Community of Religious Iconography and Regional Motives. — The Continuity of Painting. — The Renaissance of Sculpture: Classic and Byzantine Influences; Decorative Richness; Dramatic Compositions.—The Romanesque Style the First Definite Form of French Art.

THE refined activity which gives birth to the arts is only possible in a well-organised society; the best society in the eleventh century was that of the monks. Until the formation of the populous communes of Northern France, civilisation took refuge in the great monasteries. The southern cities which had preserved or developed within their walls some of the refinements of the antique world left no trace of it save in their gallant verses; the plastic arts, after the downfall of paganism, existed only for the new religion.

It was within the narrow limits of over-populous and strictly enclosed monasteries that the manual and intellectual activity necessary to the existence of art was concentrated. Architecture, sculpture, illumination, and painted glass during the Romanesque period were so many blossoms of the cloister. The monastery preserved the germs of the antique culture; it received and kept alive some sparks from Byzantine altars; elsewhere they were quenched in the whirlwind of a world of anarchy. The monastery was akin to the classic villa; its cloistered court was an enlargement

11

of the ancient peristyle; the monk's gown, his shaven face and close cropped head retained their Gallo-Roman cast among barbarian fashions. Even at the present day the old monasteries of Moissac, Toulouse and Arles remind us what places of tranquil happiness, what oases of sweetness and peace they were during the rude life of the age. Those who circulated under the beautiful arcades, around the little grassy courts, were attached to their domicile by all the more lofty aspirations of their souls; they forgot the world, its tumults and adventures, and among their methods of singing God's praises, we must reckon that of the illuminators who carefully copied Byzantine miniatures; that of the sculptors and glass-painters who patiently transferred these little scenes to the stone of capitals and the windows of churches. The monastery formed a city which had its individual means of existence and its industry. Difficult

FIG. 20.—APSE OF NOTRE-DAME-DU-PORT, AT CLERMONT-FERRAND.

arts, such as that of the goldsmith, were at home there. Romanesque art betrays to some extent the fact that it was evolved in monastic cells; it lacks youth and freshness; its sincerest sentiments often take on a traditional form, like the phrases of prayers; the most violent energy does not always succeed in breaking down the discipline of the rule.

The monks were also architects, and were the first who built vast, elegant and solid sanctuaries. The most important and the most richly decorated of the Romanesque Churches were the Abbeys. To travel through France to see the finest monuments of Romanesque architecture or decoration is to make a pilgrimage to the most famous Benedictine Abbeys, from St. Germain of Paris to St.

FIG. 21.—CHURCH OF SAINT-NECTAIRE.
(*Photo. Neurdein.*)

Etienne of Caen, from St. Bénigne of Dijon to the Madeleine of Vézelay, from St. Trophime of Arles to St. Gilles, from St. Sernin of Toulouse to Ste. Croix of Bordeaux, to St. Martial of Limoges, to Souillac, to Beaulieu, to Issoire, to St. Savin of Poitiers. The most powerful of these Abbeys have disappeared: Cluny, which in the eleventh century gave the law to Christendom, and Citeaux, which was predominant in the twelfth. Amidst the general anarchy, they formed mighty organisations; and the black monks of Cluny, and later, the white monks of Citeaux, spread their skilful architecture and propagated the motives of their iconography throughout Gaul and even beyond its frontiers.

FIG. 22.—APSE OF SAINT-SERNIN, AT TOULOUSE.

It was in the wake of the monks that Romanesque art extended over the territory of ancient Gaul. The civilisation of the period was less brilliant, no doubt, than that of the third century A.D., but it was no longer entirely confined to the towns; the monks had turned aside from the great highways to penetrate into the quarters of the *pagani*, ploughing up the soil and sowing the seed of Christianity. "They decorate the deserts with their holy perfections," writes Hugues de Saint Victor; "they adorn solitudes with their justice, their pious enterprises, their good examples." They also took into these deserts the arts of building, carving and painting.

FIG. 23.—CHURCH OF ROYAT.
(*Photo. Neurdein.*)

The relative community of style in an art so widely disseminated as that of the eleventh and twelfth centuries would be inexplicable, if we did not remember that the principal buildings marked the stages of a society always in movement. The whole of Romanesque art was born of the worship of relics.

FIG. 24.—NAVE OF SAINT-SERNIN, AT TOULOUSE.

FIG. 25.—FACADE OF NOTRE-DAME-DU-PUY. (*Photo. Neurdein.*)

It was necessary to take the pilgrim's staff continually in order to pay homage to them. The important rites of his existence brought man perpetually before tombs and shrines. Contact with these gave solemnity to an oath, and healed the sick; a long and difficult pilgrimage atoned for serious faults and soothed troubled consciences. The more famous sanctuaries attracted so many of the faithful that the aisles of churches had to be enlarged and ambulatories created; buildings were made more spacious to receive the crowds who were huddled together in the small churches of the early Romanesque style. The imposing architecture of Vézelay and Autun, of St. Gilles or Arles, is infinitely too vast for the requirements of an ordinary abbey church; it was intended to serve worshippers far beyond the parochial limits, those itinerant populations which came to pray to the Magdalen, Lazarus, St. Gilles or St. Trophime. Offerings enriched the sanctuaries; cures and miracles paid for costly churches, their sculptures, their goldsmiths' work, their ivories and

FIG. 26.—HOTEL DE VILLE AT SAINT-ANTONIN.

14

precious stuffs. The bones of Saint Foy, stolen and transported to Conques, kindled an altar-fire of Romanesque art in the heart of the desert: a bold building, decked with sculptures and guarding a treasure.

When the precious monolithic columns taken from the ancient monuments came to an end, as the art of turning them was lost, wooden posts or pillars of masonry were used to support the roofs of the basilicas; for the same reason, the arch of small dressed stones took the place of the ancient entablature made of long, rigid slabs.

FIG. 27.—THE CLOISTER OF ELNES, NEAR PERPIGNAN.
(*Photo. Neurdein.*)

Then the Latin basilica underwent the transformations which gradually developed into the Romanesque style. The building, still serving the same purposes, retained its original plan, but the new method of construction was to change its appearance entirely. To the architecture which normally set a timber roof upon slight columns and walls succeeded that of the Etruscans and Romans, which set a roof with an oblique thrust upon massive walls.

In the Carolingian period, the basilica was still covered with a timber roof after the antique fashion; it was only in certain crypts that a low, narrow vault rested heavily on sturdy pillars. It was not until the beginning of the eleventh century that architects began to suppress the timber roof and build their churches entirely of stone. Christianity then set to work to renew its churches. "About three years after A.D. 1000, the basilicas were renewed almost throughout

FIG. 28.—NAVE OF THE MADELEINE AT VÉZELAY
(GOTHIC CHOIR). (*Photo. Neurdein.*)

15

the universe, especially in Italy and in Gaul, although the greater part of these were still sufficiently fine to need no repairs. But the

Christian nations seemed to rival each other in magnificence, in order to raise the most elegant churches. Then the faithful improved (*in meliora permutavere*) the Metropolitan churches, as well as the abbeys, and the oratories of the smaller towns." This famous text of a Burgundian Benedictine, Raoul Glaber, clearly states that the churches were not rebuilt of necessity, but because a new type of structure had made its appearance, beside which the old seemed out of date. What was this "amelioration?" It was, no doubt, building with dressed stones, and the use of the vault.

FIG. 29.—ROMANESQUE HOUSE
AT SAINT-GILLES (GARD).
(*Photo. Neurdein.*)

The plan of the ancient basilica was retained; a wide nave, sometimes double side-aisles, at the entrance a porch or narthex, and behind the choir, an apse; in front of the choir the nave was traversed by the transept, which gave the church the form of a great cross laid upon the ground. But there is an essential difference between the Latin basilica and the Romanesque church; the weight of the stone vault, and the pressure it brought to bear upon its points of support necessitated the use of massive pillars and thick, low walls, capable of resisting an oblique thrust. The whole building seems to gather itself together to support this solid masonry.

The system of stability obtained simply by the verticality of the walls was replaced by another equilibrium, resulting from counterbalancing lateral forces. The antique temple rose from the ground, clear cut, alert, but without any

FIG. 30.—CLOISTERS OF MONTMAJOUR
(BOUCHES-DU-RHONE).
(*Photo. Neurdein.*)

16

exaggerated elasticity or excessive lightness, as befits an architecture which is not concerned to minimise weight. The Romanesque church, not as yet freed from this servitude, rises with a certain timidity; the walls betray the effort; they rest heavily upon the soil; they are sturdy and massive; they reveal a kind of struggle between matter and form; the history of this struggle is that of architecture in the Middle Ages; in the eleventh century, it was the material which gave its aspect to architecture; in the Gothic period, the constructor had mastered it; from the inert mass he had disengaged a resistant ossature; he reared a giddy vault upon the eviscerated walls.

FIG. 31.—FAÇADE OF NOTRE-DAME-LA GRANDE, AT POITIERS.

The earliest architects did not at first venture to throw walls and pillars into space; their buildings keep close to the ground, as if they feared to lose contact with the soil. They built empirically, without nicely calculating the forces of the over-thick walls. And yet the vault is often badly fixed. Here and there, it has bent under its own weight, and has thrust away its points of support; it has been necessary to shore up walls whose loins were broken; if we may trust the ancient records, there were many collapses; the Romanesque churches which survive at present rarely date from the beginning of the eleventh century; they replaced an earlier generation of Romanesque churches, those Raoul Glaber saw built, which are unknown to us.

But progress was rapid. Very soon, the mediæval architects recognised the mechanically essential points; they reinforced them, and lightened the building in its passive parts. To prevent subsidences and cracks in the barrel vault, they reinforced it at intervals by projecting transverse arches, or *arcs*

FIG. 32.—PORCH OF SAINT-GILLES.
(*Photo. Neurdein.*)

doubleaux. These arches rested in the interior on dosserets, or impost blocks, and were strengthened on the exterior by buttresses.

FIG. 33.—NAVE OF SAINT-PIERRE, AT ANGOULÊME.

The long nave, divided into bays, was thus enclosed from place to place in a framework of arches and buttresses. Other systems of vaulting were employed. The vault on intersecting arches; the groined vault, formed by the inter-penetration of two demi-cylinders. The cupola was employed more especially among the Byzantines. Spherical triangles, or pendentives, form the transition between its base and the square plan of the bay of the nave which it had to cover, or more frequently, corbels sustain the cupola when it reaches the angles. At the junction between two groined vaults or two cupolas, a strongly projecting transverse arch (*arc doubleau*) receives its share of the thrust and transmits it to the buttresses.

Nevertheless, the building failed to conceal effort. The lateral aisles, which in the ancient basilicas were designed to add to the proportions of the nave, now served to buttress it by means of their half-barrel vaults; the thickness of the walls and pillars made the free space appear yet more confined. The outline of the exterior tended to become pyramidal; the base of the edifice is broad and spreading; the central nave rests upon the side-aisles, and the apse expands into the apsidal chapels which it throws out around it. The architect

FIG. 34.—PORCH OF SAINTE CROIX, AT BORDEAUX.

recognises the organs which need strengthening, but as yet he dares not attempt what the architects of the thirteenth century were to do:

i.e., detach the buttresses from the mass; on the contrary, he dissimulates them as much as he can, transforms them into decorations, links them together by arcades, or rounds them, giving them the appearance of engaged columns; the Romanesque builder loved curving lines, full and convex contours. This marvellous mason, the inventor of a new system of construction, was careful to conceal his innovations under traditional forms. Nevertheless, a few towers begin to rise to the sky from his façades or the crossings of his transepts. They become lighter as they mount; the upper storeys are pierced with windows and throw out a bold spire. The Romanesque belfry soars thus proudly because it is independent of the compact structure, and detached from the system of equilibrium.

FIG. 35.—FAÇADE OF SAINT-PIERRE, AT ANGOULÊME.

Sometimes it suffices to change the character of the church, revealing a heavenward impulse in the stolid creation.

Romanesque architecture, extending over the entire surface of ancient Gaul, accommodated itself to the material resources of each region, and the local habits of its builders. Art reveals regional individualities at the very moment when the great feudal divisions begin to play an important part in history.

It was in Auvergne, on that plateau at first recalcitrant to Latin civilisation, but afterwards one of its most faithful guardians, that Romanesque architecture produced its most masterly buildings. Notre Dame du Port, at Clermont-Ferrand, or the Church of St. Nectaire, are examples of robust buildings, finely proportioned, carved from a granite that

FIG. 36.—NAVE OF SAINT-FRONT, AT PÉRIGUEUX.
(*Photo. Neurdein.*)

FIG. 37.—SAINT-MARTIN, AT BOSCHERVILLE.

makes admirable walls and coarse sculptures. The Auvergnate Church is the most complete of Romanesque organisms; its side-aisles with their groined vaults support tribunes with half-barrelled vaults, and from the ambulatory that surrounds the choir, apsidal chapels radiate in graceful symmetry. At the crossing of the transept rises an octagonal tower, which elevates and lightens the massive body. These vigorous buildings multiplied on the slopes of the central plateau. They are to be found in the valley which was traversed by the main road of Clermont and Brioude, in Limousin, in Quercy, and in Languedoc. Toulouse, inaugurating her architectonic activity at this early period, transposed the stone masonry of the day into brick. Piles of bricks give a very individual character to the belfries of Languedoc. This influence was felt very far afield. Saint-Sernin at Toulouse inspired the plan of the original church of St. Iago at Compostella. The pilgrim, lost and strange in remote regions, hailed the Romanesque sanctuary of his native land at successive stages of his road, and recognised his religion in unknown provinces. (Figs. 19 to 26.)

The close affinity between the churches of Burgundy and those of Provence recalls the relation between North and South in the basin of the Rhône; the kingdom of Arles at one time united Burgundy and Provence. The great Burgundian sanctuaries contained Provençal relics; the Magdalen and Lazarus,

FIG. 38.—FAÇADE OF LA TRINITÉ (ABBAYE AUX DAMES), AT CAEN.

who had landed of old at Camargue, had left relics at Vézelay and at Autun. The grandiose abbey of Cluny has perished almost

FIG. 39.—APSE OF THE CHURCH OF AULNAY IN SAINTONGE.

entirely; the churches which have survived attest that their architects were audacious enough at times to sacrifice solidity. They reared their vaults boldly, throwing out their walls and buttressing them only by means of low side-aisles without galleries. They thus reserved a space for lighting the nave directly with lofty windows. The Provençaux built in the Burgundian manner, but they gave greater height to their side-aisles, and the dazzling southern sunlight entered through windows much reduced in size. The builders of these churches, which often replaced Roman temples, utilised the ruins of the latter. Carved friezes and columns, imbedded in the Romanesque decoration, still remind us that antique art reigned upon this soil before Christian civilisation. (Figs. 28 and 32.)

In the south-west, from the Loire to the Pyrenees, the Poitevins and the Saintongeais reared innumerable churches, in which the lofty lateral aisles cling closely to the sides of the nave. The light struggles dimly into the constricted central space. But on the façade and sometimes on the lateral porches, the sculptors lavished exquisite decoration. The close and tender grain of limestone lent itself to the carving of delicate images and supple arabesques, and thus the somewhat loaded construction is worked as richly as an ivory casket. In this region many churches, both very vast and very humble, are crowned with cupolas, for the most part concealed by gable roofs; but at the Church of St. Front at Périgueux, the spherical domes are

FIG. 40.—1 AÇADE OF SAINT-ÉTIENNE (ABBAYE AUX HOMMES), AT CAEN.

visible, and cover the four equal arms of a Greek cross; the Oriental aspect of this architecture inevitably evokes memories

21

FIG. 41.—WILLIAM THE CONQUEROR'S ARMY IN CAMP. BAYEUX TAPESTRY.

of Byzantium, and the plan of the church is identical with that of St. Mark's at Venice. (Figs. 31 to 36.)

FIG. 42. — SCENE FROM THE APOCALYPSE; PORCH OF SAINT-SAVIN, NEAR POITIERS.
(Bibliothèque Nationale, Print Room.)

These Romanesque constructions appear more robust and flourishing in the provinces, where the ancient culture had left the strongest impress on the soil. The northern provinces never raised such perfect buildings as the churches of Auvergne and Languedoc. It was not for lack of courage. On the contrary, the Normans undertook constructions of such audacity that it was not possible to cover them with stone vaults; the over-lofty walls could not have sustained their weight. Carpenters completed the work of the masons. The proud churches of the Abbaye aux Hommes and the Abbaye aux Dames at Caen were begun in the Romanesque manner, but they had to await the Gothic vault for their completion. (Figs. 37 to 40.)

During this same Romanesque period, Chris-

FIG. 43.—GOD CREATING THE SUN AND THE MOON NAVE OF SAINT-SAVIN, NEAR POITIERS.
(Bibliothèque Nationale.)

22

FIG. 44.—EPISODE OF THE BATTLE OF HASTINGS. BAYEUX TAPESTRY.

tianity further gave rise to a vigorous development of imagery. It had first evolved a very copious iconography, which for centuries was perpetuated by miniatures, mural painting, sculpture, enamel, and stained glass. After practically suppressing sculpture as an art too deeply impregnated with paganism, it had countenanced a prodigious pictorial florescence, and had invented a dogma of imagery to illustrate the written dogma. Religious subjects were stereotyped, so to speak, in Eastern art in a large range of clearly defined compositions, which spread from monastery to monastery, thanks above all to the illuminated manuscript. It was on this common ground that Christian art was henceforth to exercise itself; it is found at the source of

FIG. 45.—RELIQUARY HEAD OF SAINT BAUDIME.
(Church of Saint-Nectaire.)

FIG. 46.—FRAGMENTS OF STAINED GLASS OF NOTRE-DAME-DE-CHARTRES.
THE ANNUNCIATION.—THE ANNUNCIATION TO THE SHEPHERDS.—THE NATIVITY.
(Bibliothèque Nationale.)

the pictorial arts of all Europe, like an original language the roots of which bear fruit in different dialects.

FIG. 47.—SATAN AMONGST THE DAMNED. APOCALYPSE OF SAINT SEVER.
(Latin Manuscript in the Bibliothèque Nationale.) (*Photo. Berthaud.*)

Pictorial themes were transmitted even more readily than architectural forms; Christian iconography, like the Christian religion itself, was almost entirely borrowed from the East. The earliest motives treated by the painters of the catacombs and the sculptors of sarcophagi among the Christians of the West—certain Old Testament episodes, such as the Israelites crossing the Red Sea, Daniel, Jonah, etc.—seem to have disappeared in the copious repertory introduced by the Benedictine miniaturists. In the Merovingian period and afterwards in the time of Charlemagne, certain painters no doubt showed some originality of invention, for they depicted the Life of St. Martin in the famous basilica of Tours, and in the palace of Charlemagne at Aix-la-Chapelle, they glorified the race and the reign of the Emperor. But all that survives of these manifestations is the record of them in the pages of historians or poets. This pictorial tradition was annihilated with the Carolingian civilisation, and when art began to live again at the close of the eleventh century, French artists seem to have adopted Byzantine forms almost exclusively.

These painters were quite untouched by any sort of realistic inspiration. They borrowed fixed images and made no attempt to transform them into representations of the world in which they lived. And yet even in the twelfth

FIG. 48.—THE MYSTIC MARRIAGE OF ST. CATHERINE.
(Church of Montmorillon.)

24

century, this iconography lost something of its uniformity when it established itself on French soil. The sculptors who transposed

Byzantine motives into their carvings had not the same habits in every region; they did not work the same stone, nor use the same instruments. The Provençals bored their marble with the auger, like the antique sculptors; the Burgundian monks hewed out long, flat silhouettes, the Languedocians robust figures; the Auvergnats carved their hard granite with infinite labour, whereas the men of Poitou and of Saintonge treated their docile limestone freely and fancifully. Hence we distinguish provincial styles in the borrowed forms of this art, as, no doubt, we should recognise them in the painting of the day, if more specimens of this had survived. Moreover, if they showed little invention, every monastery and every church selected from the common repertory the themes most in harmony with local devotion. Innumerable pilgrims flocked to Provence to pay homage to the

FIG. 49.—ADAM, EVE, AND THE ANGEL. CAPITAL OF NOTRE-DAME-DU-PORT, AT CLERMONT-FERRAND.

relics of the three Marys, which had been landed at the mouth of the Rhone together with Lazarus. The great sanctuaries of Provence show their effigies on every hand. They are to be seen on the door of St. Gilles, and in St. Trophime at Arles, going to the tomb which Jesus has just abandoned, straight and rigid, draped in long Syrian robes, all holding their vases of spices in their hands with the same gesture. The Resurrection of Lazarus was also a favourite theme with the painters of Aix and Avignon in the fifteenth century.

FIG. 50.—BAS-RELIEF IN BAYEUX CATHEDRAL.

In the regions of the West, on the great highway which leads towards St. Iago of Compostella through Poitou and Saintonge by Blaye, Bordeaux and Roncevaux, the churches also show a very characteristic motive: a knight bearing down a vanquished foe. The *Gestes* of Roland

and of Turpin represent this region as wrested foot by foot from the Saracen by Charlemagne and his companions. Every church and monastery invited the pilgrim to halt before some relic of warriors slain fighting against the Infidel; archæologists now recognise a Byzantine Constantine, where the men of

FIG. 51.—CAPITAL FROM THE CHURCH OF SAINT-SERNIN OF TOULOUSE, PRESERVED IN THE MUSÉE DES AUGUSTINS.

old no doubt saw the Emperor, "slayer of the Moors," whose exploits were recounted and whose advance was traced in contemporary song. The tradition lingered long; an incontestable Charlemagne was carved at Saintes, in the fifteenth century, on the door of the cathedral. The venerable relics of St. Martin of Tours attracted many pilgrims. The churches in western France dedicated to him are innumerable. In the sanctuaries which stud the highway, on painted window or capital, we often find the figure of the horseman dividing his cloak.

But these examples, in spite of many others that might be cited, are exceptions. As a whole, a religious iconography uniform with the dogma it accompanied was propagated. In spite of its Oriental origin, it flourished well in France. It did not take the place of an earlier art; it responded to the cravings of religious sensibility; it gave to Christians the concrete images which enabled them to picture to themselves Jesus, the Virgin, the Apostles, the

FIG. 52.—THE SIGN OF THE LION AND THE RAM, FROM SAINT-SERNIN OF TOULOUSE, PRESERVED IN THE MUSÉE DES AUGUSTINS.

FIG. 53.—CAPITAL OF THE CLOISTER, MOISSAC.

FIG. 54.—PROPHET.
CHURCH OF SOUILLAC.

FIG. 55. — PILLAR
WITH CHIMERAS.
CHURCH OF SOUILLAC.

marvellous or artless stories of the Gospel, and the fantastic visions of the Apocalypse; they saw more clearly that source of light the beams of which irradiated their whole life. For a time, the Christians of the Romanesque period were content to reproduce the Byzantine images, just as they repeated the sacred legends, without any sort of modification. But in these congealed forms there were latent forces which were later to wake to life; the Romanesque sculptors were to animate these figures, and this hieratic iconography was to end in realism.

Imagery came from the East in the form of painting, and in the Romanesque period, painting was the natural complement of architecture; vaults and solid walls afforded it vast surfaces. †The monks of the eleventh and twelfth centuries illuminated their churches like their manuscripts. The rude masonry disappeared under enlarged miniatures which recalled the distant legends of dawning Christianity, and the expected terrors of the end of the world. These have disappeared for the most part, but an attentive eye will sometimes discover on the vault of some dark crypt, bistre lines which indicate long silhouettes of Byzantine figures and the familiar attitudes of the Annunciation or the Flight into Egypt. The pilgrims who came of old to venerate the relics of the Saint were able to admire clearly defined forms and brilliant colours, by the light of the tapers.

The half-effaced frescoes to be found in certain churches,

FIG. 56.—CAPITAL OF THE CLOISTER OF
MOISSAC.

especially in the region of Poitou, give us some idea of the nature of Romanesque painting. The decorators used fresco as the ancients had done, and as the Byzantines were still doing. A monk, Theophilus, has described the process in a treatise: *Diversarum artium schedula*, a manual of the arts of this period. The colours are laid on flat and surrounded by hard outlines; modelling is reduced to a few white hatchings in the lights and a few dark blotches in the shadows. This drawing, impoverished and re-

FIG. 57.—THE LAST JUDGMENT. PORCH OF THE CHURCH OF BEAULIEU.

stricted for centuries by the monks, was adopted by the Romanesque painters and applied sometimes with a brutal hand. If the lines were tortured, the attitudes violent, the bodies distorted, it was because a violent energy had laid hold rudely of these drowsy effigies, and had shaken their torpid limbs. The most important relic of Romanesque painting is preserved at St. Savin, near Poitiers. Episodes from the Book of Genesis are painted on a barrel vault. These vast compositions are carried out in pale tints, among which greens, and red and yellow ochres predominate. The vivacity of the execution forbids us to look upon the design as mere trace-work. Other remains of frescoes near St. Savin, at Montmorillon, at Poitiers, at Montoire (Loir-et-Cher), at Le Liget (Indre-et-Loire), seem to prove that this region of richly sculptured churches was also the most fertile in paintings. But this mural decoration was soon to be transposed into glass-painting; the glass-painters were to adopt all those picturesque compositions which the Romanesque walls were

FIG. 58.—PORCH OF THE CHURCH OF MOISSAC.

unable to preserve. Some of them do not belong to the ordinary cycle of Christian painting. In St. Julien at Brioude, there are

FIG. 59.—HEROD'S FEAST. CAPITAL FROM SAINT-
ÉTIENNE, TOULOUSE MUSEUM.

remnants of a fading vision of Hell, conceived and painted by men who followed no Byzantine tradition. A monstrous Devil gambols in the flames surrounded by little terrified figures, a barbarous and chaotic nightmare which has nothing in common with the hieratic and theatrical compositions of Oriental art. It was no doubt familiar to the Romanesque imagination, and recalls the terrors of those monks who felt themselves in the claws of Satan. (Figs. 42, 43, 47, 48.)

The sculpture of the twelfth century, like the architecture of the same period, is marked by a characteristic peculiarity, in that it was an art at once very ancient and very novel, an art of primitives struggling with material as yet unsubdued, yet a decadent art, in which antiquated forms and superannuated customs still survived. It combines a strange rudeness with subtle refinements. It is awkward and contorted, because for the most part the twelfth century sculptors simply transposed into relief what Byzantine artists had designed for painting.

FIG. 60.—JESUS GIVING AUTHORITY TO
THE APOSTLES. TYMPANUM OF THE
CHURCH OF VÉZELAY.

Antique statuary, a pagan art, had disappeared completely together with the worship of which it had been an accessory. Statuary introduces concrete beings; it is the art of idolatry; painting is but an illusion, and lends itself less to a confusion of the divinity and his image. Nevertheless, in certain districts where the antique civilisation had penetrated most deeply, statues still survived. At the beginning of the eleventh century, Bernard, a scholar of Chartres, on making a third pilgrimage to Con-

FIG. 61.—GOD APPEARING AT THE END OF THE WORLD. TYMPANUM OF THE PORCH OF ST. PIERRE, AT MOISSAC.

ques, found in Auvergne certain reliquary statues which were venerated by the natives. He was scandalised by this survival of pagan custom; he derides the men who pray to a dumb and senseless thing; *rem mutam insensatamque.* The miracles wrought by the little statue of Ste. Foy were necessary to efface his first impressions and calm his scruples; in common with the men of his day and of his creed, he considered statues of gypsum, wood, or brass, absurd and sacrilegious, save as applied to the crucifix. But if the worship of relics tended occasionally to revive this statuary which the detestation of idols had destroyed, it was, no doubt, only in order to give a human form to certain costly reliquaries of gold or silver. These works in precious metals were merely the luxuries of rich monasteries, and an art, if it is to live, requires deeper roots and a more extensive development. (Figs. 45, 75.)

The beginnings of sculpture at the dawn of the twelfth century were uncertain and uneasy manifestations in unfavourable surroundings. It did not develop normally, like Greek sculpture, which disengaged a human body from a tree-trunk or a block of stone, afterwards

FIG. 62.—THE LAST JUDGMENT. TYMPANUM OF THE PORCH OF THE CHURCH OF CONQUES.

attached limbs to it, and gradually gave the suppleness of life to the whole. The motives of Romanesque art had long been established by painters when sculptors began to treat them. The first Romanesque sculptures are merely transpositions into low relief ✓ of the images of Byzantine miniature, and the vivid colours which

FIG. 63.—THE LAST JUDGMENT. TYMPANUM OF THE PORCH OF THE CATHEDRAL OF AUTUN.
(*Photo. Neurdein.*)

formerly covered the tympana of Vézelay or Moissac must originally have emphasised the fidelity of these transpositions. Their authors, too, ventured upon strange audacities. They attempted the most complex compositions of Byzantine painting with the rudimentary resources at their disposal; and their childish awkwardness gives a kind of youthful air to the figures of a senile art.

The architects of Gaul did not command materials as rich as those of the East or of Italy. They never faced their buildings with slabs of marble, and their decoration was not applied to the building, but evolved from it, hewn in the masonry. The sculptors gave the final touches to the sturdy edifice, which offered vast surfaces to their chisels. They carved the soffits and tympana of the porches and the capitals of the pillars. They transcribed in bas-reliefs the few forms that had survived from the antique shipwreck, perhaps some heraldic animals of barbaric jewellery, but above all, the images of Byzantine Christianity, which was then penetrating into the Western world in a thousand forms. In the provinces where Gallo-Roman remains were plentiful, they

FIG. 64.—THE TWO DOORS OF THE CHURCH OF SAINT-LAZARE, AT AVALLON. (*Photo. Neurdein.*)

did not fail to adapt these to the new decoration; the churches of Provence, St. Gilles, and St. Trophime at Arles, are loaded with the spoils of ancient art; architecture even burdened itself with

FIG. 65.—VIRGIN AND CHILD.
FAÇADE OF THE CHURCH OF
SAINTE-CROIX, AT LA CHARITÉ
(*Photo. Mieusement.*)

superfluous accessories in order to utilise as much as possible of the hoard; here the Roman affiliation was so close that Romanesque art desired to lose no fragment of its heritage. Augustodunum had also left many antique buildings. Throughout this region, rinceaux and rosettes give the porches of the churches the richness of certain triumphal arches. An old Romanesque door at Bourges shows that the Christian Church had not disdained to deck herself with the gauds of Avaricum. At Moissac, at Chartres, and elsewhere, the lintel over a door reproduces some antique frieze, or the side of a sarcophagus. Confronted with an antique form, Romanesque art recognised and adopted it. The capital, which was almost invariably rectangular, has thick sausage-like scrolls at the angles, which are merely degenerate Ionic volutes; the classic acanthus is preserved in a clumsy, dry, and flattened form; in St. Remi, at Reims, there are composite capitals. Even in the poorest essays of this sculpture (at Oulchy, at Morienval and at Fouesnant), the weak and tentative chisel which has been laboriously applied to the hard granite, has striven to produce a volute; this rude sculpture, like the crudest patois, is a derivation from the Latin.

The men of the twelfth century sought to achieve decorative richness by the accumulation of details; they were craftsmen who never spared their pains.

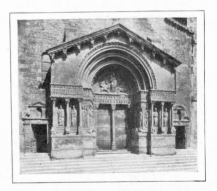

FIG. 66.—PORCH OF THE CHURCH OF
SAINT-TROPHIME, AT ARLES. (*Photo. Neurdein.*)

Their bas-relief resembles a coarse embroidery somewhat closely interwoven, which entirely fills the surface to be decorated, tympanum, archivolt, or capital. Even in dramatic compositions, with figures

in violent action, the forms are curved and interlaced in such a manner as to leave no empty spaces. In the porches and façades of the churches of Saintonge and Poitou, the decorative instinct has triumphed over iconographic scruples. In this region of fine limestone, the façades are elaborately chiselled, and time, reinforcing the work of the sculptor, continues to eat into the soft stone. The most dramatic motives are sometimes treated simply as arabesques. Hence the sculptors showed a preference for those which could be repeated indefinitely, such as the Virtues and the Vices, the Wise and the Foolish Virgins, the signs of the Zodiac, the labours of the months; in the south porch of Aulnay, in Saintonge, the twenty-four elders of the Apocalypse are multiplied at will, according to the number of voussoirs; at Sainte-Marie-des-Dames, at Saintes, the beheading of John the Baptist with the martyr between the executioner and Salome, is repeated as often as it is required to cover the archivolts of the doorway; everywhere

FIG. 69.—FRIEZES, SAINT-GILLES.

the strangest monsters are juxtaposed, with no other object than to bring them to the two extremities of the arch (Figs. 70 to 73).

33

D

St. Bernard was exasperated by "these monkeys, these lions, these monstrous centaurs, these archers, these huntsmen blowing horns . . . these quadrupeds with serpents' tails, these horned beasts with equine hindquarters." Romanesque art was running riot outside the rule of the Benedictines who had created it. Yet this fantastic fauna was nevertheless far from moribund: it originated in remote antiquity, and its progeny survived even at the height of the Renaissance. But was it no more than a mere play of the imagination in the twelfth century? It would seem at times to have been the pathetic expression of terror-stricken souls. When the sculptors of Souillac and of Moissac interlaced horrible beasts with fierce talons and gaping jaws, biting and devouring one another, were they not fixing in stone the visions which so often terrified the Romanesque monk in his cell? In these decorative extravagances, we should perhaps recognise petrified nightmares.

FIG. 70.—SOUTH PORCH OF THE CHURCH OF AULNAY, SAINTONGE.

When sculpture arose from the void to collaborate in Christian iconography, decorative motives had long been determined by painting. Doubtless, the Romanesque sculptors were not solely dependent on illuminated manuscripts for guidance; they saw and

FIG. 71.—ARCHIVOLTS OF THE PORCH OF SAINTE-MARIE-DES-DAMES, AT SAINTES.

copied the ivories and goldsmiths' wares which monks and pilgrims brought back from the East. But these miniature sculptures were themselves allied to the art of the painter, with their slight relief and clearly marked lines; Romanesque art modified the round, soft style of the antique by imitating the dry elegance of the Byzantine form.

But this youthful art handles the ankylose Byzantine types very roughly. It is curious to see how these great figures stamp and writhe and gesticulate in the process of throwing off their drowsy stiffness. Hence the furious and inexplicable gestures, the inter-

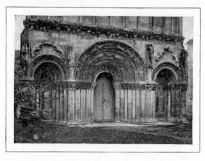

twined legs, the tremulous hands, the tempestuous draperies, the twisted robes with sharp, upturned edges. Even the rude figures laboriously carved in the granite on the capitals of Auvergne, are vigorous and lively human beings. By dint of application, the artist has succeeded in depicting a clearly defined action, and rendering intelligible gestures with his interlacement of limbs.

FIG. 72.—CHURCH OF CHADENAC (CHARENTE-INFÉRIEURE).

This pathetic violence breaks out on a tympanum at Vézelay; Christ, with His outstretched hand casts rays of stone on the heads of the apostles, who press around Him in a frenzied dance, an interminable series of little figures, which expand or crowd together, according to the exigencies of the surface they have to cover, and seem to find it very difficult to keep their angular gestures and intricate draperies within the field of the tympanum. At Autun, a Christ of the same kind presides over a Last Judgment, in which the barbarous forms give a fantastic terror to the scene. These look as if they had been flattened for ever by having lain for centuries between the pages of great folios. At Conques, the pilgrims of St. Foy were also edified by a Last Judgment, a swarm of figures, mingling in hell with acrobatic demons, or squeezed between the arcades of the New Jerusalem. At Moissac, the Christ, the most comely Romanesque Christ

FIG. 73.—PORCH OF THE CHURCH OF COGNAC.

before that of Chartres, makes a grandiose appearance in the midst of the four and twenty elders, who gaze at Him with upturned

FIG. 74.—PORCH OF THE
DESERTED CHURCH NEAR MATHA
(CHARENTE-INFÉRIEURE).

heads, twisting their necks to get a better view. At Beaulieu we have the same scene, the same figures boldly treated with high relief and angular contours, marked by a robustness wholly lacking in the thread-like larvæ of Vézelay and Autun (Figs. 60 to 63).

These complex and grandiose works have a strange charm; they express that epoch in which a semi-barbarism was breathing its ardent vitality into an exhausted civilisation. Already, however, in the middle of the twelfth century, an absolutely novel statuary began to evolve from these combinations, in which the awkwardness of an infant sculpture mingles with the conventions of a senile painting. This statuary detaches itself completely from painting, and sets in space living bodies and full forms. After the monastic sculpture of Romanesque art we have an art which is no mere repetition of religious motives, but an imitation of life. There is little affinity between the fresh plants which throw out their young and vigorous shoots in the region of Chartres, and those dried herbs which Romanesque monks found between the leaves of ancient books.

The more famous sanctuaries have for the most part lost their treasures, and collectors compete one against the other for the fragments. Some of the more modest country churches have preserved reliquaries, shrines, and vases, those precious works of rare material and difficult fashion to which the Romanesque craftsman applied his skill. They remind us that in the eleventh century the plastic arts received more than they created; the most various

FIG. 75.—STATUE OF SAINT FOY,
AT CONQUES.

elements are combined in these examples: the East and the West, the Barbarian and the Latin, the Pagan, the Christian, and even the Arab. The treasury of St. Denis possessed antique vases which Romanesque goldsmiths set in mountings of silver-gilt, adorning after their manner the relics of antiquity they had reverently collected. There are Roman cameos among the precious stones which enrich the robe of Ste. Foy of Conques, a strange and barbarous little figure with large enamelled eyes, still preserved in the wild district where it worked so many miracles and attracted so many pilgrims (Fig. 75).

FIG. 76.—FRAGMENT OF THE FAÇADE OF THE CHURCH OF ÉCHEBRUNE (CHARENTE-INFÉRIEURE).

In the twelfth century, the enamels of Limoges began to penetrate into the treasuries of the churches of Limousin and Auvergne before they found their way throughout Christendom. The enamellers continued this Byzantine industry, replacing the technique of *cloisonné* by the simpler process of *champlevé*.[1]

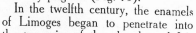

Even when they represent native saints, these figures are Oriental in design. Like the leaden net-work of the painted windows, the *cloisons* of the enamel tended to fix and stiffen the lines of Romanesque design. Here, however, flexibility and truth of design were of less moment than perfection of technique, and beauty and solidity of material. Neither goldsmiths nor glass painters were inventors of living forms, and even when sculptors had discovered the art of carving life-like figures, enamel and stained glass long remained faithful to the Romano-Byzantine style. This is what makes Romanesque goldsmiths' work

FIG. 77.—VIRGIN AND CHILD. (Wood.) (Louvre, Paris.)

[1] In *cloisonné* the design was applied to the surface, the divisions being marked by little barriers (cloisons) of metal; in *champlevé* the metal field was hollowed out to receive the enamel.

FIG. 78.—SHRINE OF SAINT-YVED. (Ivory.)
(Cluny Museum, Paris.)

so valuable; it was originally the most precious of all the arts, and was second to none plastically.

The Romanesque style, with its honest solidity, and its applied ornament,

FIG. 79.—CHRIST IN GLORY.
(Limoges enamel of the XIIth Century.)
(Cluny Museum, Paris.)

is the first definite form of French art. Fragments are all that remain to us of an earlier period, and even so, the Roman ruins in France are monuments of an alien civilisation. The Latin basilicas have survived only as memories. The Romanesque churches have endured; they are still in use, and continue to serve the purpose for which they were created. It was in the southern provinces above all that they multiplied. They are very much less numerous in the north of France, either because this style made way for its successor, Gothic, or because it flourished more luxuriantly in the regions where the antique culture had penetrated most deeply.

FIG. 80.—CASE OF AN EVANGELIARY
FROM THE TREASURY OF SAINT-DENIS.
(Louvre, Paris.)

In this architecture of the *langue d'oc*, as in the southern literature, we are conscious of a very ancient spirit, and a kind of rustic charm. The Romanesque buildings were closely associated with provincial and rural life; many of them are at a considerable distance from the main arteries of general life. Never was art so freely scattered on the surface of the soil as it was in the twelfth century. Nearly all the provinces had their individual style of architecture and sculpture; more than one lost it in the sequel for ever! How many districts and villages have known no other fine work of art but a Romanesque

FIG. 81.—FOOT OF THE GREAT CANDELABRUM
OF SAINT-RÉMI, AT REIMS.
(*Photo. Rothier, Reims.*)

church porch! After this period art became less rural and concentrated itself in the towns. Great sanctuaries, built for the reception of innumerable pilgrims, now rear their rich façades in solitary spaces, and the footsteps of the faithful are no longer numerous enough to trace a pathway in the grass. But how venerable time has made these country churches. The pavements are worn, the angles are blunted, the vault has subsided; the masonry of the façade is crumbling, and in this decaying limestone, a new stone has to be inserted occasionally, like a square of coarse linen in a frayed guipure.

FIG. 82.—ANTIQUE VASE
WITH ROMANESQUE
MOUNT. FROM THE
TREASURY OF SAINT-DENIS.

(Louvre, Paris.)

BIBLIOGRAPHY

Archives de la Commission des monuments historiques, published by A. de Baudot and A. Perrault-Dabot, Paris (in course of publication).—Pr. Mérimée, *Notes d'un Voyage dans le Midi de la France,* Paris, 1835; *dans l'Ouest,*1836; *en Auvergne,* 1838.—A. de Caumont, *Abécédaire d'Archéologie,* Caen, 1871.—Anthyme Saint-Paul, *Les Écoles romanes* (*Annuaire de l'Archéologie française,* 1878); *Viollet-le-Duc et son système archéologique,* 1881; *Histoire monumentale de la France,* 1883.—J. Quicherat, *Mélanges d'Archéologie et d'Histoire,* Paris, 1886.—E. Corroyer, *L'Architecture romane,* Paris, 1888.—Chanoine Reusens, *Éléments d'Archéologie chrétienne,* Paris, 1890, 2 vols.—Aug. Choisy, *Histoire de l'Architecture,* vol. II, Paris, 1899.—J. Brutails, *L'Archéologie du Moyen Age et ses méthodes,* Paris, 1901.—C. Enlart, *Manuel d'Archéologie française,* 2 vols., Paris, 1902-1903.—J. Brutails, *Précis d'Archéologie du Moyen Age,* Paris, 1908.—W. Lübke, *Geschichte der Architektur,* 6th edit., vol. II, Leipzig, 1886.—G. Dehio et G. von Bezold, *Die Kirchliche Baukunst des Abendlandes,*

ART IN FRANCE

2 vols., Stuttgart, 1884-1901.—G. T. Rivoira, *Le Origini della architettura Lombarda*, Rome, 1901.—L. Labande, *Etudes d'Histoire et d'Archéologie romanes*, Paris, 1902 (Provence and Languedoc).—A. de Rochemonteix, *Les Eglises romanes de la Haute-Auvergne*, Paris, 1892.— H. Chardon du Ranquet, *Cours d'Art roman auvergnat*, Clermont, 1900 : *Albums des Monuments et de l'Art ancien du Midi de la France*, Toulouse, 1893-1897.—Abbé Pottier, *L'Abbaye de Saint-Pierre à Moissac* (*Album des Monuments du Midi de la France*, Toulouse, 1897, vol. 1, p. 48).—E. Rupin, *L'Abbaye et les Cloîtres de Moissac*, Paris, 1897.—R. de Lasteyrie, *L'Abbaye de Saint-Martial de Limoges*, Paris, 1901.—Abbé Bouillet, *L'Eglise et le trésor de Conques*, Mâcon, 1892.—Abbé Bouillet, *Sainte-Foy de Conques, Saint-Sernin de Toulouse et Saint-Jacques de Compostelle* (*M.S.A.F.*, 1893).—G. Dumay, *L'Eglise et l'Abbaye de Saint-Bénigne de Dijon*, 1891.—Ch. Porée, *L'Abbaye de Vézelay*, Paris, 1909.—Bernard, *La Basilique primatiale de Saint-Trophime d'Arles*, Aix, 1893.—R. de Lasteyrie, *Cloître et façade de Saint-Trophime d'Arles* (*C. Accad. Insc. et Bell.*, 1901).—F. de Verneilh, *L'Architecture byzantine en France*, Paris, 1851.—J. Berthelé, *La Question de la date de Saint-Front de Périgueux* (*R. A. C.*, 1895).—J.-A. Brutails, *La Question de Saint-Front* (*B. M.*, 1895).—R. Phéné Spiers, *Saint-Front de Périgueux* (*B. M.*, 1897).—J. Mommeja, *Monographie de la Cathédrale de Cahors*, 1881.—A. de Caumont, *Statistique monumentale du Calvados*, Caen, 1847-1862, 5 vols. —V. Ruprich-Robert, *L'Architecture normande aux XIe et XIIe siècles*, Paris, 1884-1889.— E. Lefèvre Pontalis, *L'Architecture religieuse des XIe et XIIe siècles dans l'ancien diocèse de Soissons*, Paris, 1894-1898 ; *Manuel d'Iconographie chrétienne, grecque et latine* (*Guide de la peinture du maître Denys*), published by Didron, Paris, 1845.—Moine Théophile, *Diversarum artium Schedula*, published by Comte Lescalopier, Paris, 1843.—J. Comte, *La Tapisserie de Bayeux*, Paris, 1878.—P. Gelis Didot and H. Laffillée, *La Peinture décorative en France du XIe au XVIe siècle*, 2 vols., Paris, 1891.—H. Laffillée, *La Peinture murale en France avant la Renaissance*, Paris, 1904.—Mérimée, *Les Peintures de Saint-Savin*, Paris, 1845.—L. Giron, *Mémoire sur les Peintures murales du département de la Haute-Loire*, Le Puy, 1884 (and in *R. S. B. A. D.* down to 1901).—W. Lübke, *Geschichte der Plastik*, vols. I and II, 3rd edit., Leipzig, 1884.—L. Courajod and F. Marcou, *Le Musée de Sculpture comparée du Trocadéro*, Paris, 1892.—M. Voege, *Die Anfänge des monumentalen Stiles im Mittelalter*, Strasburg, 1894.— R. de Lasteyrie, *Etudes sur la Sculpture française au Moyen Age* (*Mon. Piot*, vol. VIII, 1902).— A. Marignan, *Histoire de la Sculpture en Languedoc aux XIIe et XIIIe siècles*, Paris, 1902.— G. Fleury, *Portails imagés du XIIe siècle*, Mamers, 1904.—R. Allen, *Celtic Art*, London, 1904.

FIG. 83.—AMIENS CATHEDRAL, WEST FRONT.

CHAPTER III

COMMUNAL OR GOTHIC ART

The Civilisation of the Ile-de-France; the Communes and their Cathedrals in the time of Philip Augustus and Saint Louis.—The Gothic Building; Saint-Denis, Paris, Laon, Chartres, Bourges, Le Mans, Reims, Amiens, Beauvais; the Cathedrals of Normandy; the Gothic Style in the West and in the South.—Stained Glass Windows.—The Renaissance of Statuary, Statues at Chartres.—The Transformation of Iconography by Statuary; the Prophets, Christ, the Last Judgment.—Idealistic Statuary; the Style of Amiens, and of Reims.—Ornamental Sculpture.

TOWARDS the middle of the twelfth century, when Romanesque art was at its zenith, a new style, destined to shed its radiance upon all Christendom, was germinating in the Royal Domain. The Romanesque epoch was a period of disseminated art; each province had its special architecture and its individual decoration; no single one dominated the rest. In the vast regions of the *langue d'oc*, from the South to the Loire, from Arles to Poitiers, from Anjou to Burgundy, the great feoffs enframed individual existences, united by the diffusion of a common religion. The antique culture which had come by the great Roman road that extends from Fréjus to Bordeaux had spread northward through Burgundy, Auvergne and Poitou. The highways of communication between the *langue d'oc* and the *langue d'oïl* met together in the basin of the Seine. The unity which was impossible in the South was inevitable in the North. Life was more concentrated in these regions, and their wide plains

41

had none of those geographical frontiers by which the particularist spirit is fostered. A personality rose above the feudal federation; a

FIG. 84.—CRYPT OF THE CHURCH OF SAINT-DENIS.

France was evolved to which the other provinces gradually attached themselves; Gothic art, born of this society, naturally followed the course of its destiny.

Since the days when the Greeks invented the Doric and Ionic temples, no society had ever developed a style of architecture more personally expressive; the immense cathedrals of the Ile-de-France and the adjacent provinces rose at about the same time; there is something of the marvellous in this phenomenon; an impulse so general and so sudden must have had some definite cause. It is to be found in the fact that the population of the communes had lately conquered a place in the world, side by side with the feudal and ecclesiastical castes. Romanesque art had been primarily the work of monks; the feudal class gave birth to the architecture of the castle; but it was the population of the communes who reared the Gothic cathedrals. Numerous towns sprang up, whose inhabitants formed a vigorous and prolific citizen class, friendly to

the king, and administered by a bishop. An urban civilisation comprising burgesses and workmen began to flourish in the shelter of their ramparts. Corporations were formed, workshops were opened, masters trained apprentices in difficult crafts; industrial activity was organised, and preserved its organisation to the end of the Middle Ages.

Lay workmen laboured,

FIG. 85.—CRYPT OF SAINT-GILLES.

but religion still guided and directed them. In the twelfth and thirteenth centuries, the cities applied their wealth and their muscles to the construction of the House of God; the entire town devoted itself to the common task. Cathedrals had to be vast, immense, for whole populations were to circulate beneath their vaults; they were to rise to a giddy height, because this seemed to give an added fervour to these Hosannas in stone; and very soon also a kind of rivalry between town and town caused vaults and spires to soar higher and ever higher. Every cathedral was the outcome of a vast charitable impulse; the bishop directed and organised the work, carried the relics about and collected contributions; the king encouraged the quest, and opened his own purse in aid of the task; the mass of the faithful accepted their share in the enterprise by offering the labour of their hands.

FIG. 86.—NAVE OF NOTRE-DAME DE PARIS.

"Whenever the great blocks of stone were hauled up by cables from the quarry, the people of the district, and even those of the neighbouring regions, nobles and commons alike, harnessed themselves to the ropes by arms, breasts, and shoulders, and drew the load

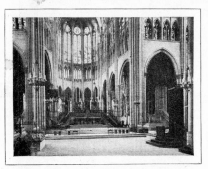

FIG. 87.—CHOIR OF THE CHURCH OF SAINT-DENIS.

like beasts of burden" (Suger). It was like a crusade in which all took part, either with their purses or their arms; the faithful pressed in from the surrounding country, dragging carts loaded with stones and beams; they encamped by the foundations of the cathedral that was to be; the work was intermingled with religious ceremonies; the building rose swiftly, for enthusiasm gives without reckoning the cost; after the sublime ceremony, when these crusaders dispersed, a prodigious building stood upon the plain.

This miraculous efflorescence is only to be explained by universal impulse. It was a brief moment, little more than a half century; the growth of the cathedrals which were not begun under Philip Augustus or not finished under Saint Louis was intermittent. As early as the end of the thirteenth century, the zeal of the overstrained community began to slacken; cathedrals were then built by forced labour; fewer were reared, and finally they ceased to be built at all. But in the thirteenth century the energies of a young and devout society raised these mountains of stone; the architects had not to fear a lack of funds; their sole preoccupation was with technical problems.

FIG. 88.—FAÇADE OF NORTE-DAME, PARIS.

Gothic architecture is the result of the mechanical researches undertaken by builders after they had substituted a stone vault for the timber roof of the ancient basilicas. To prevent the deviation of the walls, the Romanesque architects had reinforced them and narrowed their aisles. Intent upon the solidity as well as upon the beauty of their building, they preserved the Roman style, masking the buttresses as far as possible, and thickening the members of their compact masonry. Romanesque architecture remained faithful to antique forms after admitting a new principle. On the other hand, during the second half of the twelfth century, in the Ile-de-France, to the north of Paris, and in Normandy, the art of building was transformed in a few years, because architects boldly accepted all the consequences of vaulted architecture; a kind of division of labour was established in Romanesque masonry:

FIG. 89.—CHURCH OF SAINT-PIERRE, CHARTRES.

organs began to detach themselves from the compact mass; a new type of church was evolved: the Gothic church.

FIG. 90.—NOTRE-DAME, PARIS (SOUTH SIDE).

The genesis of this new architecture is marked by a constructive invention: that of intersecting diagonal ribs, the supreme achievement, after which no further progress was made. Under a vaulted bay enframed by two arcs doubleaux (transverse arches) and two formerets (lateral arches) two diagonal arches intersect,[1] and assume the weight of the vault. The four portions in which it is thus divided counterbalance each other, and the weights are concentrated partly upon the central keystone, where they neutralise each other, and partly (directed by the ribs) upon the four points of support. The architect has made himself the master of the Romanesque vault; he has hung the inert mass on a resisting ossature, and guides a diffused force at his will. This system of diagonal ribs is an element of extreme flexibility, docile to the exigencies of the plan. The architect can expand or contract these two intersecting arches at will, extending them for the bays of the nave, and curtailing them for the side aisles; he can press them back on the one side, and open them out on the other to follow the ambulatory in its course round the choir; he imposes the form he requires and

FIG. 91.—FAÇADE OF THE CATHEDRAL OF LAON.
(*Photo. Neurdein.*)

[1] This is the French "croisée d'ogives." The word ogive, though often loosely applied to any pointed arch, is derived from the Latin *augere*, to augment, in reference to this re-inforcement.

45

FIG. 92.—FAÇADE OF THE CATHEDRAL OF CHARTRES.

conducts the thrusts to the points he chooses.

The problems he had to solve were these: to fix the points of support; to suppress useless solids; to divide and direct the thrusts; to obtain equilibrium by opposing various forces; the same principles which had transformed the vault were now to be applied to the wall which sustains it. As this wall under the new system only supported the intersecting arches, the intervening solids became useless; it was obvious that wide voids might safely be pierced in them, and very soon there was little of the wall left but the framework of the windows. So much for the vertical pressure; the architect had further to deal with the lateral thrusts. All that the Romanesque architect had opposed to these was the thickness of his walls and the buttresses embedded in their masonry. The Gothic builder, bolder and more logical, frankly applied projecting buttresses; then he detached them from the wall, and from the summit of these abutments he threw arches which re-inforced the intersecting arches of the vault at their points of support; these "flying buttresses" passed over the side aisles. Here again the constructor, understanding the principles of vaulted architecture better, or accepting its consequences more frankly than his Romanesque predecessors, obtained a greater effect with infinitely less labour. A slender oblique strut easily neutralises a lateral thrust which the thickest wall could hardly resist. The flying buttress is an element as flexible as the intersecting arch; its strength is readily multiplied; it was the flying buttress alone which made it possible to rear very lofty vaults; a wall becomes weaker in propor-

FIG. 93.—NORTH PORCH OF THE CATHEDRAL OF CHARTRES.
(*Photo. Neurdein.*)

FIG. 94.—THE SAINTE-CHAPELLE.

tion to its elevation, but to rectify this it is only necessary to give the flying buttress its point of support on a more distant abutment. The Gothic organism was now complete; here again the architect had disengaged vigorous and elastic members from the wall which had hitherto achieved solidity merely by mass; he had liberated the active forces from all the dead weight which made Romanesque construction heavy.

This logical evolution resulted in a sum of decorative forms, the Gothic style. Originally these forms indicated forces, the equilibrium of which ensured the stability of the building. In the interior, they were: the lofty pillars, which rose occasionally to a height of thirty, forty or fifty metres, and covered the nave with their expanding ribs; on the exterior, the oblique descent of the flying buttresses upon the abutments, a lithic cascade which transmitted the thrust of the vault to the ground. Like the Greek temple, this style was the outcome of an ingenious adaptation of stone to the exigencies of mechanics. But whereas the ancients had established a constant relation between the height and the width of their buildings, Gothic architecture was too complex to be reduced to "orders." Its dimensions are variable. In a Greek temple, we can deduce the dimensions of the whole structure from the base of a column; the Gothic pillar rises to heights we cannot predict, for so many other elements contribute to the solidity of the building. Thus the Gothic architects, though they worked on

FIG. 95.—NORTH DOOR OF NOTRE-DAME, PARIS, BY JEAN DE CHELLES.

common principles, yet gave an individual physiognomy to each cathedral.

FIG. 96.—FAÇADE OF THE CATHEDRAL OF REIMS.
(*Photo. Trompette.*)

It was apparently in the Ile-de-France to the north of Paris that the first vaults on intersecting arches were built. As early as the first half of the twelfth century, in the valley of the Oise, and perhaps in Normandy, architects understood the advantages of the new process; making its way far afield, it retained its original name of *opus francigenum*. This name it still bore when it was about to disappear, at the time when Philibert Delorme was working at its overthrow. The first Gothic essays, then, date from the period of the Romanesque in its fullest efflorescence. While the people of the South were constructing massive walls to support their vaults, in the darker north it was necessary to provide large window spaces to light the nave; and as this reduced the resisting power of the walls, architects contented themselves with timber roofs while awaiting

FIG. 97.—NAVE OF THE CATHEDRAL OF CHARTRES.

the invention of some more ingenious contrivance. It is not easy to discover the first essays of the new style; when architects had mastered their methods, they replaced the works in which their first tentative efforts might have been traced by more finished achievements. But very often a Gothic roof covers a building of Romanesque aspect; it is fixed awkwardly upon the wall itself, instead of falling distinctively upon a formeret. The windows retain the round-headed form, and the buttresses are not yet disengaged from the wall to offer a more distant point of support and to receive the thrust by the intermediary of flying buttresses.

The new vault had certainly been known for many years, and

architects had adopted it, at least tentatively, when a memorable structure arose to demonstrate its advantages. The famous abbey of St. Denis guarded the relics of three martyrs, Denis, Eleutherius, and Rusticus. King Dagobert, after amassing treasure in the building, desired to make it his last resting-place. Its Merovingian basilica was successively Romanesque and Gothic, before the royal tombs began to make it a chronicle of French sculpture. In the twelfth century, the concourse of pilgrims to the shrine was so great that they could not all obtain access to the relics. Suger, when he

FIG. 98.—FAÇADE OF THE CATHEDRAL OF AMIENS.

was a monk, saw worshippers crushed to death by the crowds that were pressing in behind them; a denser population, a more fervid faith, required a vaster sanctuary. When he became Abbot, Suger enlarged the crypt; it is surrounded by an ambulatory with radiating chapels, and still covered by a groined vault resting on enormous pillars (Fig. 84). Above this solid Romanesque crypt he built a Gothic choir; here slender columns support the intersecting arches of the vault. In this case, the architect is no longer tentative; he knows that he may venture; the inert masses of the masonry become slighter and more nervous; a less massive support sustains a higher and wider wall (Fig. 87). This choir was solemnly consecrated on June 11, 1144, in the presence of the king and queen, the assembled nobles, ecclesiastics, strangers, and commons who had

FIG. 99.—NAVE OF THE CATHEDRAL OF AMIENS.

flocked in from the neighbourhood. The new style was not, of course, invented at St. Denis. But this much frequented abbey

FIG. 100.—THE "HOUSE OF THE MUSICIANS," AT REIMS.
(*Photo. V. Courleux.*)

certainly accelerated the transformation of architecture. In a few years, builders set to work eagerly in most of the large towns north of the Loire; the Romanesque monuments were dismantled, and their stones were set into Gothic pillars and buttresses; some few porches and towers specially dear to the faithful alone survived, incorporated in the new cathedral.

Notre Dame in Paris, begun in 1163, and almost completed during the reign of Philip Augustus, did not receive the porches of the transepts until 1260, a century after its foundation. The arrangement of this church is marked throughout by extreme clarity. Two side aisles give width to the building, and extend round the choir in a double ambulatory. After the year 1290 the body of the church was further enlarged by chapels which correspond in depth to the buttresses and occupy the spaces between them. The lower pillars are as sturdy as towers; the triforium occupies the entire space between the supporting arches and the upper windows; each compartment of the ribbed vaulting is sexpartite, and covers two bays; the points of support for the ribs of the vault are rather low. This primitive Gothic style still retains the robust aspect of Romanesque architecture; the ascending lines are intersected by horizontal courses on which they rest; each pier, to reach the summit, requires three storeys, three pauses, and three departures (Fig. 86). There is no cathedral in the world the pro-

FIG. 101.—APSE OF THE CATHEDRAL OF AMIENS.

portions of which are more admirable, none which presents a finer appearance from various points of view. The apse, which rests

FIG. 102.—APSE OF THE CATHEDRAL OF BEAUVAIS.

upon very oblique flying buttresses, springing boldly from distant points of support, has often been compared to a galley propelled by long oars; the lateral outline is the regular development of a noble building with a prolonged vertebra, proudly rearing aloft the mighty towers of its façade (Fig. 90).

It is this façade more especially which gives its distinctive character to Notre Dame. It repeats in greater perfection the H form of the Romanesque church of the Trinité at Caen. Its two wide towers, closely attached to the central body, exactly cover the side aisles and the flying buttresses; the two masses, rising to an equal height, end frankly, evoking no regret for the spires which were never added; the Gallery of the Kings and the open gallery of the third storey cut through the sturdy buttresses, dividing the square front into equal quadrilaterals; they enframe the porches, the side windows and the central rose window, deeply embrasured in the thick wall (Fig. 88).

This façade was conceived as a whole by a constructor skilful in designing with broad masses and frank angles, and the ornamental accessories of the later style were applied to its robust nudity. Compared with this vigorous and well-proportioned architecture, the north and south porches by Jean de Chelles are a charming decoration, but somewhat flat and fragile. Notre Dame has profited by the historical importance of Paris. It

FIG. 103.—CHOIR OF THE CATHEDRAL OF BEAUVAIS.

remains the finished type of that Gothic style, the varieties of which were so numerous. Outside the Ile-de-France other cathedrals may boast a richer façade, a more graceful nave, bolder towers, and more luxuriant sculpture; but not one shows a more limpid coherence of structure. Notre Dame has become as it were a classic work. Amidst the exuberance of Gothic fancy, the wise and exemplary model is the monument which Maurice de Sully reared in the Cité, in the heart of Paris and of the kingdom of France.

The Cathedral of Laon is the sister of Notre Dame, and almost of the

FIG. 104.—APSE OF THE CATHEDRAL OF BOURGES.
(*Photo. Neurdein.*)

same age. The two façades show a family likeness; but Laon is even more grave of aspect. Its deeply recessed windows and rose-window, placed with a certain irregularity in the midst of symmetry, give it a violent and uneasy physiognomy; from the upper part of the towers, which arise like alert sentinels, project the heads of oxen (Fig. 91). On the abrupt eminence of Laon, this church affects the haughty robustness of a stronghold, whereas the Parisian cathedral is peacefully extended on its island. The naves are also

FIG. 105.—THE FIVE PORCHES OF THE CATHEDRAL OF BOURGES.
(*Photo. Neurdein.*)

similar in style; but that of Laon, instead of terminating with a semi-circular apse, is now bounded by a straight wall. This square plan, replacing the traditional rounded apse adopted in the first Christian basilicas, suggests a secular hall. The Gothic church of Soissons, on the other hand, retains the circular form in the north transept as a heritage from the Romanesque epoch.

Notre Dame at Chartres, with its great north and south porches, was completed in 1260, and consecrated in the presence of St. Louis and the royal family. The central body of the building dates from a time when the architect remained prudent in spite of his boldness; the courses are solid, the height is prodigious, but the effort by which it is supported is formidable. The lofty vault makes a nave which retains Romanesque proportions in its plan seem short. The huge interior is dark in spite of the immense windows, for the light filters through the jewelled mosaic of stained glass (Fig. 97). The wide nave is crowned by a very open vault; to support it it has been necessary to thicken the buttresses, multiply the flying buttresses and link them together by arcades. On the exterior these stone struts descend in overwhelming cataracts; no effort has been made to mask their heaviness; this conflict of forces, which ensures the solidity of Gothic buildings, shows a sort of violence here. The west front was not a homogeneous conception; it began as a Romanesque design, with its three doors pressed together between its two towers; but an immense rose-window was inserted

FIG. 106.—CHURCH OF NOTRE DAME, DIJON.
(*Photo. Neurdein.*)

to decorate this façade which soars upward with the nave it closes (Fig. 92). The circular forms of Romanesque decoration are found everywhere; its round-headed arcading appears in the rose-window of the west front and in the flying buttresses. One of the towers is the boldest essay of the Romanesque style; it rises massive and solid, flanked by sturdy buttresses, and terminates in a belfry; the superposed storeys thus reach the level of the roof, and from thence, suddenly, an octagonal pyramid springs

FIG. 107.—APSE OF THE CATHEDRAL OF LE MANS.

heavenward to a height of 100 metres. The second spire, built in the sixteenth century, rises higher only by means of starting from a higher level. These piles of stones dominate La Beauce, and on the vast plain which so many pilgrims once traversed, carting materials towards the famous sanctuary, they seem to proclaim the protecting presence of Our Lady.

FIG. 108.—MONT-SAINT-MICHEL (SOUTH SIDE).
(*Photo. Neurdein.*)

The cathedral of Bourges shows a more massive silhouette upon the plains of Berry, for the towers seem to have lacked power to rise to any height. The body of the church is not interrupted by a transept; on the façade the architects juxtaposed five doors corresponding to the aisles and offering an immense field to the sculptor; the decoration is on so vast a scale that it was not possible to continue it above (Fig. 105). In the lateral porches the architects have embedded some precious Romanesque fragments; like Chartres and Le Mans, Bourges shelters some admirable archaic sculptors.

At Le Mans, the choir is an unusually important feature (Fig. 107). It is surrounded by double aisles, and thirteen chapels, which are almost as large as churches, radiate from these. The abutments are adapted to the complexity of the aisles; each of the flying buttresses bifurcates and finds points of support on two buttresses, between which is a window giving a direct light to the ambulatory. Thus in the interior the forest of pillars and ribs, and on

FIG. 109.—CATHEDRAL OF ROUEN.

the exterior that of the buttresses and flying buttresses, becomes more and more dense and daring.

Notre Dame at Reims, which was finished at the end of the thirteenth century, was prolonged by the addition of three bays in the following century. The nave was made wide enough to contain the crowd of coronation days. The general outline on the façade recalls that of Notre Dame; it has the same unity of plan, the same arrangement of windows and galleries. But the work, reconstructed at the end of the thirteenth century, dates from a time when the style had become much more florid; the horizontal lines disappear under a network of ornament. A soaring tendency common to the whole

FIG. 110.—SALLE DES HÔTES IN THE MONASTERY OF MONT-SAINT-MICHEL.

façade urges the lines upwards, and resolves every projection into spires, gables, and pinnacles. The wall itself is reduced to the small columns of the windows; the towers are mere skeletons

FIG. 111.—FAÇADE OF THE CATHEDRAL OF ROUEN, BETWEEN A ROMANESQUE TOWER AND THE "BUTTER TOWER." (End of the XVth century.)

without bodies, through which the eye passes, and the tympana of the west porches, instead of a full bas-relief, enframe stained glass. This chiselled, hollowed, and much-decorated façade shelters an innumerable population of figures (Fig. 96). Its animation, its festival aspect, is carried on to the sides of the building; the pinnacled buttresses are recessed to shelter statues. The roof is surrounded by a graceful gallery, a diadem for the church in which kings were crowned. Throughout, Reims conceals the elements of strength beneath a wealth of decoration. Stone foliage quivers on the capitals; the scene seems duly set for the pageants of monarchy.

Notre Dame at Amiens, built by Robert de Luzarches, was not finished till 1269. No nave in existence reveals an architect surer of his means, or more skilful in the calculation of his audacities. Here there is nothing to suggest the weight of the building; the walls are cut away and the pillars which support the vault are elongated to rise; they are sub-divided into clustered shafts, and the shaft which corresponds to the arc doubleau (transverse arch) of the vault springs without interruption, with a single bound, as it were, to the keystone. The very lofty side-aisles seem to enlarge the nave immeasurably; between them, over the central aisle, the enormous mass of the vault seems etherealised by distance, like some airy covering, or like a sail stretched over the ribs of the vault, and upheld by a continuous wind from below. In this luminous nave with its dilated walls, the soul is exalted and amplified.

FIG. 112.—FAÇADE OF THE CATHEDRAL OF COUTANCES.

To sustain the immense mass it was necessary to reinforce it with huge buttresses which rise boldly from the ground. But in the facade, the soaring impulse seems to have failed. The decoration of the three porches gives a certain air of heaviness; the towers barely rise to the level of the roof; materials for a further ascent were lacking; the monster had not strength enough to raise his head.

The people of Beauvais determined to raise a church to even dizzier heights; in 1272, they had finished their choir; it fell in, and the church was never finished. The restored choir still awaits its nave. It is so lofty that it was found necessary to double the supporting pillars in order to sustain it. And yet the architect had accumulated exterior

FIG. 113.—SALLE DES CHEVALIERS IN THE MONASTERY OF MONT-SAINT-MICHEL.

abutments; on the outside, the apse looks a frail creation, lost among the multitude of long arms which the gigantic buttresses throw around it (Figs. 102, 103). These daring architects recognised that a stone building is not an abstract structure; in proportion as the organism becomes more complex, its equilibrium depends on a greater number of elements; the most exact calculations are liable to be upset by defects in the material. An adventurous spirit was inherent in Gothic architecture; many towns followed the example set by Beauvais; amazing successes occasionally gave rise to the belief that the architect had made a compact with the devil, and had bartered his soul in order to rear a vault or raise a spire.

FIG. 114.—APSE OF THE CATHEDRAL OF BAYEUX.
(*Photo. Neurdein.*)

Normandy owns various cathedrals in which a lantern-tower rises boldly at the crossing of the transepts; it is to this feature that the Norman churches owe their originality of silhouette; this tower dominates the building with its mass and its crowning spire. In the

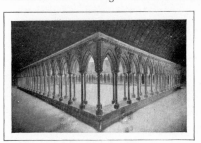

FIG. 115.—COURT OF THE CLOISTER OF MONT-SAINT-MICHEL.
(*Photo. Neurdein.*)

interior, the vault seems to have opened to admit the daylight. These beautiful Norman churches are very numerous; at Rouen there are the cathedral and Saint Ouen; the cathedral has a facade ill-attached to two towers set over far apart, an old Romanesque tower, and the so-called Tour du Beurre (Butter Tower), a structure somewhat soft and languid in form, overlaid with the accessory ornament of flamboyant Gothic; on the stone of the porch, elaborately cut by the

57

architect and minutely chiselled by the sculptor, time is now working in his turn (Fig. 111). The great nave of Saint Ouen

appears even vaster than it is as a result of its majestic unity, and the somewhat frigid elegance approved among the architects of the fourteenth century. At Coutances (Fig. 112) the façade has the soaring pride of outline that characterises St. Étienne at Caen; the two spires, and the lantern-tower which recurs at Bayeux and at St. Lô, are models of plain, nervous, and slender masonry. In its naves, as in its towers and spires, Norman architecture reveals the characteristic haughtiness it had found so hard to reconcile with the exigencies of Romanesque masonry.

On the narrow summit of Mont Saint Michel, the architect built and burrowed; buttresses resting on the flanks of the rock support a paradoxical building which continues the pyramidal form of the mount, a sanctuary famous for its pilgrims, a solid fortress for the kings of France; an abbey rich in architectonic refinements crowns this peak, encircled by ramparts against which the sea dashes (Fig. 108). Pointed architecture had penetrated to the extreme point of Brittany; it persisted for a long time afterwards in this region; everywhere else Gothic art was already making way for a new style, while the people of the peninsula were still busy carving the ornament of their graceful pierced belfries (Fig. 116).

The Gothic style also spread southwards; it crossed the Loire, but it had to compound with local custom; it was only in the north of France that it expanded, free of all pressure from the past. While adopting the new principles, each province safeguarded its own tradition as far as possible. The Normans, when they passed from Romanesque to Gothic, retained their lantern-towers; in Poitou and in Anjou, the architects preserved their customary high side aisles, a peculiarity which gives the body of these churches in the interior the appearance of a large hypostyle hall. The intersecting diagonal

FIG. 118.—CATHEDRAL OF ALBI.

ribs are combined with the cupolas dear to the architects of the South West; hence these domical vaults which characterise the Plantagenet style.

The Cathedral of Poitiers, although it is a Gothic building, is manifestly akin to Notre-Dame-la-Grande, the old Romanesque sanctuary; the architect has contrived to dispense with flying buttresses; he has retained a predilection for the semi-circular arch in the design of his windows, and he makes frequent use of small columns in his decoration. Throughout this region we find that the Gothic did not always supersede the Romanesque style; it merely induced greater slenderness and loftiness. Limoges, Clermont-Ferrand, Rodez and Narbonne possess great churches of the thirteenth century, imitated more or less from those of the North.

In proportion as we advance to the South, we shall find the French style undergoing modifications

FIG. 119.—CHURCH OF SAINT-NAZAIRE AT CARCASSONNE.
(*Photo. Neurdein.*)

more and more considerable. There are no flying buttresses on the exterior, no side aisles in the interior; the Gothic building has

FIG. 120.—KING AND QUEEN, CENTRAL PORCH OF WEST FRONT OF THE CATHEDRAL OF CHARTRES.

retained all the massive majesty of Languedocian Romanesque. Moissac, Toulouse and Albi are wide single-aisled buildings; strong buttresses were necessary to support the very open vault; instead of detaching them from the exterior walls, the architect has made them project strongly on the inside, so strongly that they serve as partitions for the lateral chapels. The principle of Gothic construction was not accepted with all its consequences. Sainte Cécile at Albi, compact and sturdy, rests upon its promontory, more like a defiant fortress than a tutelary cathedral; between the two towers of the façade there was place for a guard-room; an embattled parapet runs round the roof; the towers are those of a stronghold, the windows like loopholes (Fig. 118). In the fourteenth century, Carcassonne, finally reunited to the Crown, also wished to have a cathedral "in the French manner;" but here again the customs of the South transformed the style of the North; the buttresses are not detached from the wall to support flying buttresses, and the lofty roof is replaced by a flat covering (Fig. 119).

FIG. 121.—FIGURE OF A QUEEN, IN THE CHURCH OF SAINT-DENIS.

(From Corbeil.)

The Gothic cathedral is a true product of the Ile-de-France. It harmonises perfectly with the skies under which it was born, whether its lofty

FIG. 122.—CHRIST IN GLORY. TYMPANUM OF THE WEST PORCH OF THE CATHEDRAL OF CHARTRES.

FIG. 123.—VIRGIN OF THE
ANNUNCIATION. RIGHT
TYMPANUM, WEST FRONT
OF THE CATHEDRAL OF
CHARTRES.

(*Photo. Mieusement.*)

mass is veiled in mists, or the sun brings out the florescence of the grey stone on the façade washed by winter rains which it turns to the West. It is also an urban product, the communal monument *par excellence;* it enshrined the soul of the city; it was planted in the midst of houses which crouched beneath its flying buttresses; men did not isolate it upon a summit or an empty space; they loved to circulate round it, in the little streets that wound about its feet; above the gables of the wooden houses they saw its fasces of shafts soaring skywards, and its whole silhouette terminating in innumerable points. It is the towers and spires, dominating the forest of roofs, which give each city its special character when one sees it from afar, encircled by its ramparts. Even to the present day, these cathedrals have remained the typical buildings of the French towns; the people of the communes left in them not only evidences of a heroic faith, but features which have fixed the physiognomy of cities for all time; these old stones attract and retain pilgrims more fervent than ever.

But we must go deeper to understand the profound significance of this architecture. That of the Greeks was governed by the external decoration. The populace never entered the temple. It challenged admiration from the summit of its Acropolis, clearly detached from its base, its pure outline relieved against the deep sky. All Christians enter the cathedral, and it was in order to receive the whole city that naves were enlarged and vaults heightened; it was to illuminate its congregations with celestial visions that voids were made in the

FIG. 124.—THE VISITATION.
RIGHT TYMPANUM, WEST FRONT
OF THE CATHEDRAL OF CHARTRES.
(*Photo. Mieusement.*)

61

FIG. 125.—LEFT PORCH OF THE WEST FRONT OF NOTRE-DAME, PARIS.

walls, and filled in with immense windows of stained glass. It is also in the interior that we feel the presence of the exalted spirit which raised and organised this mass of stones; the prodigious height of the vault is not meaningless; all these aspiring lines invite the eye to look up and seek God. On festivals, the voices of children and the thunder of the organ fill the empty space, carrying up the orisons of a whole population in a common *sursum corda.* When the chants are hushed, and the church is deserted, it preserves its sentimental power; the slightest sound, the closing of a gate, a key turning in the lock, the footfall of a passer-by, echoes through the immense space; in the solemn silence the solitary soul also takes on an unaccustomed sonority, and vibrates in unison with this atmosphere in which the mystery of the divine seems to brood.

After the building of this cathedral, where the whole city could find place on festivals, the problem of decoration presented itself. It is not like the Greek temple, a simple building, almost invariable in its configuration. Its very complete organism admits of innumerable complements; architects could always add towers, spires, and even chapels; in succeeding centuries they could apply a wealth of ornament to the somewhat bare façades of the primitive style. But the architect was not the sole craftsman of the cathedral; nearly all the working guilds contributed to it. It required stained glass for its windows, paintings on its walls, wood carving for its choir-stalls, hammered iron work for its

FIG. 126.—NORTH PORCH OF THE CATHEDRAL OF CHARTRES.

doors, and above all, sculpture. Statues multiplied on every hand; buttresses were recessed to provide niches for them; porches were made deeper to receive a greater number. Decorative exigencies were thus the origin of Gothic sculpture. The cathedral expresses not only the unity of the commune, its closely knit organisation, and its fervour of faith; in its mighty flanks it bore innumerable images, figures familiar to the souls of its day. Between the primitive worship and the more philosophic religion of Calvin and of Bossuet, Christianity went through a phase of ingenuous idolatry in the Gothic period; the plastic arts were the language of faith in those days, and sculptors were led to forms of beauty and life by piety. Iconography was an inexhaustible source of figures and

FIG. 127.—DETAIL OF THE NORTH PORCH OF THE CATHEDRAL OF CHARTRES.

motives of every kind, and the cathedral offered a limitless field to decoration. For the statuary of porches, the bas-reliefs of tympana or archivolts, the theme could be amplified or curtailed, the persons be more or less numerous according to ornamental requirements. To understand the details of the original design now, we have to dip into the diffuse literature of the Middle Ages, the religious texts, some of the Old Testament, the Gospels, the Apocrypha, the Acts of the Apostles, the parables, the famous sermons of the doctors of the Church.

Stained glass and sculpture are the indispensable complements of the Gothic cathedral; architecture required these two arts, and they were so much loved by Frenchmen that architecture was modified to give them a larger place. The windows

FIG. 128.—SOUTH PORCH OF THE CATHEDRAL OF CHARTRES.

became larger to enframe a wider expanse of glass; porches became deeper to receive a greater number of statues. Further, at the

FIG. 129.—PROPHETS, KINGS; RESUR-
RECTION OF THE VIRGIN AND HER
CORONATION. WEST FRONT OF
NOTRE DAME, PARIS.

beginning of the thirteenth century, glass-painting and sculpture, like architecture, were primarily French arts. The monk Theophilus, in his treatise on the arts, attributes a peculiar skill to the French glass-painters.

The earliest basilicas were no doubt lighted through coloured glass. But it was not until the Romanesque period that this painting began to represent living figures. A coloured window was then a transparent mosaic, in which pieces of glass, stained and cut, were held together by a tracery of lead; the leading was supple enough to follow the design in its contours. The motives form little medallions superposed in such a manner as to decorate the window. An iron framework ensured the solidity of the whole. At first this consisted of rigid metal bars which cut across the mosaic; but at Saint Denis and at Chartres we already find the brutality of this reinforcement yielding to the exigencies of decoration; the framework is made to surround and isolate the medallions, and the general arrangement of the glass gains greatly in clarity.

The figures of stained glass windows typify a phase of mediæval design, that of the Romano-Byzantine paintings and of the Benedictine miniatures; this drawing is harsh and stringy in character, defining the figures with a hard outline, and swathing them in close draperies with twisted folds. The lead framework emphasises the hardness of the features. But this hardness is not gratuitous; it prevents the forms from dissolving in the radiance of this luminous painting. The little humble figures, with their conventional attitudes, preserve their well defined personality among the blues, reds, and golds, which gleam like sky, and fire, and sun.

FIG. 130.—FIGURE IN
THE NORTH PORCH OF
THE CATHEDRAL OF
CHARTRES.

FIG. 131.—THE RESURRECTION OF THE VIRGIN. LEFT PORCH OF THE WEST FRONT OF NOTRE-DAME, PARIS.

In the course of the fourteenth century painted glass became less decorative and more and more realistic in character. The forms show greater richness and variety, and the figures, less harshly drawn, are clothed in more supple draperies. The frank colours of the early glass are replaced by broken tints; colours more neutral, and even monochrome, make their appearance. As early as the thirteenth century the glass-painters had modified, to some extent, the rich effects of the first stained glass windows. At the close of the Middle Ages glass-painting sacrificed splendour to an impossible correctness; in the effort to imitate the effects of realistic painting, it lost not only its original beauty, but its *raison d'être;* after this, it was better to fill the windows with colourless glass, and so to illuminate real pictures.

FIG. 132.—SAINT THEODORE. SOUTH PORCH OF THE CATHEDRAL OF CHARTRES.

It was at the beginning of the thirteenth century that the art of glass-painting had reached its highest perfection in the workshops of St. Denis, where Suger had the glass for the abbey church made; in those of Chartres, where the glass for the innumerable windows of the cathedral and of other churches in the West was produced; and finally, in those of Paris, the town in which all the industries of Gothic art tended to centralise. The stained glass of this period produced an effect dazzling yet soft, which the illuminators attempted to transpose into their miniatures; a few seconds spent in contemplating the great figures of the high windows, or the little pictures of the low chapels, sufficed to suggest to them celestial beatitude. The Sainte-Chapelle of St. Louis is like a crystallisation of precious stones;

FIG. 133.—NATIVITY. FRAGMENT OF THE DESTROYED ROOD-SCREEN OF THE CATHEDRAL OF CHARTRES.

Gothic windows enabled the pale light of the north to realise marvellous visions.

Gothic architecture was born when builders freed themselves from traditional forms and frankly accepted those indicated by mechanics; a similar emancipation took place in sculpture. The monks of the twelfth century had produced only an incomplete statuary; all they did was to give a certain degree of relief to the forms of the Benedictine paintings. Even when stirred by violent emotion, these figures remained rigid; they suffer from an over-long subservience to the Byzantine convention, and are awkwardly crushed down on a flat surface. A different art, a real sculpture, healthy, and normal, so to speak, began to develop in the middle of the twelfth century.

While the composite sculpture of Burgundy and Languedoc was producing agitated and uneasy forms, this youthful art was setting up simple figures in stiff attitudes; before achieving life and ease, sculpture, like antique statuary, had to go through the hieratic phase, the phase of *frontality*. But these quiescent figures enjoy complete organisms; they have solid bodies, detached from the mass.

It is not possible to follow from work to work

FIG. 134.—APOSTLES. CENTRAL PORCH OF THE CATHEDRAL OF AMIENS.

the process which gradually endowed the stone with life; dates and provinces cannot be determined with precision; this resurrection of sculpture must be assigned to about the middle of the twelfth century, and to an indeterminate region embracing Bourges, Chartres, and Saint Denis. When the carvers of images felt the charm of living forms, the ancient prejudice against statuary had to give way; Christianity tolerated a kind of modified idolatry, and thus it was given to this religion to find again what Greek paganism had first discovered eighteen hundred centuries earlier. The Gothic artists were right not to fear these novel forms, for whereas those of the Romanesque monasteries were related to antique art, of which they were often mere disfigurements, the statues of Chartres

FIG. 135. — APOSTLES. TYMPANUM OF THE SOUTH PORCH OF THE CATHEDRAL OF AMIENS.

have no remote heredity; they were born Christians and autochthonous.

This initial period produced more than one remarkable work. At Bourges and at Le Mans, certain long, rigid figures are sheltered in the back of the Gothic building. There were some at Saint Denis; two statues at Corbeil (Fig. 121) also survive from those years in which the figures began to detach themselves from the inert mass, while in Provence, at Saint Trophime at Arles, and also at Saint Gilles, the Apostles were still imbedded in the Romanesque façade. But we must go to Chartres to behold the first florescence of living statuary. A wondrous stone population emerges from its walls and pillars; they are, certainly, decorative statues, but they have an independent existence, and are no longer mere architectural ornaments.

FIG. 136.—APOSTLES. CENTRAL PORCH OF THE CATHEDRAL OF AMIENS.

Here we may study the sculpture of a whole century and more; some very early statues seem to be hardly more than slightly convex tombstones. Others, dating from the middle of the thirteenth century, have supple bodies and learnedly treated forms. The statues of the west front date from the middle of the twelfth century. They are set against strongly projecting Romanesque pillars, and do not adhere to the building

FIG. 137.—MARCH AND APRIL, WEST FRONT OF THE CATHEDRAL OF AMIENS.

(Fig. 120). Thenceforward, in other porches, architecture had to reckon with large sculptured figures; pillars disappear, to make place for statues; they look as if they were drawing themselves in to take shelter between the pedestal on which they stand and the canopy which overhangs them, and seem to move more freely than the earlier figures against pillars (Figs. 134 to 136). In the west front of Chartres, the porches, with the projecting pillars of their embrasures, were constructed in the Romanesque style of the West, by an architect who had provided for sculpture only on the tympanum and archivolts.

FIG. 138.—FRENCH IVORY KNOWN AS THE "VIRGIN OF THE SAINTE-CHAPELLE," BEGINNING OF THE FOURTEENTH CENTURY.

These first figures of Gothic statuary are the precocious masterpieces of an art as yet far from mature. The youthful freshness of this sculpture is shown in the calm and rigid dignity, akin to Greek archaism, to which it returns after the agitated style of the Romanesque period. Here, again, we have the hieratic immobility of the body, the impassible irony of expression found in the Æginetan marbles and those of the Parthenon. The artist is no longer inspired, as was the Romanesque sculptor, by a flat, painted image, antiquated and clumsy, falsified by centuries of conventionalisation; like the earliest Greek idols, the first Gothic statues emerged from a stone post. They seemed to be still imprisoned in it, but half disengaged, like flowers bursting from the bud, their petals still folded. In this new conquest of the aspects of life, sculpture once more went through a period of sharp and angular forms; like the slender Korai of the first Parthenon, the long figures at Chartres

FIG. 139.—JESUS APPEARING TO THE HOLY WOMEN. JESUS AND THE MAGDALEN. HIGH RELIEFS ON THE CHOIR SCREEN AT NOTRE-DAME, PARIS.

were carved by an industrious chisel which atones for the inexactitude of the planes by the care with which it defines the accessories of the costumes and the details of the faces. The elaborately rendered draperies are not cast about very robust bodies; shoulders are imperceptible, the arms are attached to the trunk; on the long slim bodies are perched delicate heads of bearded men, or women with long braided hair. The faces, with their prominent eyes and lips compressed in an austere smile, do not belong to our world; these holy beings are rapt in contemplation of radiant visions; a juvenile art has given them but an incomplete life; yet the workmanship is subtle and incisive; these figures have a tense and nervous quality which gives them an indefinable charm.

If we now walk round the cathedral, and study the innumerable figures of Prophets, Apostles, and Martyrs in the lateral porches at Chartres, we shall feel, even if we make no attempt at an impossible chronological classification, as if we were looking on at the slow labour which awoke this world of stone, and moulded the inert matter into the attitudes of life. The Apostles preside over the central south porch, the Prophets, still vigorous and agitated, over that of the north. This elaborate art, which can also be brutal upon occasion, is admirable in its evocation of a strange and antiquated world. In the neighbouring doorways the miracle is completed, and we see the stone bend and soften and curve to imitate moving bodies and floating draperies. The faces are modelled in larger planes, and forms are more frankly defined; the beard no longer adheres to the breast, the neck is longer, enabling the head to turn upon it, the shoulders are broader, the arms begin to move. The

FIG. 140.—CHRIST BLESSING, KNOWN AS THE "BEAU DIEU D'AMIENS." WEST FRONT OF THE CATHEDRAL OF AMIENS.

FIG. 141.—THE MEETING OF
ABRAHAM AND MELCHIZEDEK.
INNER WALL OF THE FAÇADE OF THE
CATHEDRAL OF REIMS.

figure is no longer fixed rigidly against a pillar, the feet cramped upon an inclined plane; it is detached and independent, and plants its feet firmly upon the ground to support its weight. Then one leg only is rigid, and the other is bent carelessly; the axis of the body is inflected, one hip is raised; the lines of neck and shoulders become mobile; the whole figure, with its supple limbs, produces a harmonious equilibrium. And now these figures begin to combine, and to enact some quiet drama together, the Annunciation or the Visitation: the Virgin, St. Anne, the angel Gabriel, make up tranquil groups animated by a common sentiment. A century after the pillar-statues, the swaddled terms of the west front, sculptors were setting up graceful and vigorous figures, vital organisms which, even in repose, suggest their latent energies. They had become capable of carrying their imitation of human types still further, of executing portraits, reproducing costumes, and even attempting the play of physiognomy; the art of statuary had recovered all its powers.

Christian iconography, when it adopted this form of art, was completely transformed by it. All the remote figures of the Gospel and of the Old Testament presented themselves to the eyes of the faithful, not with that strangeness of aspect

FIG. 142.—THE "GILDED VIRGIN."
SOUTH DOOR OF THE CATHEDRAL OF
AMIENS.

which kept the Romanesque figures in a fantastic, supernatural world, but with faces and bodies like those of living beings. The series of the Old Testament Prophets had to be retained; they appear in the north porch of Chartres, and are still beings outside the bounds of nature; an art hampered by archaic stiffness had fixed their violent personalities; they are the turbulent and furious vision-aries of the Bible, who, prior to the dawn of the serene radiance of the Gospel, sometimes illuminated their tempest of invective by lightning flashes of truth. Throughout the Middle Ages they re-tained their formidable aspect; we shall find these wild beasts later, at the end of the fourteenth century, round the well of Moses at Dijon, bowed down by the terror of their terrible predictions.

The principal figures of the Gospel change their appearance.

FIG. 143.—PLANT ORNAMENT OF THE CATHEDRAL OF REIMS.

Christ detaches Himself from the tympanum on which the Romanesque artists had carved His figure in relief, seated amidst the Elders of the Apocalypse or the sym-bols of the Evangelists (Fig. 122). This attitude He now retains only in the Last Judgment, over which He presides on the west fronts of our cathe-drals. But later He is to be found standing alone, upon the central pier of certain doorways, instinct with an in-dividuality, a personal significance which owes nothing to figures surrounding Him, or to a scene in which He is taking part. His attitude has become calmer, His face nobler; in one hand He holds the Word of Truth, and with the other He makes the sign of benediction.

To this tranquil figure the sculptors of the thir-teenth century gave in-comparable majesty. The "Beau Dieu" of Amiens, draped in an ample, flow-ing toga, lifts a face so gentle that a soft light seems to shine from it; revelation could not be

FIG. 144.—SAINT RÉMI CONDUCTED BY ANGELS. WEST FRONT OF THE CATHEDRAL OF REIMS.
'Photo. Neurdein.)

more impressively announced (Fig. 140). In the thirteenth century a serene splendour enfolds the teaching Christ; at the end of the Middle Ages He was replaced by the suffering Saviour.

But the Virgin was more especially dear to the artists of the thirteenth century; her figure dominates the whole of Gothic art. The majority of the great cathedrals were dedicated to her, and already an imposing chapel in the choir was set apart for her. The part she plays in the Gospels is modest enough; but popular imaginations supplemented it; legend blossomed around her, and provided her with a copious biography. In the twelfth century the Virgin was represented seated, and supporting the Infant God upon her knee; she was the

FIG. 145.—FIGURE ON THE CENTRAL PORCH OF THE WEST FRONT OF THE CATHEDRAL OF REIMS.
(*Photo. Mieusement.*)

"throne of Solomon." Jesus does not look at her; He is already preaching or blessing. It is thus she was represented on the tympana of the Romanesque churches, thus she was carved in stone, in ivory, in metal and in wood. In the Gothic cathedrals one entrance was always dedicated to her. She stands carrying the Infant Jesus on her left arm, her hip slightly projecting, her right leg carelessly bent, in such a manner as to throw her robe into large oblique folds. Her head is still covered with a corner of her mantle, in the traditional Eastern fashion; but a large royal crown discounts the severity of this nun-like Byzantine head-dress. Her features show no trace of the impassible stolidity of the Romanesque Virgins; her head is inclined towards the Child, with half-

FIG. 146.—THE QUEEN OF SHEBA. WEST PORCH OF THE CATHEDRAL OF REIMS.
(*Photo. Mieusement.*)

closed eyes and smiling lips. The supple figure, the somewhat sinuous robe, the playful hands, the tender look the Virgin bends upon the little Jesus, all these amenities have evolved a new figure, dearer than all others to Gothic art. It was the French thirteenth century which invented this gracious queen, delicate, gay, and smiling, of which the "gilded Virgin" at Amiens is the finished monumental type, a type that was repeated for centuries in ivory and in wood (Figs. 138, 142). The little Virgins carved in ivory accentuate this dainty grace; the features of the plump faces are small and fine, the cheeks rounded, the forehead prominent, the neck well covered; but the nose is pointed, the lips and eyes compressed in a keen little smile.

The sculptors of the thirteenth century were always happily inspired by the legend of the Virgin. At Amiens and at Reims, the Annunciation, the Visitation, the Presentation in the Temple, lend themselves to many calm, tender, and discreet scenes. Attitudes and emotion are unnecessary, the episode is always rendered with a gentle charm. The Death and the Resurrection of the Virgin have furnished subjects for the greatest masterpiece of Gothic statuary, in the north doorway of the west front of Notre Dame in Paris (Figs. 129, 131). This tympanum, in three stages, is in a style perfectly different from the Romanesque manner, with figures in high relief, completely detached from the background; but these figures, which are like so many independent statues, compose closely related groups, interwoven with a harmony of lines rare in the Middle Ages. Here again the sculptor was inspired by the

FIG. 148.—FIGURE OF ONE OF THE SAVED IN THE LAST JUDGMENT OF THE CATHEDRAL OF BOURGES.

(*Photo. Mieusement.*)

73

FIG. 149.—VIRGIN OF THE VISITATION. CENTRAL DOOR OF THE WEST FRONT OF THE CATHEDRAL OF REIMS.

Apocryphal Gospels. The Virgin has just died; Jesus has come down from Heaven, and the Apostles, scattered throughout the world after His death, have gathered together for the last time round her bed. Their heads, to which a gentle calm common to all gives a certain family likeness, form a circle round the expected miracle. Jesus gives the signal of Resurrection, and two angels reverently uplift the Virgin's corpse. Above, in the top of the tympanum, the glorification of Our Lady is completed. She is seated to the right of her Son; humble and radiant, she bends towards him with folded hands, while an angel places the crown of glory on her head. Form and sentiment were never more happily harmonised. French statuary of the thirteenth century is greatly in advance of the other plastic arts. Not till two centuries later shall we find such noble grace and attitudes so elegant and virginal rendered by painting; Fra Angelico was the first to evoke visions so purely beautiful.

The sculptors were able to give life to the twelve Apostles who accompany Jesus or the Virgin; but it was difficult to bestow a definite character on each of the twelve. The most animated series of Apostles bequeathed to us by mediæval art is to be found in the south porch of Amiens Cathedral. Above the "gilded Virgin" twelve vivacious little figures, well proportioned, their mild heads enframed in curling hair and beards, converse in couples, bending forward, leaning back emphasising their speech with an amusing variety of gesture (Fig. 135). The alert grace of the attitudes and the diversity of the draperies compensate for the somewhat monotonous vagueness of the types. These Apostles at Amiens and those in the

FIG. 150.—SOUTH PORCH OF THE CATHEDRAL OF ROUEN, KNOWN AS THE "PORTAIL DE LA CALENDE."

tympanum of the Virgin at Notre Dame in Paris show that French sculpture of the thirteenth century might, like Greek sculpture of the fifth century before our era, have created a canon in certain similar types and identical proportions. But mediæval sculpture was practised on too vast a territory, and in workshops too remote from each other; it had also too complex a programme to have enabled it to perfect a single type of beauty.

Christianity had gained its profound hold on the minds of men by permitting the popular imagination to collaborate in sacred narrative; the tenderness that vivifies religious art is not born of theology. Out of the universal iconography the men of the thirteenth century chose, and gave prominence to, the figures more particularly interesting to their local expressions of worship. In the general tradition, each diocese had its particular interest in one of the innumerable figures that belong to all Christendom. The Parisians kept a place of honour for the

FIG. 151.—APOSTLE BEARING THE CROSS OF DEDICATION, SAINTE-CHAPELLE.

Evangelists, for the patrons of their city; when they enter Notre Dame they are received by St. Denis, carrying his head, and accompanied by angels; elsewhere they see St. Marcel piercing the Dragon with his crozier. The cathedral, which absorbed an ancient church dedicated to St. Stephen, was not unmindful of the proto-martyr; the southern tympanum is dedicated to his history. The people of Amiens easily recognise their special patrons among the apostles of the universe; in the left porch of the west front, St. Firmin raises his hand in benediction towards that Picardy he converted; one of the most famous bishops of Amiens, St. Honoré, is elaborately commemorated on the tympanum of the south porch.

At Chartres, amidst the multitude

FIG. 152.—NORTH PORCH OF THE CATHEDRAL OF ROUEN, KNOWN AS THE "PORTAIL DES LIBRAIRES."

of figures which embraces the whole Christian iconography of the day, the faithful could identify their St. Potentien and their Ste.

FIG. 153.—FIGURE OF ONE OF THE SAVED IN THE LAST JUDGMENT OF THE CATHEDRAL OF BOURGES.
(*Photo. Mieusement.*)

Modeste, a graceful Virgin; and the admirable St. Theodore (Fig. 132) who guards the south porch recalled the fact that the Cathedral preserved his head among its relics. A. Reims we find the evangelist St. Sixtus, and St. Remi, to whom a dove brings the holy phial [1] (Fig. 144); the cathedral in which the kings of France were crowned shows on its façade David anointed by Samuel, and Solomon anointed by Nathan. Local traditions came from every region and took their place in the universal revelation; the roots of Christianity struck deeper, and art received its vital sap from the soil on which it flourished.

It was for this reason that it became more and more realistic and concrete. After the evolution of an urban civilisation, the various guilds discovered patrons and protectors; the faithful organised the celestial world after the fashion of their own, and the vague personalities of saints and martyrs entered the communal corporations and assumed their attributes. St. Bartholomew became a tanner, St. Thomas a stonemason, St. Crispin a shoemaker, St. Christopher a porter; the perfumers placed themselves under the protection of the Magdalen; the goldsmiths, under that of St. Eloi (Eligius); St. George was a knight, St.

FIG. 154.—THE CORONATION OF THE VIRGIN. IVORY.
(The Louvre, Paris.)

Luke a painter, St. Martha a servant. These relations between mankind and the saints became closer and more numerous in the

[1] This phial, preserved in the Cathedral, contained the oil for the coronation ceremony. It was smashed with a hammer by the revolutionaries in 1793.

course of the Middle Ages; artists imagined less and less, and copied more and more, in representing this Christian mythology. Jesus, the Virgin, and a few other figures whose features were clearly fixed by tradition, were brought more into harmony with daily life, without ever becoming portraits or losing the general aspect determined centuries ago; but all around them a host of secondary actors assume a more realistic appearance; in sculpture as in painting, Gothic art, illustrating the Gospels, or the narrative of Jacobus de Voragine, showed the image of the mediæval world to the fourteenth and fifteenth centuries.

FIG. 155.—THE "BLACK VIRGIN" OF COULOMB.

(The Louvre, Paris.)

The subject of the Last Judgment, which is found in nearly all the great cathedrals, demonstrates the formation and transformation of a motive during the twelfth and thirteenth centuries; it manifests the successive characteristics of French sculpture, in the confused and disjointed violence of Autun, the serene majesty of Paris, the dramatic and emotional art of Bourges. At Autun, the scene is already complete: Christ, the dead who are awakening, the angels and demons who contend for the elect and the damned; but the elements are not yet harmonised; Christ occupies too large a space; around Him, the tumultuous figures create such a confusion that it is not easy to grasp the great mystery which is enacted. In the south porch of Chartres, the composition is calm and well balanced; below the figure of Christ the little bodies of the elect and of the damned are ranged in orderly groups, but the scene lacks grandeur. At Paris, the Last Judgment is represented in three stages with marvellous clarity; above, Jesus presides over the last day of the world; in the lowest stage, the dead come forth from their graves; in the intermediate space, the Archangel and the Devil divide the souls. But though it is clearly defined, the composition is perhaps lacking in movement; there is a certain monotony in the awakening of the dead (the execution, it must be remembered, is modern); the groups of the elect and the damned are arranged in compact and well distributed bands; the sinister cavalcade of the Apocalypse is confined to the archivolts. At Amiens the same grandiose composition takes on a less peaceful, a more agitated character. But at Bourges the drama becomes animated and affecting (Figs. 156, 162). Here the sculptor has endeavoured to ana-lyse sentiment, instead of contenting himself with a somewhat monotonous mass of similar figures; the risen dead, after rais-ing their sepulchral stones, gesticulate and entreat; above, on either side of the great angel who is weighing souls, the final separation between the two worlds is completed. The damned are driven away and cast into the jaws of hell by horrible

FIG. 156.—THE LAST JUDGMENT. CENTRAL PORCH OF THE WEST FRONT OF THE CATHEDRAL OF BOURGES.
(*Photo. Neurdein.*)

and grotesque demons; one of these has the grinning mask of a satyr. But the elect are touching to behold. their little curly heads irradiated by the childish smile of an intimate faith (Figs. 148, 153).

Until we come to the Netherlandish painters of the fifteenth century, we shall find no more expressive vision of the Last Judg-ment than this legacy from the Middle Ages. The Gothic painters had little further to invent; the Netherlanders added grimaces and contortions to the spectacle of hell, and the painters of Cologne devoutly coloured the little figures of the saved, putting blue above their heads, green beneath their feet, and red upon their cheeks.

FIG. 157.—TOMB OF SAINT STEPHEN; CHURCH OF AUBAZINE (CORRÈZE).

By this imitation of the flexibility and disorder of actual life, sculpture freed itself from architecture, to which it was at first merely supplementary, and from the rigidity of line it imposed. The sculptors who executed the tympanum of Notre Dame in Paris belonged to this brief and

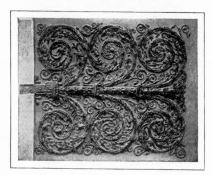

happy age of precarious equilibrium, during which technical skill allowed artists to handle forms with ease, but not to give more than an idealised image of realities; the faces are uniformly serene and beautiful, the draperies carved in planes of great geometrical regularity. The Apostles at Amiens are of the same simple and non-emphatic type; their gestures are natural and peaceful; their robes

FIG. 158.—HINGE OF HAMMERED IRON IN THE WEST PORCH OF NOTRE DAME, PARIS.

fall in strongly marked folds, slightly broken, without much flexibility; the faces are lively and intelligent, but have none of the individuality of portraiture. This elegance is not the outcome of a very search-ing art; the figures, in which, however, there is no trace of the ancient heraldic stiffness, are somewhat monotonous in their attitudes; under the great Gothic porches, they are admirably decorative.

At Reims, on the other hand, the somewhat abstract sobriety of Paris and Amiens is replaced by a varied and even incoherent vitality. Here the sculp-tors have been little concerned with unity of style; they have given free rein to their own exuberance of spirit; the faces are more expressive as well as the attitudes, and the draperies are more flexible. Many of the figures are even individual types; certain spare, bony, energetic heads, the faces tense with moral expres-sion, are set upon alert bodies in animated attitudes. Some of the faces are eager

FIG. 159.—GRILLE OF FORGED IRON FROM OURSCAMP, IN THE MUSÉE DES ARTS DÉCORATIFS, PARIS.

and spiritual as if the more subtle stone could imprison, without extinguishing, the flame of life. Here are great angels of a feminine type who bend forward daintily, with an expression of gentle malice. Here, too, among the angular figures of mediæval sculpture, is that

amazing group of the Visitation, which revives the luxuriant contours of antique statues, and the quivering folds of their clinging draperies; robust and supple female forms are draped in flowing robes of delicate texture and minute folds. These women are not of Gothic race; they are akin to those idols which antique art carved in the marble to satisfy its worship of physical beauty and moral health. The peaceful dialogue between these two majestic figures suggests a colloquy between vestal virgins.

Such a variety of types and style shows how little Gothic sculpture was fettered by formulæ such as those which had for centuries hampered painting. The Gothic sculptors were not all skilful, but they were all inspired by a vigour unknown before their time. It took possession of French artists, when, at the beginning of the thirteenth century, the plastic arts came for the first time into contact with life.

The evolution of ornamental forms is more significant of the intimate predilections of French taste than that of architecture or the representation of figures. Nothing characterises the style of a period so strongly as its grammar of ornament, those forms which are born spontaneously under the artist's hand when it is uncontrolled by any law of utility or imitation. At

FIG. 161.—SHRINE OF SAINT CALMINE. LIMOGES ENAMEL IN THE MUSÉE DOBRÉE (NANTES).
(*Photo. Gibouin.*)

the same period when architects set their vaults upon intersecting arches, sculptors transformed the appearance of the capitals which

FIG. 162.—THE LAST JUDGMENT (FRAGMENT). PORCH OF THE CATHEDRAL OF BOURGES.
(*Photo. Neurdein.*)

received the ribs. Romanesque ornament was a very complex mixture of ancient or exotic motives; its sculptors sought rather to combine than to invent. Towards the close of the twelfth century, decorators showed a tendency to eliminate the barbaric interlacements and arabesques, and all the remnants of antique art, volutes or acanthus leaves. While the sculptors were returning to the living forms of the human body, the decorators borrowed from vegetable life swelling and bursting buds, spreading leaves, closing or opening petals. In contrast to the Romanesque capitals with their trenchant designs and dry angles, the products of a minute and difficult technique—that proper to the worker in ivory or precious metals—the first Gothic capitals, swelling with a robust sap, clothe themselves with the broad leaves of arum or water-lily, and petals the fleshy contours of which preserved the solid character of the basket. By degrees, as the Gothic style became more supple, the sculptors adopted more elaborate plant forms; they reproduced the leaves of oak or parsley, and while preserving regularity of arrangement, they imitated the dense disorder of foliage. Reims Cathedral contains not only the most life-like figures of Gothic statuary; on its robust architecture, on the capitals of its pillars, ivy and vine leaves climb and inter-

FIG. 163.—CHALICE OF SAINT-RÉMI.
TREASURY OF THE CATHEDRAL OF REIMS.

(*Photo. Neurdein.*)

twine, so delicate and nervous that they seem to quiver as we gaze. How arid Romanesque decoration seems for all its

ART IN FRANCE

luxuriance, when we compare it with this freshness! Later, at the end of the fourteenth century, the last Gothic artists carved the sharp and curling forms of cabbage, chicory, and thistle; on the stone angles, as on the pages of manuscripts, the indented and serrated leaves of plants flourish in profusion. Like Gothic architecture itself, the Gothic flora became fragile and complicated.

FIG. 164.—CATHEDRAL OF REIMS. CAPITAL OF A PILLAR IN THE LADY CHAPEL.

(Photo. Neurdein.)

BIBLIOGRAPHY.

The same general works as for Chapter II.—Villard de Honnecourt, *Album manuscrit* published by Lassus and Darcel, Paris, 1858.—Anth. Saint-Paul, *Simple mémoire sur l'origine du style ogival (B.M.,* 1875). —Louis Gonse, *L'Art gothique,* Paris, 1890.—Ch. H. Moore, *Development and Character of Gothic Architecture,* New York, 1899.—G. von Bezold, *Die Entstehung und Ausbildung der Gothischen Baukunst in Frankreich,* Berlin, 1891.—G. Dehio, *Die Anfänge des Gothischen Baustils (Repertorium für Kunstwissenschaft,* 1896).—H. Stein, *Les Architectes gothiques,* Paris, 1909.—D. Mich. Felibien, *Histoire de l'Abbaye de Saint-Denis en France,* Paris, 1706.— Vitry and Brière, *L'Eglise abbatiale de Saint-Denis et ses tombeaux,* Paris, 1908.—L. Vitet, *Notre-Dame de Noyon,* Paris, 1845.—F. de Guilhermy and Viollet-le-Duc, *Description de Notre-Dame de Paris,* Paris, 1856.—F. de Guilhermy, *Description de la Sainte-Chapelle,* Paris, 1887.—M. Aubert, *La Cathédrale Notre-Dame-de-Paris,* Paris, 1909.—Abbé A. Bouillet, *Les Eglises paroissiales de Paris. Monographies illustrées,* Paris, 1897-1903.—Lassus, *Monographie de la Cathédrale de Chartres,* Paris, 1867.—Abbé Bulteau, *Monographie de la Cathédrale de Chartres,* Chartres, 1888-1902, 3 vols.—E. Lefèvre Pontalis, *Les Fouilles de la Cathédrale de Chartres (B.M.,*1901).—R. Merlet, *La Cathédrale de Chartres,* Paris, 1909.— Abbé Bouxin, *La Cathédrale de Laon,* Laon, 1890.—G. Durand, *La Cathédrale d'Amiens,* Amiens, 1901-1903.—Abbé Cerf, *Histoire et Description de Notre-Dame-de-Reims,* Reims, 1861, 2 vols.—L. Demaison, *Les Architectes de la Cathédrale de Reims (B. A.,* 1894).—Gosset, *Histoire et Monographie de la Cathédrale de Reims,* Paris, 1894.—Bégule, *Monographie de la Cathédrale de Lyon,* Lyons, 1880.—Corroyer, *Description de l'Abbaye de Saint-Michel,* Paris, 1877.—Denais, *Monographie de la Cathédrale d'Angers,* 1899.—Abbé Bossebœuf, *L'Architecture Plantagenet,* Angers, 1897.—Ch. de Grandmaison, *Tours archéologique,* Paris, 1879.—Abbé Arbellot, *Cathédrale de Limoges,* Paris, 1883.—H. Crozes, *Monographie de la Cathédrale Sainte-Cécile d'Albi,* Toulouse, 1873.—G. Dehio, *L'Influence de l'Art français sur l'Art allemand au XIIIe siècle (R. A.,* 1900).—C. Enlart, *Origines françaises de l'Architecture gothique en Italie,* Paris, 1894.—C. Enlart, *L'Art gothique et la Renaissance en Chypre,* Paris, 1899, 2 vols.—C. Enlart, *Origines françaises de l'Architecture gothique en Espagne (B. A.,* 1894).—De Baudot, *La Sculpture française au Moyen Age et à la Renaissance,* Paris, 1881 (Album of 400 motives in statuary or ornament).—P. Vitry and G. Brière, *Documents de Sculpture française du Moyen Age,* Paris, 1904.—E. Mâle, *L'Art religieux en France au XIIIe siècle,* 2nd ed., Paris, 1902.—M. Voege, *Die Anfänge der monumentalen Stiles im Mittelalter,* Strasburg, 1894.—R. de Lasteyrie, *Etudes sur la Sculpture française au Moyen Age (Mon. Piot,* vol. viii., 1902).—R. de Lasteyrie, *La Porte Sainte-Anne à Notre-Dame-de-Paris (Mém. de la Soc. de l'Histoire de Paris,* 1902).—Margaret and Ernest Marriage, *The Sculptures of Chartres Cathedral,* Cambridge, 1909.—R. Kœchlin, *La Sculpture belge et les Influences françaises aux XIIIe et XIVe siècles (G. B. A.,* 1903, II).— A. Marignan, *Histoire de la Sculpture en Languedoc aux XIIe et XIIIe siècles,* Paris, 1902.—

COMMUNAL OR GOTHIC ART

R. Kœchlin, *Quelques Ateliers d'ivoiriers français aux XIIIe, XIVe siècles* (*G. B. A.*, 1905).—Louise Pillion, *Les Portails latéraux de la Cathédrale de Rouen*, Paris, 1907.—A. Schmarsow, *Das Eindringen der französischen Plastik in die deutsche Sculptur* (*Repertorium für Kunstwissenschaft*, 1898).—For Painting : the works quoted on Romanesque Art.—F. de Lasteyrie, *Histoire de la Peinture sur verre*, 2 vols., 1857.—Magne, *L'Œuvre des Peintres verriers français*, Paris, 1885.—L.-O. Merson, *Les Vitraux*, Paris, 1895.—H. Oidtmann, *Die Glasmalerei*, 2 vols., Cologne, 1898.

FIG. 165.—CATHEDRAL OF REIMS.
CAPITAL OF A PILLAR, SOUTH SIDE OF THE NAVE.
(Photo. Neurdein.)

CHAPTER IV

FEUDAL ART AND CIVIC ART AT THE CLOSE OF THE MIDDLE AGES

The Centres of Artistic Activity: the King, the Great Nobles, the Pope at Avignon.—The Middle Classes in the Fifteenth Century.—Feudal Architecture.—Communal Architecture, Ramparts, Houses, Mansions of Rich Burghers or Princes, Town-Halls.—Cathedrals in the Fourteenth Century; the Radiating Type.—The Flamboyant Style at the End of the Fifteenth Century.—Sculpture, Tombs.—Painting, Stained Glass, Illumination.—Realistic Evolution of Miniature-Painting.—The First Distemper Pictures.—Painting in Burgundy, at Avignon and Aix, in Touraine and Bourbonnais.—Popular Inspiration in the Arts of Imagery.

In the thirteenth century, an intense artistic activity took possession of all the great communes which desired to build a cathedral, and then to people it with statues and adorn it with coloured glass windows. Art had already become the work of laymen, but, as yet, it only existed for religion, and like religion, it had spread abroad in the world. As the century advanced, artists worked less exclusively for the requirements of worship; there is a charm in the plastic arts which kings and great nobles soon desired to enjoy and to reckon among the accessories of their wealth. Now the art of luxury cannot be so widely disseminated as religious art. It requires wealth, and a certain intellectual culture; there must be prosperous towns to form skilful workmen and rich citizens or the court of a prince to pay them. Under these conditions, the artistic energies of a country tend to concentrate in certain places. It was in the

fourteenth century that the destinies of French art began to inter-
mingle with those of the great men of the kingdom, of kings and
those who aspired to rival
them.

FIG. 167.—CHATEAU-GAILLARD.

To survey the activities
of the most distinguished
among these patrons of
the arts is to pass in review the principal works
of art of the second half
of the fourteenth, as well
as those of the succeeding
century. First in order
are the kings : the first
Valois, frivolous and magnificent ; John the Good,
who took musicians with him to his captivity in England ; a painter
has left us his portrait, the earliest of French pictures (Fig. 243),
a brutal head painted in languid colours. Then Charles V., the
wise king who built Vincennes, the Bastille, and the Louvre, a
quadrangular fortress which combined many architectonic amenities
with a huge donjon, dating from the time of Philip Augustus ; the
learned king who loved beautiful manuscripts, and wrote on them
"This book belongs to me, Charles" ; the collector of miniatures,
whom the illuminators have shown us with his big nose and his
ill-shaved chin, receiving some precious book as a homage ; the
builder of the chapel of the Célestins, whose image a sculptor set up
in the porch, side by side
with his queen, holding a
model of the building in
his hand. The statue has
survived ; it is a tranquil
work, without brilliance
or fire, but probably absolutely faithful ; the man
still lives, with his weary
body, his narrow chest,
his good-natured face, half
meditative, half smiling
(Figs. 209, 210). We

FIG. 168.—CHATEAU OF ARQUES.

find him again on his tomb at Saint Denis, carved by his "imagier,"
Beauneveu ; this statue is more commonplace ; but we recognise the

great nose in the flabby face, and the subtle expression. Then come the brothers of Charles V., Louis d'Orléans, the builder of

FIG. 169.—COURT OF THE CHATEAU OF COUCY.

Pierrefonds (Fig. 176) and of La Ferté-Milon; the Duc de Berry, who was rapacious only that he might procure himself refined delights; his plump, snub-nosed, reddish face is familiar to us; in his old age, he is shown wrapped in furs, turning over his book of hours, to admire the wonderful *châteaux* his architects had built and his miniaturists had painted for him. Finally, there are the Dukes of Burgundy: Philippe le Hardi and Jean sans Peur, whose successors gave them such admirable tombs; Philippe le Bon more especially, and Charles le Téméraire, who were rich and powerful, and had the good fortune to rule Flanders, and employ those great artists Claus Sluter, Jan van Eyck, and Rogier van der Weyden.

In the South, the Popes had made Avignon a city of luxury and pleasure. They built themselves a fortified palace (Fig. 174) on the hill, encircling it with ramparts, and summoned fresco painters to decorate it in the Sienese manner. It was at their behest that Italian painting crossed the Alps; it has left a few decorations in the monasteries of Savoy; it penetrated far into the country, as far as Toulouse, where Italian artists painted the Church of the Jacobins. Avignon preserved her artistic vitality for a long period; situated upon the main road to Italy, the town seems a precursor of the Italian cities; rich in churches and in works of art, she is to the Northerner the threshold of that land where the relics of the past appeal so strongly to the sense of beauty. But if the fourteenth

FIG. 170.—KEEP OF THE CHATEAU OF COUCY.

century in Provence was in the main Italian, the preceding century had rather been Netherlandish; it was a period of intense expansion for the art of the great Flemish towns. Aix was the city of the good King René, who loved painting so much that tradition has made him a painter; in any case, he certainly summoned to his court many skilful artists, whose acquaintance he had perhaps made during a forced sojourn in the Low Countries. He sat for them frequently; on the shutters of triptychs, his painters have shown us his coarsely modelled head with the pendulous goitre, and the thin face of his

FIG. 171.—RAMPARTS OF DINAN.

wife. Many Northerners came to Aix in those days, bringing their angular and richly attired figures to bask in the sun of Provence. Towards the close of the fifteenth century, the modest court of the Duke of Burgundy at Moulins had also attracted painters, who portrayed the family of the Duke, and the undulating verdure of the Bourbonnais landscape.

In the course of the fifteenth century, however, the rich patrons necessary for the artists of the day began to fail. Charles VII. and Louis XI. were too much occupied; they had to introduce order into France; the task of embellishing her was left to their successors. The great feudatory princes were gradually declining; whereas Louis d'Orléans had built the Château of Pierrefonds, his son Charles, vanquished at Agincourt, vegetated at Blois; the Duc d'Anjou lost his states one by one; the court of Burgundy disappeared with Charles le Téméraire.

On the other hand, an enriched middle class was replacing the feudal aris-

FIG. 172.—CHATEAU OF ALENÇON.

tocracy. Jouvenel des Ursins, a prelate who was the friend of Charles VII. and Etienne Chevalier, sat to Fouquet. Jacques

Cœur, Charles VII.'s controller of finances, built a house at Bourges which is one of the most charming examples of fifteenth

century architecture (Fig. 192). At about the same period, the hospital of Beaune (Fig. 186) was built by order of Nicolas Rolin, Chancellor of the Duke of Burgundy, for whom Jan van Eyck and Rogier van der Weyden painted pictures. The middle classes gradually came to play the part

FIG. 173.—RAMPARTS OF VILLENEUVE-LÈS-AVIGNON.

formerly assumed by the nobles, who were ruined by the luxury of the towns.

The artistic efflorescence of feudal civilisation was practically confined to the fourteenth century; its architecture dates from this period. Before this, the castle was but a fortress; solid walls continued the sharp acclivity, defying escalade by their height, and the shock of projectiles by their thickness. At the time when the Communes, directed by their bishops, were raising their learnedly constructed churches, strongholds such as the Château Gaillard (Fig. 167), which Richard Cœur-de-Lion built to close the Seine to the King of France, were nothing but brutal obstructions of masonry. Upon an eminence, the crest of the plateau was encircled by walls, at the angles of which rose towers and keep. This keep, which dominated the surrounding country in a symbolic fashion, was the only inhabited portion within the narrow limits. In the Romanesque period, it was generally quadrangular; in the thirteenth century it was circular. At Coucy, in the first half of the thirteenth century,

FIG. 174.—PALACE OF THE POPES AT AVIGNON.

the keep rose to a height of fifty-five metres, and the walls on the ground floor were ten metres thick. Viollet-le-Duc points out that everything in this castle was on a colossal scale; the panels of the battlements, the steps of the staircases, the benches and supports seem to have been constructed for giants; the whole is an object lesson on feudal power; in his donjon, the lord of Coucy could bid defiance to the world.

This fortress was impregnable; but the huge mass suffocated those whom it protected. In the fourteenth century, the donjon was considered a very uncomfortable dwelling; within the ramparts, houses were erected against the walls, and the height of the curtains was raised for their protection. The building gradually improved; on the exterior, it still presented a hostile face, with solid walls, pierced only by narrow loopholes; but this sturdy outer shell now enclosed a mansion. The graceful façades that gave on the inner court had large windows and spacious balconies, crowned by high roofs which

FIG. 175.—KEEP OF THE CHATEAU OF LANGEAIS.
(*Photo. Neurdein.*)

are seen from a distance rising above the curtains; here the architect was able to indulge his Gothic fancy in decorating dormer windows and chimneys.

For the noble, imprisoned in his castle, the principal amusement was no doubt a walk along the barbican or covered way, at the top of the curtains and towers; through the loopholes he could contemplate from afar the plain, the forest, the village; he enjoyed in anticipation the pleasure of a gallop in the open

FIG. 176.—CHATEAU OF PIERREFONDS.
(*Photo. Neurdein.*)

country. The castle of Pierrefonds, built at the beginning of the fifteenth century and restored by Viollet-le-Duc, shows how skilfully architects installed a palace in a fortress. It would be impossible to tell in a few words how the offensive and defensive perfection of

the ancient castle was evolved. All we can do is to note the principal inventions, those which were retained, with slight modifications, in castles built after the feudal régime. The wall was no longer merely obstructive; it protected its defenders on the summit behind battlements; first wooden *hourds* (or timber scaffolds), and later stone machicolations supported by corbels, enabled them to cast down projectiles upon assailants, themselves unseen.

These walls and towers were the precursors of the Renaissance *Château*. Here, as in religious architecture, utility directed invention,

FIG. 177.—RAMPARTS OF CARCASSONNE.

and an organism was constituted, an organism both harmonious and logical, the forms of which were destined to persist even after the feudal fortress had ceased to have any *raison d'être;* a decorative style was evolved from the fortress, from its towers, its battlements and its machicolations, just as Gothic ornament developed on the initial theme of diagonal ribs supported

by arches and pillars. Of the earlier structures, little now remains but gutted towers and crumbling walls overgrown with vegetation; all this ingenious architecture is gradually assuming the aspect of the rock from which it was derived. How many hill tops of Brittany, Limousin, Périgord, Provence, and Auvergne are crowned and completed by the still haughty silhouette of dis-

FIG. 178.—RAMPARTS OF CARCASSONNE.

mantled fortresses! Looking at them, we see how feudalism and its castles were the natural products of the soil. In the Château of

Bonaguil, in Lot-et-Ga-
ronne, built in the middle
of the fifteenth century,
the architect's chief con-
cern was to resist and to
utilise artillery. He ex-
tended the exterior de-
fences widely, and in the
lower parts of the towers,
he made apertures for the
muzzles of cannon. And
yet these proud towers,

FIG. 179.—RAMPARTS OF AVIGNON.

and this donjon upon the rocky scarp, offer an insurmountable
resistance only to escalade. Powder would very soon blow this

FIG. 180.—VALENTRÉ BRIDGE, AT CAHORS.
(*Photo. Neurdein.*)

dry masonry to fragments.
All these castles suffered
from their too intimate relation to a form of society
which was not destined
to endure ; they were subjected to long cannonades
from the royal artillery,
and were methodically
destroyed in the time of
Richelieu and Mazarin,
after the definitive victory
of the monarchy. Feudal
architecture had to trans-

form itself in order to subsist ; the castle abandoned its obsolete
organs of defence ; the smiling Renaissance palace emerged from
its shell when at last the will of the king was powerful enough

to decree that henceforth
no one should live in a
fortress.

The Communes, after
conquering their place in
feudal organisation, had to
defend it ; the burgesses
encircled their towns with
ramparts ; but these ram-
parts were to prove no
more enduring than the

FIG. 181.—CHATEAU OF ANGERS.
(*Photo. Neurdein.*)

91

fortresses; the stone girdle had to be removed or it would have strangled the growing community. Only some few towns, such as Dinan (Fig. 171) and Saint Malo in Brittany, and Provins in the Ile-de-France, have preserved large portions of their ancient ramparts. But there are three southern cities where these are almost intact: Carcassonne (Figs. 177, 178), Aigues-Mortes (Fig. 166) and Avignon (Fig. 179).

Aigues-Mortes was the creation of Saint Louis and of Philip the Bold. The kings of France coveted an outlook upon the Mediterranean. Hence this fortified town, rising from the flat shore, is quite unlike the usual Acropolis. The nature of the ground did not necessitate an elaborate plan; the masonry is the only eminence in the plain. Upon this desert of sand and of pools rises a quadrilateral structure of uniform walls flanked by towers of equal height. The whole has a stunted look in a landscape the infinite lines of which enhance the drowsy horizontality. On all four sides the ramparts present a solid front of masonry, unbroken save by narrow loopholes for the watchful archer. The ramparts of Aigues-Mortes constitute a mediæval fortification in all its simplicity; a very thick wall to check the enemy, an obstruction offering no weak points for attack, and, behind it, ingenious hiding-places for the defenders.

Here, again, a refuge was contrived; the Tour Constance rises, round and solid. This massive shell of masonry encloses rooms with graceful vaults; the wall is honeycombed with galleries and staircases, which constitute so many traps for the feet of the assailant. Saint Louis and his successors hastened to make Carcassonne equally impregnable when it became a royal town. On a vast, wind-swept plain the citadel rears its mighty bulk, dominating the historic passage of the Garonne into the Mediterranean; the double *enceinte* flanked by fifty towers encircles an abrupt hill; the huge flat, bare

FIG. 184.—AITRE SAINT-MACLOU, AT ROUEN.

walls, unrelieved by any accidents save the natural asperities of the stone, are pierced with long loopholes and crowned by battlements, the sharp outlines of which have been restored by Viollet-le-Duc. Everything is calculated to the end of keeping a constant watch upon the aggressor. The defenders could follow his movements from a hundred hiding-places when he advanced towards the gloomy wall that betrayed no sign of life. A walk upon these ramparts is a crushing experience; such a piling up of masonry fatigues the spectator; the steel-grey stone adds its dull monotony to this rude armour in which a little town is dying, after having suffocated in safety for centuries.

FIG. 185.—HOTEL DE VILLE, AT SAINT-QUENTIN.

The Popes at Avignon also surrounded their pleasant town with military defences. But here the ramparts do not constitute a prison. Above the low walls, surmounted by strongly projecting battlements, the town can contemplate the Rhone and the sun-bathed rock of Villeneuve. The palace of the Popes bears no resemblance to the castles of the French nobles. It has neither round towers nor keeps. Lofty blocks of buildings enclose two quadrangular courts. But their towering walls are also defences; the huge buttresses which reinforce them are united at the top by pointed arches, which form machicolations. Fortresses were numerous in the domain of King René; they can bear the proximity of the magnificent Roman ruins. The same radiant light gilds the rude relics of feudal days, and the splendid buildings of antiquity, triumphal arch and battlemented donjon,

FIG. 186.—COURT OF THE HOTEL-DIEU AT BEAUNE.

the successive structures which civilisation extracted from the same Provençal limestone. Meanwhile civil architecture was evolved in the towns; in the fourteenth and fifteenth centuries the burgesses began to install themselves in comfortable dwellings behind the protecting ramparts. They varied greatly according to the character

FIG. 187.—HOTEL DE VILLE AT COMPIÈGNE.

of the locality; the general style of the habitation indicated the difference between the France *d'oil* and the France *d'oc,* just as did the language of the two regions. In the south the predominant type was the flat-roofed building, of well cut stone; in the north the house was built of light materials and crowned with a high, pointed roof; it was to some extent the difference of style between Romanesque and Gothic. A few Romanesque houses still subsist, the round-arched windows of which recall the Gallo-Roman type; in certain centres of Romanesque art, such as Cluny, Montferrand, and Saint Gilles, we may still see houses of the twelfth and thirteenth centuries. At Cordes (Tarn) very nearly an entire street of this period is intact; in this civilisation, which had retained the municipal traditions of decorum derived from the Roman occupation, solid blocks of freestone were still the customary materials for building. A Romanesque house at Saint-Antonin, with a square belfry, recalls the communal palaces of the old Tuscan towns; delicate little columns with carved capitals form a graceful gallery in the first storey; the Romanesque builders always loved to insert an elaborate piece of sculpture into a mass of

FIG. 188.—CHATEAU OF JOSSELIN.

somewhat rude masonry. The open ground-floor served as a market for traders, and a shady refuge in which to breathe the open air.

The northern towns have preserved no civil buildings so ancient; erected at a later date of municipal civilisation, the more active life of colder latitudes wore them out and renewed them several times; northern urban dwellings date back no farther than the fifteenth century. At this period houses were built with a wooden framework, the ground-floor alone being of masonry; the upper storeys were of light materials, upheld by a skeleton of beams arranged in the form of the letter X or N. Sometimes the houses widened at every storey; large windows opened on to the street, which gradually contracted as the building rose from storey to storey; the whole was covered by an overhanging roof; a gable gave the façade that pointed silhouette dear to the Gothic architect. The

FIG. 189.—HOTEL DE CLUNY, PARIS.

man of the fifteenth century could provide a cheap decoration for his house by carving grotesques on the projecting beams of the façade; within, also, the wood was carved and painted. The whole house was like the work of a cabinet-maker. The town mansions (*hôtels*) were arranged like the interiors of feudal dwellings; Jacques Cœur's house at Bourges (Fig. 192), the Hôtel de Sens, and the house of the Abbots of Cluny in Paris (Fig. 189), are the unfortified dwellings of great nobles in a town. Like the castle, the façade of the house giving on the court has become gay and

FIG. 190.—PALAIS DE JUSTICE, ROUEN.

hospitable. It is generally separated from the street by a block of buildings, and sometimes merely by a battlemented wall, which masks the whole. The visitor who wishes to admire the graceful structure must pass through a low doorway in the wall. In the course of the fourteenth century, civil architecture adopted more and more generally the square, casement window, to which an arched hood moulding was sometimes applied. Pointed windows were reserved for religious buildings. A turret sometimes detaches itself from the body of the building, crowned with a belfry; it contains a spiral staircase, and its oblique openings reveal the steps; these little projecting towers were long a favourite motive of French architects; the one which Raymond du Temple built in Charles V.'s Louvre was famous until the Renaissance.

In the Royal Domain, town-halls made their appearance very late; the towns did not attain to the municipal power of the cities of Flanders, and the cathedrals were often used for political gatherings. Notre-Dame-de-Paris had

FIG. 191.—PALAIS DE JUSTICE, BEAUVAIS.

not been built very long before its vaults resounded with the furious invectives hurled against the Pope by an agent of Philip the Fair, before the States General. However, urban administration soon required a house for the despatch of business. It is more especially in the towns of the north, rich cities which were brought into contact with Flemish life and manners, that the town-halls have a really original character, with the elaborate decoration proper to the luxury of commercial civilisation, and the enormous communal bell-towers, haughtier than feudal donjons. On the ground-floor, as at Saint-Quentin (Fig. 185), and Arras, was an open gallery; on the upper storeys, windows described a graceful curve, in the latest style of Gothic, and sometimes, as at Saint-Quentin, a row of gables crowned the façade; they formed a circle, together with the gables of private houses, round the great Place. The Town-Hall

FIG. 192.—JACQUES CŒUR'S HOUSE, BOURGES.
(*Photo. Neurdein.*)

of Compiègne (Fig. 187), on the other hand, is very different in aspect; it is built in the style which was evolved in the heart of France after the Hundred Years War, a style more akin to the massive architecture of feudal times. Like the Hôtel de Cluny, and

FIG. 193.—FIREPLACE IN THE GREAT HALL OF THE PALAIS DE JUSTICE, POITIERS.

Jacques Cœur's house, it is a graceful and soberly-decorated building, not, like the town-halls of Flanders, open to the passer-by, and permitting the seething life of the town to penetrate under its vaults, but more akin to a civic hall under a powerful monarchy, where public functions conferred a kind of nobility, and where an equestrian statue of the king was proudly enshrined. The Rouen Palace of Justice shows the wealth of graceful ornament Gothic architecture could lavish on a façade.

Superb mouldings enframe the wide windows. Between these, buttresses, recessed for statues, mount to the dormer-windows, over

FIG. 194.—CLOISTER OF THE MUSÉE DES AUGUSTINS, AT TOULOUSE.

which they throw flying buttresses, and on the lofty roof the stone turns and curls in an exuberant florescence of pinnacles and pierced gables (Fig. 190).

At the close of the Middle Ages, the types of civil architecture, mansion and town-hall in particular, as they were to continue after the Renaissance, were definitely fixed. The renovation of architecture went no further than decoration; the recessed buttresses were replaced by pilasters, and the gables by pediments. The mouldings which overrun a Gothic façade capriciously, like the branches of an old vine-creeper, were disciplined and transformed into delicate bas-reliefs; but the building was not disturbed in the logic of its organism.

The men of the fourteenth century had practically ceased to build cathedrals; the great effort of technical invention was drawing to an end, and the mystic impulse was arrested; but the Gothic style continued to live, without renewing itself. The general forms of the building took on a more precise elegance, and ornament continued to grow richer.

The Gothic style of the fourteenth century was more methodical than that of the reign of Philip Augustus. In the transition from the west porches of Notre-Dame-de-Paris

FIG. 195.—CLOISTER OF LA CHAISE-DIEU.
(*Photo. Neurdein.*)

to the north and south porches built by Jean de Chelles, we see the architect more and more intent on precision of design; he develops the decorative theme of a door or a rose-window with easy mastery; façades acquire a precise and regular elegance, not without coldness. The admirable nave of Saint-Ouen, at Rouen (Fig. 196), due to a single uninterrupted effort, on a well-defined plan, is impeccable in style and somewhat chilly in effect. The masses of the architecture, walls and pillars, the wide windows with three mullions and roses, have the purity of a fine architectural drawing.

FIG. 196.—NAVE OF SAINT-OUEN, ROUEN.

The term *Rayonnant* (radiating) is applied in France to that chastened and correct style which came into vogue when architects substituted decorative research for mechanical problems. The resulting modifications affected every part of the building. The inert elements which remained in the masonry were eliminated; windows were enlarged, pillars were transformed into a sheaf of slender columns; the profiles of mouldings became sharper; the triforium was diminished or disappeared altogether, to give more impetus to the soaring vertical lines. The *Rayonnant* style carried elegance to the extreme point compatible with the solidity of the building. To decorate this somewhat puny ossature and drape this nudity, architects added a quantity of ornamental amenities: the mullions of the enlarged windows were elaborated, and formed roses; the pierced and pointed gables of doorways made a rigid lacework against the sky; buttresses were crowned with pinnacles; spears of stone or metal bristled on every summit; towers arose, with sharp spires flanked by belfries; the stone was hollowed and reduced, carried towards

FIG. 197.—NAVE OF THE CATHEDRAL OF ALENÇON.

FIG. 198.—CATHEDRAL OF SENS.

(*Photo. Neurdein.*)

the zenith by an impulse common to the whole building.

Thus Gothic architecture continued to enrich itself, even after its creative force was spent; the cathedral is an organism which could go on indefinitely receiving new members and ornaments; the porch could always be crowned by a gable; the façade could always be flanked by towers; each tower could always have its spire. Even the plan of the building allows of additions. At Rouen, the body of the cathedral disappears among the limbs that have been attached to it, between the two towers added to its façade, the Portail des Libraires and the Portail de la Calende, which give monumental decorations to the two extremities of the transept, the Lady Chapel which increases the depth of the apse, and finally the enormous spire which surmounts the lantern.

The cathedrals left unfinished at the close of the thirteenth century were not, however, abandoned. But the master-builder who resumed the work, concerned himself little with the intentions of the original architect. He never identified himself with the initial design; his interest was confined to the part on which he was working, façade, tower, spire, porch, or chapel. Thus the construction of churches was not carried on throughout the centuries after the fashion of a theorem taken up again at the point where it was interrupted. Each epoch brought its particular style; certain cathedrals record the whole history of French architecture. The façade of Tours enables us to follow the various styles of France in their rapid succession. As it rises from the ground, its Gothic decoration

FIG. 199.—PORCH OF SAINT-MACLOU,
AT ROUEN.

gradually turns into Renaissance ornament; two towers, which set out to end in spires, terminate in round lanterns, in the Italian manner. The façade of Angers begins a similar evolution with Romanesque elements. The Cathedral of Rodez (Figs. 207, 208) continues the avatars of French architecture even after the Renaissance. The building rises from the ground severe and massive, but as it ascends it blossoms into ornamental detail; at the second storey of the tower the solid wall begins to be pierced and carved, and the ribs to ramify with an exuberance which the solid forms of a rigid geometry support. The actual façade superposes styles that bring us to the middle of the seventeenth century. Neo-classical architects added a façade in the so-called Jesuits' Style at the top: two antique "orders" crowned by a pediment; to complete the cathedral, a reduction of the Val-de-Grace or the Sorbonne was perched on the summit.

FIG. 200.—SPIRAL STAIRCASE AT SAINT-MACLOU, ROUEN.

The interior decoration of cathedrals is no less receptive; it still goes on towards completion to the present day. The fourteenth, fifteenth, and sixteenth centuries enriched the naves with curiously wrought rood screens, which were destroyed in the eighteenth century. They gave the choir carved wooden stalls of incredible richness; they surrounded it with a sculptured gallery. In the seventeenth century, marble altars were set up at the bases of pillars, with columns and pediment enframing a large picture in the Bolognese manner. The eighteenth century added its graceful screens of hammered iron, which reveal a certain affinity between the caprices of the Flamboyant and the Rococo styles.

FIG. 201.—SOUTH PORCH OF SAINT-RÉMY, REIMS.
(*Photo. Courleux.*)

The architects of the fifteenth century had long lost the habit of

FIG. 202.—SOUTH PORCH OF THE
CHURCH OF LOUVIERS.

FIG. 203.—CHURCH OF LA TRINITÉ,
VENDÔME.

vast enterprises. They loved to elaborate a portion of a building;
they displayed their skill in the treatment of stone, which they
carved like wood and twisted like iron. When, after the agitations
of the Hundred Years War, building was resumed, pointed architecture blossomed for half a century into the Flamboyant style.[1]

It may have been an importation from England. It is even less monumental, even more exclusively decorative than the *Rayonnant* style of the fourteenth century, for it turned every organ of the Gothic building into ornament. Nevertheless, it did not violate the principles of this architecture; it merely carried them a little beyond their logical consequences, piercing the solids, dividing the vital forces of the masonry. Tympana became concave, and were covered with a perfect network of tracery; towers sprang skyward, with no solid supporting walls, by means of little superposed pinnacles and flying buttresses; stone fillets became more numerous, more

FIG. 204.—RIGHT DOOR,
FAÇADE OF NOTRE-DAME,
MANTES.

(*Photo. Neurdein.*)

[1] The English form of this evolution is known as Perpendicular.

delicate, and more involved. In the enlarged windows the mullions multiplied, and were united by curves analogous to the aspiring flicker of flames. The rose-windows at Sens leave an impression of fatigue and bedazzlement on the retina; the restless, quivering forms carry away the eye on their capricious undulations, and offer it no single quiet line on which to rest. In the same manner the simplicity of the great arches in the ogival vault is elaborated into complexity; these arches bifurcate and ramify into liernes (summit ribs) and tiercerons (intermediate ribs); purely decorative ribs accompany them

FIG. 205.—SOUTH PORCH OF THE CATHEDRAL OF ALBI.

with their fanciful curves, as in the Cathedral of Moulins, and Saint Nizier at Lyons; the stone branches become more and more tangled.

Occasionally, architects allow the key or boss of the vault to hang down like a stalactite, and this projecting stone seems to have nothing to sustain it; it is a capital without a pillar, a point of support for the ascending ribs, as in the Portail des Marmousets at Rouen, the rood-screen of Albi, and that of the Madeleine at Troyes.

These refinements reveal an architecture more subtle than vigorous. The Flamboyant style produced many marvels, chapels, towers, porches, the lantern-tower of Avioth in the Meuse, the porch of S. Maclou at Rouen (Fig. 199), Jean Texier's belfry at Chartres, and at Beauvais, the transept porches built by Martin Chambiges. At Albi,

FIG. 206.—CHOIR-SCREEN OF THE CATHEDRAL OF ALBI.

the last of the Gothic architects have laid a porch, light and delicate as a piece of lace or goldsmith's work, against the side

FIG. 207.—TOWER OF THE CATHEDRAL OF RODEZ.

of the brick fortress (Fig. 205). But Flamboyant Gothic raised no cathedral. The vigour of the structure was no longer concentrated in a few robust and sturdy trunks, as in the days of the great cathedrals; it was dispersed in tortuous branches; the lofty groves of early Gothic were transformed into dense thickets. The great Gothic period had exhausted invention in sculpture as in architecture. But sculpture can live by imitation; once detached from the architecture which had hitherto dominated it, it followed, in the course of the fourteenth and fifteenth centuries, a peculiar evolution, independent of all decorative considerations, and intent on the creation of forms more realistic or more mannered.

The favourite motive was the figure of the Virgin. The image

FIG. 208.—WEST FRONT OF THE CATHEDRAL OF RODEZ.

of the Mother, standing, and holding in her arms the Child Jesus, naturally multiplied. We find it not only on the altars of her innumerable chapels and in private oratories, but at street-corners, sheltered in little niches, and enshrined in the walls of houses under her protection. The attitude and general aspect had been fixed in the thirteenth century: the Virgin of Paris, of Amiens, and of Reims, is a gracious queen smiling at her child. But when she descended from her pedestal and became a statuette, the Virgin partook more of the nature of common humanity. The men of the fourteenth and fifteenth centuries loved her best in her character of mother; when she was shown smiling at the gambols of her infant, prayer might without impropriety become familiar, and poor folks spoke heart to heart to this Virgin who inspired no awe.

These images of stone, wood, or ivory were not all fashioned by expert hands; the goodwill of the craftsman was not always crowned by success; the humble artisan was careful to preserve the type created by the great "imagiers," but he often omitted the finer gradations, and exaggerated particular features. The date of a mediæval Virgin may always be approximately fixed by the drapery; it was only very exceptionally that the Gothic sculptors treated the nude; the design of the folds characterises each phase of their statues in trailing robes. In the thirteenth century the drapery was still

FIG. 209.—FRAGMENT OF THE STATUE
OF CHARLES V.
(The Louvre Paris.)

somewhat summary; later sculptors treated the folds of gowns as they treated the lines of the architecture; they made them smaller and more graceful, and took pleasure in elaborating them. In the time of Charles V. it was customary to pile up on the Virgin's hip a mass of fluted pleats forming rounded volutes. By the end of the century, these draperies, though they had not been simplified, had lost their somewhat conventional stiffness. They then fell to the ground, and piled their deep and multitudinous convolutions round the feet. This was an outcome of prevailing fashions. It was the period of very long dresses, of ample slashed cloaks, such as we see in illuminated manuscripts, wrapping nobles and citizens at the courts of the Dukes of Berry or Burgundy. The small Virgins, sometimes very coarsely carved, are lost, as it were, in a tangle of draperies, among which it is difficult to discern their attitudes. The sculptors of the thirteenth century had slightly inflected their figures to modify their hieratic stiffness; the weight of the body was

FIG. 210.—CHARLES V.,
FROM THE CHAPEL OF
THE CÉLESTINS.
(The Louvre, Paris.)

thrown on one hip, and this easy attitude cast the drapery into graceful oblique folds. But, although in nude figures like those of Praxiteles, or figures very slightly veiled, this movement of the hip is perfectly sufficient, it becomes barely perceptible when the body is swathed in heavy draperies. The popular "imagiers" accordingly emphasised this gesture till it became caricature. At the middle of the fifteenth century, their Virgins contort themselves amidst involved draperies. It was not until the close of the century that they recovered their grace and simplicity.

The work of the Gothic "imagiers" was reproduced in small by the ivory-workers. Their statuettes are exact reproductions of the great stone figures. If all the stone figures had perished, we might have followed the traditional treatment of the Virgin from the thirteenth to the fifteenth century in the ivories. Our Lady was, in fact, the favourite motive of the workers in ivory. Her image multiplied and was disseminated in like manner with her worship. At first she was represented as at Paris, Amiens, and Reims, a gracious figure with half-closed eyes and a slight smile on her thin lips. In the course of the fourteenth century, ivory figures follow the evolution of stone statues, and we can only date them by the chronology of parallel works of great sculpture. We note that mannerism is on the increase; the folds of the robes become complicated, and the general aspect is one of a somewhat affected grace; later on, the figure became heavy, and the delicate material was unable to translate the robust realism of the fifteenth century.

The ivory-workers did not confine themselves to the imitation of stone statues; they also transposed the effects of the miniaturists,

graving delicate reliefs upon ivory plaques which form diptychs and triptychs. In the centre is the Virgin, the little Gothic queen smiling at her child, attended by chubby angels in flowing robes. The shutters are decorated with numbers of little pictures in which the ivory-worker, following the taste of the century, has compressed the history of Jesus into the space of a few centimetres. The scenes are enframed in miniature columns and pointed arches surmounted by gables, an elaborate architectural setting, which invites comparison with the miniatures in the Psalter of Saint Louis. The French ivory-workers, like the French illuminators, excelled in adapting "histories," ingenious attitudes, expressive faces, and sinuous draperies to the limits of their little Gothic compartments.

FIG. 213.—SAINT MAURICE.
(Orléans Museum.)

FIG. 214.—FIGURE OF A KING.
(The Louvre, Paris.)

During the fourteenth century, statuary gradually achieved portraiture; this was the natural evolution of an art that had become both more independent and richer in technique. It was also a result of the new conditions; the artists were in the service of great nobles, who raised their own monuments during their life-time. From the reign of Saint Louis, the kings of France had their own images and those of their ancestors carved upon their tombs in Saint Denis; the Dukes of Burgundy at Dijon, the Duke of Berry at Bourges, the Dukes of Bourbon at Souvigny, the Popes at Avignon

FIG. 215.—SAINT MICHAEL OVERCOMING SATAN.
(Musée des Augustins, Toulouse.)

FIG. 217.—SAINT FORTUNADE: CHURCH OF SAINTE-FORTUNADE (CORREZE).

did the same. Their sepulchral effigies show them recumbent, their hands folded in prayer, their feet resting on heraldic beasts such as dogs or lions.

In the time of Saint Louis, busts were not, as yet, portraits; the costumes only seem to have been accurately rendered; the round, inexpressive faces, modelled with very little character, are lifeless, in spite of a vague indication of a smile. For a long time the sculptors of *gisants* (recumbent figures) had been content to lay the same figures they had been in the habit of erecting against pillars in cathedral porches flat upon a marble slab. They made no change in the design of the draperies; the fluted parallel folds were still retained, as if the weight, continuing to be exercised in the length of the body, had become horizontal with the latter. At Saint Denis, Philip VI. and Charles V. sleep thus, wrapped in a sheaf of rigid folds like the flutings of an overthrown column, and the cushion under the head is the sole indication that the sculptor intended to represent a recumbent figure. At the end of the fourteenth century, however, good sense corrected a fashion that lacked any justification; the folds fell on the slab, clinging to the rigid corpse and suggesting its outlines.

FIG. 216.—SILVER-GILT VIRGIN FROM THE TREASURY OF SAINT-DENIS. (The Louvre, Paris.)

FIG. 218.—THE VIRGIN AND CHILD. (Musée des Augustins, Toulouse.)

Among the artistic centres created by the luxury of kings and great

108

feudatories, Dijon was the one which showed most activity and splendour, and the ancient capital of the Dukes of Burgundy still preserves the sculptured masterpieces of this second Gothic period. This Burgundian art appeared and disappeared with the power of the Dukes; it was the result of a brilliant political phase rather than of ethnical characteristics. It is to be explained by the position of a feudal family and its suzerainty over the Netherlands. The wealthy cities of Flanders, reservoirs of skilled craftsmen, had furnished painters and sculptors for the Paris of Charles V and Charles VI,

FIG. 219.—FIGURE OF THE MAGDALEN.
(Cluny Museum, Paris.)

before providing them for the Dijon of Philip the Good. During the first half of the fifteenth century Paris was in a state of anarchy, and in the hands of the English, and Burgundy alone was able to profit by the labours of Flemish craftsmen.

At the Carthusian monastery of Champmol, near Dijon, where masses were continually to be said for the repose of their souls, the Dukes of Burgundy caused the most powerful works of the Middle Ages in their decline to be executed by the Dutchman, Claus Sluter (d. 1406) and his successors. These sculptures have been preserved. In the porch of the church (now destroyed) a Virgin upon the central pillar of the doorway reveals the hand of a master on the threshold. The bold chisel that carved it has given it robust vitality, and has decked it with abundant and complicated draperies; but in the midst of the welter of folds the vigorous body indicates certain simple movements (Fig. 224). On either side she is flanked by Philip the

FIG. 220.—FIGURE OF A QUEEN
AT THE PALAIS DE JUSTICE,
POITIERS.
(*Photo. Mieusement.*)

109

FIG. 221.—APOSTLE, FROM THE ABBEY OF RIEUX.
(Museum of Toulouse.)

Bold, his wife, Margaret of Flanders, and their patrons; the faces are strongly characterised, the attitudes natural, the draperies flowing and supple. All this vigour makes the art, which a few years earlier erected the puny Charles V of the Célestins, appear timid and poverty-stricken. For this same Philip the Bold, Claus Sluter decorated the well of the monastery with sculptures, grouping six prophets round it: Moses, David, Jeremiah, Zachariah, Daniel, and Isaiah; each holds the phylactery on which is inscribed his prediction of the sufferings of Christ. The monument was dominated by a Calvary: Jesus on the Cross, the Virgin, the Magdalen and St. John; all that remains of this is the head of Christ, a marvellous head of suffering majesty. In this work, mutilated as it is, an energy very rare in history finds expression; this art was the final outcome of a naturalistic progress; it was anterior to that classic discipline which was soon to curb violence, and force the wildest accents to take

FIG. 222.—APOSTLE, FROM THE ABBEY OF RIEUX.
(Museum of Toulouse.)

FIG. 223.—APOSTLE, FROM THE ABBEY OF RIEUX.
(Museum of Toulouse.)

on harmony. In the time of Claus Sluter no scruple, no desire for beauty or correctness, kept the passion of the sculptor within bounds; enormous heads are set on squat bodies. Among the deep folds, the sinuosities and breaks of the tormented draperies, the bodies are hardly indicated; but the boldly-carved faces, hollow, ravaged and wrinkled, reveal individualities of unforgettable vigour. The colour which once overlay these brutal forms gave an appearance of reality to the aged vociferous heads. It is not often that the exigencies of the subject, the tendencies of local art, and the genius of the artist so combine to create works harmonious even in their violence. Never again was such savage energy to be found on French soil, save in the case of genius in revolt.

The Burgundian power was shattered before all the great works projected by the Dukes had been carried out. The most brilliant among them, Philip the Good, never had his tomb; but for his predecessors, Philip the Bold and John the Fearless, two marvels of architecture and sculpture were executed; they are the work of several artists. The

FIG. 224.—CLAUS SLUTER. DOOR, ABBEY OF CHAMPMOL, NEAR DIJON.
(*Photo. Neurdein.*)

second of these monuments was not finished till 1470, by the Avignonnais, Antoine le Moiturier. On a wide base of black marble, an elaborately carved gallery of alabaster shelters a whole world of mourners (*pleurants*), who clamour under the intricacies of the delicate arcades. Above, on spacious slabs, with sharp cornices, the recumbent figures (*gisants*) lie wrapped in long Court mantles; winged angels bend over their heads, supporting helmet or coat of arms. The mourners who circulate beneath the funereal slabs of the Dukes of Burgundy, and who were also to be seen round the tomb of the Duke of Berry, are the members of the family, and the Court officials in mourning dress, as they figured at the obsequies. Their bodies are lost in their voluminous robes with their heavy, broken folds. The coarse stuffs and the hidden

FIG. 225.—CLAUS SLUTER. ISAIAH AND MOSES. WELL OF THE PROPHETS, ABBEY OF CHAMPMOL, NEAR DIJON.

faces suggest grief more solemnly than any facial contortions (Figs. 230, 232).

FIG. 226.—CLAUS SLUTER.
ZACHARIAH AND DANIEL. WELL
OF THE PROPHETS, DIJON.

Nevertheless, the Dijon sculptors did not always exploit the full pathetic force of these tragic statuettes. La Huerta and Le Moiturier even treated them familiarly, and gave a comic touch to their vulgar gestures. Some years later, at the end of the fifteenth century, we find these small alabaster figures very vigorously developed on the tomb of Philippe Pot (Fig. 232); the Gothic Gallery that enframed them in the earlier tombs has disappeared; the architectural decoration is replaced by statuary. The slab on which Philippe Pot reclines in armour, rests heavily on the shoulders of eight sinister mourners swathed in heavy gowns, the hoods of which are drawn over their heads, and walking with measured steps. This expressive violence marks the close of mediæval sculpture. Before the period of a difficult and nicely adjusted science, a good workman, well inspired, yet without any subtleties of technique, was capable of striking home rudely, and of achieving the pathetic with a vigour that was finally to disappear from art. The effect was attained in spite of—perhaps indeed to some extent by means of—the summary execution.

Gothic architecture had killed the mural painting dear to the Romanesque artists. It had virtually suppressed wall-space; the figures and scenes of Christian iconography had been transported to the windows. What mural fresco could have competed with these pictures from which the living light streamed forth? But glass-painting was subject to a technique too special, and dominated by restrictions too severe, to become more than an exquisite decoration, or to blossom into a realistic art.

FIG. 227.—CLAUS SLUTER.
MOSES AND DAVID. WELL OF THE
PROPHETS, DIJON.

The theologians of the twelfth and thirteenth centuries may have suggested new episodes and ingenious symbols to the glass-painters; they did not insist that the workman should imitate living forms and natural colours. Thus we find that the figures on glass retain the emaciated forms, the knotted and twisted lines of Romano-Byzantine design, long after these had been discarded in sculpture. It is not here that we must look for the realistic effort which corresponds, in the chromatic arts, to that which had revived the dry bones of sculpture. In Italy, mural painting, encouraged rather than restricted by architecture, awoke to life at the beginning of the fourteenth century, in the work of Giotto. In the countries of Gothic art, it was the pages of the illuminated manuscripts which prepared the efflorescence of painting.

FIG. 228.—VANE OF THE CHATEAU OF LUDE.

Miniature painting had never ceased to be practised by the monks of the Middle Ages; but in the thirteenth century a new style began to develop, inspired, apparently, by the art of the sculptors and glass-painters. There is more than one striking analogy between the little figures of the Psalter of Saint Louis and the saints which were carved by contemporary sculptors. The harsh drawing of an earlier period had become suppler and more delicate, and the illuminators of the thirteenth century, renouncing the dryness of the Benedictine miniatures, were roused to emulation by the splendour of the Gothic painted windows. Their pages glow with pure colours, reds and blues, with no intermixture to break or deaden them; the gold-leaf against which the little figures are relieved gleams from every page, and as we turn the

FIG. 229.—TOMBS OF PHILIPPE LE HARDI AND JEAN SANS PEUR.

(Museum, Dijon.) (*Photo. Neurdein.*)

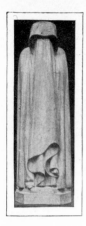

FIG. 230.—A
MOURNER ON THE
TOMB OF THE DUKE
OF BERRY.
(Museum, Bourges.)

leaves, it sparkles like the painted winuow of some dim chapel. In several cases the framework of the vignettes recalls the design of a Gothic window and its radiating mullions. It was the Parisian illuminators of the thirteenth century who first attempted to fix this gem-like painting on parchment.

But the illuminator could not rest content with the conventional design of the glass-painter. Even in the Psalter of Saint Louis, the figures are easy and life-like, with a dainty vivacity akin to the quality we find in the album of Villard de Honnecourt. This architect of the middle of the thirteenth century draws with a free pen, and traces sinuous figures draped in supple robes. It is true that his anatomy and his perspective are defective; these are weaknesses which are very frequent in the plastic art of mediæval times. But he can already make his little figures move gaily; they have cast off the Byzantine ankylosis. In the Psalter of Saint Louis, and in the best manuscripts of the close of the thirteenth century, we even find upon

FIG. 231.—CLAUS SLUTER.
CHRIST FROM THE WELL OF THE PROPHETS.
(Archæological Museum, Dijon.)

the faces the keen smile of certain contemporary sculptures. Following in the wake of the "imagiers," the illuminators gradually become masters of the suggestion of life.

Throughout the fourteenth century, this conquest was rapidly pursued; most of the miniaturists worked in Paris; they were very various in origin, many of them

FIG. 232.—TOMB OF PHILIPPE POT.
(The Louvre, Paris.)

coming from the northern provinces; but they all adopted the same style in the royal city. Their workshops laid the foundations of the glorious painting of the fifteenth century. The evolution is obscure, because its manifestations are contained in numerous manuscripts which have been dispersed far and wide. But we can readily trace the progress made. First of all, the illuminators abandoned their decorative convention for realistic endeavour. Their miniatures are less suggestive of painted glass and more akin to life; the lines lose their harshness, and discard the leaden outline which encircled the figures of coloured windows; the colours sacrifice something of their splendour and purity in favour of modelling. The gold backgrounds are modified, and finally disappear altogether; elements of landscape are introduced, the sky and the ground, blue and green. The painter is about to study nature.

FIG. 233.—CANON PRAYING.
(Figure on a Tomb, Museum of Le Mans. Early XVIth century.)

The contemporaries of Charles V were able to recognise certain aspects of their times when they turned over the leaves of a manuscript. The illuminators were no longer Benedictines in cells, but laymen at large; their eyes were wide open to men and things. They lived near the Porte Saint-Denis, and led joyous lives, if we are to believe Christine de Pisan. They were able to depict Charles V receiving manuscripts; they also added familiar scenes and figures of the streets to the usual iconography, and mingled contemporary anecdotes with traditional narrative. If the perspective of these small pictures is still conventional, it is at least intelligible; the miniaturist has little sense of composition; but his disconnected juxtapositions abound in delightfully observed episodes, from which it is easy to deduce Parisian life in the time of Charles V.

FIG. 234.—ARISTOTLE AND CAMPASPE.
(Cathedral, Lyons.)

The appearance of landscape reveals a novel conception of

FIG. 235.—STATUE OF ANTOINETTE
DE FONTETTE.
(Museum, Dijon. xvith century.)
(*Photo. de Beauregard.*)

painting. After they had renounced their gold backgrounds, the illuminators painted their little figures upon a ground of soft verdure, and under a sky of cloudless blue. At the close of the fourteenth century these summary indications became richer and more precise. Books of Hours figure very frequently among the manuscripts, their opening pages consisting of an illustrated calendar of the months. These illustrations, which had long been traditional, represent the occupations of humanity, and more especially work in the fields. The sculptors were content to show the attitudes of reaper, vintager and sower. When the illuminators had to set a landscape behind these little figures, they had to learn to distinguish the seasons by the colour of the sky and the appearance of plants. In the time of Charles V the landscapes of the miniaturists showed these distinctions, though they still relied upon certain conventions. The most famous of the manuscripts of this period, the "Very Rich Hours of the Duke of Berry," was illuminated for this prince by three artists from Limburg (1416). They enlivened their landscapes by representations of the castles of the royal house. Seated in his armchair, the old Duke, as he turned over his Hours, could travel in spirit from Poitiers to Mehun-sur-Yèvre, from Vincennes to the Louvre or the Palais de la Cité. This

FIG. 236.—IVORY TRIPTYCH OF THE XIVTH
CENTURY.
(Cluny Museum, Paris.)

116

extraordinary work gives a vivid picture of the France of those days: the people at their work, the nobles hunting and riding, and on the heights, dominating the plain where the peasant sows or reaps, wonderful castles which have now disappeared, the last of the feudal dwellings, in which the grimness of the old fortresses was relieved by Gothic fantasy. These modest little pictures have an engaging freshness which they owe to the lightness of the medium—thin body colour on parchment. Their fragile art gives an air of graceful minuteness to the world it represents. No doubt these

FIG. 237.—DRESSER, XVITH CENTURY.
(Cluny Museum, Paris.)

castles, decorated like shrines, these great nobles, furred like cats and variegated as popinjays, are faithful reproductions. But contemporary architecture and sculpture evoke a civilisation very much rougher.

Illumination was not the sole kind of painting in use at the end of the fourteenth century. Certain artists were working in tempera on wooden panels. They hardly did more than amplify the little compositions of the miniaturists. These illuminators on a large scale lack vigour; certain happily inspired details show delicacy of observation; but over-softness of colour and the abuse of gold impede the victorious progress of Malouel, Bellechose and Broederlam, all those Netherlandish artists who worked for the Dukes of Burgundy (Figs. 242, 244).

FIG. 238.—COFFER OF THE XVTH CENTURY.
(Cluny Museum, Paris.)

It was at this period, in the first quarter of the fourteenth century, that two events combined to change the destiny of French painting. The English invasion drove royalty, and most of the industries which ministered to its luxury, towards the South.

117

FIG. 239.—CALVARY.
CENTRAL COMPARTMENT OF THE NARBONNE ALTAR-PIECE.
(The Louvre, Paris.)

Paris lost its radiating power for a considerable period. At the same time, some Northern artists, the Van Eycks, invented a new technique, which enlarged the possibilities of painting enormously, by giving it a robuster and more accurate instrument. But whereas this novel painting became the national art of the great Netherlandish cities, and the natural fruit of their urban civilisation, in France it flourished only in one or two provinces; it was not, like sculpture, an autochthonous art; for a long time it seemed a transplanted product; and generous amateurs, great nobles, and wealthy burgesses, were necessary to attract and retain painters.

The disasters of the French monarchy had not checked the Netherlandish immigration; but the painters of the Low Countries made their way for the most part to the court of Burgundy, and thence towards Provence and Italy. Philip the Good, Charles the Bold, and their ministers had very great painters for their portraitists; Jan van Eyck, Rogier van der Weyden and others produced masterpieces for their Chancellor, Rolin. In these relations between Flanders and Burgundy, the Flemings owed nothing to their Burgundian surroundings; the court of Dijon never acclimatised the Netherlandish plant; it merely gathered its fruits. The same may be true of sculpture, but stone monuments are more durable than the panels of painters; the works of the Carthusian monastery of Champmol, which are still in their original places, constitute a kind of local museum, from which the genius of a school seems to radiate. In its far-reaching

FIG. 240.—FIREPLACE,
XVTH CENTURY. FROM LE MANS.
(Cluny Museum, Paris.)

expansion, Netherlandish painting founded colonies even more active than that of Dijon; it reached Italy by way of Germany and France; Flemish or Dutch painters travelled to Genoa, traversing the East of France from north to south. The great highway which served the fairs of Champagne, Lyons, and Beaucaire, was an artistic road.

On this road, Avignon, which had lately lost its Popes, and Aix, one of King Rene's capitals, were halting-places for travelling artists. As early as the fourteenth century, Sienese and Giottesque art had entered into France by Avignon. The halls of the papal palace were decorated with Italian frescoes, and, doubtless, many a motive reached Paris, and inspired its painters and miniaturists; in the famous Narbonne panels, in spite of

FIG. 241.—THE LIMBURG BROTHERS. HUNTING AT VINCENNES. MINIATURE IN THE TRÈS RICHES HEURES DU DUC DE BERRY. (Condé Museum, Chantilly.)

the sharpness of the Gothic drawing, we recognise the sinuous softness of Sienese compositions (Fig. 239).

In the fifteenth century, the painters who passed through Avignon

FIG. 242.—JEAN MALOUEL. GOD THE FATHER, THE VIRGIN AND ST. JOHN WEEPING OVER THE BODY OF JESUS. (The Louvre, Paris.)

brought with them the precise style of the North. One of them is known to us, Enguerrand Charonton of Laon, who painted a pale small-featured Virgin, crowned by the Father and the Son, and attended on either side by a multitude of heavenly figures (1453). This apparition dominates a vision of Provence, a parched landscape with arid hills over which white houses are scattered (Fig. 248). A mysterious anonymous masterpiece, a Virgin of Pity, formerly at Ville-neuve-lès-Avignon, translates into paint one of those pathetic groups

119

FIG. 243.—PORTRAIT OF JEAN
LE BON.
(Bibliothèque Nationale, Paris.)

which the "imagiers" used to carve in stone or wood. Here the breadth and freedom of the sculptured forms replace the dainty charm of the miniaturist's figures (Fig. 249). At Aix, King René attracted a group of painters, some of whom came from Flanders. Nicolas Froment, although he was a native of Uzès, successfully adopted the Netherlandish naturalism. In his picture of the *Burning Bush* (Fig. 251), the precision of the detail and the splendour of the colour reveal a disciple of the school of Bruges (1476). He was, further, an excellent portraitist of the good King René and of his wife, Jeanne de Laval. His other authenticated work, a *Resurrection of Lazarus*, like several other anonymous paintings, shows how Flemish art had become acclimatised, how it adopted the local legends, and borrowed the natural features of Provence. It is pleasant to recognise its sunny landscape, and, here and there, some truculent and hirsute head, some olive feminine face, enframed in dark brown tresses. This artistic province, which was destined to be merged more and more into France, preserved its personality for a long period. It continued to send many artists to the Court and to Paris, thus demonstrating its vitality in an organism in which the centre tended increasingly to absorb all energies.

Meanwhile, somewhat apart from the great highway on which art circulated between Flanders and Italy, monarchical France gradually recovered from the terrible crisis in which it had almost succumbed; driven out of Paris by the English invaders, royalty had installed itself south of the Loire. Whereas the eastern provinces, from the states of the Duke of Burgundy to those of King René

FIG. 244.—BROEDERLAM.
THE ANNUNCIATION.
FRAGMENT OF AN ALTAR-
PIECE.
(Museum, Dijon.)
(*Photo. Neurdein.*)

FIG. 245.—DESCENT FROM THE CROSS. (The Louvre, Paris.)

were open to foreign influences, the France of the king at Bourges had contracted towards its centre, and in its isolation was long separated from those Netherlandish provinces, the artistic life of which had been so closely intermingled with its own. Painting continued to flourish; it was an art full of delicate originality, but it had all the weakness of convalescence; it lacked a strong centre in which to take root, and profound local traditions in which to find guidance. Tours, Bourges and Moulins all took an equal part in the existence of this acephalous school; it is known as the School of the Loire; and like the Loire, the great artistic stream flowed, indolent and indecisive, in an over-vast bed.

The Tourangeau, Jean Fouquet (1415-1485), seems to have been the most distinguished painter of the reigns of Charles VII and Louis XI. It would be evident that he owes very little to the Netherlands, if certain critics had not insisted on crediting him with one or two very fine anonymous portraits, in which the impeccable mastery and precision of Flemish art, or of an art derived therefrom, is clearly manifested. Four paintings by him are practically authenticated; they immortalise the most illustrious figures of the monarchy in the middle of the fifteenth century: Charles VII, "the very victorious king" (Fig. 258); Jouvenel des Ursins, his counsellor (Fig. 257); Étienne Chevalier, Treasurer of France, and finally a Virgin, which atones for its poverty of

FIG. 246.—SAINT SIFFREIN. (Museum, Avignon.)

121

FIG. 247.—JACQUEMART DE HESDIN.
THE MARRIAGE OF CANA.
MS. LAT. 919.
(Bibliotheque Nationale, Paris.)

technique by its interest as a probable portrait of Agnes Sorel. Each of these works shows the same qualities and the same defects. The painter saw his models clearly, and has characterised them admirably : the king—a poor frail, shivering creature ; Jouvenel, an obese and apoplectic burgess. But though his eye is clear, the painter's hand is not very sure ; the drawing is flaccid ; the brush of the miniaturist is more successful with figures in which vagueness becomes grace. He illuminated a Book of Hours for Etienne Chevalier, and a History of the Jews by Josephus, on which he has lavished delicate impressions of his country and of his time. The lightness of the technique, the limpidity of the colour, are in perfect harmony with the natural aspects of Touraine, the soft curves of the blue hills which border the valley of the Loire, and make a background for the little figures in front. The river runs lazily through its meadows, the sky is a light azure, luminous and transparent. Sometimes a town with its ramparts, or a castle, white and new, rises above the river. It is easy also to recognise certain famous Parisian buildings, Notre Dame, the Sainte Chapelle, Vincennes, the Bastille, the gallows at Montfaucon. Scenes in sacred history are enacted by the contemporaries of Charles VII and Louis XI ; sometimes we see the heavy men-at-arms who expelled the English marching through the courtly throng, well-to-do citizens discussing their affairs, or gossips chatting round a newly delivered woman. It is worth

FIG. 248.—ENGUERRAND CHARONTON.
THE CORONATION OF THE VIRGIN. FRAGMENT OF THE
PICTURE AT VILLENEUVE-LÈS-AVIGNON.
(*Photo. Langlois.*)

while to linger over these landscapes and their little figures. It is not often that French painters show us their native land and its peasants with such sincerity (Figs. 252, 253).

Nevertheless, French art was about to accept the motives of an alien art. Fouquet went to Italy, and brought back with him drawings of arabesques and pilasters, a whole system of orna-

FIG. 249.—VIRGIN OF PITY.
FROM VILLENEUVE-LÈS-AVIGNON.
(The Louvre, Paris.)

mentation in the style of Michelozzo, which he used with more zeal than discretion. The spectacle of this Tourangeau, of the middle of the fifteenth century, sacrificing the fantasies of flamboyant Gothic for the more methodical and less capricious decoration of Italy, is a significant one. This assimilative facility is found

FIG. 250.—JEAN FOUQUET.
PORTRAIT OF THE PAINTER,
ENAMEL.
(The Louvre, Paris.)

elsewhere in Fouquet's circle, in one of his successors, the miniaturist Jean Bourdichon. The Book of Hours of Anne of Brittany (Figs. 260, 261; 1508), shows a sustained sweetness not without insipidity. The painter hardly looks at the living world around him; his brush delights in vague forms and soft colours. Another agreeable artist has left some charming paintings, the most important of which is in the Cathedral at Moulins. Like Bourdichon, this

FIG. 251.—NICOLAS FROMENT.
THE BURNING BUSH. CATHEDRAL OF
AIX IN PROVENCE.
(*Photo. Neurdein.*)

FIG. 252.—JEAN FOUQUET.
ADORATION OF THE MAGI.
ÉTIENNE CHEVALIER'S BOOK OF
HOURS.
(Condé Museum, Chantilly.)

"Master of Moulins" (Figs. 256, 259, 262, 263, 264) was primarily the devout portraitist of the Blessed Virgin (1480 to 1500); he painted her pale and delicate, and sometimes placed on her head the white coif of the Berrichonne women. Even when he shows her in the splendour of her heavenly court, she still preserves the ingenuous air of a pretty peasant girl. The great nobles and high-born ladies of France have not yet the aristocratic appearance which the Renaissance was presently to give them. The types of the district are as recognisable in their faces as are in the landscapes the soft and verdant undulations of the Burgundian soil. But this attractive art lacks vigour; we feel that it would be easily influenced. Its finest quality is a delicate sensibility, a natural elegance which corrects the native clumsiness of the northern figures, without, however, giving them the superb attitudes of Italian art, or its learnedly contrived *mise-en-scène.* At this date French art gave itself up to an ideal of elegance and beauty, and seemed, like the art of all the rest of Europe, to attune itself to that of Italy. Memling and Gerard David allowed their Flemish realism to be softened by the breath from the South, and in Jean Bourdichon's miniatures we seem every instant to recognise some figure of a Virgin or Saint Sebastian from Umbria. The harsh accent of Gothic art is mellowed by a new harmony. No centre could have been better adapted to reconcile the dissonances between the Germanic north

FIG. 253.—JEAN FOUQUET.
SIEGE OF JERICHO. HISTORY OF THE
JEWS, BY JOSEPHUS.
(Bibliothèque Nationale, Paris.)
(*Photo. Berthaud.*)

FEUDAL ART AND CIVIC ART

and the Latin south. The strongest antipathies could not resist the cordial eclecticism of the hospitality of Touraine. All that the French aristocracy needed in order to worship the beauty that had been in the making for a century on the other side of the Alps was to know it.

But we should be giving a very inadequate idea of this expiring Gothic art, if we should depict it as entirely feudal, executing works of sculpture and painting only to adorn tombs, to commemorate the piety of donors, or to delight the cultivated taste of wealthy patrons. In addi-

FIG. 254.—CEILING OF THE CHAPEL IN JACQUES CŒUR'S HOUSE AT BOURGES. (*Photo. Neurdein.*)

tion to the statuary of the rich, their brilliant and difficult painting, there was also in the fifteenth century a popular art less easy to know, but which expresses the soul of the age with a direct and often brutal sincerity. The sculpture of tombs,

FIG. 255.—FRAGMENT OF THE DANCE OF DEATH AT LA CHAISE-DIEU. (*Photo. Neurdein.*)

the pictures with donors, are works of official piety. The artless Virgins of Pity to be found in many village churches, and some few paintings coarsely frescoed on old walls, bear a closer relation to common humanity. If these popular works had been

FIG. 256.—THE MASTER OF MOULINS. THE VIRGIN IN GLORY, WITH THE DONORS, PIERRE DE BOURBON AND ANNE DE BEAUJEU.
(Cathedral of Moulins.) (*Photo. Neurdein.*)

FIG. 257.—JEAN FOUQUET.
PORTRAIT OF JOUVENEL DES URSINS.
(The Louvre, Paris.)

FIG. 258.—JEAN FOUQUET.
PORTRAIT OF CHARLES VII.
(The Louvre, Paris.)

better preserved, we should have a clearer insight into the soul of that period. There is one motive in particular which seems to have been dear to the humanity of the time, and to have expressed its deepest preoccupations; this was the Dance of Death, living beings conducted to the grave by grinning skeletons. It appeared first, no doubt, in Paris, in 1424, in the charnel-house of the Church of the Holy Innocents, and thence it spread throughout France; we find scattered traces of it now at Kermaria, in Brittany, where gambolling skeletons are shown tormenting monks; at La Chaise-Dieu, where figures outlined in black show a white silhouette against a background of red ochre (Fig. 255); in the cloister of the Aître Saint-Maclou (Rouen),[1] this Dance of Death is carved in wood and is slowly crumbling away.

FIG. 259.—THE MASTER OF MOULINS.
THE NATIVITY.
(Bishop's Palace, Autun.) (*Photo. Langlois.*)

[1] The ancient cemetery of Saint Maclou.

FIG. 260.—JEAN BOURDICHON. NATIVITY. MINIATURE IN THE BOOK OF HOURS OF ANNE OF BRITTANY.

(Bibliothèque Nationale, Paris.)
(*Photo. Berthaud.*)

From the moment of its birth, engraving laid hold of this motive; it propagated among the people that sermon on death, which, no doubt, harmonised with the pre-occupations of the fifteenth century. Men had suffered both from civil war and foreign invasion; in those days of pillage, famine

FIG. 261.—JEAN BOURDICHON. ANNE OF BRITTANY AND HER PATRON SAINTS. MINIATURE IN THE BOOK OF HOURS OF ANNE OF BRITTANY.

(Bibliothèque Nationale, Paris.)
(*Photo. Berthaud.*)

and pestilence, death was ever present, and the thought that all, from the beggar to the King, the Emperor, and the Pope were equal before it, gave a kind of vindictive satisfaction to the poor. A sort of burlesque and sinister frenzy accordingly informs all these poor little puppets; the dance is attuned to the crash of drums and the rattle of skeletons. Painters were not alone in their expression of this horrible gaiety at the exploits of death. The aspects of putrefaction, described with such crudity by Villon, were depicted with strange insistence by sculptors in their stone corpses. But the time was at hand when all these rude works were to disappear before a more cultured art. The sinister phantoms of the night were to vanish in the radiant light of the Renaissance.

FIG. 262.—THE MASTER OF MOULINS. PIERRE DE BOURBON AND ST. PETER.

(The Louvre, Paris.)

FIG. 263.—THE MASTER OF MOULINS.
THE MAGDALEN AND AN UNKNOWN.
(The Louvre, Paris.)

How indeed should Gothic art have survived, when the very conditions of Gothic craftsmanship disappeared with the Middle Ages? Even in the fifteenth century the arts were no longer designed, as formerly, to satisfy collective needs. They emanated from more strongly marked individualities, and were addressed to special personages; amateurs and artists began to recognise and to seek each other. Even in architecture, the bravura additions made to the great cathedrals in the Flamboyant period have the character of purely personal fantasies, decorative caprices designed by an ingenious architect to gratify a donor. They show no trace of that common thought and that mechanical necessity which were formerly combined for the erection of cathedrals. The sculpture of the period demanded greater dexterity and a more refined training. The "imagier" of the thirteenth century carved figures which, though beautiful, were simplified and summary, proper, in fact, to an idealistic age and a monumental art. In the thirteenth century, craftsmen of the second rank were capable of producing very fine statues, just as uncultivated voices were able to take their part excellently in plain-song choirs. But at the close of the Middle Ages plastic art had become more realistic, and figures more individual; sculptors and painters wished to produce portraits. For this difficult art, dexterous craftsmen were required, and a scientific technique. Certain skilful artists emerged from the anonymous crowd of popular "imagiers"; their fame spread abroad, and great nobles sent for them from

FIG. 264. THE MASTER OF MOULINS.
ANNE DE BEAUJEU AND ST. JOHN.
(The Louvre, Paris.)

afar. The same thing happened in painting. Mosaic and painted glass were complex and elaborate crafts, but they were, after all, mechanical; even fresco had been reduced to such a simplicity of process that, in the Romanesque period, artists of no particular genius could practise it successfully. And now, miniaturists and painters of altar-pieces begin to attempt a task so difficult that the goal is never reached: to copy nature and reproduce the aspects of life. The traditions of the workshop no longer suffice for art. Very soon originality will be required, and artists will be esteemed in proportion as they shall have rejected the traditions which, in the thirteenth cen-

FIG. 265. SCENE FROM THE ROMANCE, "LES ÉCHECS AMOUREUX."
(Bibliothèque Nationale, Fr. MS. 43.)

tury, were held to constitute the whole of art. A new passion, the love of beautiful forms and beautiful colours, takes the place of religious sentiment as this gradually dies down. The arts slowly change their *raison d'être.*

Meanwhile, as the mediæval soul, that rich store-house of legend, passed away, the tenderness and wonder of Christian art all but expired in the chilly atmosphere. Artlessness is not to be preserved in mature age; if it is prolonged, it becomes intellectual debility. The day came when art had to put away the caressing forms of childish speech, and resolutely accept the severe expression of adult reason. The imagination of artists turned more and more to the antique mythology, on which religion had no longer any hold. Art and Christianity nevertheless came together again from time to time,

FIG. 266.—CHOIR OF THE CHURCH OF LA CHAISE-DIEU. (*Photo. Monuments Historiques.*)

and their divorce was never complete. But henceforth they treated each other gravely, without the familiar ease of the days when they led a common life. These stately personages no longer remembered that they had played together as children.

FIG. 267.—TAPESTRY OF THE APOCALYPSE, AT ANGERS.
(Photo. Monuments Historiques.)

BIBLIOGRAPHY

V. Leclerc and E. Renan, *Discours sur l'état des Lettres et des Beaux Arts au XIVe siècle*, Paris, 1865, 2 vols.—Lecoy de la Marche, *Extraits des Comptes et Mémoriaux du roi René...*, Paris, 1873: *Le roi René*, Paris, 1875, 2 vols.—Mgr. Dehaisnes, *Histoire de l'Art dans la Flandre, l'Artois et le Hainaut*, Lille, 1886, 3 vols.; *L'Art flamand en France...(R.S.B.A.D.,*1892).—J.-M. Richard, *Mahout, Comtesse d'Artois et de Bourgogne*, Paris, 1887.—C. Enlart, *Les Origines anglaises du style flamboyant (Bulletin de l'Union syndicale des Architectes français,* 1908).—L. Desrosiers, *La Cathédrale de Moulins,* Moulins, 1871.—Dufay, *L'Eglise de Brou et ses Architectes,* Lyon, 1879.—Abbé Fossey, *Monographie de la Cathédrale d'Evreux,* Evreux, 1898.—Viollet-Le-Duc, *Essai sur l'Architecture militaire au Moyen Age,* Paris, 1854; *Histoire d'une forteresse,* Paris, 1874.—E. Lefèvre-Pontalis, *Le Château de Coucy,* Paris, 1909.—A. Robert, *Le Château de Pierrefonds,* Paris, n. d.—E. Viollet-Le-Duc, *La Cité de Carcassonne,* Paris, 1878.—Ph. Lauzun, *Le Château de Bonaguil,* 2nd ed., Paris, 1884.—A. Darcel, *L'Architecture civile au Moyen Age (G. B. A.,* 1862, II).—Gaignières, *Recueil de tombeaux* (drawings in the *Bibliothèque Nationale*).—E. Mâle, *L'Art chrétien à la fin du Moyen Age,* Paris, 1908.—C. Enlart, *La Satire des mœurs dans l'Iconographie du Moyen Age (Mercure de France,* Dec., 1909, and Jan., 1910).—L. de Laborde, *Les Ducs de Bourgogne,* Paris, 1849-1851, 3 vols.—Bern. Prost, *Quelques documents sur l'Histoire des Arts en France (G. B. A.,* 1887, I); *Documents sur les Artistes dijonnais au XVe siècle (G. B. A.,* 1890, II, et 1891, I); *Les Arts à la cour du duc de Berry (G. B. A.,* 1895, II).—A. Perrault-Dabot, *L'Art en Bourgogne,* Paris, 1894.—A. Kleinclausz, *Claus Sluter,* Paris, 1905.—A. Germain, *Les Néerlandais en Bourgogne,* Brussels, 1909.—N. Rondot, *Jacques Morel (R. S. B. A. D.,* 1889).—Abbé Requin, *Le Sculpteur Jacques Morel (R. S. B. A. D.,* 1890).—Abbé Requin, *Antoine le Moituri:r (R. S. B. A. D.,*1890).—Marquet de Vasselot, *Antoine le Moiturier (Mon. Piot,* III, 247).—P. Mantz, *La Peinture française du IXe au XVIe siècle,* Paris, 1898.—L. Delisle, *Le Cabinet des Manuscrits de la Bibliothèque Nationale,* Paris, 1868-1881, 3 vols.—G. Graf Vitzthum, *Die Pariser Miniaturmalerei,* Leipzig, 1907.—H. Martin, *Les Miniaturistes français,* Paris, 1906.—J.-J. Guiffrey, *Inventaires de Jean, Duc de Berry,* Paris, 1894-1896, 2 vols.—L. Delisle, *Les Heures du Duc de Berry (G. B. A.,* 1884, I). — A. de Champeaux and P. Gauchery, *Les Arts à la cour du Duc de Berry,* Paris, 1894.—P. Durrieu, *Les Très Riches Heures du Duc de Berry,* Paris, 1904.—H. Bouchot, *Les Primitifs français,* Paris, 1904.—M. Poëte, *Les Primitifs parisiens,* Paris, 1904.—Abbé Requin, *Documents inédits sur les peintres d'Avignon (R. S. B. A. D.,* 1889).—Abbé Requin, *Une Œuvre de Nicolas Froment (R. S. B. A. D.,* 1902). — G. Lafenestre, *Nicolas Froment (R. A. A M.,* 1897, II).—M. Friedlaender, *Die Votiftafel des Etienne Chevalier von Fouquet (Jahrbücher* of the Berlin Museum, 1897).—P. Leprieur, *Jean Fouquet (R. A. A. M.,* 1897, I).—F. Gruyer, *Les Quarante Fouquet* (at Chantilly), Paris, 1900.—G. Lafenestre, *Jean*

FIG. 268.—TAPESTRY OF THE APOCALYPSE, AT ANGERS.
(Photo. Monuments Historiques.)

Fouquet (*Revue des Deux-Mondes*, Jan. 15, 1902).—P. Durrieu, *Les " Antiquités judaïques"
de Josèphe à la Bibliothèque Nationale* (*G. B. A.*, 1906, II).—C. Benoit, *La Peinture française
à la fin du XV*ᵉ *siècle* (*G. B. A.*, 1901–2).—É. Mâle, *J. Bourdichon* (*G. B. A.*, 1902 and
1904).—R. Maulde de la Clavière, *Jean Perréal, dit Jean de Paris, peintre de Charles VIII,*
Paris, 1896.

FIG. 269.—THE SO-CALLED TAPESTRY OF THE
UNICORN.

(Cluny Museum, Paris.)

FIG. 270.—CHATEAU DE CHANTILLY.

PART II

CLASSICAL ART

CHAPTER I

THE TRANSITION FROM THE GOTHIC STYLE TO CLASSICAL ART

The Transformation of Mediæval Society, and the Dawn of Classical Art.—Its Italian and Antique Origin.—The Classical Revolution in each Province.—The Monarchy in Touraine, the Influence of Royalty.—Architecture: the Successive Transformations of Fortresses into Sporting Lodges and Classical Palaces.—Religious Architecture.—Sculpture of the Traditional Style and Statuary in the Italian Manner.—The Tombs at Saint-Denis: Jean Goujon, and Germain Pilon.—Painting: The Italians at Fontainebleau.—The Portrait-Painters: The Clouets.—How French Art, from Gothic and Christian, became Classical and Pagan.

AFTER the death of Louis XI, and the recovery from the English wars, a new energy began to stir in every province, and for more than a half century there was an artistic production as prolific as it is difficult to define. Two styles and two ages intermingled, until such time as the new overcame the old and took its place. At the accession of Charles VIII, French art was still mediæval and Gothic; in the time of Henry II. it had become classical, and was to remain so. These two styles, the one upheld by a long tradition, the other by the charm of novelty, both benefited by the revival of national energy, and Gothic art was never more exuberant than

132

at the moment when it no longer flourished alone on French soil. But the new art was exclusive; it was permeated by the spirit and the severity of system; it aimed logically at necessary consequences, and rejected all compromise; Gothic art resisted less stoutly, and was soon eliminated. Architects began by admitting a few pilasters, and ended by building classical temples.

It will be sufficient to juxtapose the names of Louis XI and Francis I, and the civilisations they evoke, to suggest the importance of the moral

FIG. 271.—CHATEAU D'AMBOISE.
(*Photo. Neurdein.*)

revolution which French Society, or at least the monarchical world, the heart of that Society, had undergone. The France of the thirteenth century, that of the bishops and burgesses, had given to Christian Europe Gothic art, the art of the Church and the Communes. Gothic art, born in the Ile-de-France, had spread more especially throughout northern Europe. It was absolutely the creation of the Christian society of the Middle Ages. Classical art was the continuation, or the resumption of antique art, firstly on Italian soil, whence it had never entirely disappeared, and then in the other countries of Europe, where it appeared for the first time.

Gothic art was so natural a consequence of mediæval society, that it had ceased to be well adapted to the France of the sixteenth century.

FIG. 272.—CHATEAU DE CHAUMONT.

Architects had invented the cathedral to receive the dense populations of the great communes; but the active and ardent faith of these populations was a necessary factor in its execution, and cathedrals the building of which had been interrupted waited in vain for completion. Modern churches, less immense in plan, no longer demanded the ingenious and complex construction of the ogival crossing, and architects found less lofty vaults without flying buttresses more economical. In monarchical France, the feudal fortresses were irrevocably condemned. Even in the representative arts, the men of the thirteenth century had a system of images by which

FIG. 273.—CHATEAU DE PLESSIS-LÈS-TOURS.
(*Photo. Le Riche.*)

they expressed their emotions; but in the sixteenth century this iconography no longer corresponded to the collective sentiment. The secular mind had outgrown the system of scholastic symbols and the imagery of the Golden Legend; even to believers, certain traditional motives began to seem somewhat childish; the men of the Reformation and those of the Counter-Reformation were almost at one in their rejection or amendment of these.

For some considerable time past, sculptors and painters had been no longer exclusively at the service of their religion. They were attracted by living forms, they were less absorbed in the Christian drama, and more intent on the beauty of human expression. The artists of Italy, and more especially those of

FIG. 274.—FORTRESS OF PERPIGNAN.
(*Photo. Neurdein.*)

Florence, had preceded them on this path; they were at the root of that classicism which was about to revivify French art. After the idealism of the thirteenth century, the Florentines, like other artists, had at first practised a direct and brutal realism; but in the course of the fifteenth century they had applied themselves to the study of the human form with such passion and method that they had taken up the thread of antique art. The Gothic artists, men of the north, Frenchmen, Flemings or Germans, contemplating Florentine figures, realised how uncertain, timid and incomplete their own plastic science still was. French art, like all the others, had to graduate in its humanities at the school of Florence. Like the others again, it lost something of its originality in the process. Florentine art, indeed, reached its goal in a universal ideal

FIG. 275.—CHATEAU DE MEILLANT (CHER).
(*Photo. Monuments Historiques.*)

which it recognised in the works of antiquity; it was therefore able to take up the Græco-Roman tradition, and, following in its wake, French artists gradually discovered antiquity beyond Italy. The French intellect in its turn was to adapt to its own uses that classic language which had been already refined by the Greek and the Florentine intellect.

The Renaissance, or in other words the penetration of Italian methods into northern art, was a European, and not merely a French phenomenon. Its manifestations are to be traced not only in the royal domain, but in every part of France, and are as clearly seen in the provinces, as yet but loosely attached to the monarchy, as in the monarchical centre. The agents of this classicism were the travelling artists so numerous at the close of the Middle Ages, the Italians invited to France by private patrons, by cities, and by the king, the Frenchmen and Flemings who

FIG. 276.—CHATEAU DE BLOIS.
LOUIS XII'S ENTRANCE.

returned from Italy with portfolios full of drawings. And thus it came about that classical forms made their appearance more or less

FIG. 277.—CHATEAU DE BLOIS.
FRANCIS I'S STAIRCASE.

everywhere during the first thirty years of the sixteenth century. Churches, tombs and town-houses were transformed even in the reign of Louis XII; mythological figures in the Italian manner took their places in all the traditional arts of France, in tapestries, in illuminated manuscripts, in the painted glass of Pinaigrier, as in the enamels of Léonard Limosin and the Pénicauds. It was the Italian pottery which put Bernard Palissy on the track of a new technique. Classic decoration was adapted to the particular art of each province. Local tradition in every district attaches a famous name to this diffuse evolution: Hugues Sambin at Dijon, Philibert Delorme at Lyons, Ligier-Richier in Lorraine, Dominique Florentin in Champagne, Jacques Marchand at Orleans, Michel Colombe in Touraine, Piérre Sohier at Caen, Jean Goujon at Rouen, Nicholas Bachelier at Toulouse, Léonard Limosin at Limoges, Bernard Palissy in Saintonge, Jean Cousin we know not where.

Toulouse, the capital of Romanesque art and a centre where Gothic art had been but coldly received, was better disposed towards the Renaissance style, in which it recognised the classical and Latin spirit. Nicholas Bachelier placed columns

FIG. 278.—CHATEAU D'AZAY-LE-RIDEAU.
(*Photo. Neurdein.*)

of stone and marble upon the Toulousian bricks; at the Hôtel d'Assézat they are superposed, and form, together with the entablatures and openings of the façade, a very skilful arrangement by which the dismal heaviness of the brick structure is relieved (Fig. 293). On several private houses the Corinthian order bears a rich decoration of sculptured marble. One of the lateral doors of Saint Sernin, and the door of the Dalbade are among the most charming adaptations of the Italian style in France.

FIG. 279.—CHATEAU DE CHAMBORD.
(*Photo. Monuments Historiques.*)

The great Eastern region, as yet but feebly welded to the centre, that ancient Lotharingia traversed by the artisans of the north on the way to Italy, was also to be permeated by the classical spirit. Lyons was the city of great fairs, a metropolis of French commerce; since the time of Louis XII, it was the centre whence the king watched the affairs of Italy. Aix, where King René's Flemings had worked, readily accepted the Italian forms; on the doors of his cathedral, Gothic ornament is superposed on the Italian arabesques. Avignon still received the artists of the north, but they now worked in the Italian manner. In the middle of the century, when there was a great dearth of painters in the kingdom, a Champenois, Simon of Chalons, established in Provence, introduced figures copied from Michelangelo and Raphael in his religious compositions with some skill (Fig. 363).

FIG. 280.—CHATEAU DE SAINT-GERMAIN.

When she lost her Dukes, Burgundy also lost her artistic personality; but Dijon still enjoyed its admirable situation on the highway to Italy. This city also had its Renaissance, marked by a robust exuberance of style and a certain heaviness.

137

It finds expression in the façades of certain mansions, and in that of the Church of Saint Michel, as also in the furniture carved by

FIG. 281.—CHATEAU DE CHENONCEAU.
(*Photo. Neurdein.*)

Hugues Sambin (Fig. 309). Franche-Comté, rich in black marbles and in alabaster which was used by the Dijon sculptors, had lived in artistic dependence upon Burgundy. The great nobles had caused splendid mausoleums to be erected for themselves. In the sixteenth century these tombs lost their Gothic character, and even their religious significance; pilasters and arabesques replaced pointed arches and pinnacles, and pagan figures were associated with Christian personages.

At Brou, a church was built to shelter tombs, rich monuments in which the Renaissance style mingles with Flamboyant art. Commissioned by an Austrian princess, the grand-daughter of the Dukes of Burgundy, betrothed in the first instance to the King of France, afterwards married to the King of Spain, and soon a widow, and executed by a bevy of artists and workmen, among whom were Germans, Flemings, Picards and Italians, this exuberant work combines the style of two ages, the Gothic and the Classical, and reveals the cosmopolitanism of a province as yet imperfectly attached to its powerful neighbours (Figs. 305, 306, 307).

Champenois art, on the other hand, shows a very clearly defined character, above all in sculpture. From this period date a number of Calvaries, of

FIG. 282.—CHATEAU D'USSÉ. (*Photo. Neurdein.*)

sepulchres, and of single figures of saints, with faces generally refined, and somewhat contorted, in the manner of the Flemish painters; they are perfectly distinct from the Tourangeau type, those round, smooth faces characteristic of Fouquet's worthies.

FIG. 283.—BIRD'S EYE VIEW OF CHANTILLY.

(From the album, "Paris vu en ballon," by A. Schoelcher et O. Decugis.)

Troyes has preserved a touching St. Martin, with a fine austere face; the careful servant exorcises the town with a gesture of dramatic simplicity (Fig. 321). A *Visitation* shows us two housewives in Sunday dress (Fig. 322) coming from mass; the folds of their gowns, the embroidery of the stuffs, the ribbons, the jewels, the long plaits, and even the bunch of keys, make up an accumulation of details that please the eye, although the colour is no longer there to complete the effect; there is no trace here of that generalising modelling which Italian masters and antique works were soon to teach. This southern province, Champagne, witnessed the efflorescence of a picturesque statuary akin to that of the Flemings and Germans; wood and stone were elaborately worked and afterwards illuminated with brilliant colours. This art was dear to a luxurious society, and at Troyes, as at Nuremburg, sculptors trifled with the accessories of costume. But about 1540 Dominique Florentin brought from Italy a new manner of treating marble; the chisel of sculptors was thenceforth applied to the modelling of supple bodies and light draperies.

In Lorraine the Dukes had tombs erected for themselves in the Italian style; Charles IV built a memorial chapel imitated from that of the Medici.

FIG. 284.—THE OVAL COURT AT FONTAINEBLEAU.

A few masterpieces were evolved from the soul of the people. In the middle of the sixteenth century arose an artist, Ligier-Richier, who showed himself capable of adapting Italian forms to Christian sentiment. A large number of religious sculptures are ascribed to

FIG. 285.—HORSE-SHOE STAIRCASE AT FONTAINEBLEAU.

him, for the most part in marble. The tomb of Saint Mihiel is by an artist who has preserved the powerful emotion of the Middle Ages, but who knows how to balance a composition in the classical manner, and to give elegance or violence to his attitudes. The Magdalen bends to kiss the Saviour's feet with a sinuous suppleness, an inclination of the neck which reveals a technical mastery that verges on mannerism. At Bar-le-Duc there is a skeleton due to this same art, which elevates the ancient motives by the elegance and nobility of the new style. The skeleton, on which some fragments of flesh are still hanging, is mediæval in its inspiration; but it was carved by a learned anatomist, who has given this figure of a Gothic charnel-house the noble attitude of an antique orator (Figs. 331-333).

Like all the provinces in which the Flamboyant Style had flourished, Normandy, with its two capitals, acclaimed the new art.

FIG. 286.—BIRD'S EYE VIEW OF FONTAINEBLEAU.
(From the album, "Paris vu en ballon,"
by A. Schoelcher et O. Decugis.)

Scarcely had the Palais de Justice and the Tour de Beurre been completed, when Italian ornament began to make its appearance on façades and tombs. The Château de Gaillon, built for the Cardinal d'Amboise in the time of Louis XII, combines all sorts of novel amenities with the picturesque arrangement of a fifteenth century *château*.

Two magnificent tombs in the Lady Chapel of Rouen Cathedral seem to have fixed two moments of this artistic reformation. The

FIG. 287.—FRANCIS I'S GALLERY AT
FONTAINEBLEAU.

FIG. 288.—HENRY II'S BALL-ROOM AT
FONTAINEBLEAU.

first, that of Georges d'Amboise (Fig. 341), has a rich ornament of arabesques and pilasters, a floriated decoration in the manner of Michelozzo, such as the men of the early Renaissance were in the habit of applying to Gothic buildings. The tomb of the Marquis de Brézé (Fig. 346), a slightly later work with its portico of columns surmounted by Caryatides, is a monument in the classical manner, in spite of its equestrian statue and its realistic recumbent figure. At Caen, Pierre Sohier (Fig. 304) was the author of an exquisite combination in which exuberant forms borrowed from Italian motives replace the restless lines of the Flamboyant Style.

At the close of the Middle Ages, Brittany had shown a great artistic vitality; parishioners crowned their churches with airy spires, nobles and citizens built solid fortresses. After the sixteenth century, at the period when France abandoned mediæval forms of sculpture and architecture, Brittany held aloof from the common movement. The peninsula

FIG. 289.—THE LOUVRE, WITH LESCOT'S WING ON
THE LEFT.

remained isolated, lying as it did outside the great international highways, by means of which that interchange between Italy and the North was carried on, destined first to transform, and then to suppress Gothic architecture. Thenceforth, Breton art was behind French art as a whole; its Calvaries continued to be rude in execution; its "imagiers" talked a patois, and were ignorant of the learned language which all Europe had borrowed from Italy. Among these Breton Calvaries, the most ancient,

FIG. 290.—HÔTEL DE VILLE OF LA ROCHELLE.

that of Plougastel, dates from the sixteenth century. At the height of the classic period, the Plougastel Calvary preserved the conceptions, the attitudes, the costumes of the Middle Ages, and a purely rustic style. There is nothing in this *naïveté*, touching as it is, to cause us to regret that French art had accepted the Italian discipline and antique culture (Figs. 326, 327, 329).

When we come to Touraine, we touch the very heart of national existence; here it was that the blood of the decrepit monarchy, impoverished by war and anarchy, had once more begun to pulse vigorously; here it was that the kings of France had fled for sanctuary, before they took to sojourning here for pleasure; and here it was that the destinies of French art were decided, in the strongly united France of Francis I and Henry II.

FIG. 291.—COURT OF THE HÔTEL CARNAVALET, PARIS.

Among the causes which favoured classicism, we must reckon the influence of a monarchy under the omnipotent Francis I. Since art had become independent of religion, it had often accepted service under a king. The king knew that one sure means of immortality was to associate himself with the work of artists, and to attach his name to imperishable works. Many an Italian Mæcenas had set the example. Francis I, Louis XIV and Napoleon successively engaged this force in their service, and concentrated the artistic energies of France for their own aggrandisement. The civilisation of towns and of ancient communes was slowly effaced day by day in the general life; it was dominated by the more brilliant centre of the court. This centralisation naturally tended to favour classicism at the expense of those provincial traditions and local arts which were so flourishing at the close of the Middle Ages; the

FIG. 292.—LOUVRE. DOOR KNOWN AS JEAN GOUJON'S DOOR.

somewhat abstract generality of its principles made it acceptable everywhere, and its very universality demonstrated the unity of the kingdom.

The entry of the French into Milan, Florence, and Rome during the wars of Charles VIII, Louis XII and Francis I was merely an incidental cause in an inevitable evolution. Even had these wars never taken place, French art would have passed from the Gothic to the classic phase; for no country in Europe, neither Spain, nor Flanders, nor Germany, was able to preserve its originality in face of the seductions of Italy. But in a monarchical and aristocratic country like France, the periodical descent of its king and its nobles into Italy naturally hastened the adoption of ultramontane fashions by imposing them at the very heart of French life, the court of the king. Louis XI was purely Gothic. But in 1495, his son, Charles VIII, wrote from Naples, saying how he had been

FIG. 293.—HOTEL D'ASSEZAT, TOULOUSE

FIG. 294.—HÔTEL BOURGTHÉROULDE, ROUEN.

dazzled by the beauty and richness of the paintings; he had already made up his mind to bring back Italian artists to decorate Amboise. Some years later Louis XII declared to the Florentines that he was anxious to employ "Master Leonard, their painter." It was, however, only Francis I who succeeded in attracting the great Florentine. The king's companions, visiting the galleries of the palaces, and the gardens of the villas, marvelled at the luxury and the smiling charm which "the fair speech of Master Alain Chartier, the subtlety of Master Jean de Meung, and the hand of Fouquet would be powerless to set forth, describe or paint." For this Gothic feudality, such a civilisation was a new thing, fashioned by masters in the art of enjoyment.

Fouquet, however, had been in Italy as early as the middle of the fifteenth century. He had admired Michelozzo's ornamental style, and on his return had decorated the background of his portraits with simulated pilasters and sculptural arabesques. His contemporaries, Bourdichon and other miniaturists, began to replace the Gothic churches they had hitherto depicted by Italian palaces, and occasionally even produced compositions or figures imitating Florentine or Umbrian paintings. Decorative elements are, indeed, very easily borrowed, and the same pictures are understood and admired without difficulty in very different countries. On the other hand, architecture and religious sculpture, which are bound up with deeply rooted habits and customs, are not to be modified instantaneously; a new system of

FIG. 295.—HENRY IV'S COURT, CAPITOLE, TOULOUSE.

144

FIG. 296.—THE GRANDE PLACE, ARRAS.

decoration will not suffice to transform them. Italian architects and sculptors, when they took part in great artistic enterprises in

FIG. 297.—HÔTEL D'ÉCOVILLE, CAEN.

France, were obliged to adapt themselves to local customs; they threw a veil of Italian decoration over tombs and *châteaux,* monuments constituted in the image of French life by very ancient usages. Pictures, on the contrary, were a court luxury, and Italian painters such as Andrea Solario, Leonardo da Vinci, Andrea del Sarto, and later, the whole school of Fontainebleau, were able to work in the heart of France without modifying any of their alien habits. The field of action lay open to painters.

The fortresses, which look so white and delicate in the Gothic miniatures, seemed very dismal dwellings in the tranquillised kingdom of the sixteenth century; their solid walls enclosed narrow and sombre existences. During the peace which lasted from the reign of Louis XI to the outbreak of the

FIG. 298.—THE BOURSE, LILLE.

FIG. 299.—HÔTEL DE VILLE, ARRAS.

religious wars, architecture, too, was able to disarm, and to lay aside its heavy cuirass. The castles were thrown open to the light of day; the dwelling emerged from the encompassing walls; it was erected in the midst of gardens, or in a park; trees, fountains and flowers contributed to the attraction of the dwelling, and in the walls which formerly presented a solid surface, large windows were made to open upon the smiling surroundings. From their windows and terraces, the nobles loved to contemplate the wide plains of the Loire or the Cher. It was the art of building which expressed most fully the joyous expansion and the graceful fancy of the monarchy and aristocracy of France. A like enthusiasm inspired all ranks. The king, the great nobles, and high functionaries spent the greater part of their revenues on the construction of exquisite *châteaux*. Humbler persons ruined themselves by building, and Philibert Delorme speaks of the distrust felt by expectant heirs for architects. The least enterprising were eager to transform their old manor-houses in accordance with the taste of the day; they gutted their ancient towers to pierce them with windows; they added a modern block of buildings to a Gothic or Romanesque keep. The new style tended to regularity and symmetry. But the necessity of preserving majestic and imposing fragments forced architects to display a certain ingenuity. They devised unexpected aspects; they were entertained by the unforeseen combinations produced by the feudal architecture of castles intermingled with the urban style of palaces, and, a little later, with classic façades in the Italian manner. From

FIG. 300.—CATHEDRAL OF TOURS.

Louis XI to Charles IX, the number of French *châteaux* is considerable, and their variety is such that it is impossible to classify them in accordance with a clearly defined type, such as that of the Florentine palace, or the Roman villa.

Nevertheless, in the variety of combinations, certain elements reappear persistently. The Renaissance *château* in its earlier manifestation was only the feudal castle transformed. It retained the great towers, the curtains with their battlements and machicolations, and occasionally, the moat in which the

FIG. 301.—ORLEANS CATHEDRAL, SOUTH PORCH.

basement of the building was submerged. Each of these organs was preserved for the beauty discovered in it now that it was no longer useful. The *château*, having descended into the plain, cast the reflection of its battlements and machicolations into the slow waters of a river, and these martial symbols became an amusement for the eye.

The main block of an urban mansion, with large square windows and a lofty roof loaded with dormer windows and chimneys, was attached to the great feudal towers. The new towers, of a less ponderous design, were sometimes corbelled out at the angles of the building. Later, antique decoration made its appearance, with its columns, pilasters and pediments; the Greek orders enframed doors and windows, and soon the somewhat geometrical regularity of these motives imposed on façades a symmetry unknown to the Middle Ages.

FIG. 302.—DOORWAY OF THE DUCAL PALACE, NANCY.

The transformation in French architecture began before the penetration of Italian influences. The last castles built in the time of Louis XI are still defiant of aspect. At Chaumont (Fig. 272) the

arrangement of the building as a strictly enclosed fortress was one day to appear very dismal, and one of the four blocks of buildings which enclosed the quadrilateral was pulled down to open out a prospect over the valley of the Loire. At Ussé (Fig. 282) again, a large breach had to be made to give light and air to the *château.* Its inhabitants no longer sought safety behind a screen of solid walls; its offices, its terraces, its courts and approaches were spread out freely around it. Even structures which retained their formidable features were surrounded by gardens; behind the great tower and the grey masonry of Langeais flowers bloomed in gay parterres. Architecture allowed itself to be disarmed at last, and associated itself with the peaceful charm of nature.

The king set the example in this transformation. To judge from the fragments of it that still exist, the famous castle of Plessis-lès-Tours, where Louis XI died, was no austere prison, but a mansion of red brick and white stone in a charming valley enclosed by softly swelling hills. Charles VII died when he was superintending the transformations he had undertaken at Amboise. The Chapel of St. Hubert (Figs. 336, 338), and the façade towards the Loire built for him were still purely Gothic, richly flamboyant, and appear all the more delicately elaborate from their juxtaposition with massive feudal masonry (Fig. 271). Louis XII, the son of Charles d'Orléans, the captive poet, was born in a fortress at Blois, which Froissart described as "fair, strong and sturdy, and one of the finest in the kingdom" (Figs. 276, 277). When he became king of France, he did not desert the

FIG. 305.—TOMB OF MARGUERITE
DE BOURBON, IN THE CHURCH AT BROU.

landscapes of his childhood. He began the reconstruction of the old castle, and raised a graceful block of buildings of brick and stone, crowned by a high roof with Gothic dormer windows. Francis I was, as said Du Cerceau, "marvellously addicted to building." This architectural king was, indeed, the creator of Chambord, Madrid, Saint-Germain, La Muette, Villers-Cotterets, Blois, Fontainebleau, and Pierre Lescot's Louvre. In each of these buildings, we can trace the progress of classic decoration. At the beginning of the sixteenth century, only a few motives are introduced; but very soon one of the latent principles of classicism, regularity, is imposed upon the façades and plans of modern buildings. Nevertheless, even when this royal architecture seems an imitation of Italian palaces, it differs from these, because it answers to different requirements. The Italian villa was a place of rest arranged primarily with a view to the delight of the eye; it is placed on a picturesque site, which is agreeably contemplated from a belvedere. In times of peace, the chief amusement of the king of France was the hunting of stag or wild boar. Thus nearly all the royal *châteaux* adjoin a vast forest; many of them were originally hunting lodges; the images of St. Hubert found in some of them,

FIG. 306.—ROOD-SCREEN IN THE CHURCH AT BROU.

at Amboise and Pau, for instance, were not without their special significance; such a statue would not have been out of place in any of the royal houses. In the pictures and tapestries in which they are represented, the king, his court and his pack of hounds

FIG. 307.—TOMB OF MARGUERITE
OF AUSTRIA, IN THE CHURCH AT BROU.

nearly always figure in the foreground.

The open staircase (Fig. 277) in Francis I's wing in the Castle of Blois is a Gothic structure with Italian decorations; loggias conceal the curtain of the ancient fortress, and give the façade an aspect of magnificence which also characterises the Château de Madrid. At Chambord (Fig. 279) feudal towers flank a symmetrical building; this regular quadrilateral is obviously not the work of a mediæval architect, but the *château* has retained one very Gothic characteristic, the accumulation of all the decoration on the roof. Italian ornament has been borrowed, to be arranged in the French manner; there is an elaborate architecture of chimneys, dormer windows and lanterns, which recalls the delightful accessories of the *chateaux* depicted by the illuminators of the Duke of Berry. At Saint-Germain (Fig. 280), a feature of southern architecture, a terrace, from which the king could contemplate his forest, and follow the windings of the horn from afar, was substituted for the customary roof. But even here, the mode of construction is French; this terrace rests on an ogival roof, to sustain the arches of which it was necessary to encase the building with buttresses; arcades and galleries in the Italian manner are applied to this Gothic skeleton, but they do not mask it.

Following in the royal footsteps, the rich men of the kingdom re-built their dwellings. Two of the most graceful *châteaux* of the sixteenth century, Azay-le-Rideau and

FIG. 308.—ROOD-SCREEN OF THE CHURCH OF THE
MADELEINE, TROYES. (*Photo. Neurdein.*)

Chenonceaux (Figs. 278, 281), were begun about 1518–1520 for financiers. They are among the most charming of French buildings, and they make but the slightest decorative concessions to the Italian fashion. Their very original charm lies entirely in the elegance of their outline, their happy proportions, and the picturesque arrangement of their turrets, windows and dormers.

FIG. 309.—CHURCH OF SAINT MICHEL, DIJON. (*Photo. A. Joliet.*)

Fontainebleau, the most famous of the royal houses, is far from being one of the happiest achievements of this period of ingenious architecture. But Francis I, "who caused it to be built, took marvellous pleasure therein, so that he sojourned there for the most part, and enriched it with all sorts of commodities, with galleries, halls, chambers, bath-rooms, and other adjuncts, the whole embellished with all kinds of histories, both painted and in relief, done by the most renowned masters the king could collect in France, and in Italy, from whence he also obtained some fine antique pieces. And in short all that the king could find that was excellent, was for his Fontainebleau." Hence this *château*, the general conception of which is rather poor, contains a number of very choice motives, not always in very close relation to the main body of the building: these include porticoes, staircases, sculptures, and above all, a marvellous internal decoration, which is its great original feature (Figs. 285–288).

FIG. 310.—NAVE OF SAINT EUSTACHE, PARIS.

By the middle of the sixteenth century, architects had almost abandoned all recollection of feudal buildings. They seem thenceforth to have ignored the turrets, the dormer windows, the

FIG. 311.—CHURCH OF SAINT ÉTIENNE DU MONT, PARIS.

machicolations, the battlements, which gave such graceful adornment to the first *châteaux* of the century. The general arrangement was no longer governed by the accidents of the site; the structure developed its symmetrical members on an even surface; architectonic beauty became less and less dependent upon the charm of details, and the picturesque unexpectedness of their disposal; it inhered rather in the art of the proportions, and the unity of the whole. The *château* was no longer to be distinguished from the urban hotel. Four blocks of buildings, one of which, smaller than the rest, formed a gallery, gave a rectangular quadrilateral. To ornament the flat façades, architects applied the principles of Roman construction as they were beginning to know them from Vitruvius, from antique ruins, and from Italian buildings: these consisted in arranging on the façade, in such a manner as to enframe the windows, columns or pilasters supporting entablatures or pediments; in superposing as many orders as there were storeys in the building; the Tuscan or Doric order for the ground-floor, the Ionic order for the first storey, and composite columns or Caryatides for the second. Between the columns, if space permitted, niches were hollowed for the reception of statues. This general ornamentation was repeated indefinitely all along a façade; the monotony was relieved only by projecting pavilions, with higher roofs. Thenceforth, architecture was reduced to drawing, and a knowledge of proportions. The decorative elements of French palaces admitted of little change,

FIG. 312.—FAÇADE OF THE CATHEDRAL OF TOUL.
(*Photo. Monuments Historiques.*)

FIG. 313.—VIRGIN AND CHILD. CHURCH OF SAINT GALMIER, LOIRE.

the distinction between one building and another, and even between one period and another, was very slight. If we omit the internal arrangements, the history of French architecture could be followed almost completely in the fashion of disposing colonnades on a façade. Nevertheless, limited to these methods, it created varied styles and forms that were always pure; in proportion as it restricted decorative invention, the art of building owed more to measurement and calculation.

In the middle of the sixteenth century, three men were brilliant exponents of this architecture, which had already become the classic French style. These were Pierre Lescot, Jean Bullant, and Philibert Delorme. Pierre Lescot was commissioned by Francis I to rebuild the Louvre. He gutted Charles V's palace, and built the south-west corner of the square court, two blocks of buildings which were to serve as models to many architects; they were the nucleus of that new Louvre, the building of which went on for three centuries. All those who successively added a pavilion, a gallery, or a façade were dominated more or less by Pierre Lescot's conceptions. "This surface of masonry is so rich in columns, friezes, architraves and all sorts of architecture, and of such excellent symmetry and beauty, that its equal is not to be found in all Europe" (Androuet du Cerceau). Those who continued it would occa-

FIG. 314.—ROOD-SCREEN OF SAINT ÉTIENNE DU MONT, PARIS.

sionally strive to be richer or more majestic; but that initial Louvre in which the genius of Lescot and of Goujon met, remains the most brilliant and one of the most graceful inspirations

FIG. 315.—TOMB OF FRANCIS OF BRITTANY.
NANTES CATHEDRAL.

of the Renaissance (Fig. 289).

Jean Bullant showed even greater submissiveness to antique forms, and was the first to make use of the "colossal order"; at Ecouen, instead of reducing the colonnade to the dimensions of the storeys, he enlarged it to the scale of the façade; and instead of superposing small columns, he erected lofty columns which rise from the soil to the summit. Philibert Delorme was also an enthusiastic admirer of antiquity; he had studied its treatises and measured its monuments. In the Château d'Anet, the Tuileries, and Fontainebleau, he not only derived certain ingenious decorative forms from antique ruins, but actually re-captured that harmony of proportion which was the soul of Greek architecture. Yet his conceptions are not merely those of a designer; they are essentially those of a constructor; in his book on architecture, if he is much pre-occupied with the measurements of columns and entablatures, he loves to exercise his skill on the difficulties of masonry, on spiral vaults and double winding staircases; he does not neglect comfort, and is concerned to build chimneys that will not smoke. His vigorous intelligence was able to master the two artistic eras, the Middle Ages and Antiquity, and to select freely and without idolatry from the traditions of the French master-masons and the works of Vitruvius. He sought to adapt, not to imitate. He is

FIG. 316.—THE VIRGIN
OF OLIVET.
(The Louvre, Paris.)

FIG. 317.—STRENGTH.
MICHEL COLOMBE.
NANTES CATHEDRAL.

154

FIG. 318.—TEMPER-
ANCE. MICHEL
COLOMBE.
NANTES CATHEDRAL.

to be reckoned among those architects, so numerous in France, who were thenceforth to complain of being sacrificed to foreign fashions. He even prided himself on having created a French order by erecting ringed columns here and there to hide the joins in the drums.

The cathedral also submitted to the classic influence. Throughout the sixteenth century, the churches still preserved their traditional constitution: vaults on intersecting arches supported on pillars and re-inforced by flying buttresses. But this Gothic skeleton was overlaid on every side with an Italian decoration.

FIG. 319.—PRUDENCE.
MICHEL COLOMBE.
NANTES
CATHEDRAL.

There is no kind of resemblance between the antique temple and the French church, and yet a gradual transition from one to the

FIG. 320.—JUSTICE.
MICHEL COLOMBE.
NANTES
CATHEDRAL.

other of these diverse architectures was effected. Unlike classic art, the Gothic style is very adaptable, and will accept an eclectic decoration. The Greek temple was a fixed and complete organism, in which nothing could be changed. It continued immutable throughout antiquity, and in the second manifestation it enjoyed among the moderns. The Gothic cathedral, on the other hand, was an organism in a perpetual state of transformation, one which readily received all kinds of architectonic grafts. In the time of Louis XI and Louis XII, ingenious artists, constructors rather than

FIG. 321.—SAINT
MARTHA.
CHURCH OF THE
MADELEINE, TROYES.

decorators, tried the fashionable ornaments of the day on its vast sides. In time, they intermingled Italian arabesques and the fantasies

FIG. 322.—THE VISITATION.
CHURCH OF SAINT JEAN, TROYES.

of the Flamboyant Style; then the ornamental grammar of the ancients was accepted in its entirety, for nothing prevented architects from designing antique pilasters upon buttresses, or carving Corinthian capitals to support the arches of a vault. In those parts of the church of Saint Pierre at Caen which were built after 1520 by Pierre Sohier (Fig. 304), we find this combination of the Flamboyant Style and Italian decoration. The pinnacles of the apse are in the form of curved vases, with convolutions and sculptured arabesques which destroy the soaring lightness of the Gothic lines. In the interior, crockets and consoles hang on the ribs of the vaults like some heavy vegetation. But in the over-rich decoration, there is a latent principle of regularity and symmetry which was subsequently to simplify this exuberant style. A little later, Pierre Lemercier, in building Saint Eustache in Paris (Fig. 310), remained a mediæval architect; but limbs of this

Gothic body, the pillars and flying buttresses, are clothed in the classic manner. The sixteenth century built few churches; it showed little originality in this work, and it was not until the following century that the innovations passed from the decorations to the skeleton of the building itself. The literary language of France underwent a like transformation; to imitate Latin

FIG. 323.—SAINT GEORGE KILLING THE DRAGON.
MICHEL COLOMBE.
(The Louvre, Paris.)

more closely, French writers loaded their orthography with etymological letters, and their vocabulary with borrowed words; but a more profound assimilation was required to win the logical regularity of classic syntax.

Sculpture was too closely associated with the religious life for any abrupt interruption of its normal evolution. In every corner of France, Italian art found sculptors who were working at tombs for great nobles, or carving the traditional figures of saints for the people. In the course of the fifteenth century, there were certain motives which made a special appeal to Christian sensibilities: the groups which illustrate the last moments of Jesus, the Crucifixion, the Virgin of Pity: the stricken Mother weeping over the corpse upon her lap, a sombre *tête-à-tête* which sums up all the sorrow of the Passion. The Entombment was further a tragic spectacle which gave rich opportunities to the artist: a corpse, the sumptuous costumes of Nicodemus and Joseph

FIG. 324.—THE MAGDALEN.
FIGURE OF THE "SEPULCHRE" AT SOLESMES.

of Arimathæa, the attitudes and the mournful faces of the Virgin and the Holy Women. These groups appear in many churches,

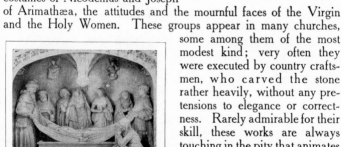

FIG. 325.—"SEPULCHRE" IN THE ABBEY OF SOLESMES.

some among them of the most modest kind; very often they were executed by country craftsmen, who carved the stone rather heavily, without any pretensions to elegance or correctness. Rarely admirable for their skill, these works are always touching in the pity that animates them. The naïve and sorrowful figures are grouped solicitously round the dead, whose body is dimly seen in the background of a low chapel, dark as a tomb.

The most famous of these "Sepulchres" are that at Solesmes (Fig. 325) and that by Ligier-Richier at Saint-Mihiel (Fig. 331). The Solesmes Entombment

157

ART IN FRANCE

FIG. 326.—THE CALVARY AT PLEYBEN.

dates, no doubt, from the close of the fifteenth century, and shows more than one pilaster in the Italian manner. But these borrowings are applied, not assimilated; the artist has juxtaposed them boldly with the Flamboyant ornament. The figures, on the other hand, reveal no traces of an alien art. This entombment is a tranquil scene; a certain placidity, a kind of expressive impotence, becomes an advantage to the artist, and gives a peaceful majesty to the drama. Italian art is prone to emphasise gesture till it verges on paroxysm. Here, on the contrary, we have neither violence nor grimace; the holy women are not convulsed by moral suffering, and the weight of the corpse has not evoked attitudes of painful effort in the bearers. The robust figures of Solesmes are akin to the minute personages Fouquet painted so agreeably, if a little languidly. The finest of them, that of the Magdalen, recalls one of the peasant girls transformed by that artist into saints. She is weeping quietly, somewhat apart from the rest, like a discreet servant. This art, lacking aspirations towards truth and beauty, is yet full of a sweet serenity.

One name dominates the art of Touraine at the beginning of the sixteenth century: Michel Colombe was of a country and of a period which eagerly collected all the motives of Italian decoration and inserted them even in Gothic monuments. But he continued to chisel his figures in the French manner, that of an artist who was not concerned to elaborate his modelling, and did not trouble himself about anatomical subtleties. The *St. George killing the Dragon*, which he carved with great care

FIG. 327.—THE CALVARY AT PLOUGASTEL.

158

FIG. 328.—CLAUDE OF FRANCE.
CHURCH OF SAINT DENIS.
(*Photo. Mieusement.*)

for the Château de Gaillon (Fig. 323), lacks elasticity and fire. The marble demands more nervous forms than those of this rigid knight on his heavy charger. In the tomb of Francis II of Brittany at Nantes, the general architecture remains that of the Middle Ages: a sarcophagus with sculptured sides supporting two recumbent figures with clasped hands. But at the first glance we feel that we are no longer in the Gothic age; the panels are overlaid with the branching ornament of the Flamboyant Style; the pilasters are decorated with delicate Italian bas-reliefs; the ornamentation, although still rich, is so far chastened as to permit a precision of lines and planes which is already classical. The mourners (*pleurants*) subsist merely in the shape of little ornamental figures; they have made way for apostles. But above all, the four great allegorical statues at the angles, Justice, Strength, Temperance, and Prudence, proclaim their remoteness from the mediæval iconography. The princes and kings for whom tombs were to be erected thenceforth would prefer radiant divinities, suggesting ideas of glory, to the hideous insistence on Death, characteristic of the Gothic tomb. A little later, they caused the sides of their sarcophagi to be carved with representations of their exploits, and with trophies of victory. But all this was more than a change of style in architecture and sculpture. A pagan joyousness took the place of the melancholy of Christian sentiment. Michel Colombe's cardinal virtues

FIG. 329.—FIGURES OF APOSTLES AT PLEYBEN.

were not as yet wholly classical in type and costume; but they were no longer mediæval. Their vigorous elegance, the tranquil majesty of their attitudes, heralds a world in which the figures disdain

159

FIG. 330.—CHARLOTTE OF
FRANCE. CHURCH OF SAINT
DENIS. (*Photo. Mieusement*.)

expression, and are content with beauty.

Michel Colombe is not a very clearly defined figure in art-history; but the anonymous works which, in their quest for paternity, naturally group themselves about him, add considerable substance to this shadowy personality. Throughout Touraine there were sculptors who carved in stone or marble beautiful Virgins, at once elegant and artless, calm and healthy, and free from vulgar realism. In earlier figures of this type, a violent movement of the hip had produced a tumultuous disorder in the draperies. This disappears; the figure is drawn up, and the robe falls about it in quiet folds. These statues are characterised, not by the sovereign majesty of the Virgin Queens of the thirteenth century, but by the somewhat rustic elegance dear to Jean Bourdichon and the Master of Moulins. The violent "imagiers" are now modelling gentle feminine faces. The Virgin of Ecouen, and still more, the Virgin of Olivet (Fig. 316) are among the most seductive figures of French statuary. Here nervous energy and will-power were not demanded; the artist gave himself up to a novel pleasure, the delight of creating and contemplating a charming form. The men who loved these works were as yet unacquainted with Italian beauty, but they were fully prepared to receive and welcome it. They were beginning to essay the refinements of the Italian craftsmen. Florentine art was about to teach them to endue the whole body in its suppleness of attitudes and draperies, with that purity of line they had already achieved in the features of the face. Had she

FIG. 331.—"SEPULCHRE" IN THE CHURCH OF SAINT-ÉTIENNE, AT SAINT-MIHIEL. LIGIER-RICHIER.
(*Photo. Monuments Historiques.*)

been born a few years later, the Virgin of Olivet would have been, not more graceful, but less homely in her elegance, and her draperies would have been more delicate in texture.

When, at the beginning of the sixteenth century, Jean Perréal became the overseer of the tomb of Francis I, Duke of Brittany, he chose marbles at Genoa, had them transported at great expense to Lyons, and carted from Lyons to Roanne; thence they followed the course of

FIG. 332.—FIGURE OF A CHILD.
LIGIER-RICHIER.
(The Louvre, Paris.)

the Loire to Nantes, where they were carved by Michel Colombe and his pupils. It was not only a new material which was then brought into France. The beautiful marble, destined to become more and more the medium of the sculptor, exacted a delicacy of execution impossible with the stone of the old "imagiers"; its close and tender grain, its whiteness, its polished surface necessitated

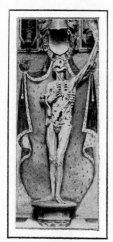

FIG. 333.—SKELETON IN THE CHURCH OF SAINT ÉTIENNE AT BAR-LE-DUC. LIGIER-RICHIER.
(*Photo. Laurent.*)

suppler and more precise modelling. The ornamental vocabulary was the first thing to be transformed. The interlaced ribs and serrated foliage of the Flamboyant Style disappeared from an architecture of regular lines. Flat pilasters and entablatures were decorated with candelabra, arabesques, and garlands in low relief; a decoration subordinated like an embroidery to the plane of the surface and its framework. The Italian workers in marble, who had come to France as early as the reign of Charles VIII, intermingled their ornamental style with that of monuments, the figures of which remained purely Gothic. But very soon these figures themselves began to cast aside their peculiarities of costume and physiognomy, generalising, idealising, and tending towards that type of beauty which Florentine discipline and the study of the antique had recently revealed. It was then only that French art was penetrated to its depths by the classic spirit.

FIG. 334.—SCREEN FROM AUGEROLLES, IN THE CLUNY MUSEUM, PARIS.

Around royal or princely sarcophagi arose beautiful allegorical figures clad in those conventional draperies known as antique, which reveal the form of the body. The recumbent figure was no longer encased in rigid armour; he wore the cuirass of the Roman pattern, outlining the breast, the abdomen and the thighs. Very often he rose on the funeral slab, and rested on his elbow after the manner of an antique river-god, or knelt before a fald-stool. The face was still a portrait, but the figure was that of an impersonal hero.

The monuments at Saint Denis demonstrate this transformation of sculpture very clearly. In order to pass from the Gothic world to that of the Renaissance, we must make a pilgrimage through this Way of Tombs. The evolution of form corresponds to a moral evolution. The sculptors of the Middle Ages had fixed images of death in these recumbent kings, and the royal insignia added little to the miserable prestige of the stone corpses. But in the sixteenth century, the king is not even represented in the rigidity of death; he is seen kneeling upon a beautiful sculptured structure, surrounded by fine allegorical figures; for the sinister "pleurants" no longer attend Louis XII, Francis I and Henry II. The tomb of Francis I, constructed by Philibert Delorme (Fig. 347), is a triumphal arch, and the base, sculptured by

FIG. 335.—THE FLIGHT INTO EGYPT, ON THE CHOIR-SCREEN IN AMIENS CATHEDRAL.

Pierre Bontemps, records the exploits of the king. In the tomb of Henry II, the great figures cast by Germain Pilon are not there to lament the dead, but to recall his virtues and his glory. The idea is as pagan as the architecture, and as the divine bodies of the figures. In spite of the sculptured corpses that lie beneath the arcades, these tombs are no expression of the humble Gothic philosophy; the man is not stretched out upon the slab, resigned and submissive; he has not accepted death; his tomb is no temporary resting-place in which he awaits his resurrection; it is a triumphal monument which commemorates and amplifies an illustrious life, and assures him of the immortality of glory after his brief existence on earth.

FIG. 336.—THE CHAPEL OF THE CHATEAU D'AMBOISE.
(*Photo. Neurdein.*)

Setting aside Cellini, goldsmith and metal-worker, the artists Italy sent to France were chiefly painters, and yet it was above all the French sculptors who most readily assimilated Florentine plastic art. There is no common measure as

FIG. 337.—DOORS OF THE CHURCH OF SAINT SAUVEUR, AT AIX IN PROVENCE.

between the amiable masters of Moulins or the graceful miniaturists of the school of Bourdichon, and the superb draughtsmen of Florence. The interval which the Flemings, the most supple and gifted of craftsmen, only bridged over by a century of application, was not to be spanned instantaneously. Two admirable sculptors, however, succeeded in assimilating the refined elegance and the supreme science of Florentine design. Jean Goujon (born about 1515) translated Primaticcio's long and supple figures with their clinging draperies, into bas-reliefs. In his figures at Écouen, in the Louvre, and on the Fontaine des Innocents, he adheres very closely to a model which we feel to be, not a solid body in space, but a drawn or painted figure. He applied himself to the achievement

of one of the most difficult subtleties of Florentine sculpture; in bas-reliefs of the most attenuated type, in which, however, the bodies take the most undulating attitudes, some few centimetres of relief very elegantly indicate the gestures of a figure in motion. Even the superb Diana of the Château d'Anet, so proud in her divine nudity, seems to be adapting her haughty head and her long limbs to the exigencies of a façade (Fig. 352). The sculptor's supple forms assume the attitude best adapted to the space with a graceful ease, just as do those of the decorative painters at Fontainebleau. But the pupil has more youthful freshness than the Italian masters he imitates; his chisel strengthens and sharpens the contours of the decadent painter; he brings all the probity of a Primitive to bear upon his transposition into marble of the somewhat languid grace of the last disciples of Correggio. In the Fontaine des Innocents, he has confined the forms of Undines in the narrow spaces between the pilasters, and on their limbs, suppler than sea-weed, he has thrown draperies as fluid as the waters that flow from their urns (Figs. 349, 351).

In the less exclusively classical work of Germain Pilon (born in 1535), the unlettered and naïvely naturalistic art of the fifteenth century "imagiers" survives. On the tomb of Birague (Fig. 354) and on that of Henry II, he has placed vigorous portraits; but these exact effigies are of bronze after the manner taught by Cellini, and the sculptor, although he has frankly

FIG. 339.—CHOIR SCREEN IN THE CATHEDRAL OF CHARTRES.

reproduced the peculiarities of faces and costumes, shows a sovereign elegance, unknown before the Italian influence. How majestic are these figures in their fine draperies! This precision of style, combined with grandiloquence, was long to persist in French sculpture, and more especially in the statuary of tombs. Germain Pilon was one of those who most admirably combined fidelity of portraiture with the rhetoric of a funereal oration. He has a further claim to distinction in the French school, inasmuch as he, as well as Jean Goujon, discovered the secret which enabled the Florentine masters to give a kind of subtle life to the marble; he borrowed their flexible forms with

FIG. 340.—TOMB OF RENE II OF LORRAINE: CHURCH OF THE CORDELIERS, NANCY.
(*Photo. Neurdein.*)

their refined extremities; he endued his works with certain tactile qualities, which makes us feel the suppleness of the tissue and the quiver of the satiny surface on the epidermis of his nymphs. The Three Graces or Theological Virtues who were destined to carry the hearts of the royal couple have a brilliant elegance which thenceforth never failed in its appeal to French taste; it is only surprising that the precious burden should have been confided to young girls whose vocation for the dance is so obvious (Fig. 355).

FIG. 341.—TOMB OF THE CARDINALS OF AMBOISE; ROUEN CATHEDRAL.

Gothic art, both religious and feudal, had asked very little of painting, and in the artistic centres of France, pictorial production was not, generally speaking, comparable to that of the "imagiers" and architects. Thus, during the seventeenth century, when the king desired to associate painting with royal luxury, he could not find in his own kingdom the resources which were so abundant in the case of architecture and sculpture. He accordingly appealed to the

FIG. 342.—FIGURES ON THE TOMB OF PHILIPPE
DE COMMINES.
(The Louvre, Paris.)

foreigner; painters came from Flanders, and, above all, from Italy; they brought the manner of their own country with them, and did not find in France a national style with which they had to compound. The works they left behind them on French soil are to be explained by their native, and not by their adopted country. Once again it is on record that Flanders sent out excellent craftsmen; while Italy bestowed on France, together with her artists, a new æsthetic process.

Francis I had already made some attempts to attract the most famous of the Italians, and after the battle of Marignan, he brought home Leonardo da Vinci, who died soon afterwards; he then addressed himself to Andrea del Sarto, but was unable to retain him; at last he succeeded in capturing Il Rosso, a pupil of Michelangelo and Primaticcio, a decorative painter trained in the facile school of Correggio. Others came to attach themselves to these two masters. The innumerable frescoes with which they covered the walls of Fontainebleau have disappeared for the most part, destroyed by time or damaged by restoration. But their work is less interesting in itself than in its relation to the new conceptions it introduced in France. Il Rosso and Primaticcio represented an art

FIG. 343.—TOMB OF LOUIS XII AND ANNE
DE BRETAGNE. SAINT-DENIS.

quite unknown there; they practised the Florentine manner, that is to say, a learned art. They were thoroughly versed in the subtleties of anatomy and perspective; they represented supple and graceful bodies moving in space, with ease and mastery. This school of drawing com-pleted the instruction derived from casts of antique works. The painters Il Rosso, Prima-ticcio, and Niccolo dell' Abbate, in conjunction with Greek statues and the treatises of Vitruvius and Serlio, were the most active agents of classicism in France. Through the teaching of these artists and of these works, French art was led to assimilate the Italian and

FIG. 344.—UPPER PART OF THE FIREPLACE IN THE CHATEAU D'ÉCOUEN.

the antique doctrine of which it had hitherto only understood and imitated the decorative amenities; and it discovered that the worship of the human body was the basis of classic art. This

FIG. 345.—FIREPLACE OF HUGUES LALLEMENT, CLUNY MUSEUM, PARIS.

pride in physical beauty, and this audacious display of nudity were new things in France. The me-diæval artists had tolerated nudity only as a method of insistence on human misery, on the shameful nakedness of the unredeemed; they imaged the glorious splendour of the elect as adorned with rich stuffs, furs, and jewels. The beau-tiful nude forms of classical art delighted a court distinguished by gallantry of manners and avowed sensuality. And this art taught a further æsthetic lesson, one which was not at first very clearly under-stood, but which gradually per-meated French art; it taught that beauty of drawing is related to the ideal proportions of the human body; the architectural treatises which were translated at this period further taught the canon of the classical orders. French art pondered long the geometry of beauty which Florence had re-discovered, and thenceforth it was never to forget it. It was at Fontainebleau that it took its first lesson. Jean Cousin seems to have been one of the most learned professors of the new style (Fig. 370).

The Italians also brought with them a new iconography. It was necessary to give names to their beautiful figures, and a significance to their gestures. It is quite possible that the painters of the period felt but little interest in the adventures of Ulysses or of Diana; but the learning of the Humanists was about to familiarise the French intellect more and more with the world of mythology and of Graeco-Roman history. That antiquity which presented itself somewhat con-

FIG. 346.—TOMB OF THE DUC DE BRÉZÉ, ROUEN CATHEDRAL.

fusedly to the imagination as a domain where humanity seemed to lack all typical individualism was the ideal epoch for the existence of those slightly abstract figures French artists were thenceforth to create. In the second half of the sixteenth century, obscure poets and mediocre painters prepared the ground for the two forms of art in which the French classical spirit was to find its highest expression: tragedy and historical painting.

The great compositions at Fontainebleau delighted the imagination with splendid visions, but they were only indirectly related to contemporary life, by means of allegory or mythological allusion. There was room for a realistic art, that of portraiture.

From the reign of Francis I, a veritable mania for portraits obtained at the French Court.

FIG. 347.—TOMB OF FRANCIS I SAINT-DENIS.

FIG. 348.—GERMAIN PILON.
BUST OF A CHILD.
(The Louvre, Paris.)

At that period of elegance and gallantry, men and women elaborated the art of pleasing by every refinement of toilet and of physical culture. They delighted to see themselves reproduced in miniatures or pictures; throughout the century, artists were occupied in depicting with delicate colours and dainty brushes gala costumes and carefully manipulated faces. In the inventory of Catherine de' Medici's furniture, three hundred and forty-one portraits figure among the tapestries, enamels, and mirrors.

Once again it was the painters of the North, the Flemish immigrants, who applied the minute sincerity of their methods to French sitters. Their style was similar, if their skill varied. The majority of these portraits represent the face only; the attitude of the body was very rarely used to complete the individuality of the type. The Flemings of the fifteenth century had also loved to enclose the face and the hands of their models in a little frame. But though the later artists show the same scrupulous precision, their honesty is less brutal. In the cultured society of the day, they learned to be truthful and yet amiable; Flemish realism was tempered by the tone of good society, by French courtesy. To judge by contemporary portraits, men, down to the reign of Francis I, were extraordinarily ugly; after this date, agreeable drawing and colour give a certain elegance to the most vulgar types. The painting is light, delicate, and slight in texture; but the smallest gradations are cunningly utilised, and every stroke of the brush tells.

The Clouets are the

FIG. 349.—JEAN GOUJON. FONTAINE DES
INNOCENTS, PARIS.

FIG. 350.—GERMAIN PILON.
BUST OF HENRY III.
(The Louvre, Paris.)

most famous of these Flemish crafts-men, polished by French amenity (Figs. 365, 366): the father, Jean Clouet, no doubt from Brussels, who worked at the Court, in Touraine; his son, François, called by his con-temporaries Jannet; and Corneille, called Corneille de Lyon, and some-times Cornelis de la Haye, who was working at Lyons about 1540. As befits mere portraitists, these painters are more shadowy to the historian as personalities than their sitters; the few authenticated works by them, and the numerous pictures which are grouped around these by analogy, evoke the aristocracy of the sixteenth century with great vitality. There are few historical periods the actors in which are more familiar to us than those of the reigns of Francis I, Henry II and Henry III. If they could revisit us, we should recognise all the men who lived round Francis I: the king with his large nose, and his sleepy eyes, broad-shouldered, and *décolleté* like a woman, and all the gentlemen of the religious wars, scented and affected like their kings, the three sons of Catherine de' Medici, whose shivering senility and puerile coquetry they imitate. Jannet and Corneille de Lyon have admirably rendered the aristocratic pallor and milky complexions of the Court ladies, with tints as light as water-colours; their painting, consisting entirely of glazes, is diaphanous as a fair skin. In the portrait of Elisabeth

FIG. 351.—JEAN GOUJON. FONTAINE DES INNOCENTS, PARIS.

of Austria, the brilliant accessories of the costume, the silk, and the gems of the ornaments make the fine porcelain textures of the flesh appear still more fragile and delicate. Corneille de Lyon was fond of setting these white faces against a green background, for the sake of the rosy irradiation such a scheme imparts to them. Few colours were used in these portraits; sometimes these were dispensed with altogether; simple drawings, with a few touches of red chalk, suffice to suggest the vivacity of the glance and

FIG. 352.—JEAN GOUJON. DIANA, FROM THE CHATEAU D'ANET.
(The Louvre, Paris.)

the nervous fold at the corner of the mouth in a smooth and carefully made up face. We are indebted to this fashion of chalk drawings for our knowledge of the figures in history down to the time of Louis XIII. Stripped of all non-essentials, and reduced to a few lines, this art gives a keen and penetrating subtlety to the definition of types, even when the artist's hand lacks decision.

It seems a strange development in the destinies of French civilisa-

FIG. 353.—TOMB OF PHILIPPE DE CHABOT.
(The Louvre, Paris.)

tion, that this, after having created the Gothic form, should have abandoned it altogether in favour of classical art. The other European countries went through the same metamorphosis. But the classic regions, such as Italy, had never fully accepted

FIG. 354.—GERMAIN PILON. RENÉ DE BIRAGUE.
(The Louvre, Paris.)

FIG. 355.—GERMAIN PILON.
THE THREE VIRTUES.
(The Louvre, Paris.)

FIG. 356.—SIDEBOARD, TIME
OF HENRY II.
(The Louvre, Paris.)

pointed architecture, and the true homes of Gothic art, England, Flanders and Germany, never achieved classical purity. France, on the contrary, spoke the modern language of the seventeenth and eighteenth centuries with the same sincerity she had shown in the use of the mediaeval tongue of the thirteenth and fourteenth centuries. She alone was able to change her ideal, and to create works which expressed her genius and propagated it beyond her frontiers in the age of faith as in the age of reason.

Like Christianity, the art of the thirteenth century extended beyond the political frontiers, which were, indeed, by no means clearly defined; religion, which was its soul, made it a universal

FIG. 357.—SIDEBOARD, ATTRIBUTED TO HUGUES SAMBIN.
(Museum of Bourges.)

FIG. 358.—BERNARD PALISSY.
ENAMELLED POTTERY.
(The Louvre, Paris.)

language. At the close of the Middle Ages, the enfeebled religious spirit made way for naturalism; the plastic arts, more deeply rooted in the soil, drew inspiration from it, and the unity of Christian art was broken up. Classicism came to re-unite European art, imposing a common ideal, borrowed for the most part from antiquity. From this

FIG. 359.—WALNUT WOOD COFFER.
(The Louvre, Paris.)

time there has been at the base of artistic language a kind of essential syntax, a sort of abstract universality, which becomes very apparent as soon as there is a dearth of original temperaments.

In this classical art, the pre-occupation with pure beauty became more and more engrossing to the artist; construction, painting and sculpture were so many learned and difficult exercises, designed to evoke feelings in which very little religious sentiment had survived. Orthodoxy was forced to make so many concessions, that theologians

FIG. 360.—BERNARD PALISSY. DISH.
(The Louvre, Paris.)

conceived scruples as to the maintenance of relations between faith and art. The men of the Reformation, and then those of the Counter-Reformation, watched and condemned the fancies of painters and sculptors. Theologians, as well as artists, thought it more seemly that plastic production should be exer-

FIG. 361.—JEAN I. PÉNICAUD. ENAMELLED DIPTYCH.
(Cluny Museum, Paris.)

FIG. 362.—TAPESTRY OF THE LEGEND
OF SAINT QUENTIN.
(The Louvre, Paris.)

cised upon images other than those of Christian iconography. Religion withdrew from art, and circumscribed its domain that it might the more easily defend it. From the sixteenth century onwards, artists and poets alike demanded new resources from antique mythology; the Græco-Roman divinities, born of a collaboration between artists and poets, never ceased to belong to them. In all countries and in all ages, those who seek to vivify an ideal body turn back to paganism. The worshippers of pure beauty all meet on Olympus. Christianity was a creed still too vital and too jealous to lend itself to the caprice of artists; paganism, on the other hand, belongs

FIG. 363.—SIMON DE CHALONS.
ADORATION OF THE SHEPHERDS.
(Museum of Avignon.)

to them; plastic genius suffices to bring the heathen gods to life again.

It is true that when French art abandoned its religious and mediæval traditions, it caused many vigorous roots to wither in the ground. It has often been made a reproach to the French classical school that it lacked the artless

FIG. 364.—DIANA AND HER NYMPHS.
(Museum of Rouen.)

FIG. 365.—JEAN CLOUET.
FRANCIS I.
(The Louvre, Paris.)

FIG. 366.—FRANÇOIS CLOUET.
ELISABETH OF AUSTRIA.
(The Louvre, Paris.)

and absolute sincerity of the Gothic artists, that it offered a superior sort of pastime to cultivated minds, and did not represent the French soul in its entirety. It may be urged without any subtle intention, that French sculptors and painters show more sincerity in the representation of Venus or Apollo than in that of Christ or the Virgin; in the first case they are concerned with the production of pure plastic forms, and the lack of candour is no longer an outrage, when all are agreed that art is merely a diversion. As early as the fourteenth century, the French middle classes were so far instructed in the history and religion of antiquity that the pagan origins of their own civili-

FIG. 367.—CHARLES IX.
WAX MEDALLION.
(Cluny Museum, Paris.)

FIG. 368.—CATHERINE DE' MEDICI.
WAX MEDALLION.
(Cluny Museum, Paris)

175

FIG. 369.—BALL AL THE COURT OF HENRY III.
(The Louvre, Paris.)

sation were one day to be more familiar to them than the links that bound them to Christianity; while the pseudo-antique art was in process of formation, Humanism was instructing a public to the end that it might understand its intentions. It was, no doubt, an artificial culture; it made distinctions between popular and scientific art; it severed the innumerable ties, which, in the Middle Ages, united a Christian people and its religious art. And yet this classicism was never, in France, isolated by its aristocratic character. The most sincere poets of classical art, Poussin, Lorrain, David, Prudhon and Ingres were not very profound Humanists. Erudition plays no part in the pagan charm of their masterpieces; but an instinctive and profound predilection sometimes reveals to us the close kinship between the French genius and antique modes of thought and feeling.

FIG. 370.—JEAN COUSIN.
THE LAST JUDGMENT.
(The Louvre, Paris.)

FIG. 371.—FRANÇOIS CLOUET.
CHARLES IX.
(The Louvre, Paris.)

BIBLIOGRAPHY

L. de Laborde, *La Renaissance à la cour de France*, 2 vols., Paris, 1850-1855; *Compte des Bâtiments du Roi de 1528 à 1571*, 2 vols., Paris, 1877-1880.—E. Müntz, *La Renaissance en Italie et en France à l'époque de Charles VIII*, Paris, 1885.—Mrs. Mark Pattison, *The Renaissance of Art in France*, London, 1879.—W. Lübke, *Geschichte der Renaissance in Frankreich (Architektur)*, Stuttgart, 1883.—H. von Geymüller, *Die Baukunst der Renaissance in Frankreich*, Stuttgart, 1901.—L. Palustre, *La Renaissance en France*, 3 vols., Paris, 1879-1889.—A. Berty, *La Renaissance monumentale en France*, Paris, 1864, 2 vols.—P. Vitry, *Tours et la Touraine (Les Villes d'art)*, Paris, n.d.—F. Bournon, *Blois et Chambord (Les Villes d'art)*, Paris, n.d.—Pfnor, *Monographie du Château d'Anet*, Paris.—Champollion-Figeac and Pfnor, *Monographie du Palais de Fontainebleau*, Paris, 1863, 2 vols.—Philibert de Lorme, *Nouvelles Inventions pour bien bastir*, Paris, 1561; *L'Architecture*, vol. I, Paris, 1567 (vol. II not published).—M. Vachon, *Philibert de l'Orme*, Paris, 1887.—H. Lemonnier, *Philibert de Lorme (R.A.A.M., 1898, I).*—H. Clouzot, *Philibert de l'Orme*, Paris, 1910.—J.-A. du Cerceau, *Les plus excellents bastiments de France*, 2 vols., 1576-1579.—R. de Geymüller, *Les Du Cerceau*, Paris, 1887.—L. Vitet, *Le Louvre*, Paris, 1853.—A. Berty, *Topographie historique du Vieux Paris* neighbourhood of the Louvre, 2 vols., Paris, 1866-1868.—L. Batiffol, *Le Louvre et les plans de Lescot (G.B.A., 1910, I).*—G. Charvet, *Les Edifices de Brou (R.S.B.A.D., 1897).*—J. Gauthier, *L'Architecture civile en Franche-Comté au XVIᵉ siècle (R.S.B.A.D., 1899).*—Abbé Bouillet, *Saint-Etienne-du-Mont*, Paris, 1897.—V. Calliat and Leroux de Lincy, *Eglise Saint-Eustache*, Paris, 1850.—L. Courajod, *Alexandre Lenoir, son journal et le Musée des Monuments français*, vols. II and III, Paris, 1886-1887.—R. Koechlin and Marquet de Vasselot, *La Sculpture à Troyes dans la Champagne méridionale au XVIᵉ siècle*, Paris, 1901.—Paul Denis, *Ligier-Richier*, Nancy, 1906.—A. Castan, *L'"Architecteur" Hugues Sambin (R.S.B.A.D., 1890).*—E. Thiollier, *Sculptures foréziennes de la Renaissance (G.B.A., 1901, I).*—P. Vitry, *Michel Colombe et Sculpture française de son temps*, Paris, 1901.—Réveil, *Œuvre de Jean Goujon*, engraved by Réveil, Paris, 1868.—R. Lister, *Jean Goujon, His Life and Work*, London, 1903.—H. Jouin, *Jean Goujon*, Paris, 1906.—P. Vitry, *Jean Goujon*, Paris, n.d.—L. Palustre, *Germain Pilon (G.B.A., 1894, I).*—A. de Boislisle, *La Sépulture des Valois à Saint-Denis (Mém. de la Société de l'Histoire de Paris, vol. III, 1876).*—Vitry and Brière, *L'Eglise abbatiale de Saint-Denis et ses tombeaux*, Paris, 1908.—J. Gauthier, *Conrad Meyt et les Sculpteurs de Brou (R.S.B.A.D., 1898).*—De Champeaux, *Histoire de la Peinture décorative*, Paris, 1890.—L. Dimier, *Le Primatice*, Paris, 1902.—E. Müntz, *L'Ecole de Fontainebleau et le Primatice (G.B.A., 1902, II).*—H. Bouchot, *Les Portraits aux crayons des XVIᵉ et XVIIᵉ siècles conservés à la Bibliothèque Nationale*, Paris, 1884; *Le Portrait en France au XVIᵉ siècle (G.B.A., 1887, II); Les Clouet et Corneille de Lyon*, Paris, 1892.—A. Germain, *Les Clouet*, Paris, n.d.—F. Wickhoff, *Die Bilder weiblicher Halbfiguren (Jahrbücher* of the Museums of Vienna, 1901).—L. Bourdery and E. Lachenaud, *Léonard Limosin*, Paris, 1897.—E. Dupuy, *Bernard Palissy*, Poitiers, 1902.—Edm. Bonnaffé, *Les Faïences de Saint-Porchaire (G.B.A., 1895, I).*

FIG. 372.—THE LUXEMBOURG PALACE, PARIS.

CHAPTER II

THE EVOLUTION OF CLASSICAL ART

Royalty in Paris.—The New Architecture in the Towns: Town Houses and Country Houses.—Religious Architecture: the Jesuit Style.—Sculpture: the Decoration of Façades; Memorial Sculpture; Royal Statues.—Painting Becomes an Integral Factor in French Life.—The Immigration of Flemish Painters in Provence and in Paris.—The Royal Academy of Painting and Sculpture.—Italian Influence.—Simon Vouet; Lesueur.—Contemporary Life, Callot, the Brothers Le Nain.—Sébastien Bourdon.—The Classical Style: Poussin, the Antique, Christianity.—Composition and Execution; Influence of Poussin on the Taste of His Time.—Claude Gellée, called Le Lorrain.

FROM the time of Francis I, art had been too closely allied to the monarchy not to feel its misfortunes. It languished during the years of religious strife, evil administration, and foreign warfare. All great enterprises were abandoned, and the painters of Fontainebleau vegetated idly around the palace. Then the peace came, there was a revival of artistic activity. When Henry IV found himself at last safely established in that Paris which he had entered with so much difficulty, he hardly quitted it for the rest of his life. The monarchy, nomad in the sixteenth century, had become sedentary and Parisian. It established itself in the Louvre and the Tuileries, and began the construction of the great gallery which was intended to unite them. In spite of the multiple cares of the monarch, and the brevity of his reign, the capital of the kingdom gained considerably from becoming the royal residence. With Henry IV the masons entered the city, and masons are followed by painters and sculptors.

178

A modern Paris was soon to take the place of the mediæval town; its present physiognomy began to develop. The classical style, which was popularised by mansions, churches, and private dwelling-houses, has never ceased to dominate French architecture from this period. In the renovated city, the only Gothic buildings that were left after a short time were religious structures, spared by virtue of their sacred character.

FIG. 373.—THE SMALL GALLERY OF THE LOUVRE (GALERIE D'APOLLON), FROM AN ENGRAVING BY ISRAEL SILVESTRE.
(Bibliothèque Nationale, Print Room.)

Houses with heavily loaded roofs, and slight walls strengthened by cross-beams ceased to be built.

In the engravings of the seventeenth century we already find the modern street with its more regular alignment, and the high square façades with their symmetrical windows. Very soon private houses began to show pilasters, capitals, and cornices. But at first, architects were content with the quiet and unostentatious cheerfulness obtained by the picturesque combination of red brick, white stone, and blue slate. It was suitable to a society which, constrained to recuperate financially, and rejoicing in its recovered tranquillity, was content to put off its artistic pretensions to the future. This style was not so Netherlandish and "Huguenot" as is sometimes supposed. Its amenity had already found favour in the days when Louis XI inhabited his "Plessis" at Tours. But in the seventeenth century, Vitruvius and Serlio were so widely read that French architecture could not long abstain from the adoption of the classic orders. Brick was considered a vulgar material. We may judge of the favourite effects in this medium from the remains of the Place Dauphine (Fig. 375), the Place Royale (376), and

FIG. 374.—THE LONG GALLERY OF THE LOUVRE, FROM AN ENGRAVING BY ISRAEL SILVESTRE.
(Bibliothèque Nationale, Print Room.)

the central pavilion of the palace of Versailles (Fig. 478). In the heart of Louis XIV's majestic building, the modest country house of his father still exists.

FIG. 375.—THE PLACE DAUPHINE FROM THE PONT-NEUF, FROM AN ENGRAVING BY PERÉLLE.
(Bibliothèque Nationale, Print Room.)

But the transformation of the towns was not confined to the style of their façades. It is certain that the good king Henry IV had conceived a new plan for his great city. Like all mediæval towns, Paris was choking within its walls; the Seine was its sole great highway; the city could only breathe on the banks of its river. The congested Gothic buildings rose to a great height; no clear spaces were reserved round churches and palaces to secure their scenic effect. Classical architecture, with its regular façades, requires a spacious setting if the eye is to appreciate its unity of composition. The design of streets and squares was also complementary to the architecture: the Place Royale and the Place Dauphine are built on a unique plan. Public buildings, such as the Collège des Quatre-Nations (Fig. 388), were provided with broad wings, that they might present an imposing theatrical appearance to the king's sight. At the beginning of his *Discours de la Méthode,* Descartes speaks of the perfect town, geometrical and regular as an architect's plan. In Poitou, in the very heart of the country, Richelieu realised this ideal; like many other works of pure reason, it lacks nothing but life.

FIG. 376.—PLACE DES VOSGES (FORMERLY PLACE ROYALE), PARIS.

In Paris, architects were unable to expand freely. The Louvre made laborious attempts to extend its long façades in the midst of a congested district. It remained entangled in a maze of private

180

houses, while Marie de' Medici erected her palace of the Luxembourg outside the town, in a region of gardens and convents. The Florentine queen was thinking of her Pitti Palace at home; but the haughty ostentation of strength characteristic of Tuscan architecture could not find favour in Paris. Salomon de Brosse built an *hôtel* on the French plan, between courtyard and garden; the façades with their lofty roofs are enlivened by the simple design of the windows, and the beauty of the

FIG. 377.—COURT OF THE HÔTEL SULLY, PARIS.

dressed stone; though it lacked the ornamental richness of the new Louvre, the general effect has a very refined elegance (Fig. 372).

Following the royal example, the nobility and the middle classes began to make new dwellings. Richelieu had lived in the Petit Luxembourg in order to be near the Queen-Regent; he had the Palais Royal built to be near the king. The quarter of the Marais and the Ile Saint-Louis were soon covered with stately houses. In the interiors were galleries adorned with stucco and paintings; on the façades, the somewhat frigid decoration of the classic orders. Domestic architecture in its turn adopted this system of ornament, hitherto reserved for royalty. The mansions in the Marais which have survived still preserve a kind of melancholy dignity,

FIG. 378.—PALAIS CARDINAL (BIBLIOTHÈQUE NATIONALE), PARIS.

though tradesmen's vans have replaced coaches in their courtyards. On those façades which architects designed in accordance with the rules of Vitruvius, commercial advertisements now hang upon the crumbling cornices and weather-worn stone (Figs. 377, 378).

The wealthier citizens had also country-houses ("maisons des champs"), where they could entertain their guests on a larger scale. These houses retained no trace of the feudal construction still visible in the *châteaux* of the sixteenth century. They are regular buildings, square in plan; the façades, though they are ornamented with pilasters and pediments, owe their agreeable elegance to the design of the windows and the beautiful roofs.

FIG. 379.—FOUNTAIN IN THE GARDEN OF THE LUXEMBOURG, PARIS.

Lateral buildings project, enclosing a fore-court; the building itself seems to be coming to meet the visitor and conduct him to the hospitable threshold. How different are these cheerful dwellings from the closely guarded, distrustful Italian palaces! At the back of the house, the garden presents itself as a kind of perennial gala decoration; flowers or clipped shrubs make a heavy lace-work on the soil; jets of water fall into flat basins; then there are radiating alleys, with trees ranged on either side to amuse the eye without shutting out the horizon. The engravings of Pérelle and Israël Silvestre show us the kind of life for which these *châteaux* were designed; they depict carriages and horsemen arriving, and passing through the iron gates into the fore-court, or gentlemen and ladies grouped about the fountains and flower-beds of the gardens, exchanging ceremonious

FIG. 380.—HÔTEL DE VILLE, AT LYONS.

greetings and conversing. It was for the reception of visitors that M. de Maisons built the *château* on the banks of the Seine which bears his name, and that Fouquet erected the Château de Vaux; it was to make his receptions more magnificent

FIG. 381.—CHATEAU DE CANY.

that the King of France created Versailles (Figs. 381–385).

The first half of the seventeenth century was marked by an extraordinary Catholic revival. Religious orders, either new or re-constructed, recaptured some of the territory lost by Catholicism since the Reformation. This Christian emotion found expression in architecture, sculpture, and painting; but all it contributed to these was a renewed fervour; Catholicism accepted the transforma-

FIG. 382.—IRON GATE IN THE GALERIE D'APOLLON LOUVRE. FROM THE CHATEAU DE MAISONS-LAFFITTE.

(*Photo. L'Architecte.*)

tion of art effected by contact with Italy and antiquity. It was content to exercise a gentle control over the pagan exuberance which had taken possession of the plastic arts, and might have shocked thoughtful

FIG. 383.—CHATEAU DE MAISONS-LAFFITTE. (*Photo. L'Architecte.*)

Christians. The Jesuits, who, in their colleges, reconcile Christian theology and antique thought, taught very elegant combinations. Wherever they have directed the intellect, in education as in art, they have found a classical language for their Catholicism.

They it was who determined the architectonic forms which were to replace the Gothic style.

FIG. 384.—CHATEAU DE DAMPIERRE.

Père Martelange designed for urban churches and convents reductions of St. Peter's at Rome, and of the Chiesa del Gesù. This Roman style was widely distributed, thanks to the religious orders, just as was the rejuvenated authority of the Pope. Nothing was left of the Gothic principle of directing pressure to the ribs, pillars, and flying buttresses; once more, the building relied for solidity upon compactness, and the problem was how to give this mass an elegant silhouette, and to mask the masonry with a decorative façade. This so-called "Jesuit architecture" seems to be a revival of Romanesque, because both are derived from antiquity, the one by filiation, the other by imitation; they have the same affinity as the learned terms created by the Humanists, and their popular equivalents. But the Romanesque masonry was extremely simple; the new architecture implied a scientific system of stone-cutting; it was the work of draughtsmen who

FIG. 385.—CHATEAU DE VAUX-LE-VICOMTE.

had made very correct plans on paper, inspired by classical treatises and the proportions of Roman monuments. Nevertheless, these divergences were not irreconcilable; at Notre-Dame-des-Doms, the people of Avignon succeeded in applying a classical decoration to an old Romanesque building.

In the interior, the eye, accustomed to the soaring movement of Gothic vaults, finds the barrel vaults resting on the supporting walls very heavy; the windows pierced in this vault increase the effect of heaviness by revealing the thickness of the masonry; the pilasters, the capitals, the cornices display the elegant purity of their design on every side, but they are powerless to lighten the square pillars and the solid forms. The Italians amplified this style by ornamental pomp; in France, decoration remained more sober; it was by happy proportion that French architects sought to satisfy the religious sentiment of their day, as in the churches of Saint-Paul, Saint-Louis, the Sorbonne, the Val-de-Grace, Saint Louis des Invalides, and Saint Sulpice (Figs. 386–389).

FIG. 386.—FAÇADE OF THE CHURCH OF SAINT-GERVAIS, PARIS.

A similar transformation took place externally; the vault still had to be supported, but the flying buttresses, instead of describing a frank angle, were curved inwards as if to disguise their function, and thus lost something of their supporting power. The façade became a kind of architectural exercise, where the same elements had always to be arranged; two or three antique orders surmounted by a triangular pediment. The angle formed by the upper storey and the lateral aisles was adorned by a console which affords a kind of transition. This type of façade was not constituted all at once; the first architects who had to apply them to the latest Gothic churches show indecision and

FIG. 387.—CHURCH OF THE SORBONNE.

FIG. 388.—CHAPEL OF THE COLLÈGE DES QUATRE-NATIONS (PALAIS DE L'INSTITUT, PARIS).

fantasy. At Saint Étienne du Mont (Fig. 311), the architect is still very far from the chilly simplicity of the classical style. The stone is gay with decorative amenities, like a piece of Renaissance furniture. Pierre Biard's rood-screen is of a period when architects were still pre-occupied with dainty details. But Saint Gervais is correctly cold and bare; Salomon de Brosse adapted his columns and entablatures with some elegance to the projecting cornices; this ingenious decoration was, however, too narrow for the body of the building, which protrudes on either side (Fig. 386).

In this architecture, imaginative effort is confined to the dome; this was the problem to which all constructors, after the creation of Santa Maria dei Fiori at Florence, and St. Peter's at Rome, had aspired to devote their talents. All the principal Parisian churches of the seventeenth century have a cupola, Val-de-Grâce, the Sorbonne, the Invalides, the Chapel of the Collège des Quatre-Nations; they dominate the city, and like the Gothic towers and spires, indicate the church of God from afar. But when French architects borrowed the Italian cupolas, they modified them a little; they retained the national taste for a high timber roof, and were thus enabled to give additional height to the exterior silhouette of their spherical vaults. Their little cupolas, ornamented with sculpture and decked with metal, swell proudly heavenwards, without pressing heavily upon their points of support.

FIG. 389.—CHURCH OF VAL-DE-GRACE.

THE EVOLUTION OF CLASSICAL ART

There has been some injustice in the frequent reproach brought against this architecture of its lack of sincerity and of expressive power. It is to the full as Christian as that of the thirteenth century; but the Christianity it stands for is no longer that complete Christianity which concentrated the whole thought and life of man. The Frenchmen of the seventeenth century demanded a system of definite ideas from their religion; their churches had to be lecture halls, of majestic, but reasonable proportions. Their somewhat low-pitched vaults re-echoed the periods of eloquent

FIG. 390.—BUST OF HENRY IV.
(The Louvre, Paris.)

Orators; a cultivated public assembled beneath them on appointed days to listen to well-constructed sermons on morality, which confirmed their faith by making it as intelligible as possible.

The activity of the architects benefited the sculptors and painters. Statues were required for the new churches, and for town-houses and their gardens. The king set the example: Henry IV ordered the works at the Louvre, interrupted in the reign of Henry II, to be resumed. The financiers, in their turn, coveted a richly decorated gallery, a reduction of that Fontainebleau, or of the small gallery in the Louvre, which was just finished. On the ceilings, nymphs and Atlantes intermingled with the arabesques, and

FIG. 391.—GUILLAUME DUPRÉ.
HENRY IV AND MARIE DE' MÉDICI.

supported the framework of the paintings; the same mythology re-appeared in the gilded stucco-work and in the pictures. The gardens began to be peopled with statues, in the Italian fashion. Finally, on the more sumptuous façades, statues enrich the architectonic decoration. At the Louvre, Jacques Sarrazin, crowned Lemercier's pavilion with a pediment on graceful Caryatides. But this classical sculpture found its only brilliant culmination at Versailles.

187

FIG. 392.—JEAN WARIN. GASSENDI.

The Renaissance had not disturbed the mediæval tradition of funereal monuments. The most famous men of the seventeenth century had their tombs in the churches. But small chapels cannot contain huge monuments and, for the most part, these memorials were reduced to a decorative façade of black and white marble applied to the wall. Some few princely monuments retain a certain pomp, with mourning Virtues, and genii in tears, as on the tomb of Henri de Condé by Sarrazin at Chantilly (Fig. 402), and that of Montmorency at Moulins, by François Anguier (Fig. 399). The others are modest, but always serious in their inspiration. If they lack the subtle charm of the Florentines, or of the French sculptors of the sixteenth century, the faces and attitudes express profound sentiments with a sincerity which takes the place of eloquence. There is more conviction than grace in these calm portraits and folded hands. Their sculptors have not always succeeded in giving

FIG. 393.—JEAN WARIN. RICHELIEU.

lightness to the Louis XIII costume, so gallant in wool or silk, but heavy and massive in stone or bronze; only a few among them ever thought of following the example of Germain Pilon, and throwing a loose mantle over the shoulders of their figures, to simplify a complicated equipment, or soften a too rigid skirt. Their works were frank and uncompromising images of serious and believing burgesses.

All the portraits, however, were not executed for tombs. A fashion introduced from Italy, that of portrait-busts, soon became popular.

FIG. 304.—JEAN WARIN. BUST OF RICHELIEU (BIBLIOTHÈQUE MAZARINE, PARIS).

Naturally, it is the great personages of the realm, the king and his ministers, who appear in these works of marble or metal. Dupré and Warin, who engraved medals with elegant exactitude, also modelled bronze busts with delicate minuteness (Fig. 391-394). But patrons were not content with these reduced portraits. From Henry IV onwards, all the French kings had their statues. All who crossed the Pont-Neuf, completed in the reign of Henry IV, passed before a bronze effigy of the king, mounted on a horse cast in Italy. At the corners of the pedestal, Francheville placed long, contorted, uneasy, seated figures, following the tradition of Michelangelo. At the Hôtel-de-Ville, which the king completed, there was

FIG. 395.—BARTHÉLEMY PRIEUR.
MARIE DE BARBANÇON-CANY.
(Museum, Versailles.)
(*Photo. Mieusement.*)

a bronze bas-relief by Pierre Biard on the tympanum of the central door, representing Henry IV on horseback. The son of this sculptor executed a Louis XIII for the Place Royale; here again the King of France bestrode an Italian horse. The Louis XIV of the Place Vendôme at last was given one of French race. At the entrance of the Pont au Change there was a monument on which three bronze figures by Simon Guillain, represented Louis XIII as a soldier, and Anne of Austria in court costume, turning towards the little Dauphin. In each of these statues there is a robust, if slightly heavy sincerity, which was habitual when art did not allow itself to be guided, and ruined, by Florentine idealism (Fig. 398).

FIG. 396.—PIERRE
FRANCHEVILLE. ORPHEUS.
(The Louvre, Paris.)

At this period, the glorification of French kings by statuary in accordance with a ritual first Roman, and then Italian, was a novel idea. Henry IV, Louis XIII, Louis XIV, and Louis XV had not, like their ancestors, monumental tombs in Saint-Denis. No re-

FIG. 397.—BARTHÉLEMY
PRIEUR. ABUNDANCE.
MONTMORENCY MONUMENT.
(The Louvre, Paris.)

cumbent effigy on a marble slab commemorates them as it did the mediaeval kings; we
have not even one of those living images of
them, kneeling before God, with which the
Valois kings adorned their monuments.
Royal statues now glorify only royalty; they
rise in the public squares like idols, or the
symbols of a new worship. The monarchy
benefited by this imitation of the Marcus
Aurelius, who, from the top of the Capitol,
still extends his dominating gesture over
Rome.

Painting more especially reminds us that
we are entering upon a new era. In the
Middle Ages, the true painters were the
makers of coloured windows and the illuminators. These mediums of colour died with
Gothic art. After the Renaissance, the
monarchy, the Church, and the middle
classes patronised painting, to which they
looked for decorations for their palaces and
their churches, and pictures for their dwellings. It is in this art,
more docile than sculpture, and apter in the expression of emotion,
that we shall henceforth find the most delicate manifestations of
French thought. The new religious architecture employed painters
very freely. Innumerable "saintetés"
(sacred pictures) were required for
the newly built churches and convents. In certain towns, such as
Paris, Avignon, and Aix, citizens
were in the habit of associating
painting with their pious exercises.
Every year, in the month of May,
the Goldsmiths' Guild in Paris gave
a large picture to Notre-Dame.
These "Mais," which the whole
town saw, sometimes served to
demonstrate some youthful talent.
It was by amiable customs of this
nature that the cities of Flanders
and Italy, from the Middle Ages
onward, recognised their spiritual

FIG. 398.—SIMON GUILLAIN.
LOUIS XIII, ANNE OF AUSTRIA, AND
THE DAUPHIN. MONUMENT
FORMERLY ON THE PONT AU CHANGE.
(The Louvre, Paris.)

solidarity in their collective admiration of a masterpiece. France had too long been deprived of such sentimental communion, which fires artistic energies. A Parisian public of increasing refinement was henceforth to assure the continued vitality of French art.

A continuous immigration from the North is to be found at the source of this French painting. Flanders had always allowed her surplusage of artists and craftsmen to overflow into other lands; they propagated their industry in the majority of the French provinces; they set out to study Italy, or merely in search of work. Dutchmen, Flemings, Picards, Lorrains, and Champenois, they went from

FIG. 399.—FRANÇOIS ANGUIER. TOMB OF THE DUC DE MONTMORENCY, CHAPEL OF THE LYCÉE, AT MOULINS.
(Photo. Neurdein.)

town to town, painting portraits or Church pictures. Sometimes a long undertaking kept them stationary, and they settled where they were, forgetting their native land and the Italy of their dreams. They founded colonies in many of the large French towns, and it was because they Gallicised the Germanic syllables of their names that we do not at once recognise their origin.

FIG. 400.—FRANÇOIS ANGUIER.
MONUMENT OF THE LONGUEVILLE FAMILY.
(The Louvre, Paris.)

It was one of these travelling artists, who, passing through Normandy, determined the vocation of Poussin. At Bordeaux, Flemish artists were painting portraits of the jurists, while Dutchmen were draining the marshes of Saintonge. When Sébastien Bourdon came to Montpellier, he found that Netherlandish artists had long been established there. At Toulouse, the Flemings

FIG. 401.—MICHEL BOURDIN.
TOMB OF LOUIS XI, AT NOTRE-DAME-
DE-CLÉRY.

(Photo. Limousin.)

and their pupils painted the notables of the district in a stiff and serious manner, representing them clothed in black, and kneeling at the foot of a Crucifix, with the insignia of the magistracy. But it was more especially on the high road to Italy that they left traces, at the great halting places, Paris, Lyons, and Provence. The dynasty of the Stellas, the men and women of which alike painted and engraved, settled at Lyons. The churches of Provence contain a number of pictures which illustrate the continuous infiltration of Flemish art, from the manner of Van Eyck to that of Rubens, with all the intermediate styles. At Aix, several pictures by Finsonius, a native of Bruges, show the strong colour of the Flemings struggling with the black shadows of Caravaggio, and the glowing yet murky atmosphere of Tintoretto. Other painters of the same group, such as Jean Daret (of Brussels), watered down Flemish effects in Bolognese compositions. Rubens alone was strong enough to elevate this heavy realism by a mighty breath of inspiration. Avignon continued to be a centre of art, and a town which welcomed painters. It had a public capable of understanding them, of attracting them, and of giving them work. Its churches still contain a great number of pictures painted for pious donors. They are large compositions, in most of which the rounded figures dear to Guido Reni move among the opaque shadows of Caravaggio. Some of them have retained a certain naturalistic solidity, which the

FIG. 402.—JACQUES SARRAZIN. TOMB OF HENRI DE
CONDE. FROM THE CHURCH OF SAINT-PAUL.
CHATEAU DE CHANTILLY.

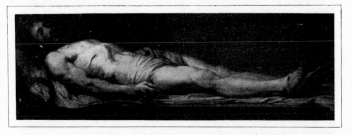

FIG. 403.—PHILIPPE DE CHAMPAIGNE. DEAD CHRIST.
(The Louvre, Paris.)

commonplace elegance of the prevailing mode has not succeeded in enervating.

One of these artists, Nicolas Mignard, called Le Romain, became famous even in Paris by painting sacred subjects with logical exactitude. His somewhat frigid culture is more naturally displayed in portraiture. The nobility of Comtat and Provence did not lack painters to fill its galleries with family portraits. The province continued to capture artists on their way to and from Rome. This did not suffice to constitute an original school; but it made the region fertile in painters.

In spite of much restoration and demolition, Flemish works are still very numerous in the Parisian churches of the seventeenth century. They consist of small, facile panels, gaily coloured with a fat impasto, or large altar-pieces in which the painter has attempted to speak the tongue of Rubens. The Louvre and various private houses also welcomed Flemish decorations of mythology or landscape. Henry IV retained Pourbus, who was passing through Paris, and Pourbus has soberly recorded the jovial malice of the "Vert Galant," and the somewhat heavy majesty of the queen. In 1620, when Marie de' Medici was seeking a painter for her great gallery in the Luxembourg, she

FIG. 404.—PHILIPPE DE CHAMPAIGNE. PORTRAIT OF MOTHER CATHERINE, AGNÈS ARNAULT AND OF SISTER CATHERINE, SAINTE SUZANNE.
(The Louvre, Paris.)

summoned Rubens. There could, of course, have been no question of keeping him permanently; but he left a considerable sum of work behind him, and also several of his pupils, such as Justus of Egmont and Van Mol. The painter of the Queen-Regent at a later date was the Brussels master, Philippe de Champaigne (160–21674). He was associated with the Jansenist party, and his works reflect their gravity of thought and the austere piety of their lives. The robust method he had acquired in his native school was not used by him to play with the beauty of appearances, but to elevate painting to

FIG. 405.—CLAUDE MELLAN.
PORTRAIT OF PEIRESC. (ENGRAVING.)
(Bibliothèque Nationale, Print Room.)

the nobility of Christian and philosophical meditation. His Dead Christs and his portraits combine a profound sense of reality with an intensity of moral life very unusual in Flemish art. Champaigne and Poussin had so many similar preoccupations, that we must suppose the Fleming often to have waived his naturalistic tendencies under the influence of a psychological idealist. He must be classed with those innumerable immigrants from the north who brought their manual dexterity to France, and, in exchange, took over French modes of thought (Figs. 403, 404, 406). A crowd of competent craftsmen of secondary rank worked in addition to the famous masters most in favour; they sold landscapes, sea-pieces, and copies at the fairs; they painted flowers, birds, draperies, and vases in cartoons for the Gobelins

FIG. 406.—PHILIPPE DE CHAMPAIGNE.
PORTRAIT OF RICHELIEU.

(The Louvre, Paris.)

tapestries, around figures by Le Brun.

Throughout the seventeenth century, French painters, when compared with Flemings and Italians, may be seen to have possessed original qualities; but they lacked dexterity of execution; they were like children whose education has been begun too late; they were no longer of an age when artlessness is attractive, and they had none of the easy assurance of maturity. The French School further lacked that technical or theoretical certitude which was the strength of the Flemings and Italians.

FIG. 407.—LAGNEAU. PORTRAIT.
(Drawing in the Louvre, Paris.)

Even in the first third of the century, the sculptors, and more especially the painters who gathered in Paris were numerous enough to generate a certain *esprit de corps*. They were no longer isolated workers, attached for some temporary task to the person of the king or some other Mæcenas; a large circle of middle class and ecclesiastical patrons upheld their industry. But in order to sell their works, they had been obliged to enrol themselves in the ancient guilds of their craft. They belonged at first to the venerable corporation of St. Luke. But this approximated them to mere artisans, and this confusion, impossible even in societies where painting is a tradition, and has deep roots in the soil, must have seemed still more intolerable in France, where this art, a new comer, so to speak, presented itself with the titles of nobility acquired during the Renaissance. An Academy of Painting and Sculpture was formed, under the royal protection. This institution, which dated from 1648, existed until the Revolution. It was, from its very foundation, and it continued to be, a corporation which defended the interests of

FIG. 408.—JACQUES CALLOT.
ACTORS OF THE COMÉDIE
ITALIENNE.

(Bibliothèque Nationale
Print Room.)

FIG. 409.—DANIEL DUMONSTIER.
PORTRAIT OF THE DUC
DE LONGUEVILLE.
(The Louvre, Paris.)

its members, an academy or learned society bent on elaborating a doctrine, a school which formed pupils; under Louis XIV it became, in addition, a sort of administration which regulated artistic work, and it was more especially in this character that it was not irreproachable. Its organization, in fact, permitted the State to govern the artist. But, on the other hand, it is incorrect to say that it ever set itself in opposition to national taste by its doctrines. Under the ancient régime, it included all artists worthy of the name; the number of its members was unlimited. The rare dissidents remained outside the fold for personal and not for doctrinal reasons. It represented successively the most diverse forms of French art, the style of Le Brun, the style of Boucher, the style of David.

During the time when this modern painting was born and was growing in France, a variety of influences was at work, and it is impossible to find any common tendency in the innumerable caprices of French artists. While craftsmen innocent of doctrine were pouring in from the North, French painters were seeking for a creed in Italy. The great Italian masters were no longer brought into France; but French novices went in great numbers to study their methods. For France, as for all Europe, the universal source of art was Rome. Those who never crossed the Alps were not the least Italianised; they were

FIG. 410.—JACQUES CALLOT.
THE SIEGE OF LA ROCHELLE (FRAGMENT).
(Bibliothèque Nationale, Print Room.)

FIG. 411.—JACQUES CALLOT. EXECUTION OF MARAUDERS IN "LES MISERES
DE LA GUERRE."
(Bibliothèque Nationale, Print Room.)

inspired by copies and engravings;

FIG. 412.—ABRAHAM BOSSE. THE PALAIS ROYAL.
(Bibliothèque Nationale, Print Room.)

they were less under the influence of contemporary Italian art, and more under that of the sixteenth century, which was itself retrospective.

It was the art of the Bolognese, then in its full vitality, which French painters saw in action. Some were still held by the tradition of Florentine idealism; they sought for moral expression, and drew beautiful forms, after antique models. Others painted from nature, like Caravaggio, with great brutality and emphasis, and violent contrasts of light and shade. But all had adopted the practice of drowning their compositions in a gloomy atmosphere. How many French painters, like La Hire in Paris, and more especially Valentin at Rome, accepted this

FIG. 413.—ABRAHAM BOSSE.
VISIT TO THE NEWLY DELIVERED WOMAN.
(Bibliothèque Nationale, Print Room.)

nocturnal tone! The latter painted, with a certain vigour, gipsies or soldiers in caves, revealed by a sudden gleam of light (Figs. 420–422).

FIG. 414.—THE BROTHERS LE NAIN. INTERIOR, WITH A FAMILY.
(The Louvre, Paris.)

Italy, it is clear, did not impose any single manner; there is scarcely any form of art she did not represent. Artists as diverse as Poussin, Lorrain, Valentin, and Callot were able to spend their lives, and work successfully there, without any sort of resulting similarity. After Fréminet and Dubois, the successors of the school of Fontainebleau, the most influential master was Simon Vouet (1590–1649). He showed much skill in utilising the inventions of the great Italian decorators. Judging from Dorigny's engravings, some of his compositions seem to have been little more than copies of Veronese. But his talent was purely superficial, and such of his paintings as have survived show but too clearly that he had not assimilated the Italian's charm of colour. With its heavy reds in the shadows, its insipid pallor in the light, his colour at once becomes discordant when he attempts to make it brilliant (Fig. 424). Many of these faults reappear in his pupils, Le Sueur, Le Brun, and Mignard. But he has a true historical importance as the master of some of the greatest artists of the French classical school.

FIG. 415.—ATTRIBUTED TO THE LE NAINS. CARD PLAYERS.
(Museum of Aix.)

He embodies the transition between the decorators of Henry II and those of Louis XIV. Together with his pupils, he propagated the monarchical mythology of Fontainebleau in the houses of private citizens.

Le Sueur (1616–1655), no doubt, owes his somewhat flaccid facility to Vouet. He never visited Italy; he was, nevertheless, thanks to the engravers, a fervent admirer, and sometimes even a copyist of Raphael, especially when he exerted himself. In the numerous works this painter, who died young, executed for financiers and for religious houses, there is something of the sincerity and artlessness of the Primitives. He does not make use of the Bolognese method of great masses of shade; his general tone is

FIG. 416.—LE NAIN. PORTRAIT OF A MEMBER OF THE PÉRUSSY FAMILY.
(Museum of Avignon.)

light and pallid; the draperies often show that acid crudity to which devout painters have always been prone. The sentiment is never obscured by the technique; his mourning Virgins with their pallid tints express grief in the terms of a melancholy saturated with tears.

Sometimes he gives us certain figures peculiarly his own, some little frail and gentle maiden saint, with the fair head of a sentimental school-girl. These fragile types are the real creations of his genius, and stand out as such among the glut of white beards and classical profiles, which were the common stock of all the painters of the day. The series illustrating the *Life of Saint Bruno* consists of rapid and not very skilful paintings. The nudity of the narrative and the simplicity of the composition are appropriate to the subject, and to the place for which it was designed, a Carthusian church; but the asperity of the

FIG. 417.—LE NAIN. THE BLACKSMITH.
(The Louvre, Paris.) (*Photo. Neurdein.*)

FIG. 418.—SUPPOSED PORTRAIT OF
JACQUES STELLA.
(Museum of Lyons.)

work is modified by a certain tenderness (Figs. 427–429, 431).

The religious architecture which had established itself in France was more hospitably disposed towards pictures than Gothic architecture had been. The light in the new churches was not broken, diffused, and tinted by pillars and coloured glass. Two columns surmounted by a pediment over the altar offered a suitable framework for a large composition illuminated by an equal light. Pictures were also hung in the Gothic churches, and here they remain, swallowed up in the gloom of chapels, for pictures and stained glass are irreconcilable. Many of them are respectable, if not for their beauty of execution, at least for their sincerity of feeling.

Painting and sculpture have left us many portraits of the men and things of this period. In this first half of the seventeenth century, fashion had not given a uniform type to every head, as Clouet's mannered elegance had done, and as the conscious majesty of Louis XIV portraiture was to do. Sculptors like Dupré and the Fleming, Warin, draughtsmen like Lagneau and Daniel Du Monstier (Figs. 407, 409), engravers like Claude Mellan (Fig. 405), painters like Sébastien Bourdon and the three Le Nains, have recorded very vigorous individualities; martial and gallant cavaliers, with twisted moustaches and lace collars; students, writers, humanists, and *savants* of a sturdy, plebeian type, with sedate velvet caps on their heads, always ready to anthematise each other

FIG. 419.—ATTRIBUTED TO
THE LE NAINS. TOPER AT TABLE.
(Museum of Amiens.)

200

in Latin; old-fashioned burgesses with full beards à *la* Sully; others whose faces have been sharpened by the pointed beard à *la* Richelieu, and kneeling *échevins* in profile, looking sideways at the spectator.

Engravers, less in bondage to traditional motives, were able to copy the world in which they lived. Abraham Bosse shows us a somewhat stiff Parisian society, in his precise style (Figs. 412, 413). Callot, a Lorrain like Gellee, gave himself like Gellée to Italy. He is a creature of weird imagination; his thin, pointed, broken line scratches or presses, rendering the agitation of a swarming crowd, the pic-

FIG. 420.—VALENTIN. A GIPSY AND SOLDIERS.
(Museum of Avignon.)

turesqueness of rags and of military accoutrements, the gesticulations of Italian mountebanks, or of little devils harassing Saint Anthony. It is an art in which precision and caprice are strangely mingled, which reflects the world of that day and its two great distractions, war and the theatre, and in which something of the old mediæval diabolism still lingers (Figs. 408, 410, 411).

It is interesting to study contemporary reality in the works of the Le Nain brothers. Natives of Laon who had migrated to Paris, Antoine, Mathieu, and Louis Le Nain, also painted some church pictures with harsh illumination and very realistic figures, in the manner of Caravaggio. But like all the northern artists before Rubens, they lacked the decorative imagination capable of elevating and animating the numerous figures of a large composition. Their portraits have neither fire nor beauty; but their

FIG. 421.—LA HIRE. POPE NICOLAS V
AND SAINT FRANCIS.
(The Louvre, Paris.)

narrow style is scrupulously sincere, and their little familiar scenes breathe an emotion very unusual in the art of their age. They represent peasants eating, drinking, resting, or "carousing" sadly

enough. The prosaic heaviness of the brush gives a kind of torpor even to enjoyment; sober and "subdued" tints render only too faithfully the haggard faces and drab rags of the models. The work of these men is a strange accident in the history of painting. Their peasants are not of the same race as those of the Dutchmen and the Flemings. The Brueghels, Teniers and Ostades are brilliant craftsmen who are amused by their grotesque models. In the seventeenth century these subjects were known as *bambochades,* and spectators looked for comic effects in them; in our age, we approve the Le Nains for evoking pity (Figs. 414–417, 419).

Ex-decorators of Fontainebleau, portrait-painters in the Flemish manner, imitators of the Italians, pupils of the Carracci or of Caravaggio, French painters show a certain indecision throughout this evolution of a national style. Artists more dexterous than sincere, like La Hire or Sébastien Bourdon, combine all these discordant elements in their works. The latter was capable of an elaborate *bambochade* in the Flemish

manner, and of a *pasticcio* on the style of Poussin with its clear-cut design and its simplified landscape. But he lacked the picturesque fertility of the men of the North, and his mind was never vigorous enough to achieve the vigour of Poussin's composition; his nervous and even incisive brush disperses where it should concentrate. His manual dexterity and his powers of observation stood him in good stead in his portraits. Many of these are finely-conceived figures, lacking all amenity of colour, and enveloped in the smoky, russet shadows of Caravaggio (Figs. 423, 425, 430).

How was a French School to emerge from this fusion of North and South? It was in the work of Poussin that the French classical genius first awoke to a conscious individuality. As he developed, French painters showed less indecision; by the

FIG. 424.—VOUET. WEALTH.
(The Louvre, Paris.)

middle of the seventeenth century, all recognised him as their master.

Poussin's mind dwelt habitually in antiquity. His aim was to place before our eyes the personages of history and of Greek mythology. He could not live anywhere but in Rome; and this was not because he wished to mix in the somewhat noisy society of

FIG. 425.—SÉBASTIEN BOURDON.
CHILDREN DRAWING.
(Museum of Montpellier.)

artists who thronged from all countries to the great picture-fair, but that he might live in contemplation of the statues which were excavated day by day, and of a region still haunted by the names of the past. It was here alone that he felt himself surrounded by the memories, the monuments, and the relics he worshipped. Here he could piously draw the ruins and measure the statues to discover the secret of their beauty. One day when he was walking with a stranger, "he picked up from among the grass a handful of earth, with fragments of lime, and grains of porphyry and marble: 'Here,' said he, 'take this back to your museum, and say: this is ancient Rome.'" Nothing could tempt him from his beloved city. He

FIG. 426.—COURTOIS. CAVALRY SKIRMISH.
(The Louvre, Paris.)

wished to live and die on that soil in which a whole world slumbers, in that atmosphere, heavy with memories, the grave poetry of which entered into his soul. He dreamed literally of giving a picture of antique life; he read ancient authors to glean characteristic traits of manners. He did not place a wand surmcunted by a hawk's head in the hand of a priest without due reflection. It was to indicate that this priest was an Egyptian, and the procession one sees in the distance in the *Burial of Phocion* serves to indicate the date of the Athenian hero's death. He is always well pleased when his archæological knowledge prevents him from inventing. But more than this: to illustrate ancient events is, of course, to return to the forms of Greek sculpture. The heroes of Plutarch and Livy have this advantage over modern celeb-rities, that they present them-selves to us in all the grace of antique statuary. Thus the claims of truth and beauty, which are at the root of classic thought, are reconciled. The painter made no distinction between art and history, be-tween Alexander and Apollo.

FIG. 427.—LE SUEUR. MELPOMENE, ERATO, AND POLYHYMNIA.
(The Louvre, Paris.)

He had, however, to work for the religion of his time, and to depict a martyr or a miracle occasionally. But church paintings demanded a rhetorical grandiloquence, and Poussin had to strain his voice to address the crowd from afar. He preferred to condense some

FIG. 428.—LE SUEUR. SAINT
SCHOLASTICA AND SAINT BENEDICT.
(The Louvre, Paris.)

Biblical or Gospel thought in small compositions. He has treated the sacred books as he has treated profane literature, with no more tenderness or mysticism, and with the same anxiety to be perfectly intelligible. All that is necessary in order to understand him, is to have read the works that inspire him. Yet his manner was not absolutely novel; it was that of Raphael, the painter of the Loggie and of the Cartoons. Raphael was the inventor of this iconography in which the plastic, psychological, and archæological discoveries of the Renaissance were turned to account.

Poussin, indeed, admired Raphael as much as he admired the antique. He was little concerned with the youthful Umbrian of radiant Madonnas and luminous landscapes; he carried away nothing from the Vatican Stanze beyond a few beautiful attitudes, and the group of the Muses on Parnassus. But he penetrated to the very soul of the narrative art of the Loggie and the Cartoons. It was in this "illustrated Bible" that he learned how to tell a story in attitudes, physiognomies, and agitated draperies, enframed in landscapes and architecture.

Poussin was not, like certain of his contemporaries, Rubens or Rembrandt for instance, the creator of a pictorial world; his originality lies primarily in his organising faculty; his genius manifests itself almost entirely in his powerful composition, a picturesque composition which knits lines and planes of light closely together, a moral composition which subordinates a variety of attitudes and types to a dominant idea. A strong intelligence

FIG. 429.—LE SUEUR.
SAINT PAUL PREACHING AT EPHESUS.
(The Louvre, Paris.)

205

governed his execution. Even when the painter is most inspired, he never seems to be carried away by his ardour; he has none of those bravura passages so frequent among the Italians and the Flemings, who are intoxicated by a fine effect, and give themselves up to the delight of rendering it skilfully. Even his vocabulary has an abstract character. He drew a great deal from antiques and from Nature, but did not paint with the model before his eyes. Nothing in his works ever makes us feel the contact of reality; no accent reveals the joy of a painter in the contemplation of the beautiful. His study of antique statues has given him a taste for

FIG. 430.—SÉBASTIEN BOURDON. FOUQUET.
(Museum of Versailles.)

clearly-defined forms, simple planes, and rhythmic attitudes; his nymphs and satyrs have an elegance of form and attitude which implies a long plastic education; they were fashioned by antique and Renaissance art. His drawing is marked by a virile grace; the forms are a little hard and sculpturesque, and in spite of colour that sometimes lacks consistence, they have that concentrated energy, that density peculiar to large figures reduced to a small scale. An occasional *Bacchanal* or *Triumph of Flora* just serves to indicate that the master was sometimes fired by the ardour of Titian; in these cases the nudities which recline on the dusky grass become more amber or ruddy of tone, and a golden twilight overlays the deep, dark blue of the sky. But this was a transient phase in his art; in general, Poussin does not look to colour for the enrichment of his thought. He groups his attitudes mentally in very simple landscapes. The light is diffuse in broad patches, bringing the masses of

FIG. 431.—LE SUEUR. DEATH OF SAINT BRUNO.
(The Louvre, Paris.)

FIG. 432.—POUSSIN.
HIS PORTRAIT, BY HIMSELF.
(The Louvre, Paris.)

the ground and of the fabrics into a few planes, and throwing the figures into relief by frank contrasts of light and dark surfaces. When his conception had taken definite form in his mind, he felt no anxiety as to its realisation. He painted with a steady hand, innocent alike of nervousness and dexterity, but the tissue of colour was less closely woven than the structure of the light and the design. Hence, when his aging hand began to tremble, his pictures suffered very little; the vigour of conception remained unimpaired, and ensured the cohesion of his loosely-painted compositions.

He composed his noblest landscapes in his old age. The harmony of his lines becomes broader and calmer when it is not encumbered by the gesticulations of a human drama. His nature has no freshness, it is instinct with an austere majesty, untouched by any fantasy of light or colour; all brilliance is suppressed that the structure of trees and soil may be the more nakedly presented. The great overhanging clouds are echoed by the simple planes of the ground and the dense foliage. An impression of serene eternity breathes from this balanced harmony. This landscape in which the ruins slumber is that described by Virgil, when Saturn, reigning over Latium, had not yet abandoned the earth to mortals. The Humanists of the seventeenth century were not surprised to find gods, satyrs,

FIG. 433.—POUSSIN. RESCUE OF THE
YOUTHFUL PYRRHUS.
(The Louvre, Paris.)

nymphs, or some river deity leaning on his urn, by the roadside, or on the banks of the Tiber.

FIG. 434.—POUSSIN. ORPHEUS AND EURYDICE.
(The Louvre, Paris.)

Although he spent very little time in Paris, Poussin had many fervent admirers in the capital. Scarcely was his glory assured in Rome, and his work well known in his native land, when he had no rival in France. Collectors overwhelmed him with commissions; a picture was looked upon as a great favour, and when one arrived in Paris, the little society of Poussin's devotees was all astir. They assembled in front of the new painting to discuss its merits. The importance of these little works in the history of the French mind is very considerable. In the first place, Poussin satisfied the contemporary taste for antiquity. He had assimilated all that could be known or divined on the subject, and had condensed it in his compositions. His pictures were not destined, like those of the Flemings, for princely galleries or Jesuit altars; they are not, like those of the Dutchmen, marvels of dexterity and precision; they never astonish, nor do they teach the science of painting. But they afford a kind of discipline, and always associate the intelligence

FIG. 435.—POUSSIN. THE SHEPHERDS OF ARCADIA.
(The Louvre, Paris.)

with the pleasure of the eye. Adapted to the dimensions of our field of vision, so that a single look can take in the whole composition, without losing a single detail, they require to be analysed and examined in a small room. Like the great French writers of the seventeenth century Poussin condensed into brief works sentiments which were floating

FIG. 436.—POUSSIN. THE CHILDHOOD OF BACCHUS.
(Condé Museum, Chantilly.)

vaguely in space, not having yet found their perfect forms. The virile poetry of this great logician blossomed under the sky of Rome, and passed afterwards into the French soil.

The enthusiasm of archæologists and artists does not fully explain the fascination of Rome for the men of the North. Throughout the ages, Celt and Teuton have dreamed of Italy, and have succumbed to her charm. The Germans of Barbarossa and the Frenchmen of Louis XII knew the nostalgia awakened by that smiling land, where they tasted a joy not easily evoked under their own sterner skies. Thus the countries whose artists crossed the Alps in great numbers were those who had to wait longest for men to depict their own landscapes faithfully; the vision of transalpine landscape painters was long obsessed by memories of Rome or Naples. Among those poets born of the contact of North and South, Claude Gellée was one of those who most fully appreciated the warm light of Mediterranean skies. Claude Gellée, called Le Lorrain (1600 – 1682), lived at Rome in a cosmopolitan circle, where men of every nation went by the name of their native land. An ignorant and simple spirit, he was little concerned with the historic memories

FIG. 437.—POUSSIN.
DIOGENES THROWING AWAY HIS BOWL.
(The Louvre, Paris.)

P

FIG. 438.—POUSSIN. APOLLO IN LOVE WITH DAPHNE.
(The Louvre, Paris.)

which breathe from Roman soil. His work appeals to no Humanist curiosity, and his compositions, in spite of their nobility, have little to say to the discursive classicism of Frenchmen. His landscapes deal with the soft splendour of southern skies. His dazzled eyes beheld a magic architecture. Sometimes it is a port; the sun, before disappearing into the ocean, darts its expiring rays caressingly on façades of marble, and gilds the crests of innumerable little waves. Or it is a plain, and dark groves of trees make the illimitable distance lighter and more limpid. All the shade and solidity are in the foreground, near the edge of the frame; in the centre of the picture, the objects become lighter as they recede, penetrated by the light and set ablaze as it were by the ardent atmosphere. These landscapes were lovingly contemplated: they have been copied and plagiarised extensively. Claude brought something of the radiance of Italy everywhere with his colour; even in the works of mediocre imitators, there is some reflex of those glowing memories which never fade from the mind of the Northerner who has once crossed the Alps.

Between the brilliant Renaissance and the sun of Louis XIV,

FIG. 439.—POUSSIN. THE DELUGE.
(The Louvre, Paris.)

the first half of the seventeenth century seems to lie somewhat in the shade. But in this twilight, that classic spirit, the discipline of which was thenceforth to govern all forms of intellectual activity in France, was definitely evolved. The generation of Louis XIII appears to have been sacrificed, because the magnificence it made possible was only realised under Louis XIV. The monarchy which made France so great asked little from its artists. It suspended the sumptuous caprices of Fontainebleau, and left Versailles a pretty brick country house. Artists worked more especially for the private citizen and for the religious orders, building mansions and churches and adorning them with Chris-

FIG. 440.—CLAUDE LORRAIN. CAMPO VACCINO.
(The Louvre, Paris.)

tian or mythological pictures. Under the somewhat depressed vaults of Saint Paul or Saint Nicolas du Chardonnet, the serious mind and the robust faith of the times still make themselves felt: sombre paintings and tombs devoid of splendour lurk in their dark chapels. These rugged images lack neither vigour nor sincerity, and it is easy to forgive those we can respect for making no attempt to dazzle, nor even to please.

In the Place Royale and in the mansions of the Marais, again, we can evoke the art-loving burgesses of the day. Never were painters and sculptors more constantly employed than those of this apparently unproductive period. They went from one great house to another, occupied for years on the decoration of a gallery. When we read their biographies, it even seems as if society were asking of art more than art could yet give: the culture of luxury, admiration for the antique, and refinement of taste were even more pronounced among amateurs than among professionals. From this time forth we see Parisian society directing and accelerating the movement of art.

Paris assumed that extraordinary preponderance of intellectual life which contributed so greatly to the unification of French art. It concentrated the

FIG. 441.—CLAUDE LORRAIN.
WASHED PEN AND INK DRAWING.
(The Louvre, Paris.)

FIG. 442.—CLAUDE LORRAIN. SEAPORT AT SUNSET.
(The Louvre, Paris.)

intellectual life of the country; artists and writers came to settle there. How many of these must the Quartier des Augustins have seen wandering in its narrow streets! The most favoured of them obtained a royal brevet and lodging in the Louvre, in the gallery overlooking the river. Some bore the proud new title of Academician. Their apprentices worked for the shops on the quays and bridges; the Flemings sold their little panels at the fair of St. Germain. This active agglomeration constituted a kind of Parisian School, which became the exemplar of all the provincial groups. Artistic centralisation was a fact before it became an institution. A uniform classical style was about to spread throughout the country in spite of local diversities, and to extend to all the frontiers of France.

After the quarrel with the Fronde, the king had made his peace with Paris. In 1660, he was living in the Louvre. From his lofty windows, the young Louis XIV looked out upon a marvellous urban prospect, each monument of which recalled the successive stages of his greatness, the history of his house, and that of France; there beneath him lay the Seine with its dense shipping, the cupola of the "Quatre Nations," the college whose title commemorated the recent triumphs, the conquered provinces, and the extended frontier; to the left the Pont Neuf with its swarming crowds; his

FIG. 443.—CLAUDE LORRAIN. SEAPORT.
(The Louvre, Paris.)

grandfather, Henry IV, prancing at the extremity of the Cité; the imposing mass of the Palais de Justice with the spire of Saint Louis

THE EVOLUTION OF CLASSICAL ART

rising above it, and further off, beyond the still Gothic roofs, the severe towers of Notre Dame, the cathedral of Philip Augustus, friend of the Communes, and the builder of the primitive Louvre. Louis XIV understood that the first work of his reign ought to be to complete this landscape by finishing the Louvre. True, he soon perceived that the mighty city could not contain the monarchy without threatening to suffocate it, and that he must create a royal town. All the artists of the day were pressed into the service of Versailles. But the continuity of national art was not interrupted. Versailles was still Paris; Versailles was not a new centre of energy, but the collective product of the Parisian and the French School.

BIBLIOGRAPHY

H. Lemonnier, *L'Art au temps de Richelieu et de Mazarin*, Paris, 1893.—Louis Savot, *L'Architecture française des bastimens particuliers*, Paris, 1642.—Le Muet, *Manière de bien bastir pour toutes sortes de personnes*, Paris, 1647.—De Chambray, *Parallèle de l'architecture antique et de la moderne...*, Paris, 1650.—For the architectural history of Paris in the classical period: Germain Brice, *Description de Paris*, Paris, 1685, 2 vols.—Sauval, *Histoire des Antiquités de la ville de Paris*, Paris, 1724, 3 vols.—Dom Félibien, *Histoire de la ville de Paris*, Paris, 1725, 5 vols.—Piganiol de la Force, *Description de Paris*, Paris, 1742, 8 vols.—Le Beuf, *Histoire de la ville et de tout le diocèse de Paris*, Paris, 1754, 15 vols. (édit. Cocheris, 1883, 6 vols., and 1 vol. of rectifications and additions by Bournon).—Jaillot, *Recherches critiques, historiques... sur la ville de Paris*, Paris, 1772, 3 vols. For the views, see the engravings of Israël Silvestre and de Pérelle.—Charvet, *Etienne Martellange*, Paris, 1874.—E. Bonnafé, *Les Amateurs de l'ancienne France, le Surintendant Foucquet*, Paris, 1882.—Chatelain, *Le Surintendant Foucquet*, Paris, 1903.—L. Vitet, *L'Académie royale de Peinture et de Sculpture*, Paris, 1861.—*Mémoires inédits sur la vie et les ouvrages des Membres de l'Académie royale de Peinture et de Sculpture*, Paris, 1854, 2 vols.—Armand Samson, *Les frères Anguier*, Paris, 1889. —H. Stein, *Les frères Anguier (R. S. B. A. D.*, 1889).—P. Vitry, *Les Boudin et les Bourdin (G. B. A.*, 1896, II).—J. Guiffrey, *Guillaume Dupré, graveur en médailles (N. A. A. F.*, 1876) —Chabouillet, *Guillaume Dupré, sculpteur et graveur en pierres fines (N. A. A. F.*, 1880).— Fleury, *Guillaume Dupré*, Paris, 1883.—L. Courajod, *Jean Warin...*, Paris, 1881.—Blanchet, *Jean Warin, Notes biographiques*, 1888.—A. Félibien, *Entretiens sur la vie et sur les ouvrages des plus excellents peintres*, Paris, 1666-88, 5 vols. The fourth volume contains an important biography of Poussin.—Bellori, *Vite de' Pittori, Scultori ed Architetti moderni*, Rome, 1672.— R. de Piles, *Abrégé de la vie des peintres*, Paris, 1699.—P. de Chennevières, *Recherches sur la vie et les ouvrages de quelques peintres provinciaux de l'ancienne France*, Paris, 1847-62, 4 vols.; *Quentin Warin, L. Finsonius, J. Daret (N. A. A. F.*, 1887); *Notes sur l'Art français*, Paris, 1894.—P. Lafond, *François et Jacob Bunel, peintres de Henri IV (R. S. B. A. D.*, 1898).—H. Bouchot, *J. Callot*, Paris, 1889.—M. Vachon, *J. Callot*, Paris, Sd.—A. Valabrègue, *Abraham Bosse*, Paris, 1891.—Champfleury, *Essai sur la vie et l'œuvre des Le Nain*, Paris, 1850. —J. Guiffrey, *Antoine, Louis et Mathieu Le Nain, Nouveaux documents (N. A. A. F.*, 1876).— G. Grandin, *Documents sur les artistes de Laon (N. A. A. F.*, 1894-95); *La famille Lenain (R. S. B. A. D.*, 1900).—A. Valabrègue, *Le frères Le Nain*, Paris, 1904.—Gazier, *Philippe et Jean-Baptiste de Champaigne*, Paris, 1893.—L. Vitet, *Eustache Le Sueur*, Paris, 1853; *Sur Le Sueur (A. A. F.*, 1855, and *N. A. A. F.*, 1877-78).—Ch. Ponsonailhe, *Sébastien Bourdon, sa vie et son œuvre*, Paris, 1891.—Nicolas Poussin, *Lettres publiées par Quatremère de Quincy*, 1824.—Maria Graham, *Life of Nicolas Poussin* (1821).—H. Bouchitté, *Le Poussin*, Paris, 1858. —P. Desjardins, *Poussin*, Paris, 1903.—Mrs. Mark Pattison (Lady Dilke), *Claude Lorrain*, Paris, 1884.—R. Bouyer, *Claude Lorrain*, Paris, 1904.

FIG. 444.—CENTRAL PAVILION OF THE COLONNADE OF THE LOUVRE.

CHAPTER III

THE MONARCHICAL ART OF LOUIS XIV

Colbert's Projects and Institutions.—The Continuation of the Louvre.—The Function and the Work of Charles Le Brun.—Mignard.—The Sculptors Girardon and Coysevox.—Pierre Puget.—Mansart's Versailles: the Marble Court; the Decoration of the Apartments; the Royal Allegory; the Great Gallery.—Le Nôtre's Park, the Groves and Fountains; the Allegorical and Mythological Statues.—The Symbolism of Versailles.—Paris; the Provinces. —Results of Colbert's Work; Technical Progress and Centralisation.

THE "Century of Louis XIV" glorified by historians was no spontaneous growth. Its artistic prosperity was prepared and organised by ministerial instruction. As soon as Colbert had got the superintendence of royal buildings in his hands, he set to work to produce French artists for the service of the king. He hoped by means of monuments to fix that glory which survives civilisations, and dominates the ages as do the grandiose ruins of Rome and of Egypt. French classical art was inclined at the moment to forget its country and its age. The monarchy brought it back to both. Sculptors, painters and architects dreamed of antiquity; they were now required to think of Louis XIV. The State, in return, undertook their education. Colbert became the protector of the Royal Academy of Painting and Sculpture, and was able to intervene in

214

the instruction of its pupils; he sent the best of these to Italy, and founded the French Academy at Rome in their interest. The king's scholars worked for

him there, completed their apprenticeship, and executed copies of masterpieces for the royal parks and galleries, when the originals were not to be bought. Thus the king became almost the sole Mæcenas of French artists, and the habitual organisation of French art was centred in State institutions.

FIG. 445.—THE COLONNADE OF THE LOUVRE.

Colbert's authoritative and practical mind left its impress on every one of these institutions. Their object was to realise fully and rapidly all that the French genius could yield. It is unjust to say that they put French art in subjection to Italy. For over a century France had been labouring to assimilate the manner of Rome or Bologna, and it was Colbert who did more than any other to enfranchise her from this vassalage. He thought jealously that French art, like

French luxury, should be the product of French craftsmen. Not content, like Francis I, with buying fruits from Italy, he determined to grow them on French soil. The Academy, under the direction of Le Brun, was ordered to evolve from the masterpieces of antiquity, of the Renaissance, and of Poussin, the surest method of attaining beauty and constructing a Manual for the perfect painter and sculptor. Modest craftsmen endeavoured conscientiously to found a system of

FIG. 446.—PORTE SAINT-DENIS, PARIS.

æsthetics in accordance with contemporary modes of thought. But æsthetics is a philosophic exercise which is of little use to artists.

This enterprise of the Academy throws a good deal of light on classical thought; but it cannot have done much service to art.

The Italians, it was said, had been led to the pursuit of beauty by Greek and Roman works. In France, the soil yields but scanty relics of the past; Colbert supplied the deficiency to the utmost of his power. He collected a great number of statues in Paris and at Versailles, and when originals were unobtainable, he ordered copies. It was not to be supposed that Trajan's column could be brought to Paris; but the professors and pupils of the Academy were

FIG. 447.—CHURCH OF THE INVALIDES, PARIS.

enabled to copy its bas-reliefs from casts obtained at great expense. Colbert, indeed, showed such avidity in his purchases, that there was a kind of revolt among the Roman populace, enraged at seeing these elements of the national wealth carried off. These works, pillaged of old by Roman pro-consuls, and now bought by the French king, transmitted from age to age, from Greece to Italy, from Italy to France, the languid elegance of Hellenistic art.

But it was not enough to prepare for the future. The king's glory required immediate masterpieces. The first project was to complete the Louvre, which had been in progress since the reign of Francis I. Bernini, the Pope's architect, was brought to Paris at great expense. He drew out a plan, executed a bust of Louis XIV. and pronounced judgment on French art and the education of French artists very freely. None of his utterances were lost on Colbert; some of the

FIG. 448.—PORTE DE PARIS. LILLE.

FIG. 449.—GIRARDON. REDUCTION OF THE STATUE OF LOUIS XIV.
(The Louvre, Paris.)

ministerial instructions bear their imprint: but the minister could not bring himself to allow a foreigner to build the palace of the King of France. Even when the first stone was laid, he would not put the Italian's name on the commemorative medal placed in the foundations, and after Bernini left, his plans were very soon abandoned. Colbert, like all the rest of the world, admired Italy, but his admiration took the form of desiring to emulate her, not of installing her in Paris.

Bernini was disposed to raze the whole quarter to the ground, to make room for a great Roman palace, solemn and austere. Claude Perrault (1667–1674) designed a more agreeable façade; between the ground floor and the entablature, detached columns form a gallery. The defect of the design is that it is not adapted to the divisions of a modern house; an over-zealous admiration for antique architecture led men to apply the colonnade of a temple without storeys to a building of several storeys, and the mistaken flatness of the roof was masked by the entablature and its balustrades (Figs. 444, 445).

But we must not overlook the decorative merit of this architecture, and the elegance of this colonnade between the massive base and the rigid band of the entablature. Perrault made no attempt to astonish the spectator by the grandiose majesty of his design. The proportions were calculated by an artist too skilful to allow them to appear gigantic. He built only the one façade; but this one sufficed to acclimatise the "colossal style" in France for ever. Mansart, Gabriel and

FIG. 450.—TUBI AND COLLIGNON.
TOMB OF LE BRUN'S MOTHER,
AT SAINT-NICOLAS-DU-CHARDONNET, PARIS.

Louis adopted its methods later, when they wanted to reconcile majesty and grace, to avoid heaviness and affectation. Since the Renaissance, architectural style has lost its decorative amenity, but it has gained strength and breadth. A façade by Lescot is well adapted to a narrow court, which forces the spectator to note the minute adjustment and ingenious detail; but the colossal style, with its large flat lines, makes a superb framework for a vast space.

FIG. 451.—THE PLACE VENDÔME [DES CONQUETES], BIRD'S EYE VIEW.
(From the album, "Paris vu en ballon," by André Schœlcher and Omer Decugis.)

The Louvre, however, was not completed by Louis XIV. The king could not lodge his executive and his court there commodiously. He felt cramped in this palace, the growth of which was held in check by Paris. He preferred the plain of Versailles, where everything, soil and water included, could be arranged to suit him. Colbert deplored the king's defection; he thought it a mere caprice, and never dreamed that the pleasant country house built by Lemercier for Louis XIII would one day be magnificent enough to give an advantageous idea of the greatness of Louis XIV. In this case, Colbert was mistaken, the king did not change his mind. From 1670 to 1685, the artistic activity of France was consecrated to the work of Versailles.

All the artists in France collaborated here. Le Vau, Mansart and Robert de Cotte successively directed the building. Le Brun (1619-1690), painter in ordinary to the king, director of the Gobelins factory, president of the royal Academy of painting and

FIG. 452.—GIRARDON. BATHING NYMPHS, VERSAILLES.

sculpture, and the confidant of Colbert, superintended the decoration. He crowned Colbert's administrative genius by his technical mastery; his facility of invention and execution made him an excellent organiser, always ready to furnish models for painting, sculpture, furniture, wood or ironwork.

FIG. 453.—GIRARDON. TOMB OF RICHELIEU.
(Church of the Sorbonne.)

We see in his work how classical art became one of the adjuncts of the monarchy. Before he undertook the direction of French art for the king, Le Brun, like others, had worked for the Church and for finance; he had painted "saintetés" (sacred subjects) and "mythologies." His two idols were Raphael and Poussin. He imitated the noble design and, in particular, the emphatic and animated movement of Raphael in the *Battle of Constantine;* in Poussin, whom he had known in Rome, he especially admired his skill in enshrining a moral drama in a picturesque composition. The professor in him preferred Poussin, whose reasoned art appears so rich in lucid precepts; left to himself, he would, no doubt, have produced scenes of ancient tragedy, with a great deal of psychology and archæology; but he had a facile brush, and circumstances made him a decorator. After a period of service with Fouquet, he passed into that of the king. In his academic discourses, he declared that painting should appeal to the intelligence, while at the Louvre, the Gobelins and Versailles, he was obliged to appeal to the eye.

FIG. 454.—GUILLAUME COUSTOU. THE RHÔNE.
(Hôtel de Ville, Lyons.)

Le Brun's large compositions are unattractive,

FIG. 455.—COYSEVOX. TOMB OF MAZARIN.
(The Louvre, Paris.)

in spite of their genuine power of invention, because they lack all the sensuous qualities of painting, and imply a process of reasoning to which few spectators in a magnificent gallery are addicted. But Le Brun was not only a painter; he designed the entire decoration of his ceilings, and the splendour he was unable to give to his canvases glowed in the framework of gilded stucco, the statues and mosaics. Hence the galleries he painted, the Galerie d'Apollon in the Louvre, and the great Galerie des Glaces at Versailles, rival the splendour of the Doge's Palace. His *Battles of Alexander* show how he preferred to paint when he was not magnifying Louis XIV or decorating his palaces. Vague analogies between Alexander the Great and Louis the Great, a slight resemblance between the two faces, discounted the inevitable royal panegyric, and left him free to produce "historical" pictures after his own fashion. He began by studying antique texts and monuments, Quintus Curtius and the Trajan Column. He then applied his theories of the proportions of the human body and of psychological expression. Le Brun was able to group large numbers of figures lucidly; his imagination gave vivacity to his vast "machines." But his over-abstract art lacks charm; Alexander's battles should begin by amusing the eye; but they are monotonously dull and heavy. On each side are

FIG. 456.—NICOLAS COUSTOU. THE SAÔNE.
(Hôtel de Ville, Lyons.)

the principal episodes; the bodies of the wounded and vanquished are heaped up to fill the angles of the composition, and these,

FIG. 457.—DESJARDINS. BUST OF PIERRE MIGNARD.
(The Louvre, Paris.)

sacrificed and lost for the moral expression, which a decorator relieves by magnificent accessories, are drowned in hot, opaque shadows. When a passage shows some pictorial charm, it is because he left the execution of it to his assistants, who were for the most part Flemings. Genoels sometimes illuminated a distant horizon; and some of the horses betray Van der Meulen's brush by their brilliant, satiny coats and fresh colour.

Le Brun had a rival and enemy in Pierre Mignard (1610–1695), who arrived too late to take the place of painter in ordinary, and only lived long enough to occupy it for a short time after the death of Le Brun. He was a facile and superficial artist, ready to undertake any task, and capable of executing it with credit. He had lived so long in Italy, and had copied so many Roman, Bolognese and even Venetian pictures, that reminiscences came to him all unconsciously. He, too, was employed on vast decorations in the cupola of the Val-de-Grâce, and in the Château of Saint Cloud, which he painted for Monsieur while Le Brun was working for Louis XIV in the gallery at Versailles. The decoration in the Val-de-Grâce is a gigantic composition, but it is diffuse and incoherent, the colour is "degraded" and flat, without any pictorial richness, without any luminous effect to bring the innumerable figures together. Essentially a man of the world, Mignard had all the qualities to make him acceptable at Court, and he was a great favourite in aristocratic society. He was the forerunner of Largillière and Rigaud in the domain of fashionable

FIG. 458.—COYSEVOX. BUST OF THE DUCHESSE DE BOURGOGNE.
(Museum of Versailles.)

FIG. 459.—PUGET. SUPPOSED BUST OF LOUIS XIV.
(Museum of Aix.)

portraiture. Between the grave and rigid personages of Philippe de Champaigne, and the nervous or richly-adorned figures of Rigaud and Largillière, we have Mignard's types, whose splendour is sometimes oppressive; the faces are delicate, but the "in-folio" periwigs are very massive, and the costumes are of stuffs so rich and rigid that they make the attitudes heavy (Figs. 474–475). The portraits of Claude Lefebvre, at the beginning of the reign, are among the best of the French School. They have not, as yet, the nobility, the impersonal majesty of the Versailles courtiers. The sitters have not yet been reduced to uniformity by the taste of the sovereign, and the artist, little concerned to paint "history," was content to be a good observer and a very skilful executant in the Flemish manner (Fig. 467). The draughtsman-engraver Robert Nauteuil sketched from nature portraits which he afterwards engraved so vivaciously that they are as full of life and colour as paintings; Edelinck, too, translated the strong and variegated splendour of Largillière's and Rigaud's portraits into black and white.

Le Brun also designed for the Versailles sculptors. Girardon (1628–1715) was the one who best understood the intentions of the king's painter. His marble seemed naturally to take the facile and redundant softness of form dear to Le Brun. The Louis XIV he executed for the Place des Conquêtes (Place Vendôme) was an imposing equestrian figure (Fig. 449). For the Grotto of Apollo at Versailles, he sculptured, together with Tubi and de Marsy, a triple group of nymphs, horses,

FIG. 460.—COYSEVOX.
BUST OF THE GREAT CONDÉ.
(The Louvre, Paris.)

and Tritons, in the midst of whom the Sun-God descends from his car, cold and elegant as the Belvedere Apollo. In the allegorical figures he placed on certain tombs—the most famous is that of Richelieu (Fig. 453) —the lines of the draperies and the bodies are very gracefully rounded; it is the eloquence of a cold and rhetorical orator, but one whose noble or gracious tone is always appropriate. Nevertheless, in the Bassin du Nord, at Versailles, a leaden bas-relief reveals a robust sensuality, under the sustained eloquence of the decorative style. Nymphs are shown frolicking in the water, and here Girardon has given the bodies a lively suppleness and a suggestion of the warmth and tenderness of living flesh (Fig. 452).

FIG. 461.—PUGET. MILO OF CROTONA.
(The Louvre, Paris.)

Coysevox (1640–1720), on the other hand, was too intelligent an artist to be submerged in the collective work of Versailles. Like the others, he placed reclining nymphs and river-gods on the margins of pools and fountains, and allegorical Virtues at the foot of tombs; but his figures have a nervous distinction. He had a

FIG. 462.—PUGET. GALLIC HERCULES.
(The Louvre, Paris.)

taste for truth, and understood the expressive power of form. Few artists have modelled with so much daring and assurance. In spite of periwigs, lace jabots and all the accessories of gala dress, his heads are strongly-marked types. When the sitter is energetic, the sculptor uses the trenchant emphasis of the fifteenth century Florentines. The image of Condé, sharply accentuated in the bronze, gleaming with sudden flashes of light, gives a strange reality to the eagle glance, and the great nose, like the beak of a bird of prey, in the haggard face (Figs. 460, 469).

FIG. 463.—PUGET. DOOR AND BALCONY
OF THE HÔTEL DE VILLE,
TOULON.

FIG. 464.—PUGET. DIOGENES AND
ALEXANDER.
(The Louvre, Paris.)

On the other hand, Coysevox treated marble with a sensual and caressing gentleness; his *Nymph with a Shell,* and his Duchess of Burgundy as Diana, are not remarkable only for their fine decorative attitudes; the flesh and the stuffs are full of quivering life (Fig. 458). This was the profound charm of the Florentines,

FIG. 465.—J. JOUVENET. PORTRAIT OF
FAGON.
(The Louvre, Paris.)

FIG. 466.—LE BRUN. PORTRAIT OF
TURENNE.
(Museum of Versailles.)

as it was of certain French sculptors, Germain Pilon, Coysevox and Houdon. They were not content with majesty and elegance in sculpture, put gave a subtle vitality to marble and metal.

The great sculptors of Versailles sometimes turned from their labours for the park to the decoration of distinguished tombs. The age was never more religious than at this period. The famous families erected stately monuments in the churches over the graves of their illustrious dead, Richelieu at the Sorbonne (Fig. 453), Mazarin at the Collège des Quatre-Nations (Fig. 455), Colbert at Saint Eustache, Turenne

FIG. 467.—LEFEBVRE. A MASTER AND HIS PUPIL.
(The Louvre, Paris.)

at the Invalides. Round the sarcophagus which serves as a plinth to the praying statue, mourning figures recall his virtues, and the regrets of the survivors. In his funeral sermon of Michel Le Tellier, Bossuet describes and translates one of these tombs when he evokes "wisdom, fidelity, justice, modesty, foresight, pity, the sacred band of virtues which watched around him, so to speak." It was Le Brun generally who gave the plan and the design for the figures. In the design for his mother's tomb, executed by Tubi and Collignon at Saint Nicolas-du-Chardonnet, he imagined a touching Resurrection scene. From the tomb an angel has just

FIG. 468.—MARTIN DESJARDINS. THE PASSAGE OF THE RHINE.
(The Louvre, Paris.)

opened rises a poor, old, terrified, imploring figure, still half-encumbered by her winding sheet, and barely aroused from her death slumber. Filial tenderness substituted human pathos for the allegory of funeral orations (Fig. 450).

One great French artist only, Pierre Puget (1622–1694), held aloof from the activities of Versailles; he

FIG. 469.—COYSEVOX. LOUIS XIV.
(Hôtel Carnavalet.)

sent but a single group for the park, his *Milo of Crotona*, and rarely left Toulon, where Colbert employed him on the decoration of the royal ships. Working remote from the Court, and independently of Le Brun's school, Puget appears as a kind of exile or opponent, and has gained a certain posthumous fame in consequence. As a fact, he was by no means a victim of official art; but he was more akin to Bernini and the Italian successors of Michelangelo than to the peaceful decorators directed by Le Brun. His dramatic group of *Milo of Crotona*, convulsed with effort and agony, must have astonished the serene or playful divinities which surrounded it at Versailles (Fig. 461). And in his Diogenes relief, a huge marble picture, tumultuous as a Rubens, the swelling muscles and violent gestures show that his impetuous genius could not subdue itself to the calm lines of an architectural decoration (Fig. 464). When Puget placed figures in a group, it was to give them attitudes of effort or impulsive movement, like those Victories on the prows of vessels which carried the fame of the king to distant places, and those suffering athletes at the Town Hall of Toulon, who struggle desperately to bear up the crushing weight of the balcony (Fig. 463). The architects of the Louvre or of Versailles would not have allowed such violence on their calm façades. Puget's impetuosity had full play, unfettered by the restraints of good taste; the artist's fiery temperament animates the marble, and endows it with a superhuman energy; a muscular frenzy swells the limbs and torsos, and would recall Michelangelo more legitimately if the figures grimaced less, if their strength were less akin to that of a porter, and if the dramatic eloquence

FIG. 470.—LE BRUN.
GRACE BEFORE MEAT.
(The Louvre, Paris.)

226

of their creator had less of the accent of Marseilles.

We must go to Versailles to judge the art of Louis XIV, the work of Le Vau, Mansart and Le Brun. Approaching from Paris, we see the buildings spread out on a slight slope, the roofs levelled to a uniform horizontal line. As we gradually advance between the two projecting wings towards the heart of the palace, we understand the process of its development. Immense wings grew from either side of a little body, Louis XIII's building, a modest façade of white stone and red brick, which Mansart enriched, but which he had to respect. It

FIG. 471.—TOURNIER. DESCENT FROM THE CROSS.
(Museum of Toulouse.)

imposed its simple and cheerful style on this entire side of the palace; here were lodged the royal executive, the ministries of Peace and War, Colbert and Louvois. In the eighteenth century Gabriel erected columns against these parti-coloured façades;

FIG. 472.—PORTRAIT OF A WOMAN.
(Museum of Montpellier.)

Louis XIV had reserved this ceremonious style for the façade which confronts the park.

At the very threshold, the eye was dazzled by the pomp of the decorations. The "Ambassadors' Staircase" rose, a structure of polychrome marbles. The apartments sustained this decorative richness. On the walls, Le Brun's pupils recorded the king's actions; these great paintings, which would have been adequate enough as cartoons for tapestries, do not give a very impressive idea of the French school. On the ceiling, the gods of the ancients continue to drive chariots and hurl

FIG. 473.—NICOLAS MIGNARD. PIETA.
(Museum of Avignon.)

thunder-bolts. The great gallery was meant to be the most luxurious part of the palace. The decoration of the ceiling occupied Le Brun for a long time. When it was unveiled, the courtiers saw the history of the whole reign magnified by mythology. The king, an Imperator in helmet and cuirass, gives orders, hurls thunder-bolts; surrounded by France, Minerva, Hercules, Monsieur. Condé, and Turenne (Fig. 480). Confronting him are various towns bowed upon their shields, terrified and suppliant; Spain, Holland and Germany, the three-headed Hydra of the Coalition; fugitives and captives, Rivers imploring deliverance, and Fame, or Mercury, ready to carry to distant lands the terror and the glory of the king's name.

FIG. 474.—PIERRE MIGNARD.
PORTRAIT OF HIS DAUGHTER.
(Museum of Versailles.)

FIG. 475.—PIERRE MIGNARD. MME. DE MONTESPAN
AND HER SON.
(Museum of Avignon.)

A certain epic strain runs through this rhetoric; Le Brun has embodied the essence of the triumphant years; he shows the king in attitudes addressed to posterity; the poet of this reign was a painter, not a writer. In this gallery, the products of the Gobelins, of Beauvais and of

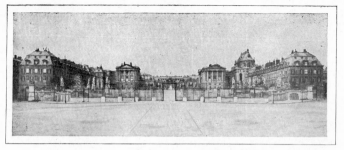

FIG. 476.—CHATEAU OF VERSAILLES.

Saint-Gobain, furniture, tapestries, mirrors and goldsmith's work, were spread in rich profusion. Of all this splendour, the ceiling is the sole remaining relic; it contrasts strangely with the nudity of the floor. To imagine all this vanished magnificence, we must evoke those portraits by Rigaud, in which crimson velvet and rich brocades billow to the very edge of the frame, and break their

FIG. 477.—VERSAILLES. LA COUR DE MARBRE.

shimmering folds at the base of marble pilasters and precious vases (Fig. 485).

The Gobelins factory, enlarged and directed by Le Brun, made the furniture for Versailles; the thousand products of this human hive composed a naturally harmonious framework; the forms of marble, metal and wood were all determined by the king's painter. Among the Gobelins artists, the cabinet-maker Boulle has a personality. With ebony and

FIG. 478.—BIRD'S EYE VIEW OF VERSAILLES.

(*Photo. A. Schœlcher and O. Decugis.*)

FIG. 479.—CHATEAU OF VERSAILLES. FAÇADE FROM THE GARDENS.

brass, with inlays of pewter and tortoise shell, he built up cabinets

FIG. 480.—LE BRUN. LOUIS XIV GIVES ORDERS TO ATTACK HOLLAND. FRAGMENT OF THE CEILING IN THE GALERIE DES GLACES.

which were much appreciated by his contemporaries; they were marked by the qualities dear to the age; these pieces of furniture, with their precious materials and careful workmanship, were an epitome of the decorative wealth displayed in the galleries (Fig. 481).

From the lofty windows of the Galerie des Glaces the king could contemplate the majestic arrangement of Le Nôtre's park. On this side the palace presents its ceremonious façade, unrelieved save by the play of light on its innumerable windows and pilasters (Fig. 479). Mansart was not oblivious of the Louvre colonnade; like Perrault, he has decorated a storey above a solid ground-

FIG. 481.—VERSAILLES. LOUIS XIV'S BEDROOM.

FIG. 482.—VERSAILLES. FRIEZE OF THE SALON DE L'ŒIL-DE-BŒUF.

floor with columns and pilasters, hidden his roof behind an attic storey, and broken the monotonous line of the upper balustrade with a few vases and trophies. Below is a bare terrace, for nothing was allowed to detract from the proud majesty of the architecture. Two large sheets of water reflect the evening flames kindled by the setting sun in the windows of the palace. Colossal bronze figures, representing the rivers of France offering the homage of their waters to the king, recline upon the margins obedient to the imperious horizontality of the site. Then the ground falls away on every side, leaving the palace in superb isolation. From the depths of the park, through a leafy vista at the end of an alley it appears, white and luminous, with the magical aspect of some fairy structure in the garden of Armida.

From the terrace, the eye commands the vast park, Le Nôtre's masterpiece; to the left, towards the south, is a flower-garden, where box and blossoms spread an embroidered carpet upon the soil; on a sunk terrace below this are the orangery and the piece of water known as the Pièce d'eau des Suisses; to the right, towards the north, are terraced parterres, descending to the Fountain of Neptune. In front, towards the west, stretches a wide turfed avenue, bordered by walls of dense foliage; it extends from the Foun-

FIG. 483 —ROBERT DE COTTE.
THE CHAPEL OF VERSAILLES.

FIG. 484.—VERSAILLES. THE TAPIS VERT.

tain of Latona, at our feet, to the Fountain of Apollo, where Apollo advances on his car, drawn by four galloping horses; beyond lies the tranquil mirror of the canal, and the prospect melts into the illimitable horizon beyond the park. On each side of the Green Carpet, behind the leafy screen, Le Nôtre arranged his labyrinth of groves; their regularity is only recognised upon a plan; the visitor soon loses himself in the labyrinth. At a point where four alleys meet, is a fountain; in the centre, lustrous, dripping bronze figures recline, gazing upward at a jet of water. A population of white statues gleams against the foliage; antiques, modern works, and copies, they line each side of the avenues. From their pedestals, they looked down on the splendid procession of king and courtiers. The great nobles of Rome were the first to set the statues excavated from the soil among their vines. The men of the seventeenth century were not astonished when they came upon naiads and rural divinities. When a certain indifferent painter, one Cotelle, represented some perspectives in the park, he enlivened

FIG. 485.—VERSAILLES. THE GALERIE DES GLACES.

them with mythological figures, as if the statues, when they were alone, came down from their pedestals to frolic on the gravelled alleys, ride upon the clouds, or gambol in the fountains. La Fontaine loved to people the melancholy majesty of great parks with the figures of Flora, Pomona and nymphs, whose white forms he had seen among the green branches.

Like the paintings in the apartments, the statues in the park were no mere accidental accessories; they played a part in the general iconography of the monarchical cult. At the entrance to the palace,

THE MONARCHICAL ART OF LOUIS XIV

the two groups between which the visitor passes recall the triumph of France over Spain and the Empire, and the sculptured figures which guard the Marble Courtyard are symbols of the royal

FIG. 486.—VERSAILLES. THE ORANGERY GARDENS.

virtues. At a time when Louis XIV came to Versailles only for relaxation, Girardon showed Apollo completing his daily course, and the nymphs pressing round to serve him. Apollo on his car reappears in the centre of the park. Latona, the Seasons, the Hours, the quarters of the globe, the elements gravitate about the Sun-God. A continuous allegory gives significance and unity to this mythology; a common sentiment animates this world of statues. To-day, the vast galleries with their blackened paintings, the alleys with their weather-worn and mutilated statues, are like a deserted temple and the ruined accessories of a vanished faith. The perennial beauty of trees and flowers is powerless to dissipate the melancholy which hangs over this marvellous setting of an interrupted *fête*. Besides, we moderns demand from works of art a subtle expression of personal sentiment. Here, painters and sculptors worked in bands under Le Brun's direction, and it is difficult to seize any individual traits among these figures. Hence, in this palace, as in the great enterprises of the Middle Ages, we must not look for personal expression, but must yield to the spell of a diffused inspiration. To

evoke the stirring majesty of Versailles, the spectator must be able to re-kindle many extinct emotions, either by the power of history or of sympathy. There are no false gods save those who have no worshippers. If we wish to hold communion with this art, we must think the thoughts of monarchical France, who admired herself in the image of her

FIG. 487.—THE LOUVRE. GALERIE D'APOLLON.

FIG. 488.—LE BRUN. THE TRIUMPH OF ALEXANDER.
GOBELINS TAPESTRY.
(*Photo. Fenaille.*)

king, and put Louis XIV on a colossal pedestal, that he might appear greater.

Moreover, the art of this age was not merely decorative. There was never a period when more works of public utility were undertaken. Colbert constructed ports; Louvois fortified the frontiers, and even now their structures are not all obsolete. Colbert caused the first observatory to be built, and that same Claude Perrault, who had designed a stately colonnade for a king, was wise enough in this case to avoid all useless ornament, and to look for beauty only in fitness. Louvois lodged the wounded veterans of the army in the Hôtel des Invalides; Liberal Bruant did not attempt to mask

FIG. 489.—LE BRUN. MELEAGER'S HUNTING.
GOBELINS TAPESTRY.
(*Photo. Fenaille.*)

the severity of his façades under a veneer of classical orders; he was concerned only with a just arrangement of a building which was not quite either a barrack, a monastery, or a hospital. The church added by Mansart to Bruant's, is, on the contrary, an official building designed for the glorification of the king; its façade and cupola are perhaps the masterpieces of the "Jesuit style" (Fig. 447).

Meanwhile, Paris, abandoned by the mon-

FIG. 400.—LE BRUN. LOUIS XIV VISITING THE
GOBELINS FACTORY. GOBELINS TAPESTRY.
(*Photo. Manufacture des Gobelins.*)

archy, continued to throw off its mediæval aspect. But its greatest enterprises still centred round the king; they were designed to greet him when he passed through the city, returning from his campaigns. Blondel and Perrault set up triumphal arches at the entrances of the old fortifications; the royal victories were recorded upon them in bas-reliefs. These monumental

FIG. 491.—VAN DER MEULEN. THE KING ENTERING ARRAS.
(The Louvre, Paris.)

gates, built in honour of the king (Fig. 446), multiplied around the city in which he no longer lived. He came occasionally, however, for the inauguration of his statues. In the heart of the city, two squares were designed and built on a special plan, with the general object of isolating the royal effigy; these were the Place des Victoires and the Place des Conquêtes (Fig. 451).

The provinces participated from afar in this monarchical art. Artists, following the example of Le Brun, styled their corporations Academies; but the best among them could never resist the glamour of the capital. Henceforth, fame was only to be won in Paris. The transformation of urban architecture made its way into the provincial capitals; at Aix and Toulouse, the new mansions were modelled on those of the Marais. The Place des Victoires and the Place des Conquêtes were also imitated. After 1680, an important event in the life of the large provincial towns was the inauguration of a statue of Louis XIV, paid for by the State, executed by the Versailles sculptors, and accepted by the king.

FIG. 492.—LE BRUN. HANGINGS REPRESENTING THE SEASONS. WINTER.
(*Photo. Fenaille.*)

FIG. 403.—FONTAINEBLEAU. TAPESTRIES OF THE ROYAL HOUSES. (*Photo. Fenaille.*)

They fell with the monarchy, and museums now shelter their crumbling remains.

Thus, in this period of unique effort, all the artistic energies of France were concentrated round the king. Such a crisis could not endure; but its consequences were infinite. True, the art of Louis XIV did not produce any of those masterpieces which appeal beyond the limits of a nation and an epoch to humanity at large. This was the price this official art had to pay. The king had not the leisure to wait. And yet Colbert's gigantic effort was not in vain. At the close of the seventeenth century, French artists were very much better craftsmen than their predecessors. There were admirable painters among the portraitists of the king as an old man; his childish portraits had been contemptible as works of art. The charm of execution, formerly confined to a Flemish or Italian work, was now to be found in the Paris of the seventeenth century. In the fine arts, as in other institutions, Colbert, working for the present, had prepared the future.

BIBLIOGRAPHY

P. Clément, *Lettres, instructions et mémoires de Colbert,* Paris, 1868-1871, 7 vols.—Ch. Perrault, —*Mémoires,* Avignon, 1759.—J.-J. Guiffrey, *Comptes des bâtiments du Roi sous le règne de Louis XIV,* Paris, 1881-1901, 5 vols.; *Inventaire général du mobilier de la Couronne sous Louis XIV,* Paris, 1885, 2 vols.—A. de Montaiglon, *Procès-verbaux de l'Académie royale...* (1648-1792), Paris, 1875 *et seq.*—H. Jouin, *Conférences de l'Académie royale...,* Paris, 1883.—A. Fontaine, *Conférences inédites de l'Académie royale...,* Paris, n. d.—H. Testelin, *Sentiments des plus habiles peintres...,* Paris, 1696.—Alph. Dufresnoy, *L'Art de peinture,* translated... with notes, Paris, 1668.—A. Fontaine, *Les Doctrines d'Art en France, De Poussin à Diderot,* Paris, 1908.— Chantelou, *Journal de Voyage du cavalier Bernin en France...,* Paris, 1885.—Bertolotti, *Objets. d'art transportés de Rome en France* (*N. A. A. F.,* 1880); *Correspondance des Directeurs ae l'Académie de France à Rome...,* Paris, 1887-1906.—Comte Franchi-Verney della Valetta, *L'Académie de France à Rome,* 1666-1903, Turin, 1903.—Lecoy de la Marche, *L'Académie de France à Rome,* Paris, 1878.—E. Bourgeois, *Le Grand Siècle,* Paris, 1896.—A. Genevay, *Le Style Louis XIV,* Paris, 1886.—A. Félibien, *Description des divers ouvrages de peintures faits pour le Roi,* Paris, 1671.—H. Jouin, *Charles Le Brun et les Arts sous Louis XIV,* Paris, 1889.— L. Hourticq, *L'Art académique* (*Revue de Paris,* 1904).—P. Marcel, *Charles Le Brun,* Paris, 1909.—Ch. Lhuillier, *Le Peintre Claude Lefebvre* (*R. S. B. A. D.,* 1892).—Ch. Ponsonailhe, *Jean Zueil..., Samuel Boissière* (on a school of painting at Montpellier) (*R. S. B. A. D.,* 1904). —Abbé de Monville, *La Vie de Pierre Mignard,* Paris, 1730.—St.-Lami, *Dictionnaire des Sculpteurs français sous la règne de Louis XIV,* Paris, 1906.—P. Auquier, *Puget,* Paris, Sd.— Fermelhuis, *Eloge de Coysevox,* Paris, 1721.—H. Jouin, *Ant. Coyzevox,* Paris, 1883.—Cl. Perrau

THE MONARCHICAL ART OF LOUIS XIV

Les dix livres d'Architecture de Vitruve corrigés et traduits, Paris, 1684.—L. Dussieux, *Le Château de Versailles,* Versailles, 1881, 2 vols.—Gille and M. Lambert, *Versailles et les deux Trianons,* 2 vols., Paris, 1900.—L. Pératé, *Versailles,* Paris, 1904.—A. Bertrand, *Versailles,* Paris, 1906.—P. de Nolhac, *Le Versailles de Mansart* (*G. B. A.,* 1902) : *La Décoration de Versailles au XVIIe siècle* (*G. B. A.,* 1895, II); *l'Art de Versailles, l'Escalier des Ambassadeurs* (*R. A. A. M.,* 1900); *l'Art de Versailles, la Galerie des Glaces* (*R. A. A. M.,* 1903). —L.-A. Barbet, *Les grandes eaux de Versailles,* Paris, 1907. Two periodicals are devoted to the history of Versailles : *Versailles illustré* and the *Revue de l'Histoire de Versailles.*—De Boislisle, *La Place des Victoires et la place Vendôme...* (*Mém. de la Société de l'Histoire de Paris,* 1888).—A de Champeaux, *Le Meuble,* 2 vols., Paris, 1885-1901.—E. Molinier, *Le Mobilier au XVIIe et au XVIIIe siècle,* Paris, 1899; *Le Mobilier français au Musée du Louvre,* Paris, 1903.—H. Havard, *Les Boulle,* Paris, 1893.—J. Guiffrey, *Les Caffieri, sculpteurs et fondeurs-ciseleurs,* Paris, 1877; *Les Gobelins et Beauvais,* Paris, n. d.—Gerspach, *Répertoire détaillé des Tapisseries des 'Gobelins...,* Paris, 1893.—M. Fenaille, *Etat Général des Tapisseries de la Manufacture des Gobelins,* Paris, 1904-1909 (2 vols. published).

CHAPTER IV

THE END OF LOUIS XIV'S REIGN, AND PARIS UNDER THE REGENCY

Art in Paris: Artists in the City.—Transformation of Domestic Architecture and its Decoration; the Rococo Style.—Religious Architecture.—Sculpture.—Painting; Transformation of the Decorative Style from Le Brun to Le Moyne.—The Influence of Rubens; Desportes, Rigaud and Largillière.—Watteau; Flemish Technique and Parisian Poetry.—His Imitators.

THE prolonged old age of Louis XIV, the frequent intervals of court mourning, even the reverses of the monarchy did not tend to give a gloomy cast to the temper of French artists. Architecture, sculpture and painting escaped the melancholy that brooded over the last years of the reign. The disappearance of the king caused no break in the continuity of the intellectual history of France; it was responsible, perhaps, for an outbreak of libertinage; but the brilliant fantasy of French painters found expression before this. The work of Watteau, the most perfect manifestation of the Regency spirit, was almost finished when Louis XIV died. For a long time, ever since the death of Colbert, in fact, French art had ceased to belong to the king. Contemplating the long-drawn setting of the sun at Versailles, men took no heed of the dawn in Paris.

During those very years which weighed so heavily on the Court, the nervous vivacity of the eighteenth century had already taken possession of the soul of the city.

In the middle of the seventeenth century, Paris already had a considerable number of collectors of pictures and precious objects. These connoisseurs formed a society of their own, at which men of the world were inclined to laugh a

FIG. 495.—ROBERT LE LORRAIN.
HIGH RELIEF ON THE HÔTEL DE ROHAN,
NOW THE IMPRIMERIE NATIONALE.
(*Photo. Neurdein.*)

little. The amateurs of painting multiplied very rapidly, and though they were not all rich enough to be collectors, they formed a very cultivated circle, ready to admire or to criticise. When the royal Mæcenas ceased to employ artists, private patrons were ready to give them commissions, and a numerous public was eager to interest itself in their works. The "good society" of the city had succeeded the world of the court. The picture-exhibitions brought it together. Art could no longer live on abstract and purely academic doctrines; it had become necessary to give pleasure, and

FIGS. 496 AND 497.—GUILLAUME COUSTOU. THE HORSES OF MARLY,
PLACE DE LA CONCORDE, PARIS.

FIG. 408.—COUSTOU THE YOUNGER.
TOMB OF THE DAUPHIN.
(Cathedral of Sens.)
(*Photo. Neurdein.*)

if Le Brun's theories were still repeated, they were applied less and less. The best pupils of the school very soon cast off their scholastic pedantry. The high moral position formerly claimed by the founders of the Academy was freely accorded to them. Most of them belonged to the best society, and took part in the fashionable life of their time. The portraits of themselves painted by these artists show them indeed at their easels, but in flowing wigs and elegant costumes. One hand holds the palette or the modelling-tool, the other gesticulates to emphasise some lively speech. The faces are amiable and intelligent; they solicit approval smilingly. The absent, reflective countenances of Philippe de Champaigne and Poussin look morose among these loquacious artists. One of them, Antoine Coypel, was even an author; there was an incipient Boileau in him who versified the poetics of painting. These literary painters translated the ideas of Virgil and Racine into pictures rather too brilliantly. The well-read society of the day sought in history-painting the same intellectual pleasure they demanded from literature.

At the end of Louis XIV's reign, there was therefore a "School of Paris." It was not of the same nature as those of Italy and Flanders during the Middle Ages and the Renaissance; it depended less on studio-traditions than on the moral solidarity of society in general. Its characteristic style is also more difficult to define; the elements are

FIG. 409.—JOUVENET.
DESCENT FROM THE CROSS.
(The Louvre, Paris.)

240

sometimes incongruous, for the most diverse techniques and temperaments were accepted by French taste; transformations were rapid, because a subtle and attentive public soon wearies; yet there was a certain continuity in successive fashions and a certain unity in the variations of individuals.

FIG. 500.—DE LA FOSSE.
THE METAMORPHOSES HANGINGS.
RETURN OF DIANA FROM THE CHASE.
(*Photo. Fenaille.*)

Academic principles had no longer sufficient authority to enforce respect from a society which had a horror of boredom. While Louis XIV was seeking diversion from the majesty of Versailles at Marly or Trianon, and asking his artists to be gay and amiable, nobles and citizens were building themselves houses arranged with great ingenuity and decorated with elegance, to serve as the background for their fashionable existence. The transformation of furniture shows how intelligently craftsmen appreciated the taste of the day and the requirements of comfort; chairs, tables and bureaux take forms in which grace and utility are happily combined; the backs and arms of chairs are inflected to support the human body, the ingenious seats contrived at this period seem to have retained the very attitudes of conversationalists. The cabinet-maker associated himself with the worker in metals to produce solid tables with a nervous grace of outline; he collaborated with the upholsterer to make comfortable seats; the curved forms and delicate lines of the furniture passed into the decoration of the apartments. The architecture of pilasters, columns, attic storeys and entablatures made

FIG. 501.—ANTOINE COYPEL.
ESTHER AND AHASUERUS.
(The Louvre, Paris.)

R

FIG. 502.—CHARLES-ANTOINE COYPEL. PERSEUS
RESCUING ANDROMEDA.
(The Louvre, Paris.)

way for joinery; marbles and heavy stuccoes were replaced by wooden panels painted in delicate colours and relieved by slight gilded mouldings curved at the angles, and expanding here and there into rococo foliation. Whereas Le Brun and Lepautre had accumulated decorative motives untiringly, Robert de Cotte, Oppenord, and Boffrand were quite content to leave ceilings and walls luminously bare, and to increase the light that entered through their larger windows, they placed high mirrors over the chimney-pieces. Stone followed the example of wood, and masonry was subjected to the same convolutions as furniture. Great houses such as the Hôtel de Soubise retained a classic majesty on the ex-

FIG. 503.—JOUVENET. RESURRECTION OF
LAZARUS.
(The Louvre, Paris.)

terior, which does not always prepare us for the amenity of the internal decoration; but the simpler houses seem to be exerting themselves to please the approaching guest; the doors have often some slight rococo touches, and gracefully twisted iron balconies gave a sort of smiling cheerfulness to façades at a small expense.

FIG. 504.—LE MOYNE. OLYMPUS. CEILING
DECORATION.
(The Louvre, Paris.)

Even religious architecture accepted this lively style. The nave of Saint Louis-en-l'Île is decorated like a drawing-room. Meissonier proposed to give the Church of Saint Sulpice a façade in which the entablatures and classical capitals were to undulate like his rococo pieces of plate. It was not executed;

FIG. 505.—DE LA FOSSE. TRIUMPH OF BACCHUS.
(The Louvre, Paris.)

but the architects of the day did not always see that it was absurd, in building, to adopt the forms of carved woodwork, engraved metal, or

FIG. 506.—F.-J. DE TROY.
THE OYSTER FEAST.
(Condé Museum, Chantilly.)

moulded pottery. The chapel at Versailles is a good example of the limits within which it is permissible to enliven the Jesuit style without making it absolutely profane. Versailles was not, like the Escurial, a king's monastery, a palace built round a church. It was a country-house, enlarged to contain the Court and the executive of the sovereign. But a place had

FIG. 507.—LE MOYNE.
HERCULES AND OMPHALE.
(The Louvre, Paris.)

FIG. 508.—SANTERRE.
SUSANNA AT THE BATH.
(The Louvre, Paris.)

never had church decoration
shown such profane gaiety as
Coypel's paintings in the vault.
The apartments have nothing to

FIG. 510.—RAOUX. MADAME BOUCHER
AS A VESTAL.
(Museum of Versailles.)

also to be found for God. The
church built by Mansart and
Robert de Cotte, was connected
with the palace, to enable Louis
XIV to enter it from the level of
his apartments. Architecture, like
all the other arts, was unaffected
by the melancholy of the monarch.
Never had the Jesuit style achieved
such a degree of worldly elegance;

FIG. 509.—RAOUX. VESTAL.
(Museum of Montpellier.)

compare with them in cheerfulness.
At Versailles, God was served after
the king; but He was lodged more
agreeably (Fig. 483).

The same elegance characterises the sculpture of the period.
Artists had profited by the great
decorative effort made at Versailles.
The works of the seventeenth
century after Coysevox and Girardon, all display a dexterity of
execution, a sleight of hand which
were sometimes lacking among the

honest craftsmen of the early Versailles. A pupil of Girardon, Robert le Lorrain, has left us a charming example of decorative sculpture. In his famous group of horses at a drinking trough, over a former stable door of the Hôtel de Rohan, he has translated the airy vivacity of painting into stone with admirable skill (Fig. 495). Coysevox was continued in the work

FIG. 511.—CHARLES-ANTOINE COYPEL.
DON QUIXOTE TAPESTRIES. THE BALL.
(*Photo. Fenaille.*)

of his pupils, the brothers Nicolas and Guillaume Coustou. The latter in particular assimilated the trenchant precision of his master. The horses of Marly express a vigorous vitality in forms carved by a graceful chisel. The line is sharp and nervous; from this time forth sculpture, even when it aims at rhetorical pomp, will not allow brilliant and incisive detail to be lost in commonplace rotundities (Figs. 496, 497).

FIG. 512.—CHARLES-ANTOINE
COYPEL. DON QUIXOTE TAPESTRIES.
THE ENTRY OF THE SHEPHERDESSES.
(*Photo. Fenaille.*)

Painters were obliged to conform to the exigencies of the new style of decoration. The lightness of fashionable rooms put an end to the shadows of Bolognese painting. The panels between the white woodwork and the mirrors had also to radiate light. When they were painted, they imitated the lightness and transparence of the sky. The gilded bosses and carvings which hung heavily over the Louis XIV galleries all disappeared, and blue skies and clouds with fluttering figures replaced them. Decorative painters, the pupils of Le Brun, already showed skill in giving movement to figures at a height, in the vault of the Invalides

Church. The best of these artists was Jean Jouvenet (1644-1717), who, in the Norman group, represents the School of Rouen, as the Restouts represent the School of Caen. He was a painter, who, in spite of his powerful imagination, had adopted the healthy habit of painting always from nature; he showed much facility in the creation of robust compositions full of dramatic force. Not many French painters have been so successful in giving vitality to the corpse-bearers of the Descent from the Cross or the fishermen of the Miraculous Draught of Fishes, and in combining vigorous gestures for a common effort. In some instances, we might almost mistake him for Rubens, if his colour were purer and clearer (Figs. 499, 503).

It was only in the works of Le Brun's successors, Charles de la Fosse, and afterwards Le Moyne, that the human figure moves with the supple elegance Correggio had first realised, half sportively (Figs. 500, 505). Academic teaching had created a reposeful type, somewhat heavy in its correctness. Fashionable French decorators soon adapted it for good society. Faces lost the cold regularity they had inherited from Apollo and Niobe; noses less straight, modelling less rounded, eyes alert enough to suggest a constant vivacity of thought, were followed by joints gallantly supple, delicate articulations, incisive modelling, the twisted draperies and broken folds which suggest flexible bodies; even when figures are in repose neither faces nor draperies are immobile; and the supple limbs always seem ready for decorative gambols on a ceiling. This nervous trepidation of forms, so characteristic of the temper of French art, persisted until the time of David, when a sculpturesque style

FIG. 513.—CLAUDE AUDRAN.
TAPESTRY GROTESQUES.
THE MONTHS, JULY AND
AUGUST. (*Photo. Fenaille.*)

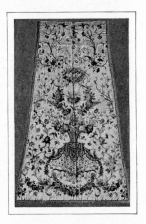

FIG. 514.—EIGHTEENTH CENTURY
EMBROIDERY.
(Musée des Arts décoratifs, Paris.)

246

imposed immobility even on the most furious gestures.

In the historical pictures, sacred or profane, of Coypel and De Troy, we recognise the divinities of Poussin and the heroes of Le Brun, costumed like the short-breeched centurions of the Trajan column, and even the psychological and historical intentions dear to the Academy; but these figures have now manners of draping and posing themselves learnt in drawing-rooms and on the stage. The personages of historical painting have laid aside their scholastic air and adopted the manners of fashionable

FIG. 515.—TOURNIÈRES. A MAGISTRATE.
(Museum of Caen.)

society. In Antoine Coypel's *Æneid* in the Palais Royal, contemporaries recognised many a court lady. Even religious painting was adapted to the taste of the day, and Santerre's *Susanna* leaves us in doubt as to whether the author most admired the grace of antique Venuses or the seductions of his Parisian models (Fig. 508).

FIG. 516.—LARGILLIÈRE.
PORTRAIT OF A MAGISTRATE.
(The Louvre, Paris.)

Le Sueur's female Saints had already shown something of this fragile grace; it had made their lachrymose piety all the more touching. But, at the dawn of the eighteenth century, feminine faces no longer imperilled their dainty beauty by the violence of passion. Many fascinating actresses had learnt how to regulate the play of attitude and physiognomy, into which the Academy had put so much meaning, in such a manner as to leave their beauty unimpaired. More than one painter like Jean Raoux, aspired to be considered a painter of history, when he had done no more than give a supple cast to

FIG. 517.—RIGAUD.
PORTRAIT OF J.-F.-P. DE CRÉQUI WHEN A CHILD.
(The Louvre, Paris.)

FIG. 518.—RIGAUD. MARQUIS DE
DANGEAU.
(Museum of Versailles.)

silken robes, and a touch of sharpness to the soft features of pretty faces (Figs. 509, 510).

These amiable successors of Le Brun had soon to reckon with a new conception of painting from Flanders, which found ready acceptance. The Academy had extracted its æsthetics from

FIG. 519.—RIGAUD. GASPARD DE GUEYDAN
PLAYING THE BAGPIPES.
(Museum of Aix.)

FIG. 520.—LARGILLIÈRE.
PORTRAIT OF MME. DE GUEYDAN
(Museum of Aix.)

the work of Poussin; but this work, excellent as an intellectual education, could not make a skilful craftsman. French decorators, the while they discoursed on Poussin's pyschology, were obliged, for the most part, to seek inspiration from other models. These they sought first in Italy, among the Bolognese. Caravaggio's sombre painting invaded the decorations of the seventeenth century. It was only the brilliance of Rubens which dissipated the smoky shadows of Bologna. Even in the time of Le Brun, there had been enthusiastic "Rubenists" who had rebelled against the propositions of the academic dogma. The freshness and vivacity of Rubens' colour made many amateurs and painters feel the in-

FIG. 521.—RIGAUD. PORTRAIT OF BOSSUET.
(The Louvre, Paris.)

adequacy of "Poussinism." At the same time, Van der Meulen brought some of the finest qualities of the Flemings to the workshops of the Gobelins manufactory. But the art-world was too much occupied with moral expression and fine drawing to note the limpid illumination of his landscapes, and the picturesque charm of his accessories. Humble Flemings painted animals, flowers, and fruits in cartoons for tapestries, without any idea that their technique contained the germs of revolt against the aesthetics of the painter-in-

ordinary. When the decorative work of the Gobelins and of Versailles was abandoned, all these minor talents were set at liberty, and thenceforth displayed their skill in small genre pictures. Amateurs bought these readily for their galleries. Collectors are not necessarily theorists. They do not admire by deductive reason; they buy the things that please them.

FIG. 522.—LARGILLIÈRE. PORTRAIT OF THE ARTIST, HIS WIFE, AND DAUGHTER.
(The Louvre, Paris.)

FIG. 523.—FRANÇOIS DESPORTES,
BY HIMSELF.
(The Louvre, Paris.)

Those little masters whose manual dexterity is their chief asset have always had their suffrages.

Desportes (1661–1743) was a pupil and successor of the Flemings. His still-life pieces of vegetables, fruit, and game, and his pictures of animals, have much of the vigour and vivacity of Snyders, though these qualities have taken on a sedater tinge, as beseems a historiographer of the royal kennels. Together with the dog and the game, he sometimes painted the sportsman (Figs. 523, 524).

Certain portraitists, again, are among the finest painters of the French school, for they spoke that vivid and exact speech which Rubens had used some half century earlier; Hyacinthe Rigaud (1659–1743), because he copied Van Dyck assiduously; Nicolas Largillière, because he was brought up in Antwerp. They translated the characteristics of physical life into painting. Rubens had shown them that pigment might become flesh and blood. Vouet, Poussin, and Le Brun had scorned to show the dry, harsh skin of a thin face, the pearly epidermis of a fair complexion. Largillière's and Rigaud's portraits are, above all things, alive.

Rigaud painted with firm touches and frank colour; the vigour of his sitters seems due, to some extent, to the solidity of his technique. His brush is nervous, subtle, and incisive; it indicates a bony face, the cartilages of the nose, the joints of the fingers, and the creases of satin, in clearly defined planes. Rounded contours, which are always banal, are relieved by this

FIG. 524.—DESPORTES. PORTRAIT OF
A HUNTER.
(The Louvre, Paris.)

clean-cut modelling; the face is sharpened by it, and intellectualised, so that we note the fire of the eye, and the animation of all the features; take away the wig, and there is an animated mask, sparkling eyes, an intelligent mouth, a face as eloquent as a pastel by La Tour, or a bust by Houdon. Even amidst the profusion of

FIG. 525.—WATTEAU. PAGE IN AN ALBUM.
(The Louvre, Paris.)

heavy hangings, tapestries, gold and silver plate, and embroidered mantles, there is always a vigorously modelled face, which dominates the tumultuous splendour. It is Rigaud's rendering that has realised the majesty of Louis XIV in his old age, and also the malicious faces of Boileau and La Fontaine, and the frank, robust countenance of Bossuet (Figs. 517-519, 521).

Largillière shows more tenderness, in spite of the vigour of his art; he loves to paint the delicate gradations of flesh, of fine stuffs, and of the atmosphere, the bluish reflections of a very fair skin, the changing lights in a satin drapery, or the gold of autumn dying away into mist. Sometimes even, a certain insipidity seems to herald Nattier's fatigued palette, for the eighteenth century was about to dilute the strong colours of Antwerp for its faintly tinted decoration. His brush has not the mordant quality, which, in Rigaud's works, sometimes gave as much firmness to the curls of a wig as to the convolutions of brass or gilded wood; it touched rounded forms more languidly; hence Largillière was a more successful painter of women than Rigaud; he gives a certain blue tone to his lights, and modifies his red reflections to produce an aristocratic pallor, so that even his *échevins*, and his magistrates in their robes show a sort of

FIG. 520.—WATTEAU. PAGE IN AN ALBUM.
(The Louvre, Paris.)

FIG. 527.—WATTEAU. L'INDIFFÉRENT.
(The Louvre, Paris.)

FIG. 528.—WATTEAU. GILLES.
(The Louvre, Paris.)

coquettish elegance, an almost feminine desire to please (Figs. 516, 520, 522).

At about the same time, François de Troy and many others sought to render the elegance of their age in the supple tongue of the Antwerp painters. But with most of them, gaiety and vivacity were blunted by the majesty of the past style, and preoccupation with "noble design."

FIG. 529.—LANCRET. THE ACTORS OF
THE ITALIAN THEATRE.
(The Louvre, Paris.)

FIG. 530.—PATER.
CONVERSATION IN A PARK.
(The Louvre, Paris.)

Watteau (1684–1721) came from Flanders to Paris, and gave the most subtle expression to the Parisian spirit. Had he remained in his native country, he would no doubt have continued the work of Teniers. Had he come twenty years earlier, he would, like Van der Meulen, have been enrolled among Le Brun's troop, and have painted Louis XIV's battles, hunting-parties, and fêtes.

FIG. 531.—WATTEAU. THE DANCE.
(Collection of the German Emperor.)
(*Photo. Berlin Photographic Society.*)

But in 1702, there was no longer an administrative organisation to fetter his independence. Gillot gave him lessons in the art of drawing brilliantly. The only law he recognised was that which bade him satisfy his own taste, and that of his friends. Amateurs had learned to appreciate delicacy of technique, by studying Teniers' little pictures.

There was a public ready to recognize and admire Watteau's exquisite dexterity. Even in Paris, the painter was able to continue his education in craftsmanship before the Rubenses in the Luxembourg, and the Venetians of the Crozat collection. Some reflections of these masters greet us in his little panels: the pearly freshness and

FIG. 532.—WATTEAU. RURAL PLEASURES.
(Collection of the German Emperor.)
(*Photo. Berlin Photographic Society.*)

the liquid splendour of Rubens, the warm russet tones of Titian, the silvery satins of Veronese; but the breadth of these robust geniuses has taken on a certain keenness; from the sanguine, lacteal Flemish material the master distilled a subtle elixir, from which the coarse odours of reality have been banished. Invented by exuberant naturalists, this language was applied by

FIG. 533.—WATTEAU.
THE EMBARKATION FOR CYTHERA.
(The Louvre, Paris.) (*Photo. Neurdein.*)

him to the interpretation of a refined society in its most factitious aspects, those of the fashionable world and the theatre. Watteau worked for operatic decorators, and his most delicate reveries seem to have been evoked by a graceful minuet in some fairy play. The actors he loved do not play the heroic parts of tragedy; they do not declaim pathetic sentiments in the midst of classic palaces; they sometimes wear the costumes of the actors of the Italian theatre, but more often dresses invented by the painter, and like those of his period, admirably designed to display the elegant ease of his little figures. The men are supple and impetuous, they stand erect on nervous, muscular legs, as ready to drop on their knees as to execute a pirouette; the sharp, eager faces of these cavaliers proclaim them as cunning and caressing as cats. The ladies meet their advances with no less dexterity, half consenting, half resisting. They look alert and vigilant, and their delicate heads, with the hair drawn up under their little caps, are as mobile as the heads of birds on their slender necks; their fans flutter incessantly, and among the folds of their silken dresses the light gleams and darts and glances, shifting in obedience to their dainty, rhythmic gestures. These vivacious attitudes, these glittering broken folds are relieved against the velvety shade of trees, or the faint blue of distant horizons. The sudden flashes of

FIG. 534.—WATTEAU. THE CONCERT.
(Collection of the German Emperor.)
(*Photo. Berlin Photographic Society.*)

the satin are subdued to some extent by the mystery of the landscape, as are the whisperings of lovers by the majestic silence of evening.

Watteau's little world is all his own. His operatic parks bear no resemblance to historical landscapes, and it is amazing to see how little his small figures have in common with those of the Academy:

FIG. 535.—LANCRET. THE FOUNTAIN OF PEGASUS.
(Collection of the German Emperor.)
(Photo. Berlin Photographic Society.)

they have neither expressive gestures, nor statuesque attitudes, nor any of the learned modellings after nature or antique examples; the painter prefers the play of light on silk, the curve of a well-formed leg, the inclination of a slender neck, all the charming gestures which mean nothing but a desire to please. For the abstract humanity of the French school, he substituted fanciful figures, but fanciful in the Flemish manner, and full of delicate observation.

In his *Embarkation for Cythera,* Watteau has brought together all the groups of lovers scattered throughout his works. The couples in this exquisite gathering show a certain hesitation; they set off not without delays and recalcitrances, but the incline is so gentle, and the example of others so alluring! In this work, Watteau did something more than summarise all the seductions of his nervous

FIG. 536.—LANCRET. THE PEEP-SHOW.
(Collection of the German Emperor.)
(Photo. Berlin Photographic Society.)

and caressing art. This poetic fancy is symbolical of his whole work; what more natural conclusion could there be to his innumerable "Conversations galantes" than this voyage to the island of love? The Paris of Versailles and the Regency must have seen something more than a graceful fantasy here. In that society, where men

FIG. 537.—LANCRET. MLLE. CAMARGO.
(Collection of the German Emperor.)
(*Photo. Berlin Photographic Society.*)

and women delighted in nothing so much as in essaying their weapons of seduction, this embarkation for Cythera showed the fundamental reason of all social relations.

But if the men of the eighteenth century greatly admired Watteau, it was nearly always a covert attachment they felt. In each of them there was a classical theorist, nourished on antiquities and psychology, and they could find nothing in their doctrine which was not hostile to their secret tenderness.

Watteau could not be really imitated save by Flemings not wholly Gallicised; he was copied by his compatriots, Lancret and Pater. They are easily distinguished from the other painters of *fetes galantes* and pastorals in the eighteenth century. Their landscapes, even when fanciful, achieve an effect of truth and a sense of reality. Their little figures are the work of painters who never attempted to model the forms of the human body; they make the light play over satin folds, lengthen their silhouettes, and sharpen their extremities to a ner-

FIG. 538.—LANCRET. WINTER.
(The Louvre, Paris.)

vous acuteness, and are amused by the grimaces of their shepherds and actors, just as Brueghel and Teniers were formerly delighted by the antics of their ragged boors.

THE END OF LOUIS XIV'S REIGN

BIBLIOGRAPHY

D'Argenville, *Abrégé de la vie des plus fameux peintres*, vol. IV, Paris, 1762.—Mariette, *Abecedario...*, Paris, 1851–1860, 6 vols.—J. Guiffrey, *Livrets des Expositions de peinture depuis 1673 jusqu'à 1800*, Paris, 1669–1875.—P. Marcel, *La Peinture française au début du XVIIIe siècle*, Paris, 1906.—C. Ponsonailhe, *Les deux Ranc* (*R. S. B. A. D.*, 1887).—F. Engerand, *Les Commandes officielles faites à Jean Restout* (*R.S.B.A.D.*, 1896).—A. Valabrègue, *Claude Gillot* (*G. B. A.*, 1899, I and II).—G. Duplessis, *Les Audran*, Paris, n.d.—E. and J. de Goncourt, *L'Art du XVIIIe siècle*, Paris, 1880–1883, 2 vols.—P. Mantz, *Watteau*, Paris, 1892.—P. Foucart, *Watteau à Valenciennes* (*R. S. B. A. D.*, 1892).—A. Rosenberg, *Watteau*, Bielefeld, 1896.—E. Hannover, *Watteau*, Berlin, 1889.—G. Séailles, *Watteau*, Paris, n.d.—L. de Fourcaud, *Watteau* (*R. A. A. M.*, 1901 and 1904).—P. Dorbec, *L'Exposition de la Jeunesse au XVIIIe siècle* (*G. B. A.*, 1905, I).—P. Foucart, *Antoine Pater* (*R. S. B. A. D.*, 1887).—M. Hénault, *Antoine Pater* (*R. S. B. A. D.*, 1899).—P. Mantz, *Largillière* (*G. B. A.*, 1893, II).—Lady Dilke, *Les Coustou* (*G. B. A.*, 1901, I).

FIG. 539.—THE PLACE DE LA CONCORDE, PARIS.

CHAPTER V

PARISIAN ART UNDER LOUIS XV AND LOUIS XVI

Artists and the Parisian Public.—The Part Played by the Monarchy.—History-painting and Decorative Painting.—Boucher: Amorous Mythology and Pastorals.—Book Illustration.—La Tour.—Nattier.—Chardin: Painter of Interiors and Still-life.—Greuze's Sentimental Painting.—Fragonard.—Joseph Vernet's and Hubert Robert's Landscapes.—Sculpture.—Bouchardon.—Pigalle and Falconet.—Sèvres China.—Pajou, Clodion, and the Caffieri.—Houdon.—Civil Architecture, the Classical and Rococo Styles.—Transformation of Paris, Gabriel.—Town Houses.—Transformation in Provincial Towns.—Religious Architecture.

THE institution of exhibitions of pictures and sculpture (Salons), and their steady success after their permanent establishment in 1737, show the growing interest taken by the Parisian world in the work of artists. Never, since it had parted company with religion to become the pastime of a cultured coterie, had art appealed to so wide a public, or found such extensive support in society. It may be that less painting was executed as decoration for princely galleries, but a great deal more found its way into private houses. The amateur was no longer necessarily an ostentatious financier or a fanatical collector of rarities; statues and pictures, preferably small in size and dainty in technique, were essential features of luxurious furnishing; and were designed to suit dining-room, drawing-room, and boudoir. The yearly exhibition of the Royal Academy tended to educate the public. A crowd of visitors were interested in these shows, who had no idea of becoming purchasers; among them were the critics, the theorists, and the large public invited to this Parisian entertainment. Works of art were no longer produced for the satisfaction of a few great patrons; they appeared in the midst of general expectation; artists were applauded or criticised; they breathed the exciting and somewhat factitious atmosphere which has become a necessity of life to modern art.

FIG. 540.—OUDRY. HUNTING SCENE UNDER LOUIS XV. TAPESTRY.
(*Photo. Fenaille.*)

The king was not indifferent to the fine arts; he made various alterations in the palace and park of Versailles; he even destroyed the famous Ambassadors' Staircase to arrange some apartments in the new taste; his council chamber at Fontainebleau was decorated with paintings by Boucher and Van Loo. After the Duc d'Antin, who re-established those relations between art and the State, which had become somewhat relaxed at the close of Louis XIV's reign, the successive comptrollers of the royal buildings, Tournehem, Marigny, and Angivillers, carried out their functions actively and

FIG. 541.—OUDRY. LOUIS XV HUNTING. TAPESTRY.
(*Photo. Fenaille.*)

intelligently, thanks to Colbert's institutions. The Beauvais factories never produced more charming tapestries than when they were directed by the painter J. B. Oudry (Fig. 540, 541) and the china of the royal factory of Sèvres was exquisitely characteristic of the Louis XV style. Marigny had revived an idea much in favour with former kings, who had often commissioned landscape-painters to depict the cities and castles of France. He caused Joseph Vernet to paint the principal French sea-ports, at the very time when the Seven Years War had drawn away all their

FIG. 542.—OLLIVIER. TEA-PARTY A L'ANGLAISE
AT PRINCE CONTI'S.
(The Louvre, Paris.)

ships. He even had dreams of turning art back again in the direction of classical severity. But government intervention was no longer capable of forming a style. Inspiration came now from the great public; an artist coveted the fame of Paris rather than that of Versailles. The king was merely a very rich patron. He demanded from Boucher and Fragonard, not, like Louis XIV, his glorification by mythological allusions, but, like the financial magnates, gay and gallant images to amuse his eye. When monarchical decoration abandoned the majestic style, it deprived the history-painters of their principal *raison d'être.* Yet they did not disappear, and they even showed a kind of artificial vitality again, when the State once more ordered their works and established museums to receive them.

The history-painters followed Le Moyne's example; they forgot the reverence with which the seventeenth century had approached the antique. Divine and heroic forms were elongated, twisted, and refined at the will of the painter, and draperies were elegantly crumpled or broken into silken reflections. The brush produced a nervous modelling, with sharply defined planes, seeking the angularities of form that break the folds of stuffs, and give definite contours in rounded limbs. Jean Restout, Subleyras, and Natoire practised in this manner with considerable skill, although certain pictures by Restout and some by Pierre Parrocel at Avignon, overstep the pardonable limits of insipidity;

FIG. 543.—BOUCHER. MADAME
DE POMPADOUR.
(Schlichting Collection.)

260

their Jesus is too blonde and curly-haired, and their saints are mere languishing actresses. Carle Van Loo was among the more gifted of these painters who excelled in making an agreeable decoration of any theme. Like the others, he set graceful figures among the clouds, and left us many charming pictures of Court life (Figs. 559, 561).

FIG. 544.—BOUCHER. THE TOILET OF VÉNUS.
(The Louvre, Paris.)

In the French School, this was a period of dexterity and facile vivacity; no trace of the heavy application of the first classical painters had survived. Something of Rubens' fire glowed in the decorative painters from La Fosse and Le Moyne onward; they had learnt in Marie de' Medici's gallery to colour daringly, to paint blonde nymphs with delicate bluish reflections in the light, and vermilion in the shadows. They refined Rubens, repudiating his over-carnal realism, subduing colours whose freshness and splendour they could not equal, and, finally, building up by sharp, staccato touches what the Fleming's brush had modelled softly and caressingly.

Boucher (1703–1770) was the painter who most frankly treated classical mythology as decorative material; for him it was hardly more than a pretext for rococo draperies and contours; and, as a

FIG. 545.—BOUCHER. VENUS, MERCURY AND LOVE.
(Collection of the German Emperor.)
(*Photo. Berlin Photographic Society.*)

result, he was the most popular painter of his day until the year 1760. In his work the style of his master Le Moyne was worked out to its logical conclusion. The proximity of Le Brun and the majesty of Versailles had imposed a certain gravity on Le Moyne's painting. But his figures were graceful, and his colours tender enough to take their places in the "little apartments" of Louis XV without detracting from the general gaiety of effect. Boucher

FIG. 546.—GRAVELOT.
DESIGN FOR HEADING OF A VOLUME.

was the outcome of Le Moyne, as Le Moyne had been the outcome of La Fosse, and with Boucher the transformation of serious history-painting into erotic decoration was complete.

Boucher further appealed to the taste of his time by his choice of themes. He does not appear to have always made up his mind to treat some definite subject; but under his brush, amorous conversations between some white-limbed goddess and some ruddy god seem to have materialised spontaneously, while all around chubby Cupids gambol on substantial woolly clouds. He knew and had studied Watteau, but he did not borrow the master's fanciful figures; he preferred rosy nudities to rustling silks. As he was a classical student, he recorded the loves of Olympus. Venus was his favourite divinity; she appears in his works, sleeping, waking, bathing, or in colloquy with Vulcan, Paris, or Anchises (Figs. 544, 545, 547); and even when his heroine is another, she is closely akin to Venus; she has the same white, plump, delicate body, the same sparkling face, the same dimpled contours. When they are draped, Boucher's figures are the shepherds and shepherdesses of pastoral romance; Lubin, kneeling by Annette, offers her flowers or birds, or teaches her to play the flute, for the painters of the day borrowed from the poets the pleasing convention, according to which shepherds pass their time in the agreeable occupation of love-making. In place of the convenient clouds that enfold the Olympians, Boucher gives his eclogues a setting of bluish verdure, of serrated foliage, of rococo ruins and be-ribboned sheep. In the centre of the

FIG. 547.—BOUCHER. DIANA AND NYMPH.
(The Louvre, Paris.)

panel, a strong light radiates from the body of a nymph or shepherd, and the painter cares little whether there are draperies or trees or clouds around it, provided the colours be caressing, like those of delicate and slightly faded fabrics. We should not be so ready to criticise their excessive sweetness, or their somewhat acid crudity, if we could see Boucher's paintings upon the softly-tinted panelling for which they were originally painted. Torn from their appropriate framework, these pictures, like all pictures in a museum, invite a careful examination never solicited by a decorator.

FIG. 548.—BAUDOIN. THE TOILET.
(Bibliothèque Nationale, Print Room.)

The admirable decorators of this period embellished everything they touched. Their lively figures, their linear fancies blossom in gold and silver plate, chased metalwork, china, tapestry, and engravings. The Flamboyant Style had flourished in its greatest luxuriance on the margins of illuminated manuscripts; the Rococo Style threw its graceful tendrils across the pages of the gravest folios. Without colour, by pure suppleness of line, the burins of Cochin, Gravelot, Gabriel de Saint-Aubin, Eisen, and Moreau the Younger reproduced plump carnations and glistening materials, and have left us the most lively records

FIG. 549.—LA TOUR. THE ABBÉ HURET.
(Museum of Saint-Quentin.)

of Parisian life in the eighteenth century. Worthless books were illustrated with engravings which are masterpieces; the most austere literature, as well as the freest, accepted these coquettish adjuncts. Boucher's broods of Cupids were numerous enough to swarm both here and in the treatises of astronomy and natural history. Science itself in those days

FIG. 550.—LA TOUR. PORTRAIT
OF THE ARTIST.
(Museum of Amiens.)

FIG. 551.—LA TOUR.
MLLE. FEL.
(Museum of Saint-Quentin.)

took on the fashionable tone, and spoke beguilingly to secure a
hearing; experiments in physics and chemistry became drawing-
room pastimes, and a passion for botany was confounded with a taste
for pastorals. Thus in the frontispieces of heavy tomes we find

FIG. 552.—LA TOUR. MARQUISE DE RUMILLY.
(Collection of J. Doucet.)

FIG. 553.—LA TOUR. PORTRAIT OF RESTOUT.
(Museum of Saint-Quentin.)

FIG. 554.—AVED.
MME. CROZAT.
(Museum of Montpellier.)

FIG. 555.—PERRONNEAU. MME. DE
SORQUAINVILLE.
(David Weil Collection.)

Cupids painting, chiselling, building, and wielding surgical instruments. In his morose old age, Louis XIV desired to see Versailles enlivened by groups of chubby children. French art did not forget his counsel. On the frontispiece of the *Encyclopœdia*, Cochin engraved with his most delicate burin a sort of gallant Olympus, in which plump, coquettish forms disport themselves among the clouds. Nor is this engraver wholly fanciful when he shows us some vast engine of war, installed and manipulated by pretty women and Cupids.

Painting has left us records of this society full of intense life. Rigaud's figures, in spite of their veracity, retained something of the grandeur of the "Great Century." The individual is clothed in his hierarchic dignities as in a majestic uniform. Between 1740 and 1760, portraitists were able to define typical personalities

FIG. 556.—DROUAIS.
MME. DE POMPADOUR.
(Museum of Orleans.)

FIG. 557.—NATTIER. MME.
DE CHATEAUROUX AS DAWN.
(Museum of Marseilles.)

more closely. In each Salon, the lively, eager faces of this society, in which aristocracy, finance, literature, science, art, and the theatre met, studied and entertained each other, re-appeared. All Paris—the "Tout Paris" of the hour—recognised itself in La Tour's pastels, and still survives in the Museum of Saint-Quentin, where the painter's "preparations" are preserved. La Tour (1704–1788) adopted as his medium that pastel which had shortly before been made fashionable by the Venetian, Rosalba Carriera. He was a neurotic, who delighted in this dry, sharp, rapid method, and who scorned the rich accessories with which nobles and burgesses of an earlier day loved to amplify their images. The light colours of the chalk, its vivacious hatchings, its contrasted lights, sufficed him for the revelation of a moral physiognomy. Some few rich farmers-general or Court functionaries still posed among the paraphernalia which served to emphasise their riches, their power, and the distinction of their tastes. But La Tour's real interest centred in the face; it was in the fire of the eye, and the nervous mobility of the mouth, that he sought and seized the life of the mind. His vision was not for calm faces, relaxed in the peaceful atmosphere of domesticity, but for such as were animated by the subtle fire of vivid colloquy. The heads he shows us are lively and alert, the facial muscles ready for speech or laughter, the features mobile, the intelligence behind them at attention. His personages are taken from various circles, the Court, the theatre, the salons of Mme. du Deffand and Mme. Geoffrin.

FIG. 558.—NATTIER. MME. HENRIETTE AS FLORA.
(Museum of Versailles.)

But in every case the individual asserts himself, liberated by his intelligence or his talent from the social hierarchy, and even from the social conventions which deaden personality. Hence La Tour's gallery of sitters shows extraordinary variety. The elegant and weary king, the proud financier, the mocking philosopher, and the whole range of theatrical women, from the careless, laughing girl to the fragile, dreamy Mlle. Fel, who gazed at him so tenderly. Many portraitists, it is true, have been greater painters; but neither Van Dyck, Hals, nor Holbein had penetrated so deeply into character; their sitters show a stronger family likeness. In spite

FIG. 559.—VAN LOO. LOUIS XV.
(Museum of Versailles.)

of the uniform rouge and the identical coiffure, La Tour noted the striking differences even in the faces of pretty women. He said of his sitters: "I plunge into their depths, and I bring them out whole" (Figs. 549–553). Perronneau's pastels, which are no less graceful

FIG. 560.—NATTIER. MME.
ADÉLAÏDE TATTING.
(Museum of Versailles.)

and dexterous, and perhaps even more delicate in colour, have not quite the same spiritual fire (Fig. 555). We must go to Houdon's terra-cottas for a continuation of La Tour's iconography.

La Tour's frankness of speech sometimes scandalised his aristocratic models, the Dauphin or the Pompadour; his vision penetrated the majestic decorum behind which the heir to the throne or the titular favourite lay concealed. Nattier (1685–1766), on the other hand, contemplated the princesses who sat to him with due respect. He was no indiscreet reader of character, and he was even willing to show his sitters not as they were, but as

267

FIG. 561.—VAN LOO. HALT OF SPORTSMEN.
(The Louvre, Paris.)

they wished to be. He conferred that fashionable elegance which every woman demands from her hairdresser and her dressmaker. For fashion, as we know, is a worker of miracles, and produces uniformity of features as well as of vesture. Nattier may be said to have fixed the type of the Louis XV style, and consequently, it is not always easy to distinguish among the innumerable "Daughters of France" whom he portrayed. A Nattier portrait characterises not an individual, but the collective type of a period: tender colours, a pink-cheeked face under a powdered wig, soft, rounded lines, a charming admixture of mythological dignity and fashionable amenity (Figs. 557, 558, 560). Tocqué, Roslin, and many others, who were not only painters but admirable costumiers, have depicted paniers, flowered satins and pretty faces, illuminated by an even and somewhat chilly light (Fig. 562).

At the end of the seventeenth century, artists had managed to reconcile Rubens' painting and classical art. The quiet influence of the little Dutch masters gave rise to a new kind of painting, innocent of any classical tendencies. The pictures of Metsu and Gerard Dou, which were greatly admired, showed how to give a familiar scene in a small space, how to please the eye by the faithful reproduction of ordinary objects, and to draw out their latent poetry, how to get values

FIG. 562.—TOCQUÉ. MARIA LECZINSKA
(The Louvre, Paris.)

of exteme delicacy by subtle gradations of colour, and how to treat common things with as much respect as the heroes of antiquity. The eighteenth century was accordingly familiar with the painting of still-life and of domestic scenes. Desportes and Oudry were, indeed, excellent painters, but somewhat after the manner of Snyders and Fyt, whose fish and game

FIG. 563.—CHARDIN. THE SILVER GOBLET.
(The Louvre, Paris.)

pieces suggest the orgies of some fabled Gargantua; their pictures combine sincerity and dexterity in a very masterly fashion, and their realism is occasionally relieved by touches of rhetoric.

But there is a style which is less brilliant and more delicate in its gradations; it is that of the Dutch masters, who by means of simple colours intermingled with light and shade, expressed the intimate sentiment of an interior, and the familiar mystery of its atmosphere.

FIG. 564.—CHARDIN. THE STONE-CUTTER.
(De Ganay Collection.)

These Dutch masters helped Chardin (1699–1779) to divine the poetry of small domestic objects. Like them, he was a modest craftsman, without any scholastic culture; he knew nothing of classical literature; he had seen no Roman ruins, and had never made drawings from the antique; his imagination, unencumbered by mythology, lay open to the suggestion of humble accessories and everyday figures. Nevertheless, he too had begun by painting still-life pieces of a somewhat ambitious character, aiming at effect, like Monnoyer's flowers or Desportes' game. But he

FIG. 565.—CHARDIN. THE INDUSTRIOUS
MOTHER.
(The Louvre, Paris.)

FIG. 566.—CHARDIN. GRACE BEFORE
MEAT.
(The Louvre, Paris.)

soon adopted a simpler tone to give eloquence to the plenishings of
the larder. No still-life painter has evoked their secret soul more
perfectly; the fruits and vegetables, the coppers and glasses of the
Dutchmen do not shine with a more solicitous cleanliness and a more
picturesque brilliance. Chardin's objects are not painted with so

FIG. 567.—CHARDIN. PORTRAIT OF THE
ARTIST.
(The Louvre, Paris.)

FIG. 568.—CHARDIN. MADAME
CHARDIN.
(The Louvre, Paris.)

delicate a brush, or such limpid colour; they seem to be reflected in a duller mirror; but they give a stronger sense of the silent intimacy and the diffused sympathy of their ambient atmosphere. When Chardin introduces figures into his little compositions, they hardly disturb the serene tranquillity of his interiors. He shows us the servant in the pantry, or the mistress in her bed-room. The surroundings he paints are those of the lower middle class to which he himself belonged; the master of

FIG. 569.—CHARDIN. THE LETTER.
(Emperor of Germany's Collection.)
(*Photo. Berlin Photographic Society.*)

the house never appears; to find him we should have to go out, and follow him to his work in counting-house, workshop, or street; no neighbours even penetrate into Chardin's interiors; the servant returning from market, the child preparing for school, are the only factors that suggest the outside world. How peaceful is the life behind these closed doors! The mistress of the house speaks and moves hardly more than her household utensils; persons accustomed to live together understand even each other's silences. The life with which Chardin endows them does not manifest itself in gesticulations and the play of physiognomy; it is suggested by natural and habitual gestures, and their whole train of thought is revealed in the direction of their gaze. The mother waits quietly until grace has been said before giving her child the plate of soup, and the child concentrates all its powers on the effort of remembering its prayer (Fig. 566). "The industrious mother" and her daughter gaze mutely at a piece of embroidery, deliberating as to the matching of some shade of wool (Fig. 565). "The house-

FIG. 570.—CHARDIN. THE HOUSE-WIFE.
(The Louvre, Paris.)

FIG. 571.—CHARDIN. BOY WITH A TEETOTUM.
(The Louvre, Paris.)

keeper" brushes the school-boy's hat angrily, and he sullenly waits to take it from her and be off. This same boy, when he is shut up to do his lessons, takes a teetotum from his pocket, and, "the world forgetting," sits absorbed in contemplation of his toy. Not one of these persons is conscious of being looked at; they are themselves in all simplicity, and have no more idea of posing than their furniture. A new language was required to record these scenes, so common in daily life, but so unfamiliar to French art, and Chardin in fact speaks a language invented by himself. His painting has nothing in common with any of the styles admired in his day; his method is that of an honest craftsman, who despises tinsel; his gowns have no brilliantly broken folds, and his furniture dispenses with rococo ornament; his colour is sober, and laid on by a quiet hand which fears to seem too easy; gliding peacefully over the surface, the brush has left fat contours on the coarse canvas; the creamy impasto softens angles, and gives that look of use characteristic of objects which have done good service; it does not aim at illusion, but it differentiates the substance of each thing represented, suggesting the dented surface of brass and copper vessels, the soft bloom of the peach, the rough skin of the pear, the polished red of the unripe apple, and the cracked glaze of an earthen pitcher; it lends pictorial interest to textures sacrificed by other painters, grey cloth, white linen, old wood; his well-woven tissue renders the peaceful continuity of light in an

FIG. 572.—GREUZE. THE BROKEN PITCHER.
(The Louvre, Paris.)

interior, gleaming on polished surfaces, dying away on dull ones, enclosed by the discreet shadows that steal along the walls.

The painters of the simple life who have shown themselves capable of redeeming its banality by their affectionate solicitude, have been rare in the French School, and indeed in all schools. Too often, the professors of realism show an excessive pleasure in their imitative skill. Teniers and Brouwer ridiculed their boors and drunkards. But on the other hand, Jean Fouquet in his miniatures, the Le Nains and Chardin, never seem bent on amusing or astonishing the spectator. The humble lives they have described are made all the more attractive by this sincerity; there is no resisting an art so thoroughly unpretentious. We cannot wonder that such painters should have been rare. Chardin said that an artist does not paint with colours, but with sentiment, the thing most difficult to teach. Painters who have tried to imitate Chardin have rarely resisted the temptation of being brilliant, like Jeaurat, or pathetic, like Greuze. Aved, the friend of Chardin, is the one artist who, in a portrait here and there, has caught something of his honest precision and of his kindly

FIG. 573.—GREUZE. THE MORNING PRAYER.
(Museum of Montpellier.)

humour (Fig. 556). But Chardin's art, like that of the Le Nains and of Fouquet, had no far-reaching influence. All three, in fact, were submerged in the three classical inundations which took place in France; these delicate plants disappeared under the flood which fertilises French soil periodically. Chardin was no more able to withstand it than the rest of his contemporaries, the brilliant, elegant and voluptuous spirits of the ancient régime. The middle classes of the Revolution were too much infatuated with the classical ideal to take pleasure in the peaceful images of the Third Estate under Louis XV.

An art unfailingly brilliant and witty is an incomplete and exciting diet; even fashionable society wearies of superficial distractions which stimulate sensibility but never satisfy it. In the midst of fancies that amuse, it feels the want of emotions which penetrate

FIG. 574.—GREUZE. THE VILLAGE BRIDE.
(The Louvre, Paris.)

more deeply. About 1760, painting of the Louis XV style, graceful and gallant decoration, no longer satisfied the public. In literature, sentimentality replaced the somewhat dry metaphysics of Marivaux; novelists and dramatists gave to the "sensitive man" the important part which had hitherto been divided between the young lover and the discursive uncle. The public which applauded La Chaussée's and Diderot's pathetic and didactic plays, acclaimed Greuze's lachrymose pictures with no less enthusiasm.

On his return from Rome, Greuze (1725–1805) accordingly began to work upon the sensi-

FIG. 575.—GREUZE. THE FATHER'S CURSE.
(The Louvre, Paris.)

FIG. 576.—GREUZE. THE SON'S PUNISHMENT.
(The Louvre, Paris.)

bilities of his contemporaries by the methods of melodrama. He depicted hapless and edifying virtue. The family whose history he related did not belong, like that of Chardin, to the Parisian lower middle class in which he himself lived. It was a rustic family—virtue at this period was the monopoly of the peasant. In Chardin's nothing ever happened, and a painter was therefore its fitting annalist; Greuze's, on the other hand, was a product of the novel and the drama, and this was why it appealed so strongly to Diderot. No one could resist the pathos, the pity, and the despair which breathe from *The Village Bride* (*L'Accordée du Village*), or *The*

FIG. 577.—FRAGONARD. CORESUS AND CALIRRHOË.
(The Louvre, Paris.)

Father's Curse (*La Malédiction paternelle*) (Figs. 574–576). But Greuze's sermons are wanting in discretion. When he paints filial affection, he shows us a mother half suffocated by the exuberant caresses of her children, and his paralytic grandfather, a helpless victim of the officious attentions of his progeny, must have succumbed at last to their devotion. Besides, he who speaks of virtue must do so with a singleness of mind as foreign to this unctuous preacher as to those moralists, at once complacent and indignant, who denounce vice eloquently, while gloating over its details. Greuze's best artistic quality, in fact, reveals itself in the demure prettiness of his young girls; when he shows them away from their

FIG. 578.—FRAGONARD. THE BATHERS.
(The Louvre, Paris.)

father—the tedious old man like Diderot—he lingers caressingly over their tearful eyes and crumpled linen; his colour, generally cold and flat, takes on some little animation to make the blood circulate in their fair flesh. He painted them so young and beautiful, that it would be hard to doubt their innocence (Figs. 572, 573). And yet these same infantile faces re-appear in the

FIG. 579.—FRAGONARD. TWO WOMEN
TALKING.
(The Louvre, Paris.)

female fauns of Fragonard and Clodion; the favourite model of these artists had a woman's body with a child's face. The age which Watteau had shipped to Cythera, was still lingering there on the eve of the Revolution. It was still gazing appreciatively at dimpled forms, when David suddenly gave it marble statues to contemplate.

Greuze's sentimentality had infected Fragonard (1732–1806), a charming painter, even more gifted than his master Boucher, who succeeded Boucher, as Mme. Du Barry succeeded Mme. de Pompadour. He lavished his talents more especially in minor works, sketches, washed drawings, studies in red chalk, dashed off with amazing vivacity. His brush played with a patch of light in a tangle of chiaroscuro, often without any very definite intention.

The French School had never produced so dexterous a craftsman. His facility might have tempted him to become a mere ingenious illustrator; but he was also an excellent painter, a master of subtle and exquisite colour, touching plump nudities with a vermilion glow after the manner of Rubens, or throwing interlaced forms into a tumult of grey clouds and pale foliage, a combination of languid colour and vague light which recalls some of Correggio's works. But Fragonard etherealised Rubens' vigour, and galvanised Correggio's languor with his nervous energy. Finally, he adopted the tone of the day, and his young lovers, after frolicking in barns

FIG. 580.—FRAGONARD. LE CHIFFRE
D'AMOUR.
(Wallace Collection, Hertford House.)
(*Photo. Spooner.*)

like Baudoin's couples, settled down to domestic happiness with a swarm of children.

This generation of men and women of sensibility, sympathetic readers of *La Nouvelle Héloïse*, loved to appear in appealing attitudes. Drouais, a successful disciple of Nattier, travestied little aristocrats as Savoyards. Madame Vigee-Lebrun had a prodigious success in the Court-world (Figs. 589, 591). She borrowed from Flemish painting the brilliance of colour by which she gave freshness of complexion and liquid softness of eyes and lips to her sitters. Marie Antoinette posed as the beloved mother surrounded by her children, while in Nattier's time no painter would have ventured to place Marie Leczinska in a family group among her innumerable daughters. Madame Vigee-Lebrun did not forget to paint herself and to show how she adored and was adored by her daughter. Her facile brush and tender colour have preserved images somewhat lacking in individuality, of those heroines of the emigration or the guillotine, who bared "necks white as the flesh of chickens" on the revolutionary scaffold.

FIG. 581.—MOREAU THE YOUNGER. THE ADIEU. ENGRAVING.
(Bibliothèque Nationale, Print Room.)

FIG. 582.—LAVREINCE. THE BILLET DOUX. ENGRAVING.
(Bibliothèque Nationale, Print Room.)

Literature helped this sentimental generation to discover a fresh source of emotion. Writers of fiction such as Rousseau and Bernardin de Saint-Pierre taught them that meditation rises to sublimity in the solitude of Nature, and that water, trees, storm and darkness seem to become animate, and to participate in our passions.

FIG. 583.—ROSLIN.   YOUNG GIRL.
(The Louvre, Paris.)

The society of the day accordingly craved for representations of ruins, waterfalls and shipwrecks. Landscape-painting became prodigiously popular. Certain painters attempted to fix the spectacles which inspired so much romantic reverie. But painting was unable to give the public the images it demanded; the eye of the diverting artists of the day could not contemplate Nature devoutly. Joseph Vernet (1714–1789) began with conscientious copies of Roman scenery, which he coloured from Nature, with somewhat chalky, but sincere, tints. He reproduced their picturesque aspects without poetry, without giving the banks of the Tiber that majesty which ennobles Poussin's compositions (Fig. 585). When he came to Paris, the public demanded storms, shipwrecks, and night effects from him. He was the first purveyor of Romanticism, which thenceforth proved an eager consumer of tempests and moonlight scenes. In spite of his sincere respect for truth, he reduced all these varied aspects to the conventional effects which were within the limited compass of the artists of his day, whose colour, though it was capable of rendering the vivid variations of rich stuffs, became languid and monotonous when it imitated the delicate harmonies of the open air. The poets were no more successful in producing a true impression; they thought too much of Virgil's landscapes, and they had only the insipid vocabulary of mock pastorals wherewith to express themselves. The series of French seaports painted by Joseph Vernet to M. de Marigny's order, are panoramas

FIG. 584.—MME. LABILLE-GUIARD
MME. ÉLISABETH.
(Museum of Versailles.)

which are certainly carefully drawn and ingeniously composed. But they seem very empty to us now, though Vernet did his utmost to make them attractive. This is because they lack the most essential element; they fail to

FIG. 585.—J. VERNET. VIEW OF THE BRIDGE AND CASTLE OF ST. ANGELO, ROME.
(The Louvre, Paris.)

suggest those differences of light and atmosphere which give local character. In Provence, Saintonge and Brittany, Vernet saw the same light of the same dull colour; he made no distinction between the Mediterranean and the Ocean, the Azure and the Emerald Coasts.

Hubert Robert's colour (1733–1808) is gayer, because it is more fanciful. "He painted a picture as quickly as he wrote a letter." He was the virtuoso of ruins. His manner was novel in France, but in Italy Piranesi and Panini delighted in the picturesqueness of old and crumbling walls, and long before them, Salvator Rosa had painted jagged rocks which looked as if they had been hewn out by an explosion. Hubert Robert trifled with the noble ruins of Rome and Provence; his pictures suggest no melancholy broodings over tombs. His eye was pleased by broken columns, shattered cornices, crumbling, moss-grown masonry, and the Italian vagabonds who

FIG. 586.—HUBERT ROBERT. THE PONT DU GARD.
(The Louvre, Paris.)

swarm in their picturesque rags among these venerable stones. His compositions, in which the most famous Roman ruins, temples, thermæ, and aqueducts (Figs. 586–588) are grouped capriciously like the flowers in a bouquet, are brilliant fantasias, at once absurd and charming. A cheerful light touches the ancient masonry with rose and gold, and throws transparent patches on fluted marble and decrepit walls. Hubert Robert shows the same vivacity in depicting those Chinese or English gardens, where

FIG. 587.—HUBERT ROBERT.
THE TRANSFORMATION OF THE PARK OF VERSAILLES
UNDER LOUIS XVI.
(Museum of Versailles.)

trees, paths, streams and rocks are mingled in artificial profusion to astonish the visitor. He made models for landscape gardeners. Just as Louis XV had introduced gay little apartments among the vast saloons of Versailles, so, in the geometrical park, did Louis XVI cause Hubert Robert to instal a few rustic grottoes and groups of various trees; poplars rise boldly into the air, side by side with weeping willows overhanging some still pool.

Vernet's storms and Robert's ruins attempted to quench that thirst for Nature which men were feeling; but they had to wait for a long time yet before painters could draw a sincere and profound poetry from the spectacle of light and plants; and for this task, the piety and careful scrutiny of a humble soul were required, and not the devices of a brilliant decorator. Some few painters were already rambling on the banks of the Seine or in the forest of Fontainebleau, as solicitous for truth as the Dutchmen. In certain simple works by Moreau and one or two unknown contemporaries, there is something of the soft, mild radiance that hovered over Rousseau's chastened and pacified old age, and his solitary reveries. But before we find the river or the forest in the works of their successors, we must go back for a time, under David's guidance, to the museum of antiquities.

The statuary of the eighteenth century had no need to escape from the bonds of classical tradition before it could please the fashionable taste of the day. Sculptors, although by no means

FIG. 588.—HUBERT ROBERT.
THE MAISON CARRÉE, NÎMES.
(The Louvre, Paris.)

280

impervious to the brilliant elegance which had become the characteristic of Parisian art, had never quite forgotten the majestic Olympus of Le Brun and Girardon. Sculpture is less susceptible to the caprices of fashion than painting, because it tends to respond less and less to any requirement of modern life. In the thirteenth century, it gave a human aspect to God and the saints; a

FIG. 580.—MME. VIGÉE-LEBRUN.
MARIE-ANTOINETTE AND HER CHILDREN.
(Museum of Versailles.)

little later, it laid portrait-statues on the slabs of tombs. Then the monarchy had peopled its parks with mythological forms, and set

FIG. 590.—DROUAIS. PORTRAIT OF THE
COMTE D'ARTOIS AND HIS SISTER.
(The Louvre, Paris.)

up the effigies of kings in the public squares. In the eighteenth century, not one of these customs was sufficiently dominant to govern sculpture and determine its style; but, on the other hand, none had completely disappeared, and the same sculptors were employed, as occasion arose, in representing the Virgin, a bathing girl, and

FIG. 591.—MME. VIGÉE-LEBRUN. MME.
VIGÉE-LEBRUN AND HER DAUGHTER.
(The Louvre, Paris.)

FIG. 592.—BOUCHARDON.
CUPID.
(The Louvre, Paris.)

Louis XV. Moreover, the sculptor, like the history-painter, works for the most part without any definite object. His immediate aim is to exhibit his work to the public at the next Salon. The majority of the statues which are thus produced each year are not the result of any collective want; they appeal to the generosity of collectors and of the State.

Being thus less susceptible than painting to the influences of fashionable life, sculpture has retained a larger measure of respect for academic traditions. There is a more obvious continuity of style in its productions, and among sculptors we do not find that diversity which at this period began to make a picture exhibition a very varied entertainment. The statuaries of the eighteenth century, in spite of differences of temperament or method, had a common ideal of beauty. Their type is very similar to that which was evolved in decorative painting from Le Brun to La Fosse, and later from Le Moyne to Boucher, a type which persisted even in the lively nymphs of Fragonard. In sculpture, as in painting, the race of heroes had become less robust; figures were longer and more flexible, and draperies more suggestive of rustling silks.

There was even, in the first part of the century, a sculpture of involved forms and intricate modelling, derived from rococo decoration. The Adams and Michel-Ange Slodtz got their agitated style from Italy; it owed its origin to Correggio, and had been glorified by Bernini. It is comprehensible, and even excusable, in religious statuary, with its ecclesiastical costumes and the heavy draperies a tempest could barely ruffle. The numerous statues of these men are, moreover, never devoid of artistic qualities; but more dexterous than sincere, they never

FIG. 593.—GUILLAUME
COUSTOU. MARIA LECZINSKA.
(The Louvre, Paris.)

dreamed that an excess of skill might injure their expressive power, and that posterity would admire some measure of intelligent amenity in works they intended to be eloquent and inspired. These descendants of Correggio and Bernini peopled the Jesuit chapels with agitated figures, and arranged a graceful disorder of fluttering robes over their altars. It was considered the acme of ecclesiastical luxury to crown the high altar with one of those explosive "glories" which project gilded rays on puffy clouds enlivened by plump cherub-heads.

FIG. 594.—PIGALLE. TOMB OF MARSHAL SAXE. TEMPLE SAINT-THOMAS, STRASBURG.
(*New Photographic Society A. G, Berlin.*)

Le Moyne resisted the tendency to some extent, though he occasionally succumbed to the temptation of showing his freedom and facility. Bouchardon (1698–1762), on the other hand, replied to this brilliant and mannered art by a somewhat over-emphatic simplicity. It was he who executed the bronze Louis XV for Gabriel's "Place"; the group bore a strong resemblance to that of Louis XIV by Girardon; but the king was easier and more elegant, and the horse a more nervous and highly-bred beast; Coustou had abolished the heavy chargers of Le Brun and Van der Meulen. Bouchardon had a superstitious reverence for the ancients, like his friend and patron, the Comte de Caylus. His careful studies of their polished marbles had given him a horror of the abrupt and intricate manner of the Adams, and even of Coustou's sharply-defined modelling. But he was not always in intellectual

FIG 595.—PIGALLE. TOMB OF MARSHAL D'HARCOURT.
(Notre-Dame, Paris.)

FIG. 590.—FALCONET.
PYGMALION AND THE STATUE.
FROM THE SÈVRES GROUP.

sympathy with his age; and when he exhibited a Cupid cutting himself a bow out of the club of Hercules, his contemporaries wondered that he had preferred the slender, elastic grace of adolescence to the soft plumpness of the Cupid dear to the painters of the day (Fig. 592). This cold admirer of the ancients linked the period of Le Brun to that of David, passing a little above the heads of his contemporaries.

The younger generation, that of Pigalle (1714–1785) and Falconet (1716–1791), was more thorough than the Adams and less cold than Bouchardon. They showed admirable skill in depicting alert figures in charming attitudes of arrested movement. Pigalle's Mercury stops to fasten his sandal with all the lightness of a body ready to bound forward and used to flying. Graceful and brilliant as was his art, Pigalle did not shrink from such monumental tasks as the tomb of the Duc d'Harcourt and that of the Maréchal de Saxe (Figs. 594, 595). Surrounded by the symbols of his victories, and still striking terror into the hearts of his foes, the marshal descends with a firm step into the tomb; France, in the distracted attitude of a tragedy queen, tries to keep him back, and intercedes with Death, who presides over the open tomb below, where a mourning Hercules also finds a place, and satisfies the requirements of symmetry. In the individual figures as in the general arrangement there is a great deal of technical skill. But the pantomime by which we are invited to admire the hero, pity France, and detest Death, is too vociferous; the noisy agitation of the group drowns those

FIG. 597.—FALCONET. THE
CLOCK OF THE THREE GRACES.
(Camondo Collection.)

accents of contemplative melancholy which emanate from the silence of Gothic monuments. This grandiloquence would be perfect if talent and intelligence could create an epic, and give soul to the mythology of a *Henriade*. Pigalle was too ingenious to confine himself to the traditional iconography of academic statuary. His Louis XV at Reims was not an equestrian figure in the manner of the Marcus Aurelius; the king was on foot; instead of fettered slaves at the angles of the pedestal, there were seated figures, representing, not Commerce, but a merchant, not Labour, but a workman. Contemporaries were delighted with this figure of a fellow-citizen, who had seated himself for the first time in the place so long occupied by a majestic woman in antique draperies, holding in her hand a scale, a sword, or a cornucopia as occasion required.

FIG. 598.—FALCONET.
BATHER.
(The Louvre, Paris.)

Falconet also determined to be sublime when he went to St. Petersburg to cast his colossal statue of Peter the Great. Heroes were no longer content to bestride their charges quietly, like Louis XIV and Louis XV. The Czar's horse caracoles on a gigantic rock. Sculpture became bolder and more ingenious every day. In spite of this rhetorical outburst, Falconet was primarily the delicate modeller of nymphs and bathers; he was faithful to a feminine type of very graceful refinement, a supple body, soft and unresisting, with pointed extremities, and caressing gestures, in which the charm of the Medici Venus is softened by the gentle sensuality of Correggio's female figures. For these tender forms, marble seems a substance too hard and cold; china is a perfect material for such fragile groups. Falconet's art, indeed, provided more than one model for the Sèvres manufactory; thus sculpture was enabled to play a part in the decoration of interiors, and to meet a fashionable requirement (Figs. 596, 597).

Just as the demi-gods of the painters had become smaller, whiter, and pinker when

FIG. 599.—HOUDON.
WINTER.
(Museum of Montpellier.)

285

they were enthroned over the chimneypieces and doors of boudoirs, so statuary was adapted to the drawing-room, and the heroes of academic sculpture became *bibelots.* Boucher's pastorals were also transposed into biscuit china; licence can only be brilliant in small dimensions. The loves of Lubin and Annette were multiplied by the potter as they had been by the engraver, until the day when the Sèvres paste materialised the grave deities of revolutionary civism (Figs. 602, 603).

In the works of the next generation Pajou, Clodion, J. J. Caffieri and Houdon, sculpture became more and more nervous, sensitive and brilliant; yet it had retained none of the somewhat pretentious mannerism of Slodtz and the Adams; it never attempted to be sublime, but was content to produce dainty nudities and sparkling faces. Pajou (1730–1809) gave his marble the melting softness of flesh; and Clodion (1738–1814), when he modelled his nymphs and Cupids, handled the clay as Fragonard handled paint in his brilliant sketches, and showed the same joyous mastery of his material (Figs. 604–606). Both Pajou and Clodion often preferred the rapid modelling of terra-cotta to the slower processes of marble. J. J. Caffieri's busts—

generally seventeenth and eighteenth century writers—have an easy softness and a certain mobile vitality. The busts of an earlier age reveal more of an artist's vision, of his personal style, and do not bring us face to face with reality as do those of Caffieri and Houdon. In his portraits of the French classic writers, Caffieri has given them the impetuous brilliance of their age.

Houdon (1741–1828) essayed not only to fix beautiful forms in marble and bronze, but to suggest the palpitations of life in them; in a work by him there is not a fraction of surface which is inert. His *Diana* trips along on tiptoe with a careless lightness which does not disturb the proud grace of her body, and the light, gleaming on her limbs, sends a quiver of life over her bronze flesh (Fig. 600). In a bust by Houdon, there is not a furrow nor a plane which does not serve to express thought. Such vivacity and such psychological insight are only to be found in La Tour's sketches. The feverish life of the age animates the clay; it is France on the eve of the Revolution: Diderot listening, and ready to break out; Rousseau frowning, his face that of a self-indulgent country priest; Mirabeau's insolent, unwholesome mask, and above all, Voltaire's fleshless

FIG. 602.—SÈVRES CHINA. THE KISS.

head. Houdon modelled this more than once. He even carved a full-length figure of the philosopher in marble; but he neither dared to strip the bony form, like Pigalle, nor to clothe the skeleton in ordinary dress. He wrapped the seated old man in a loose robe; the falling folds suggest the impatient body, ready to spring from the seat, but conceal it entirely, save for the two nervous hands which grasp the arms of the chair; the face with its thin lips, toothless mouth and piercing eyes, is thrust forward, and under the loose skin, puckered by an ironical smile, the bones and tendons are strongly marked. Never had art thus fixed the image of a restless, mobile, combative intelligence, in all its terrible lucidity (Figs. 607, 608).

FIG. 603.—SÈVRES CHINA.
THE BOSKET-SELLER.

A very brief survey of Louis XV architecture will suffice to show that French art was never more classical, or more anxious to adapt antique forms to the exigencies of modern life than at this period. Certain attempts to impose the fancies of the rococo style on architecture had no durable success, at least in Paris; a door or a balcony of hammered iron may have yielded to caprices of line; but architecture never sacrificed majesty and purity of style. Louis XV art amused itself freely with minor works, brilliant or sensual, because it was confident of the solidity of

FIG. 604.—CLODION.
BACCHANTE.
(The Louvre, Paris.)

FIG. 605.—CLODION.
FEMALE SATYR.
(Cluny Museum, Paris.)

its principles. As had happened before in the case of the Flamboyant Style, it was abroad—and more especially in Germany—that the Rococo manner ran riot. Even in the middle of the century, Cochin the younger, the engraver, denounced this style in the name of good sense, and his strictures recall those which Vitruvius

FIG. 606.—PAJOU. MME. DUBARRY.
(The Louvre, Paris.)

FIG. 607.—HOUDON. VOLTAIRE.
(Comédie-Française, Paris.)

addressed in classic times to that fantastic decoration which the men of the Renaissance christened "grotesque." During the second half of the century, the tranquil geometry of French architects overcame the nervous agitation of cabinet-makers and metal-workers.

Paris was actively at work destroying her mediæval city, and multiplying classical façades. Bouchardon erected a monumental fountain in the Rue de Grenelle. His

FIG. 608.—HOUDON. BUST OF LOUISE BRONGNIARD. (The Louvre, Paris.)

FIG. 609.—DEFERNEX. MME. DE FONDVILLE. (Museum of Le Mans.)

structure, with its learned lines, its sculptures of impeccable purity, errs only by its excessive importance. Two thin jets of water are an insufficient pretext for such an imposing scheme.

Under Louis XV there were innumerable pretexts for embellishing Paris with statues, porticoes and decorative façades. After the peace of Aix-la-Chapelle, the municipality wished to do for Louis XV what had been done for Louis XIV in the seventeenth century, after the peace of Nimeguen. Bouchardon was commissioned to cast an equestrian statue; as was the custom, the royal effigy was surrounded by architecture. The towns of Bordeaux, Nancy, Reims and Rennes followed the example of Paris; a statue of the king entailed a framework of façades designed to harmonise with it, as those round the site of the

FIG. 610.—CAFFIERI. CLOCK OF CHASED BRASS. (Museum of Versailles.)

FIG. 611.—CABINET DESIGNED BY THE BROTHERS
SLODTZ.
(Bibliothèque Nationale, Paris.)

Capitol surround Marcus Aurelius. To make an appropriate stage for Bouchardon's Louis XV, Gabriel laid out the vast piece of ground between the Tuileries Gardens and the Champs Elysées, now known as the Place de la Concorde. He designed a graceful balustrade; at the angles, on sentry-boxes, there were to have been mythological and monarchical allegories according to the ritual of Versailles. But these were never set up, and Bouchardon's statue was destroyed. Louis-Philippe finally completed the Place. The Citizen King replaced the symbols of the ancient régime by the "Towns of France"; they form a circle now about

FIG. 612.—THREE-BRANCHED
CANDELABRA.
(Jones Collection.)

FIG. 613.—CHANDELIER OF CHASED
BRASS.
(Bibliothèque Mazarine, Paris.)

monuments with inoffensive symbols, two fountains and an obelisk. But the essential features of the scheme were Gabriel's two symmetrical palaces, with colonnades on lower storeys; they show an advance on the Louvre colonnade. Gabriel (d. 1782) treated large architectural masses with greater ease than Claude Perrault; his long façades, with their flat lines, harmonise, strange to say, with the pleasant houses built during the eighteenth century in the two adjacent quarters of Saint Honoré and Saint Germain, some of which, such as the former Hôtel de Salm (now the Palace of the Legion d'Honneur), are little masterpieces in their ingenuity of arrangement and their original beauty. Gabriel ranks with Mansart as the French architect who most successfully applied the

FIG. 614.—BUREAU OF LOUIS XV.
(The Louvre, Paris.)

FIG. 615.—SOUP TUREEN.
(Sèvres Museum.)

classical decoration of the "orders" to modern palaces and houses. In the Petit Trianon, as in the Ecole Militaire (Figs. 622, 623), he achieved suitable dimensions, purity of outline, and that just relation of elements

which produces the effect of a well-proportioned human body. Compared with the charming pavilions of the Ecole Militaire, Bruant's façades at the Hôtel des Invalides seem somewhat heavy and dismal.

The eighteenth century witnessed the popularisation in provincial and domestic architecture, of that style, the syntax of which, so to speak, had been fixed by Claude Perrault and Mansart. Down to the time of the Revolution, the world of the nobility and finance continued to renew

FIG. 616.—ROUEN POTTERY.
(Cluny Museum, Paris.)

FIG. 617.— GERMAIN. SOUP TUREEN OF CHASED
SILVER.
(d'Haussonville Collection.)

its dwellings. Town houses were arranged more and more with a view to convenience. Behind the heavy gates which they presented to the streets of the Faubourg Saint-Germain or the Faubourg Saint-Honoré, was a court enframed by cheerful façades with wide windows; on the garden side, the architect rarely resisted the temptation of throwing out a little colonnade; in drawing-rooms, on the other hand, the cabinet-makers continued to exclude architectural decoration. The most important and the best of these town houses have been assigned by modern France to her ministers, her ambassadors, her deputies, and the President of the Republic. The reigns

FIG. 618.—PLACE DE LA CONCORDE. BIRD'S EYF
VIEW.
(From "Paris vu en ballon," by A.
Schœlcher and O. Décugis.)

of Louis XIV and Louis XV produced a large number of such houses which are models of good taste; the nineteenth century never touched them without compromising their perfect elegance. The graceful habitations of the old régime saved the new the trouble of building.

It was also during the long reign of Louis XV that the French provincial towns made their greatest advances towards modern com-

FIG. 619.— THE PAVILLON DE HANOVRE,
PARIS.

fort and the classical style. The Renaissance, which built so much, brought about no such important transformations. The eighteenth century must have destroyed a good deal; even styles are intolerant when they contain a fund of active energy, and find the ground already occupied around them. The new architecture did not ex-

FIG. 620.—HOTEL SOUBISE. ARCHIVES NATIONALES, PARIS.

pand without injuring the buildings of the Gothic age. Some-

FIG. 621.—COUNCIL CHAMBER. PALACE OF FONTAINEBLEAU.

times it was content with juxtaposition, as in the case of the beautiful episcopal palaces in Gabriel's manner which arose by the side of many old cathedrals. The towns which were suffocating within their encircling walls demolished these and transformed them into public promenades. The escarpments were utilised to form picturesque terraces and open up distant prospects. The fortified cities of the Middle Ages came to breathe the fresh air on their ancient ramparts, just as the feudal nobles of the Renaissance had done when they transformed their castles.

By the end of the century a great many towns

FIG. 622.—LE PETIT TRIANON, VERSAILLES.

293

FIG. 623.—ÉCOLE MILITAIRE, PARIS.

possessed monuments, squares, and gardens like those of Versailles and Paris, in the taste of Mansart and Le Nôtre. Their governors—d'Aiguillon at Nancy and Tourny at Bordeaux—built "Places" with classical façades; the Compagnie des Indes created Lorient, and the town houses constructed by wealthy shipowners still look seaward above the ramparts of Saint Malo. Towns in the extremities of Brittany, Saint Malo, Brest, Lorient, Rennes and Nantes, bear the impress of classical art, the art which unites

FIG. 624.—ERMENONVILLE. THE GARDENS.

FIG. 625.—THE HAMLET OF THE PETIT TRIANON.

this refractory peninsula to French life. The city of Bordeaux, growing continuously in wealth, embellished itself in the Louis XVI style; the architect Victor Louis (1731–1807) completed the work begun there by Gabriel the elder. He built the large theatre, one of the finest examples of the French classical style. The façades are

very pure in design, and
the internal arrangements
so happy both as regards
convenience and deco-
rative effect that architects
have imitated them ever
since, without improving
on them. Louis also de-
signed houses for the rich
citizens. The prosperity
and the reconstruction of
Bordeaux fortunately coincided with the moment
when French architecture,

FIG. 626.—THE COLONNADE IN THE PARC MONCEAU,
AT PARIS.

which could no longer build fine churches, was constructing delightful town houses. All the France of the Atlantic coast, Bordeaux,
Nantes, Lorient, was turning a smiling face to the Ocean at the very
hour when the command of the sea was slipping from her (Fig. 627).

The France of the South was not behindhand. Toulouse, as was
her habit, transposed the fashionable buildings of the day into brick,
and gave her Capitol a façade imitated from the colonnade of the
Louvre, though the columns have become simple pilasters, and the
Toulousain brick gives a certain heaviness to Perrault's noble design.
At the "Fontaine" of Nîmes, and the Peyrou of Montpellier (Fig.
629), architects laid out delightful public promenades, with fountains,
flowers, trees and terraces, bounded by flights of steps or bordered
by balustrades, with a slender pavilion dominating the whole;

FIG. 627.—THE PLACE DE LA BOURSE, BORDEAUX.
(*Photo. Neurdein.*)

FIG. 628.—THE GRAND THEATRE, BORDEAUX.

throughout, an ingenious regularity guides and amuses the pedestrian, and a lofty situation was always chosen to afford that view of a distant landscape which was lacking at Versailles.

Strasburg and Metz were transformed at this period, and French art, crossing the Rhine as in Gothic times, conquered Germany. But Nancy boasts the finest example of the Louis XV style; the good king Stanislas possessed but one attribute of royalty—the faculty of building; side by side with mediæval Nancy, he created a new town, of squares and promenades, triumphal arches, galleries, fountains, iron gates, an attractive architecture of pretty, useless things, which arrest the traveller that he may stop and admire them (Figs. 632-634, 636). The king's architect, Héré, was a worthy rival of Gabriel, who framed his wide windows with majestic pilasters. But the Rococo of Nancy is less serious than the

FIG. 629.—LE PEYROU, AT MONTPELLIER.

Classicism of Paris; the Rococo ornament which in Paris was reserved for internal decoration breaks out upon the façades of Nancy. Some tempest seems to have carried off and dispersed the fleecy clouds and fluttering Cupids of Boucher's ceilings. We find these lively little people perched everywhere, on the balus-

FIG. 630.—PALAIS DE LA LÉGION D'HONNEUR, PARIS.

trades of terraces, on cornices, even on the bars of iron gates. The mythological fountains seem to have come out of the landscape of some pastoral poem. Lamour completed this architecture with wrought ironwork, the most delightful of superfluities; he hammered out bars and fixed them with a fancifulness which, true to the principles of French taste, hides a good deal of logic under its caprices. This energetic art was a more successful vehicle than sculpture for the intricate subtleties of the Rococo. No style so well adapted to the material of the blacksmith and the worker in

FIG. 631.—GRAND THEATRE, BORDEAUX. STAIRCASE, FIRST FLOOR.
(*Photo. L'Architecte.*)

metals had been known since the days of Gothic grilles and hinges. At each juncture when suppleness and nervous energy were desiderata, in the days of the Flamboyant and Rococo Styles, metal has achieved greater triumphs than wood or stone. Lamour's ironwork and Gouthières's chased metals are the masterpieces of Rococo. A graceful balcony of hammered iron was a luxury permissible even to a modest house of this period.

The religious architecture of the eighteenth century had little indeed of the vitality and vigour which characterised that of the town houses. The Jesuit style had run its course. Architects were no longer inclined to repeat the Church of the Val-de-Grâce, of the Sorbonne, or even of the Invalides. On the façade of Saint Sulpice, Servandoni superposed two colonnades, crowned by a balustrade, and flanked by two towers (Fig. 637). San Giovanni Laterano and Notre Dame de Paris were combined to modify

FIG. 632.—FOUNTAIN OF NEPTUNE, AT NANCY.

FIG. 633.—PLACE CARRIÈRE, NANCY.

the flat, pyramidal façades of the Jesuit churches. In place of the old church of Saint Geneviève, Soufflot (1713–1780) erected a colossal building, in which, like Bramante in St. Peter's at Rome, he succeeded in raising the dome of the Pantheon on the vaults of the basilica of Constantine. The peristyle recalls that of Agrippa's Pantheon (Figs. 638, 640). The colossal order replaced the superposed orders of the Renaissance on the façades of churches, as it had already replaced them on the façades of palaces. But little more was required to give Christian churches the appearance of pagan temples. As they had no new problems to resolve, architects sought for novelty only in a more or less exact imitation of the antique. In the seventeenth century, Colbert dreamed of transporting the Maison Carrée of Nîmes to Paris, stone by stone. The last classical church built, the Madeleine, after some vacillation on the part of the constructors, ended by becoming an enlarged version of a small Roman temple. The work of classical architecture was accomplished. In the sixteenth century, small antique columns and entablatures had been ingeniously arranged to mark the storeys of modern structures; gradually, these decorative facings had reverted to their original forms, till they finally imposed pagan architecture on the modern churches. The Madeleine, indeed, very nearly became a "Temple of Glory"; it is now a fashionable church. But the huge Pantheon is still empty and lifeless. The memory of Saint Geneviève, which haunted the ancient sanctuaries of the hill, has evaporated under Soufflot's icy vaults; the church is vacant, neither Christian nor

FIG. 634.—LAMOUR. GRILLE, PLACE STANISLAS, NANCY.

pagan. It has been converted into a museum of paintings glorifying Paris and France, and a Saint Denis for great Frenchmen. But in spite of the talents of its decorators, and the famous tombs it shelters, this secularised building is mainly a place of pilgrimage for tourists, and evokes little sentiment beyond an indifferent curiosity.

This revival of a worship of the antique among architects and painters was not the work of the Academy. Those amiable decorators, the official artists of the eighteenth century, received the youthful David and his exalted manner coolly enough. They

FIG. 635.—THE FOUNTAIN DE LA GROSSE HORLOGE, AT ROUEN.
(*Photo. Neurdein.*)

took little interest in the theory of their art. The public was so well disposed towards them, that it would have been folly to imperil their success by the pursuit of a difficult ideal. It was the world of writers and philosophers which produced æsthetes and archæologists such as Diderot and Caylus, who attacked artists for their subservience to fashionable taste; these domineering theorists ended by emancipating painters from the bondage of futile amateurs, and imposing upon them an ideal of austere beauty. French thought has

FIG. 636.—PLACE STANISLAS, NANCY.

FIG. 637.—FAÇADE OF THE CHURCH OF
SAINT-SULPICE, PARIS.

such a desire to reduce everything to a lucid system, that the critics of the Salons took upon themselves to argue about beauty when the Academicians ceased to do so. Art criticism demonstrates the continuity of classical taste from Le Brun to David, even when painters and sculptors seem to have cast it off.

But it is indeed a question whether French art ever ceased to be classical. Its fantasies were never without a method. The most capricious manifestations of the Rococo Style had grown upon the geometrical forms of classical architecture, just as Flamboyant decoration had sprung from the vigorous limbs of Gothic art. The most licentious episodes of the "little masters" are often, like Poussin's gravest pages of history, masterpieces of clarity and intelligence in their composition. The quality of the idea declined, but not the faculty for expressing it justly. Hence this eighteenth century, which respected nothing, was much more conservative in art than might have been expected at a time when the spirit of the age was essentially critical and rebellious. Voltaire, who destroyed so many beliefs, left Boileau's Credo untouched. The brilliant erotic compositions of Boucher and Fragonard prevent us from seeing the great academic pictures; these are now skied on the walls of museums; but in Diderot's Salons they occupied the places of honour. The most dissipated of their pupils retained some latent veneration for the severe masters whom they no longer obeyed. The teaching of Le Brun was by no means forgotten when critics began to demand a return to antique gravity.

FIG. 638.—THE PANTHEON, PARIS.

FIG. 639.—BOUCHARDON. FOUNTAIN IN THE RUE DE GRENELLE, PARIS.

It is not possible to see this worldly art succumbing before scientific art without a feeling of regret. It had the faculty of giving pleasure more fully than any other manner; it is not necessary to be a connoisseur, a theorist, or a dreamer, in order to appreciate it; the culture of an educated man suffices. The society in which it was born transmuted the most difficult sciences into witty conversation; graceful women talked without pedantry of grammar or political economy; such a world inevitably created an art that was seductive and delightful to all alike. Other schools produced more extraordinary craftsmen and profounder poets; but these are as a rule mighty geniuses, for the comprehension of whom a strenuous effort is required. The artists of the eighteenth century were too amiable, too well-bred, ever to lose touch with the world to whom they appealed. To charm the society of their day, they had to retain its grace and refinement. The Parisian society of the reigns of Louis XV and Louis XVI owes to its artists that it appears so fascinating to us; years and fashions have passed without dimming its powers of seduction. Whereas literary language

FIG. 640.—THE PANTHEON. BIRD'S EYE VIEW.
(From "Paris vu en ballon," by A. Schœlcher and O. Décugis.)

301

had become too much exhausted for poetry, Gabriel's Trianon, and the works of Watteau, Boucher, Chardin, Houdon, Clodion and Fragonard fixed those brilliant and voluptuous images, touched at times with emotion, but for which the men of the eighteenth century would seem to us very dry and prosaic, in spite of their lachrymose and didactic old age.

BIBLIOGRAPHY

Patte, *Monuments érigés en France en l'honneur de Louis XV*, Paris, 1765.—J.-F. Blondel, *Architecture française*, Paris, 1752-1756; *Distribution des maisons de plaisance*, Paris, 1738, 2 vols.—G. Boffrand, *Le livre d'Architecture...*, Paris, 1745.—P. de Nolhac, *Le Château de Versailles sous Louis XV*, Paris, 1898.—Lady E. Dilke, *French Architects and sculptors of the XVIIIth century*, London, 1900.—Jeanne Bouché, *Servandoni* (*G. B. A.*, 1910, II).—Héré, *Recueil des plans, élévations et coupes* (2 atlases), Nancy, n. d.—A. Hallays, *Nancy* (*Les Villes d'Art Célèbres*), Paris, n. d.—Lamour, *Recueil des ouvrages en serrurerie*, Nancy, 1767.—Stanislas Lami, *Dictionnaire des sculpteurs; français au XVIIIe siècle*, 1 vol. publ., Paris, 1910.—A. Rosero, *J.-B. Bouchardon*, Paris, 1894; *Bouchardon intime* (*R. S. B. A. D.*,1901).—S. Rocheblave, *Pigalle* (*R. A. A. M.*, 1902, II). —H. Thirion, *Les Adam et les Clodion*, Paris, 1885.—J.-J. Guiffrey, *Clodion* (*G. B. A.*, 1892, II).—A. Jacquot, *Les Adam, Les Michel et Clodion* (*R.S.B.A.D.*, 1897).—E. Bourgeois, *Le Biscuit de Sèvres au XVIIIe siècle*, Paris, 1908, 2 vols.—G. Lechevallier-Chevignard, *La Manufacture de porcelaine de Sèvres*, Paris, 1909.—Comte de Caylus, *Vies d'artistes du XVIIIe siècle, discours sur la peinture et la sculpture*, published by A. Fontaine, Paris, 1910.—S. Rocheblave, *Essai sur le Comte de Caylus*, Paris, 1889.—Abbé Dubos, *Réflexions critiques sur la poésie et la peinture*, Paris, 1719, 2 vols.—Diderot, *Salons*, X and XI of the Assézat edition.—J. et E. de Goncourt, *L'Art du XVIIIe siècle*, 3e édit., 2 vols., Paris, 1880-1883.—Louis Courajod, *Histoire de l'enseignement des Arts du dessin au XVIIIe siècle...*, Paris, 1874.—Lady Dilke, *French Painters of the XVIIIth Century*, London, 1900. —J. Foster, *French Art from Watteau to Prudhon*, London, 1906.—J. Locquin, *Le Paysage en France au début du XVIIIe siècle et l'oeuvre de J.-B. Oudry* (*G. B. A.*, 1908, II, 353).— P. Mantz, *Boucher, Lemoyne et Natoire*, Paris, 1880; *Nattier, Tocqué* (*G. B. A.*, 1894, II). —Prosper Dorbec, *Louis Tocqué* (*G. B. A.*, 1909, II).—A. Michel, *Boucher*, Paris, 1886. —G. Kahn, *Boucher*, Paris, 1904.—C. Gabillot, *Les trois Drouais* (*G. B. A.*, 1905, II).— P. de Nolhac, *Nattier*, Paris, 1904.—G. Schéfer, *Siméon Chardin*, Paris, 1903.—E. Pilon, *Chardin*, Paris, 1908.—M. Tourneux, *L'Exposition Chardin-Fragonard* (*G. B. A.*, 1907, II); *M. Q. de la Tour*, Paris, 1904; *Jean-Baptiste Perronneau* (*G. B. A.*, 1896, I); *L'Exposition des cent pastels* (*G. B. A.*, 1908, II).—L. Dumont-Wilden, *Le Portrait en France au XVIIIe siècle*, Brussels, 1909.—R. Portalis, *Fragonard*, Paris, 1899.—C. Mauclair, *Fragonard*, Paris, n. d.—Lagrange, *J. Vernet*, Paris, 1855.—Joseph Vernet, *Correspondance de Joseph Vernet au sujet des ports de France avec Marigny et Angivilliers* (*N. A. A. F.*, 1893). —H. Bouchot, *Mme. Vigée-Lebrun* (*R. A. A. M.*, 1898, I).—C. Gabillot, *Hubert Robert et son temps*, Paris, 1895.—Hautecœur, *Le Sentimentalisme dans la peinture française de Greuze à David* (*G. B. A.*, 1909, I).—S. Rocheblave, *Les Cochin*, Paris, 1895.—Lady Dilke, *French Engravers and Draughtsmen...*, London, 1903.—Lazare Duvaux, *Livre-journal de Lazare Duvaux...*, with an introduction on the taste and the trade in works of art in the middle of the XVIIIth century, by L. Courajod, Paris, 1873, 2 vols.—Lady Dilke, *French Furniture and Decoration...*, London, 1902.—A. Molinier, *La Collection Wallace, meubles et objets d'art français*, Paris, 1903.—J.-G. Wille, *Graveur du Roi, Mémoires et Journal*, Paris, 1857, 2 vols. —H. Cordier, *La Chine en France au XVIIIe siècle*, Paris, 1910.

FIG. 641.—DAVID. CORONATION OF NAPOLEON I.
(The Louvre, Paris.)

PART III

MODERN ART

CHAPTER I

THE NEW CLASSICISM DURING THE REVOLUTION AND THE EMPIRE

Æsthetic Idealism.—The Influence of Antique Art.—The Revolutionary Spirit.—Administrative Transformations.—Compromise Between the Idealism of Artists and the Exigencies of Actuality.—Architecture: Greek pasticci; Percier and Fontaine.—Empire Furniture.—Painting: David; Reform in Technique; Realism and the Classical Spirit.—Guérin, Lethière, Gérard.—A Romantic Attempt: Girodet.—The Survivors of the Eighteenth Century.—Prudhon.—Gros.—Some "Little Masters."

At the close of the eighteenth century French art submitted for the third time to the classic discipline, and even more completely than in the time of Louis XIV and Francis I. This recrudescence or archæology and rationalism coincided, as before, with a new attempt at national centralisation; for the Convention and the Empire consolidated and drew more closely together those forces of the State which the declining monarchy had allowed to relax.

303

FIG. 642.—SALON. EMPIRE.
(Temporary Exhibition of the Musée des
Arts décoratifs.)

Once more a kind of secret sympathy or pre-established harmony between political absolutism and classic art makes itself felt; it seems as if the country, when it sought to realize its unity, preferred an abstract, universal art, or at least an art general enough to dominate all the local variations of the French intellect. The classic spirit had intensified; in the time of Francis I, antique or Italian influences had been ingeniously reconciled with local traditions; under Louis XIV, Colbert accepted antique art, but on condition that it became naturalised in France. And now the æsthetes of the Revolution and the Empire put forward an absolute ideal, bearing no relation either to national history or geography. The ideas developed in the academical discussions of the seventeenth century and in Charles Perrault's dialogues re-appeared, but in a more absolute and vigorous form, because they were now saturated with metaphysics and treated by professional dialecticians.

French rationalism, always ready to follow up its deductions, advanced boldly to the limits of the absurd; in art as in politics, it triumphed with a sort of intransigeance. The theorists who swarmed in those days of philosophical frenzy and legislative fury, defined ideal beauty; they declared it to consist of an absolute harmony of forms, and taught that it could be attained by calculation, application, and knowledge of the antique; the lax and facile art of the eighteenth century was proscribed unreservedly; it might give

FIG. 643.—MARIE LOUISE'S JEWEL-CABINET
AT FONTAINEBLEAU.
(*Photo. Neurdein.*)

a passing pleasure by its happy carelessness and its brilliant fancy, but its beauty was relative to the taste of a certain society, and the taste of this society was not good; true beauty is untouched by changes of fashion, because it is founded on reason; it was realised once for all by the ancients; hence their art preserves an eternal youth, in spite of the centuries; and we have

FIG. 644.—NAPOLEON I'S BEDROOM AT COMPIÈGNE.
(*Photo. Neurdein.*)

nothing to do but to imitate it; let us return to Greek art; it is not Greek, but universal; it is not antique, but eternal; beauty is of no time and no country.

These were the ideas of æsthetes rather than of artists; they were developed by critics rather than by painters; but David and the Davidians adopted them, and the most vigorous artists were influenced by them. The art of the period bears the stamp of this ideology, with few exceptions; the spirit of abstraction proclaims itself in the bloodless forms and the generalised modelling of its painters. Outline drawing, without shading, was never in such high favour; the sinuous line gives a kind of theoretical definition of all things. Deprived of colour, of relief, of light and of substance, this calligraphy indicates only purity of form and harmony of proportion. Architects designed buildings without any particular function while legislators were drawing up ideal constitutions; ideas fly lightly when they are not weighted by reality.

The excavations at Pompeii sent a wave of archæological fever over scientific and artistic Europe. For years poets and artists had been describing the life of the Greeks and

FIG. 645.—CLOCK.
(Sèvres Museum.)

FIG. 646.—INKSTAND.
(Sèvres Museum.)

Romans, and now, for the first time, men found themselves in contact, not with ideal statues, or the ruins of exceptional monuments, but with a whole city, its houses, its paintings, and even in some cases with its furniture. The dream that had been cherished ever since the Renaissance was at last to be realised; it had become possible to resuscitate this world which all had supposed lost for ever, but which had been surprised in its sleep. A quantity of new evidences enabled students to approach more closely to that reconstitution of the antique which Mantegna, Raphael, Poussin and Le Brun had essayed. It was not only the art of the ancients that was now to renew modern art, but their life which was about to modify actual life, furniture and costume. The ruins of Pompeii not only rejuvenated history-painting. This open tomb transformed the world of the living.

The revolutionary spirit brought its ardent passions to the aid of the antique. The art of the eighteenth century against which Vien, David and their pupils reacted, was an art of the aristocracy and the clergy. The neo-classicists had already repudiated it in the name of aesthetics when the Revolution deprived it of all *raison d'être* by destroying the régime of which it was a luxurious accessory. The art sprung from the classic democracies did not seem tainted in its origin like that of the churches and palaces; like the republican eloquence of the "Conciones," it had not been contaminated by despotism and superstition. Thus the Revolution completed the work of the Renaissance, and swept away the few Gothic remains which still separated modern from antique thought. The Classicists of the eighteenth century were, no doubt, pagan in imagination, but they

FIG. 647.—EXPIATORY CHAPEL OF LOUIS XVI, PARIS.

306

were royalist and Christian in externals. Although they believed in the superiority of Greek temples, they continued to build Christian churches. They harmonised sufficiently the two points of view. Revolutionary Classicism condemned the whole activity of the Middle Ages, and suppressed what still remained of it;

FIG. 648.—THE BOURSE (STOCK-EXCHANGE), PARIS.
(*Photo. Neurdein.*)

for some years, it might have been supposed that the art of Athens and of Rome was to be directly introduced into French civilisation. At a time when furniture was Pompeian and costume Greek, when political speeches were translations from Livy or Plutarch, it is not surprising that David and Guérin should have resuscitated Leonidas and Romulus. This crisis lasted but a few years, but it sufficed to break the continuity of modern art; to renew its growth, a new graft had to be made on the ancient trunk.

The men of the Revolution did not share Rousseau's opinions as to the corrupting influences of the fine arts; they often proclaimed that artists should contribute to the education of the nation. David was an important member of the Convention because he was a great painter. He caused the suppression of the Royal Academy of Painting and Sculpture, which disappeared with all the other ancient corporations. But the unity of art was not affected by this: the authority of David and his teaching was such that painters were never more submissive to official doctrine than in the interval between the disappearance of the ancient Royal Academy, and its reappearance during the Consulate as Class IV of the Institut. The new Academy, however, was a closer and a more honorific corporation than

FIG. 649.—CHURCH OF THE MADELEINE, PARIS.

FIG. 650.—ARC DE TRIOMPHE DU CARROUSEL, PARIS.

its predecessor; far from being open to every capable artist, like the Académie Française, it only received a limited number of members. Thus it by no means included all the great artists of the nineteenth century. Its history is not coincident with the history of French art.

This masterful idealism could not altogether ignore reality; we shall see in what manner it effected its compromise. More than once, David and his pupils had to abandon their helmeted heroes for some revolutionary scene or some imperial ceremony. David was commissioned to paint the Constituents taking the oath of the Tennis Court (*Serment du Jeu de Paume*). He began the work with a certain enthusiasm; but he had hardly painted ten of these heroes when he began to send many of them to the scaffold; after this it would have been inconsistent to immortalise them in painting. A little later, Baron Gros, painting the cupola of the Pantheon, was obliged to change the Cæsarian Napoleon of the original design into a stout Louis XVIII presenting the Charter. Between the execution of two modern pictures dealing with current events, these classical painters returned to their studios to polish the rounded limbs of some Leonidas or Psyche. Thus the Conventionnels, while passing provisional measures, found time to add an article to their ideal Constitution. After 1815, all these Davidians had leisure to cultivate pure beauty. But then their ardour began to flag; for events had urged them on and had never ob-

FIG. 651.—ARC DE TRIOMPHE DE L'ETOILE, PARIS.

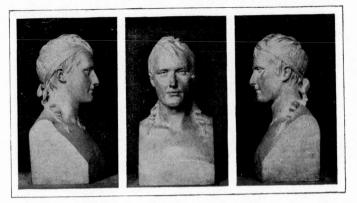

FIG. 652.—HOUDON. BUST OF NAPOLEON.
(Museum of Dijon.)

structed their flights. Theory seems a feeble thing when it is no longer animated by passion.

Architecture is generally in abeyance in times of war, civil or foreign; neither the Revolution nor the Empire found much time for building. The Revolution lived in a provisional state; it held its assemblies in any convenient hall, and was content with wooden sheds and plaster statues for its great festivals. Gradually, as it solidified, the modern government installed itself in the ravaged palaces of the ancient order. Napoleon used the dwellings of the monarchy, with the exception of Versailles, the sinister associations of which made it uninhabitable. He had dreams of an immense palace for the King of Rome, on the hill where the Trocadéro was afterwards built; but Percier and Fontaine had barely time to draw up the plans. He saw no more than the foundations of the Arc de l'Etoile begun by Chalgrin in honour of the Grande Armée; it was not finished until thirty years later, and the Emperor's ashes passed under the triumphal arch, when they were brought back from St. Helena. His effigy on the Vendôme Column suffered as much from revolution as the statue of Louis XIV it had supplanted. The Empire managed to complete one church in the form of an antique Temple of Glory, but the Restoration intervened, and dedicated this *pasticcio* of the Maison Carrée at Nîmes to Mary Magdalen (Fig. 649).

The buildings begun, interrupted, continued, and transformed, from Louis XVI to the end of the Restoration are all ambitious reconstitutions of the antique. Gravity became an affectation of

FIG. 653.—CHINARD.
MME. RÉCAMIER.
(Museum of Lyons.)

austerity; the Tuscan order was not always considered severe enough. Artists turned back from Greek art to that of Egypt, with its tombs, its massive walls, its lotus flowers and its sphinxes. When the architect's archæological zeal was rather less fervent, he was content to place complete façades behind a peristyle; colonnades were erected before churches, private houses and theatres, and around the Bourse. There were colonnades at the Odéon, and at the Théâtre Française, where Talma, in Roman costume, was then giving lessons in history to Guérin and Lethière. There was one even for the Variétés; and that little theatre squeezed in a cramped peristyle between two buildings on the boulevard, as if, long before Offenbach, it had been dedicated to the parodies of the antique. The basilica, the most ancient type of Christian architecture, and that which approaches most nearly to antique buildings, was the type chosen by the Restoration for the numerous churches it built. It could not give them peristyles so imposing as those of the Panthéon or the Madeleine; but all boast at least a few columns. When Brongniart undertook the Bourse, he could devise nothing more suitable to shelter stockbrokers than a peripteral temple (Fig. 648). They applied the maxim of André Chénier and for these modern uses felt obliged to make antique buildings.

The best buildings of the period are those of the two inseparables, Percier (1764–1838) and Fontaine (1762–1853); the triumphal arch of the Carrousel is a delicate work by refined designers. In the courtyard of the Louvre, which they were connecting with the Tuileries, they amused themselves, as Philibert Delorme had occasionally done, by elaborating some little piece of architecture, adjusting columns and entablatures, enframing delicate bas-reliefs between the strongly marked mouldings of the structure (Fig. 650). Fontaine built the Chapelle Expiatoire over the graves of Louis XVI and Marie-Antoinette for Louis XVIII. "This cloister, formed of a chain of tombs," is a significant symbol of the Restoration. Both were monuments of regret, ex-votos to the past. Isolated in the very heart of Paris, this Campo Santo turns away our thoughts from the present and confines them in the sad memories of the past (Fig. 647).

The architects of the Empire were more busily employed in designing furniture than in building. It was they who, following in the wake of the archæological painters, applied the austere rigidity of the Pompeian style to furniture. Even when the eighteenth century style was at its apogee, there had been a good deal of criticism of rococo convolutions; that a line should twist and turn so much on its way from one point to another had appeared unreasonable to

FIG. 654.—BOSIO. THE NYMPH SALMACIS.
(The Louvre, Paris.)

the contemporaries of Louis XV, and unseemly to those of Louis XVI. The legs of tables and the backs of chairs were straightened; and in the reign of Louis XV a style was evolved—the so-called Louis XVI style—which combined elegance and simplicity. After this came the Neo-Greeks, who attempted to reconstruct antique furniture; their adherents consented to be heavy in order to be majestic. Forms became massive and decisive, with pronounced angles. In a reception room this furniture seems to be protesting against fashionable futility; it reveals the spirit of a new

FIG. 655.—CHAUDET. CUPID.
(The Louvre, Paris.)

society, the pedantry of an archæologist and the narrow arrogance of an important functionary. Even the china of the period masks its fragility; Sèvres vases, more pretentious than urns, were overlaid with gold, and decorated with large historical pictures reduced to small dimensions. This age of fragile governments had a passion for solid forms; no arm-chairs were ever more massive than those in which the Directors, the Consuls, Napoleon and the last Bourbons sat in succession; and, strange to say, it was the same classical logic which produced such rigidity in

FIG. 656.—DAVID. THE SABINE WOMEN.
(The Louvre, Paris.)

art, and such instability in the State.

The name of Louis David (1748–1825) dominates this period so completely that artists like Vien, who was his master, and Guérin and Regnault, who were not his pupils, seem to us to have been his disciples. Long before the Revolution, he had heralded revolutionary art; there was always in him the authority of the leader of a school. An apostle of severity, of a difficult, moral, and archæological art, he had all the intolerance of a seeker of the absolute. At an early age, he showed a passionate hatred for and even a kind of Jacobinical fury against the frivolous aristocratic painting of the eighteenth century; in certain pictures, the *Horatii, Brutus,* and the *Death of Socrates,* he reveals the stoicism which, for some years, was to ennoble passions, stimulate powers, and give heroism to the human drama. His first works appeared when Vien was preparing the way for the new style, by stripping his compositions of Boucher and Fragonard's elaboration, renouncing fanciful accessories, purifying his line, informing his work with gravity, and giving earnest attention to the model. The crisis of austere idealism had begun. But David was no mere theorist; he was a painter whose artistic vision was keen and vigorous, an honest and scrupulous craftsman, who scorned to substitute empty dexterity for direct and sincere expression; he lopped off the embellishments of the Rococo, stripped art of its decorative prettinesses, and found

FIG. 657.—GÉRARD. MME. RÉCAMIER.
(The Préfecture de la Seine, Paris.)
(*Photo. Neurdein.*)

majesty and serene nudity beneath the furbelows of fashion. He professed to paint entirely from nature. But unfortunately he could not look at nature save in the light of Græco-Roman æsthetics. In the poor model perched on a plank in his studio, he sought the generalised forms of antique statuary; at first he showed a preference for bodies with tense and swelling muscles, and

FIG. 658.—DAVID. THE DISTRIBUTION OF THE EAGLES.
(Museum of Versailles.)

strongly defined forms; later, at the time of his *Sabines* and *Leonidas*, he modelled rounded limbs; following his example, Gérard and Girodet, and the rest, polished the varnished skins of their figures with flat colour. With a model before his eyes, and the attitudes of statues in his memory, David eliminated movement from his art; his heroes pose, and never act.

He also suppressed the picturesque mobility of nature and of light. His figures are in space, but not in the air, and have no illumination save that of the draughtsman who suggests a round object by contrasts of light and shade; each figure has received the same studio light; in the "Roman" pictures, which represent the interior of an antique house, they are juxtaposed in uniformly dark surroundings; in his "Greek" period, the background is a cold, light gray, which represents the open air. Thus with David, a system impoverished the painter's powers; nothing was left to him but the proportions of the body, purity of modelling, and beauty of attitude; his sole medium of expression was a rhythmic and majestic rhetoric, which lacked colours and

FIG. 659.—DAVID. M. SÉRIZIAT.
(The Louvre, Paris.)

ART IN FRANCE

FIG. 660.—DAVID. MME. RÉCAMIER.
(The Louvre, Paris.)

images for the translation of violent sentiments; a strange art, in which men of strong passions attempted to speak the language of pure reason.

Thus classical art once more essayed to abandon the world of the living. But, idealist and archæologist though he be, it is very difficult for an artist to ignore his age, especially at a dramatic period like that of the Revolution and the Empire. Reality becomes so stirring, so full of surprises, that art cannot ignore it; the whole of France was so deeply moved, that idealism had to make some concessions to contemporary history. The Conventionnels commissioned David to immortalise some of the revolutionary scenes; Napoleon was not the man to give up his painters to the conquerors of the antique world. He "protected" the fine arts after the manner of Louis XIV, that they might add to his glory. In the competitions he instituted, a prize was offered for the best historical painting; but another was awarded to a "subject reflecting credit on the national character." This, of course, pointed to the Napoleonic epic. The imperial army, with the Emperor at its head, charged into the Salons of 1808–1810, and Murat's cavalry put Leonidas and Romulus to flight. Embroidered uniforms and violent attitudes mingled with the pale nudities. But David, Gérard, Girodet, and Gros himself, retained their classical majesty, even in depicting their contemporaries. They gave the members of the Constituent Assembly and the soldiers of the Grand Army the gigantic dimensions hitherto reserved

FIG. 661.—GUÉRIN.
RETURN OF MARCUS SEXTUS.
(The Louvre, Paris.)

314

for the heroes of tradition. They endeavoured to suggest the robust modelling and proportions of the classical canon beneath their modern costumes. We might discover a Greek profile under the shako of more than one old campaigner. The silk stockings of the high court functionaries are drawn, not over the slender calves of the Louis XV period,

FIG. 662.—DAVID. DEATH OF BARA.
(Museum of Avignon.)

but over the "rotulæ of the Atrides," and the stout muscles of Roman statues. In David's *Distribution of the Eagles* (Fig. 658), he dressed Giovanni da Bologna's *Mercury* in a hussar uniform to represent a figure rushing impetuously forward. And without doing violence to reality, Napoleon's painters were able to give him the clear-cut, beardless face of Cæsar, and the laurelled brow of an Imperator.

Nor were the emotions which agitated the contemporary world incomprehensible to a student of Plutarch who had become the official painter of the Convention and of the Empire. Words and actions readily assumed a heroic guise. David was able to pass from the *Oath of the Horatii* to the *Oath of the Tennis Court* without quitting the chilly heights of stoicism. When, a little later, he abandoned Leonidas at the pass of Thermopylæ, to follow Bonaparte in the pass of Mount St. Bernard, his soul was still exalted by Lacedæmonian virtue. Moreover, the greater men of the school, Gros and David, retained the tendency which made French classical art so serious; they were no mere anecdotists; they endowed each of their compositions

FIG. 663.—GIRODET. ATALA AT THE TOMB.
(The Louvre, Paris.)

315

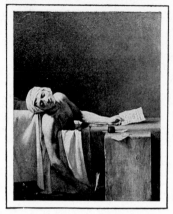

with some vital thought. The battles and incidents of the Revolution and the Empire seem to be events of a totally different order when they are recorded by Swebach and Boilly. In David's art more especially there is a power of generalisation, a manner of looking at things "under the aspect of eternity," which amplifies a momentary action into a historical symbol. The generous ardour of the Constituent Assembly is admirably expressed in the *Oath of the Tennis Court,* and all the outstretched arms which ratify Bailly's vow. No better exposition of Napoleon's power could be offered than the pictures of the *Coronation of Napoleon* (Fig. 641) and the *Distribution of the Eagles;* the wild enthusiasm of the officers for the Emperor, the gesture of the new Cæsar bestowing the crown in the presence of a passive pope and of an assembly of high functionaries proud of their new honours and glad to share in this consecration which was also their own. Thus David's realism remains classical; the spectacles of contemporary history are subjected to the same laws as imaginary scenes with antique personages; he gives us correct forms and expressive attitudes, composition as stable as architecture, and a great thought animating actors, spectators, and scenery.

Guérin (1774–1833) had learnt the new æsthetics, idealism and classicism, in the studio of his master Regnault, as Lethière had done in that of Vincent. Guérin sought success in the expression of emotion more intently than David. His most

famous works are scenes of tragedy. His figures strike theatrical attitudes, and seem always on the point of a tirade. Talma and Mlle. Georges had taught them the art of declamatory poses. Lethière represented certain episodes of Roman history with a grandiose setting, architecture interrupted by heavy shadows; the importance of the surroundings seems to suggest a reconstitution of Republican Rome; the figures have some slight reality, and the stormy sky gives a catastrophic atmosphere to the scene. Gérard (1770-1837) was less docile to the Davidian discipline. The somewhat trivial facility of his talent made it easy for him to desert the studio for the drawing-room. It did not prevent him from executing some

FIG. 666.—GÉRARD.
MARIE LÆTITIA BONAPARTE,
MOTHER OF NAPOLEON I.
(Museum of Versailles.)

rather feeble compositions, but it made him a popular portraitist. He was the official painter of the aristocracy under the Empire and the Restoration, and the embroideries of the Court costumes which he conscientiously reproduced forced him to heighten the tone of his naturally dull colour.

FIG. 667.—GROS.
PRINCESS LUCIEN BONAPARTE.
(The Louvre, Paris.)

Some excellent disciples were faithless to the creed, sometimes all unconsciously. Chateaubriand, when he endued his magnificent prose with the reverie, the melancholy, and the storms of passion, revealed the irresistible charm of romantic sensation. The cold statues of the Davidian school were swathed in Ossianesque mists, and the pale rays of the moon were shed caressingly upon their marble forms. But these figures are of classic race; they were conceived by lucid minds, fashioned by artists who loved precision of form, and painted in the prosaic light of the studio. In Girodet's labo-

FIG. 668.—GROS.
THE PLAGUE-STRICKEN AT JAFFA.
(The Louvre, Paris.) (*Photo. Neurdein.*)

rious work (1767–1824), we are conscious of the constraint of a language obliged to express sentiments for which it was not made. To suggest tenderness or melancholy, he envelops his Endymion or his Atala in strange lights. In his *Deluge* and his *Battle of Cairo,* he intermingles great bodies in violent attitudes, to show the abandonment of passion. But the rigidity of the design gives a kind of stony fixity to the tumult, and the languorous softness of the atmosphere disappears under the icy precision of the painting. The discord between Romantic sentimentality and the Classical tongue may be read in Girodet's ineffectual work.

On the other hand, many mediocre painters attempted to rise to the nobility of the new Classicism, while retaining the amorous complexion of the art of Louis XVI. David himself painted the loves of Helen and those of Psyche. Efforts were made to raise lachrymose sensibility or elegant libertinage to the level of the new art, while the belated imitators of Boucher exerted themselves to sing the glory of the First Consul and of the Emperor. On the confines of these two epochs, works full of contrasts came into being; some, like Greuze and Fragonard, too old to change their instrument, attempted epic airs upon their little flutes; others, to whom David had allotted the heroic trumpet, applied themselves to the laborious elaboration of pastoral motives. Greek figures were depicted writing love-letters, or weeping over the empty cages of lost birds; lamentable nudities, with smooth limbs and flat muscles, make us regret

FIG. 669.—GROS. EMBARKATION OF THE
DUCHESSE D'ANGOULÊME, AT PAUILLAC.
(Museum of Bordeaux.) (*Photo. Moreau.*)

the plump Bacchantes of
Clodion and Frago.
Licence seems dismal
enough when rhetoric
takes the place of wit!

Prud'hon (1758–1823),
however, by the grace of
genius, escaped these fa-
talities of the schools.
Like André Chénier in
poetry, he created a very
vital and spontaneous
manner, in which we see
a reflection of all that was

FIG. 670.—GROS. NAPOLEON AT EYLAU.
(The Louvre, Paris.)

dear to the souls of his age; the refined sensuality of the art of Louis
XVI was ennobled by romantic reverie. Prud'hon remained a fervid
admirer of antique forms; but his instinct led him to the exquisite
grace of Praxiteles, while the æsthetes were celebrating the cold
and declamatory beauty of the Belvedere Apollo. The supreme
charm of his work lies in the tender seduction of the colour and
light; among all the coldly contemplative painters of his day,
Prud'hon alone had a voluptuous eye. The graceful forms of his
nymphs bathe in an atmosphere which they illuminate with their
warm whiteness, and their flesh, drinking in the light, gives back
to obscurity the rays they have received. It was thus that Correggio in his time animated the cold statues of Florentine design, by
putting into them a diffused light which seems to reveal an inner
life. Prud'hon was guided to Greek beauty by his instincts as a
painter more infallibly
than was David by his
archæological theories,
for Praxiteles too, when
he carved the marble,
strove to suggest the tenderness of flesh and the
limpidity of the glance. In
his moon-silvered mists,
Prud'hon achieved that
voluptuous softness which
Girodet attempted to pro-
duce by eccentricities of
illumination (Figs. 672–

FIG. 671.—BOILLY. THE TRIUMPH OF MARAT.
(Museum of Lille.)

676 and 679). The mystery of the park where Josephine reposes is full of dreamy sadness, and the light touches tenderly the easy lines of her relaxed figure. Prud'hon attempted not only to outline, but in his colour there is light and the warm softness of flesh. In the midst of wooden painters his work glows with the graceful sensuousness of Dorat or Gentil Bernard and at times has the gentle sadness of a meditation of Lamartine.

Gros (1771-1835) had also too strong a temperament to submit altogether to David's impersonal method. Among the many correct draughtsmen who were busy modelling impeccable nudities, he worked with spirit, and retained the fire of improvisation in an immense picture. His apprenticeship was only just over, when he shared the life of Bonaparte's soldiers during the Italian campaign of 1796; he handled arms and equipments, became a practised horseman, and saw actual war. The other Davidians, who were military painters by accident, so to say, knew Napoleon's soldiers only from the reviews they witnessed in the Place du Carrousel. Gros greatly admired Rubens, the painter who, before him, had most vividly rendered the fury of battle and the splendour of martial trappings. In his best moments his rapid brush suggested movement and violent gesture, his thin and brilliant colour rendered light flesh, the satiny coats of horses, and

FIG. 674.—PRUD'HON. PSYCHE.
(Condé Museum, Chantilly.)

FIG. 675.—PRUD'HON.
ZEPHYRUS CARRYING OFF PSYCHE.
(The Louvre, Paris.)

a number of visual sensations which classical idealism tended to eliminate; painting full of flavour, where every moment the brilliant and facile brush of a son of Rubens breaks through the ideal rigidity of the Davidian composition. Without Gros, the military epic of the Empire would not have had a painter worthy of it.

But he was something more than a mere battle-painter; like David, he put thought into his vast panoramas. The classical battle-pieces show us warriors, but not soldiers; another genre was evolved, that of Salvator Rosa and of Bourguignon, who painted unnamed battles and cavalry skirmishes of considerable spirit and invention, in which the hind quarters of horses disappear in clouds of pistol-smoke. On behalf of the king, Van der Meulen gave commissions

FIG. 676.—PRUD'HON. JUSTICE AND DIVINE
VENGEANCE PURSUING CRIME.
(The Louvre, Paris.) (*Photo. Neurdein.*)

Y

for historical battle-scenes, where we may admire Louis XIV giving orders on an eminence. The realities of battle had never entered into art, till Gros introduced them. True, this painter sometimes allows himself to be carried away by the pleasure of showing movement and colour, and the *fantasia* of his brush very well expresses the *furia* of Murat's squadrons cutting down the flying burnooses; but in his *Pestiférés de Jaffa* (Fig. 668) and his *Field of Eylau* the artist gives us, much more than the violent pantomime of combat, the pity and the sadness of the conqueror, the despair and rage of the conquered, a lowering sky, the smoke of conflagrations, snow and blood. War was no longer merely a picturesque theme; it excited emotions hitherto unimagined by art. Gros was full of its fever; when the era of battles was past, the soul of his work died out with military enthusiasm. He had not the courage of his genius; he thought it necessary to return to classical themes. His master David, when he went into exile, left the school to his direction. He had always been

somewhat over-awed by the helmeted heroes of the Academy, and a little ashamed of his shakoed veterans. He accordingly ceased to paint these, and his inspiration failed (Figs. 667–670).

But it was not only the great days of the Revolution or the victories of the Empire which seduced painters from antiquity. The example of the Flemish and Dutch Little Masters encouraged

FIG. 678.—BOILLY. HOUDON MAKING A BUST OF MONGE.
(Musée des Arts décoratifs, Paris.)

modest painters, like Demarne, to record incidents of daily life. David's studio produced Granet, who had a predilection for small dark interiors, and worked in the gloomy cloisters of the dispossessed Capuchins; he may almost be said to have created a motive which has not yet lost favour, and seems to herald the convent-interiors of Bonvin, those little pictures full of shadows and silence in which monks and nuns move quietly about (Fig. 680). Drolling and Boilly depicted the Paris of the middle and lower classes with spirited fidelity. Drol-

FIG. 679.—PRUD'HON.
THE EMPRESS JOSÉPHINE.
(The Louvre, Paris.)

ling's manner also is that of a pupil of the Dutchmen. It has endured to our own times; and we shall probably never lack Little Masters who will delight in following a ray of light striking on the stone flags of a kitchen, and kindling reflections on copper and glass (Fig. 682). Boilly's sharp and

FIG. 680.—GRANET. INTERIOR OF A SCHOOL.
(Museum of Aix.)

over-emphatic precision suggests the reduction of a large design, and his smooth uniform colour has the brilliance of the mahogany dear to the cabinet-maker of the Empire (Figs. 677–678). Finally, there were witty observers who found

FIG. 681.—MOREAU. LANDSCAPE.
(The Louvre, Paris.)

FIG. 682.—DROLLING. INTERIOR OF A KITCHEN.
(The Louvre, Paris.)

amusement in the picturesque spectacles of Paris under the Directory and the Restoration. Between Robespierre and Napoleon, between revolutionary civism and martial exaltation, there was an outburst of libertinage, and both in costume and manners, a picturesque disorder very stimulating to the caricaturist. At the time when David, liberated from the Revolution and not yet enrolled by the Empire, was taking the opportunity of returning to Romulus, Carle Vernet and Debucourt were sketching the bizarre Muscadins and Merveilleuses of the Palais-Royal (Fig. 683).

To us, Little Masters such as Boilly and Carle Vernet seem more interesting, perhaps, than the ambitious idealists of the school of David, for the reaction against this school has led us to misjudge all sincerity which is not realistic. And yet the soul of the Revolution survives in David's work, and not in that of Boilly. Even though certain men forced themselves into an expression of artificial grandiloquence, yet as a whole the school of David, with its epic style, did not misrepresent its epoch. Emphasis is not out of place in speech, when there is heroism in actions. Among all these painters from Guérin to Gérard, there were some unwilling captives of the sublime; but the sincerity of David and of Gros lies in their very disdain of prosaic realism. Their vision was great, not because they were megalomaniacs, but because their perfervid generation demanded colossal

FIG. 683.—DEBUCOURT. THE GALLERY OF THE PALAIS ROYAL.
(Bibliothèque Nationale, Print Room.)

324

temples and triumphal arches. Cartellier's marbles, and the heroes of David and of Gros are superhuman in their proportions. Before "The Distribution of the Eagles," David used to say: "Posterity looking at this picture will exclaim, 'What men and what an Emperor!'" They were soaring in idealism when fierce storms broke out, and the tempest of heroism

FIG. 684.—CARLE VERNET. THE RACE.
(The Louvre, Paris.)

carried all before it. But they never abandoned, even in the full flood of realism, their vigorous ideology which was able to put enthusiasm into stiff forms and to express epic ideas by realistic figures. And when the era of violent years was at an end, all this sentimental exaltation, finding its occupation gone, turned to the delirium of Romanticism.

BIBLIOGRAPHY

Quatremère de Quincy, *Considérations sur les Arts du dessin en France*, Paris, 1791.—Renouvier, *L'Histoire de l'Art pendant la Révolution*, Paris, 1863.—F. Benoit, *L'Art français sous la Révolution et l'Empire*, Paris, 1897.—L. Bertrand, *La fin du classicisme et le retour à l'antique*, Paris, 1897.—L. Courajod, *Alexandre Lenoir, son journal et le Musée des Monuments français*, Paris, 1878–1887, 3 vols.—A. Fuetey and J. Guiffrey, *Documents sur la création du Musée du Louvre* (1792–1793), Paris, 1909.—Spire Blondel, *L'Art pendant la Révolution*, Paris, n. d.—M. Dreyfous, *Les Arts et les Artistes pendant la période révolutionnaire*, Paris, n. d.—M. Foucher, *Percier et Fontaine*, Paris, 1905.—P. Lafond, *L'Art décoratif et le Mobilier sous la République et l'Empire*, Paris, 1900.—A. G. Meyer, *Canova*, Bielefeld, 1898.—Emeric David, *Sur les progrès de la Sculpture française depuis le commencement du règne de Louis XVI jusqu'à aujourd'hui*, Paris, 1824.—Chesneau, *La Peinture française au XIXᵉ siècle; les Chefs d'école*, Paris, 1862.—J. David, *Le peintre Louis David*, Paris, 1880.—Delécluze, *Louis David, son école et son temps*, Paris, 1855.—Ch. Saunier, *Louis David*, Paris, n. d.—L. Rosenthal, *Louis David*, Paris, n. d.—Ch. Ephrussi, *Gérard* (G. B. A., 1890, II).—H. Lemonnier, *Gros*, Paris, 1905.—Gauthiez, *Prud'hon*, Paris, 1886.—E. Bricon, *Prud'hon*, Paris, 1907.—P. Dorbec, *Les premiers Peintres du Paysage parisien* (G. B. A., 1908, II).—H. Harrisse, *L. Boilly*, Paris, 1898.

FIG. 685.—PORTRAIT OF INGRES.
BY HIMSELF.
(Condé Museum, Chantilly.)
(*Photo. Neurdein.*)

FIG. 686.—PORTRAIT OF DELACROIX.
BY HIMSELF.
(The Louvre, Paris.)
(*Photo. Neurdein.*)

CHAPTER II

THE ROMANTIC PERIOD

The End of the School of David.—Géricault.—Romanticism in Painting; Individualist and Lyric Art; Imagination and Passion; Delacroix; his Themes and his Technique.—The Minor Romanticists; Decamps.—The Classical Opposition; Ingres; the Serenity of his Art; Linear Design; Ingres' Conception of Decorative Painting; his Disciples.—Mediæval and Modern Subjects in History Painting; Horace Vernet; Delaroche.—Charlet; Raffet; Daumier.—Landscape Painting: Dutch Influence.—Corot.—Rousseau.—Diaz, Dupré, Daubigny, Troyon.—Sculpture from the Time of the Empire.—Statues of Great Men.— David d'Angers.—Rude.—Barye.—The Revival of Mediævalism.—The Gothic Phase.

THE school of David made a melancholy end. The master himself died in a sort of apotheosis; but he was in exile in Brussels, where the glow of his glory still survived, though its source in Paris was extinguished. In December, 1824, at Girodet's funeral, Gros and Gérard asked each other sadly, "What mighty hand would be able to hold back the school on the incline down which it was being dragged by Romanticism?" Neither had authority enough to impose David's austere ideal upon rebellious youth. Gérard was merely a Court portrait-painter, and Gros, a premature wreck, was bewailing the sins of his youth. Girodet had already disquieted David by his Ossianism; but if he felt differently from his master, he painted like him; and artists are lenient to divergencies of inspiration. When, however, technical innovations began to appear, they could not be regarded as venial audacities; they menaced art in its fundamental institution, that of teaching.

It was the museum of the Louvre, rich in the masterpieces of Flanders and Italy until the year

FIG. 687.—HEIM. CHARLES X PRESENTING THE AWARDS AT THE SALON OF 1823.
(The Louvre, Paris.)

1815, which revealed the inadequacy of the Davidian doctrine to the younger artists. Passing from the dismal studio in which a rigid model was posed upon a plank, to the Museum, the pupil of David or Guérin noted the expressive power of naturalism in the hands of Caravaggio or Rubens. Géricault's vigorous painting (1791-1824) ought to have warned the Davidians that their serene idealism could not satisfy a generation which had grown up in the fever of the Revolution and the Empire. True, he died too young not to leave some doubt as to the significance of his work and the value of his innovations. But it

FIG. 688.—GÉRICAULT. CHASSEUR OFFICER.
(The Louvre.) (*Photo. Neurdein.*)

was obvious that he had tried to give robustness to the thin and abstract style of French painting, and tone to its anæmic constitution. The vigorous executants of Spain and Bologna taught him to model fiercely or delicately, to build up his bodies with solid matter, and define them with frank outlines. He owed a good deal to Gros, but he did not preserve Gros' smooth and brilliant manner. The innovations of modern naturalism often resolve themselves into borrowings from the old Flemish or Dutch, Spanish or Neapolitan schools. Géricault is the leader of those nine-

FIG. 689.—HEIM. READING A PLAY AT THE
COMÉDIE-FRANÇAISE.
(Museum of Versailles.)

teenth century realists, educated in museums, the first of those superb craftsmen among whom we find Courbet, Ribot, Manet, and Lucien Simon. Twice in David's time he had distinguished himself by vast and violent canvases of hussars and cuirassiers in action; his daring pencil had seized the momentary gesture of a cavalryman leading a charge, rising upon his rearing horse; and his glowing colour had shown brilliant uniforms and tragic lights in the sinister atmosphere of battle (Fig. 688). When the Restoration disbanded the troops, it deprived him of uniforms and swords. Géricault then turned to that world of athletes, unchained of old by the tumultuous genius of Michelangelo. His drawings and sketches set in motion great muscles straining in some herculean effort, and he painted his masterly work, the *Raft of the Medusa,* a pile of corpses and dying men above which several figures raise themselves, upheld by a last hope, gathering their remaining strength to make a signal for help and to stretch out their hands towards safety (Fig. 691). Like Michelangelo when he painted the Sistine Chapel, Géricault mingles in confusion beautiful bodies, stiff or relaxed. But he does not merely show the innate power which lifts and twists them; his painting has a professional robustness and the trivialities of a materialistic technique. Gros had set the model. Very soon romantic figures became a prey to furious gesticulations. Finally Géricault visited London,

FIG. 690.—DELACROIX. MASSACRE
OF SCIO.
(The Louvre, Paris.)

and there liberated himself altogether from his French education. His impressions of England, green landscapes under a watery sky, race-courses, and stables, are rendered by means of nervous painting and fresh colour; it was Géricault who introduced the race-horse into French art, and inaugurated a *genre* afterwards popularised by engraving and lithography; horses

FIG. 691.—GÉRICAULT. THE RAFT
OF THE MEDUSA.
(The Louvre, Paris.)

with well groomed coats, neck and shoulders stretched out, both fore and hind legs extended. Until then horses ran in pictures by prancing like stone figures on a pedestal. Since then painters have caught from instantaneous photography more than one aspect among the innumerable positions of a horse who gathers and flings himself in galloping, which the eye had not been able to catch, and they have given up the flying gallop of Géricault. Still, that is a real position of horses who gallop *ventre-à-terre* over the turf of the race-course (Fig. 697). Géricault died before Romanticism had declared war against Classicism, and his work, still undecided when it was interrupted for ever, hardly allows us to judge which side he would have taken in the battle.

In the Salon of 1822, a young friend of Géricault's, Eugène Delacroix (1798–1863), exhibited a scene from the *Divine Comedy*. But there was nothing in this livid vision of *Virgil and Dante in Hell* very surprising to a public familiar with Caravaggio, and the *Raft of the Medusa*. It was not until two years later, before the *Massacre of Scio*,

FIG. 692.—DELACROIX. VIRGIL AND
DANTE IN HELL.
(The Louvre, Paris.)

FIG. 693.—DELACROIX. DON JUAN'S SHIPWRECK.
(The Louvre, Paris.)

that the critics inveighed against the "massacre of painting" (Fig. 690). Delacroix had, in fact, transformed his pictorial language in the interval; inspired by the English landscape painters he had loaded his palette with brilliant colours and illumined Gros' robust impasto with the glint of Oriental tissues and the marble tints of putrefaction. This time, the work was frankly revolutionary; the young Romanticists rallied round Delacroix, and the struggle against the classical tradition began; no durable school resulted from it, but the consequences were such as to transform the very conception of art.

To these young Romanticists art was not the realisation of an abstract ideal, but the expression of an individual soul, and the more original the artist, the greater the value of his works. He should not fear to manifest his vigorous personality; on the contrary, he should defend it jealously against external influences, against all the forces that, by limiting his personality, tend to obscure his genius. Romanticism was the revolt of sensitive faculties, hitherto disciplined by the play of definite ideas. Latent and irresponsible forces rose from unconscious depths to reject classical logic. For logic, with its fixed principles, is identical among all men; it has a sort of eternal existence, superior to the minds which successively exercise it; and the Romanticist affects to despise this faculty which makes individuals similar.

Now from the sixteenth century onwards, a long artistic tradition had fixed

FIG. 694.—DELACROIX. LIBERTY LEADING THE PEOPLE.
(The Louvre, Paris.)

a body of rules which weighed upon the artist as law weighs upon the citizen. Towards the end of the eighteenth century, after David, this dogma became more fixed than ever, and æstheticians, deducing with strictness principles of absolute beauty, constrained the imagination of the painter and only left him a narrow outlet towards that ideal of beauty which was Greek and Italian before

FIG. 695.—DELACROIX. ARAB FANTASIA.
(Museum of Montpellier.)

it became French. Romanticism, exploding, burst through this academic compression. Delacroix's work, from beginning to end, was a passionate protest against this legislation which lays fetters upon genius. For more than thirty years, he painted as if he were fighting, with spasms of energy and disgust, sometimes with the exaltation of triumph, more often with the rage of defeat. He felt a savage joy in tearing up the code of the Classicists. We learn this not only from his feverish, convulsive drawing, not only from the violence and the fury of his "drunken brush," but from the irritable

FIG. 696.—DELACROIX. THE TAKING OF
CONSTANTINOPLE.
(The Louvre, Paris.)

confidences he made to his Journal. He execrated that form which becomes impersonal under pretence of purity and dead under pretence of nobility; to him there were lines which are veritably monstrous—straight, wavy and especially parallel ones. He rejoices when he can say of the work he is doing that it is turbulent and rough. "My picture is writhing—that blessed coarseness—I hate systematic painting." It

FIG. 697.—GÉRICAULT. HORSE-RACE AT EPSOM.
(The Louvre, Paris.)

seemed as if he wished to communicate his fury to the paint which he spread on the canvas, and that disorder in execution seemed to him an indication of sincerity. If Delacroix had not been commissioned to do large decorations he would have wasted his genius in little sketches. He forced himself always to preserve in his vast compositions the dash of the sketch. His sympathies are with the "incorrect and careless geniuses," all those who betray the pathetic struggle of passion against form.

Delacroix prized the independence of emotion and of personal fancy so highly, that he never conceived of painting as a representation of reality. This, indeed, is the Romantic paradox. The painter cannot, of course, borrow his images from anything save nature; but to Delacroix, these images were only a means; he took forms and colours from visible things, but, just as the poet chooses metaphors, only in order to speak more magnificently of himself. The Romanticists attacked the Classicists in the name of truth, for truth is the battle-cry of all art-rebellions. And yet Delacroix and his group had a hearty contempt for objective accuracy; no school was ever less docile to the exigencies of representation, or less capable of portraiture. Delacroix's imagination elaborated a world too full of colour and poetry for him to have ever dreamt of sacrificing it to the universe of our actual vision. A perpetual fount of fictive images

FIG. 698.—DELACROIX. BATTLE OF TAILLEBOURG.
(Museum of Versailles.)

hid the real aspect of things from him; this short-sighted painter was a visionary. The presence of the model checked his inspiration; he only resorted to it occasionally to repair his lapses of memory, and he had the same contempt for historical accuracy. He made no pretence, like Delaroche, of attempting to reconstruct the Middle Ages accurately. Historical accuracy is a heavy fetter for a poet. The "local colour" of historians is merely retrospective realism.

Thus Delacroix's world is marvellously coherent and harmonious, in spite of its strangeness. In his nature, which is not

FIG. 699.—DELACROIX. THE JUSTICE OF TRAJAN.
(Museum of Rouen.)

that in which we live, sky, plants, rocks and animals, flesh and draperies participate in a kind of feverish exaltation and ardent melancholy. This world is the projection of his soul, the translation of his temperament into images. "The most real things in me are

FIG. 700.—DELACROIX. MEDEA.
(Museum of Lille.)

the illusions I create with my painting." His own emotions, and those of his time, live in his pictures. The impressions of a student of romantic literature become a sort of instantaneous illustration in his work; he gives us visions of Dante, dramas of Shakespeare or Goethe, poems of Byron, novels of Walter Scott, and then the events which stirred the hearts of the first generations of the century; the heroic struggle of the little Greek nation against the Turks, the flag of 1830 rising through the smoke over the barricades of paving-stones; mediaeval visions, vivid as pages of Michelet, battles, Nancy, Taillebourg, Constantinople, and a quantity of mediaeval and modern scenes, Gothic or

333

FIG. 701.—VICTOR HUGO. THE FORTRESS.
(Victor Hugo's House, Paris.) (Washed Drawing.)

Revolutionary halls, tumultuous welters in which the colour yells, and the drawing is dislocated by furious gestures; then the East, that Morocco where he had travelled and seen fantasias of horsemen, where he had divined the drowsy harems and the innumerable wild beasts, the lions and tigers which roar at us from his little canvases. The setting for these convulsive bodies is a tragic landscape, a green and glassy sea, a lowering sky, the lurid twilight of storm and massacre. Finally, when he undertook large decorative compositions, Delacroix was able to express modern and living ideas, never borrowed from the conventional store-house of allegory, but so full of thought that they might have appeared irreconcilable with the genius of painting. In the middle of the Galerie d'Apollon in the Louvre, on that ceiling dedicated by Le Brun to the glorification of the Sun King, he produced a sumptuous decoration, worthy of the Doges, and at the same time he expanded the victory of the God of Light over the Python into a magnificent symbol.

Rubens would, no doubt, have given greater freedom in the movement, greater splendour in the colour; but he would never have conceived the tragic forms that writhe in the primeval slime.

This lyric painter loved colour for its emotional power; it sprang from his imagination charged with passion, like a musical rhythm or a cry. His picture is no arrangement of correctly posed figures; in the first sketch there are patches of colour which represent storm, calm, melancholy, terror or horror; skilful drawing is an impersonal thing, like a well-reasoned argu-

FIG. 702.—MÉRYON. THE STRYGE.
(Bibliothèque Nationale, Print Room.)

ment, but colour is as individual as the sound of the voice. Delacroix loved it brilliant and sumptuous, in the manner of Venice or Antwerp; but he had an exasperated sensibility and an uneasiness of mind which prevented his songs from rising in those clear and joyous accents. He did not care for frank tones or simple harmonies, but essayed broken tints, purple-reds, greenish-blues; there is no colour in the prism with which he did not try strange combinations and subtle contrasts; his feminine carnations, blond and pale, are drowned in a kind of milky mist, and in his penumbra

FIG. 703.—DEVÉRIA. SKETCH FOR THE BIRTH OF HENRY IV.
(Museum of Montpellier.)

he gets the soft translucence of a fine pearl. Sometimes he strikes a harsh, metallic note; in other passages the colours neutralise each other, dulled by an intermixture in which cunning dissonances make themselves felt.

His hand trembles at times, and the brush deals slashing, staccato strokes, and does not always find the right, all-expressive touch at once. When the composition is peaceful, we are shocked by the recurrent inaccuracies, the uncertainty and monotony of the forms, the vague involved folds of heavy stuffs which do not drape the limbs or indicate their movements, the exaggerated arch of the horses' necks, their uncertain anatomy, their plunging hoofs, their flabby softness and ridiculous contortions, the faces seen in profile on shoulders seen from behind. But when Delacroix is fired by his inspiration, his paint-

FIG. 704.—DECAMPS. THE BELL-RINGERS.
(The Louvre, Paris.)

335

FIG. 705.—DECAMPS. CHILDREN COMING OUT
OF A TURKISH SCHOOL.
(Musée des Arts décoratifs, Paris.)

ing is swift and sure as a flash of lightning. Examine one of his little Arab fantasias; the horses bound like sheep dogs among the fluttering burnooses; everything crackles, sparkles, caracoles and plunges; the form agrees with the gesture, limbs are twisted or stretched out; the wild beasts that he painted with such delight, lions and tigers rushing upon their prey or battling with huntsmen and horses, are like forces let loose.

Delacroix attempted a paradox when he tried to make painting lyrical like poetry and music; painting and sculpture are dedicated to the representation of the external world. Our own visual experience forces us at every moment to correct the painter's fancy, and instinctively, we feel it to be intolerable that reality, which is common property, should be treated according to the caprice of a fevered dreamer. Delacroix's art, with its partial failure, reveals the mind of a poet of genius. His explosive sensibility created a new manner of seeing, but one too individual and special to become general. Hence Delacroix, who determined so many artistic vocations, never formed a pupil; he could substitute nothing for the traditional method of the Classicists. At the end of his life, his painting excited even more hostility than at the beginning. In the very thick of the Romantic fray, contemporaries were unable to distinguish the provocations of the turbulent, and the skilful adaptations of the eclectics from the audacities of the real innovators. Delacroix's personality was not

FIG. 706.—DECAMPS. CHILDREN AT
THE WELL.
(Museum of Chantilly.)

very clearly defined among the group of rebels. But the little band was gradually sifted; Boulanger, Devéria, and many others, failing to produce their promised masterpieces, were soon forgotten. Delaroche, whose Gothic accessories had caused him to be taken for a Romanticist, betrayed the prudence

FIG. 708.—INGRES. STRATONICE.
(Museum of Montpellier.)

FIG. 707.—INGRES.
THE VOW OF LOUIS XIII.
(Cathedral of Montauban.)
(*Photo. Neurdein.*)

his education more and more clearly.
full of German sentimentality; but he spoke in abstract terms, as if he desired to show souls through transparent bodies, and he naturally found himself at last in the camp of the Classicists (Fig. 720). Delacroix finished the race begun thirty years earlier with a youthful ardent throng quite alone. He had preserved his lyrical fire to the end, although the Romantic fever around him had long subsided.

But about the year 1830, the pulses of France beat fiercely. The burning and lurid imagination of Romanticism did not always achieve important works; it found exuberant expression in

of his temperament and the academic character of Ary Scheffer seemed at first

FIG. 709.— INGRES.
MARTYRDOM OF SAINT SYMPHORIEN.
(Cathedral of Autun.)
(*Photo. Neurdein.*)

337

FIG. 710.—INGRES. THETIS AND JUPITER.
(Museum of Aix.)

small illustrations. The novel art of lithography, and the re-vivified art of wood-engraving, a few lines, a few shadows, revealed the delirious visions of certain artists better than painting or sculpture. In some old romantic books, the drawings of Célestin Nanteuil, Gigoux, Johannot, Devéria and even Delacroix startled the classical reader. Here also the linear anatomy of Girodet and Flaxman, the long figures of Achilles and Agamemnon, were replaced by personages in picturesque Gothic garments. Solitary poets, lyre in hand, dreaming upon tombs; delicate lovers embracing, spied upon by jealous rivals; women dragged by the hair; masked faces; hang-dog executioners; black dungeon cells—the illustrators imitated and surpassed literature in excesses. Then there was the *macabre* style, the dead rising from tombs, grinning skeletons, witches on broomsticks; acrobatic Mephistos, shaggy, angular, horned. From Gothic roofs the gargoyles and monsters came down; from old German castles came flights of bats and of witches riding broomsticks; hell opened its gates, and in this little world of the illustrator, devils were as numerous as Cupids had been in the time of Boucher.

While the battle was raging between Classicists and Romanticists, Decamps (1803–1860) won universal admiration with his little robustly-painted pictures. Like the Romanticists, he showed himself a colourist, and a lover of rare effects; like them, he was attracted by the vision of

FIG. 711.—INGRES. APOTHEOSIS OF HOMER.
(The Louvre, Paris.)

the East. But his temperament had none of the fiery passion of Delacroix. Sometimes he seems to have been thinking of Rembrandt, and sometimes of Chardin. But he suppressed emotion, thought, history, and even nature; or rather, he took from the material world only certain small aspects, so fragmentary and so individual that they seem to be merely pretexts for his technical essays. He gets an equal amount of picturesque effect from a smoky garret or a tragic landscape, from a piece of wall with a few beggars'

FIG. 712.—INGRES. MME. DE SENONNES.
(Museum of Nantes.)
(*Photo. Neurdein.*)

rags, and from jagged, bloodshot clouds lowering over burning rocks (Figs. 704-706). Marilhat also loved the torrid East; he built up solid landscapes with shattered rocks and majestic ruins. But he died young, before he had learned to illuminate his solid colour. At that same Salon of 1824, where the younger painters flocked to admire the *Massacre of Scio*, a pupil of David's, Jean-Baptiste Dominique Ingres (1780-1867), who had been for some

time in Italy, also made a brilliant success with his *Vow of Louis XIII.* We are accustomed to look upon Ingres as the successor of David; but all he had derived from David was his position as the head of the traditional school; no doubt there was room within this school for more than one ideal, for the master and pupil were far from agreeing. The Classicists sought for a beauty somewhat mannered and Alexandrine, the theatrical elegance of the Belvedere Apollo, or the mincing prettiness of the Venus de Medici; Ingres, on the contrary,

FIG. 713.—INGRES. GRANET.
(Museum of Aix.)

FIG. 714.—INGRES. MME. DEVAUÇAY.
(Condé Museum, Chantilly.)
(*Photo. Neurdein.*)

was very sensible of the charm of the primitive schools, when art, absorbed in the desire for truth, had no idea of effacing the characteristic accent. This admirable draughtsman made it a rule to copy the human body and actual draperies; in his purest contours, the line preserves the nervous force of life. The art of David depersonalises figures; that of Ingres strips them of their material character, but not of their individuality. His *Œdipus*, a contemporary of the heroes of Guérin and Girodet, has neither the Grecian profile nor the rounded limbs of an antique marble. Ingres felt himself more akin to the Italian primitives than to the Græco-Roman sculptors, and many persons were wondering at his realism, when Delacroix made his appearance. Then Ingres felt himself called upon to be the apostle of the beautiful, in opposition to him whom he called the apostle of the ugly. Never were two temperaments more antagonistic, and

as each wielded considerable authority, this antagonism became a doctrinal rivalry.

Delacroix's art is the troubled reflection of all the passions of his day. Ingres despised his own age; he came back from Italy to Paris, with no idea of settling in the French capital; a success kept him there, and a failure drove him away; like Poussin, his dream was to retire to Rome, the city of ruins and of history. There, lost in the contemplation of his own ideal, he would gladly have forgotten the world. Delacroix showed Greece weeping over smoking ruins, or Liberty

FIG. 715.—INGRES. MME. DELORME.
(Drawing.) (The Louvre, Paris.)

victorious on the barricades. While shots were flying in the street below, Ingres sat at his window, and touched his Venus Anadyomene with a loving brush. Vibrating to every breath of passion, carried away by the impression of a moment, Delacroix cried: "I begin to paint a woman, and I make a lion." Late in life Ingres finished a study begun in his youth, and in this *Source* we can discover no discord between inspiration and method. Delacroix was always inventing, and would not tolerate imitation. Ingres imitated continually either nature or the old masters, and believed there was no such thing as invention. He exhibited an *Apotheosis of Homer* which was designed to be a kind of Credo for his classical religion; it repre-

FIG. 716.—INGRES.
DUC D'ORLÉANS.
(Museum of Versailles.)

sents great artists and writers doing homage to the poet of the *Iliad* and the *Odyssey* for the works with which he had inspired them. However, neither Ingres nor Delacroix felt it essential to make his art conform to the æsthetic doctrine he had adopted. Ingres talked a great deal about principles, and laid down axioms acceptable to the Classicists of every age, but, like any Romanticist, he obeyed the intimate promptings of his genius. No doubt he lacks profundity, if we compare him with Delacroix. We may admit that his culture was not of a very high order, that his intelligence was limited, that he had neither strong sensibilities, nor a rich imagination. But if he seems a little narrow, it is because he was too exclusively an artist; he thought nothing in the world could compete with the sweep of a beautiful line. He aspired to make every work that left his hands a feast of perfection for the eye, like a piece of exquisite chasing, or an

FIG. 717.—FLANDRIN.
NAPOLEON III.
(Museum of Versailles.)

FIG. 718.—INGRES. ODALISQUE.
(The Louvre, Paris.)

antique cameo; and whereas Delacroix dashed off his sketches with an impatient brush, Ingres, in spite of the prodigious dexterity of his pencil, repeated a motive again and again before he attacked its final form. Ingres had tasted the secret satisfaction of sinuous lines drawn by a master hand in the works of the great Renaissance draughtsmen, and it is easy to recognize echoes of Leonardo and Raphael in his Madonnas and his draped figures. He owes less to that antique sculpture which had petrified David's painting; for in sculpture the silhouette is determined by the modelling of the full form, and Ingres, on the contrary, attenuates the relief, while defining the contours with extreme delicacy. His first work, *Œdipus*, still emphasised salient forms in the Davidian manner, and in the *Saint Symphorien* there is a lictor who is famous for his sturdy muscular system (Fig. 709); but as a rule, Ingres would not allow modelling too emphatic to falsify the supple continuity of his line. The antique works to which he owed most were the paintings on vases, draughtsman's paintings, touched with the point of a fine brush. In some of his most exquisite small pictures, the colour is diaphanous and fluid that the figure may not lose its linear lightness. Very often he only drew his portraits, and colour could only have added heaviness to their elegant precision. The fine point of the pencil on the paper left definite forms. Shadows even are scarcely needed to give bodies to these outlines. The line, soft or sharp, clean-cut or blurred, suffices to express solidity. It is never lifeless but always expresses a living form and brings out the individual character of a face or a dress. Ingres combined the trenchant exactness of

FIG. 719.—INGRES.
LA SOURCE.
(The Louvre, Paris.)

a Holbein with the grace of the Florentines. We cannot but admire the manner in which he fixes reality with a few strokes of the pencil, and informs the majesty of a Greek drapery with truth.

His rhythmical design was more attuned to the round contours of feminine nudity than to the salient muscles of an athletic body. The limbs he draws show no effort; his favourite attitudes were those of an arm in repose, or of a supple body reclining languidly. His preparatory sketches return again and again to the inclination of a neck, the curve of a shoulder, the pose of a hand upon a drapery. His best portraits of women owe

FIG. 720.—ARY SCHEFFER.
SAINT AUGUSTINE AND SAINT MONICA.
(The Louvre, Paris.)

much of their elegance to the curve which undulates from the line of the neck along the arm to the finger-tips. The bust bends slightly forward, as if to allow these relaxed lines to fall more easily. The face is less interesting to him, for here the modelling gave less opportunity for the exercise of his sinuous elegance. He executed admirable portraits, but somewhat against the grain, to make a livelihood, or to please his patrons. He preferred to imagine inflexions of hips, or breasts thrown forward by an inclination of the head. The pictures in which he has put most of himself are simple nudities such as the *Odalisque* or *La Source;* his more ambitious compositions are merely interlacements of feminine bodies, like the *Bain Turc* or the *Age d'Or.* Ingres has given us feminine attitudes of the most haunting grace: the divinely beautiful

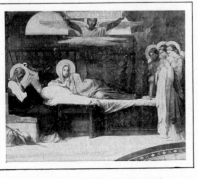

FIG. 721.—FLANDRIN. THE NATIVITY.
(Church of Saint-Germain-des-Prés, Paris.)

Virgin in the *Vow of Louis XIII;* the superbly defiant *Iliad* at the feet of Homer, and the dreamy *Odyssey;* the fragile *Stratonice,* shrinking as from a blow; the *Odalisques* stretching themselves languorously, or drooping and weary; the *Source,* fresh and ingenuous, like some beautiful plant, her lips parted like an opening flower; his feminine faces all have the astonished candour of childhood; the wide eyes look out at the spectator without speculation or anxiety.

But the head of a school could not confine himself to the painting of Odalisques and portraits. Ingres had to set an example, and to give French painters models of more ambitious compositions. Although his imagination did not rise to the conception of a vast whole, he showed skill in linking together a number of the figures he drew with such perfection in a common action. But the *Martyrdom of St. Symphorien* lacks movement; the gestures are too ingeniously harmonised, and the equilibrium is too perfect; there is an excess of discipline in this drama. On the other hand, Ingres had created an enduring style of decorative painting some years earlier in his *Apotheosis of Homer* (Fig. 711). This developed throughout the entire nineteenth century, and even now apparently it has not come to the end of its manifestations. Ingres, who had studied the artists of the fifteenth century for years in Italy, modified the natural realism of oil-painting to imitate

the somewhat abstract sobriety of Florentine frescoes. His composition is without depth, without atmosphere, and even without light. The symmetrically arranged figures take attitudes adapted to the tranquil lines of architecture, like the figures in a very flat bas-relief. There is no movement to disturb the attitudes,

FIG. 724.—COUTURE. THE ROMANS OF THE DECADENCE.
(The Louvre, Paris.)

nor breath to move the draperies. The colours are generalised, the forms immaterial, the figures without movement, the textures without reflections, the flesh without life; a serene elegance and an icy purity mark the work. Although Ingres thus unfolded all the resources of his marvellous drawing, although he recognised that realism in colour and effects of relief were to be avoided, he never worked out his process to its logical conclusion, by giving the delicate pallor of fresco to his general tone. His pupils continued to colour without charm elegant or merely correct silhouettes, until the day when Puvis de Chavannes completed this beauty of line by the poetry of a natural illumination, and, like Poussin before him, set rhythmic figures in a real landscape.

FIG. 725.—HORACE VERNET. MARSHAL MONCEY AT THE CLICHY BARRICADE.
(The Louvre, Paris.)
(*Photo. Neurdein.*)

Ingres lived to see his decorative style continued by his pupils, Amaury, Duval, Mottez, and above all, Hippolyte Flandrin (1809–1864). The numerous religious works executed under the Monarchy of July and the Second Empire repeat the *Apotheosis of Homer.* The faults of this manner become very apparent in the disciples; coldness is not the least of these; in

FIG. 726.—HORACE VERNET.
THE TAKING OF THE SMALA (FRAGMENT).
(Museum of Versailles.)

the work of these correct and skilful draughtsmen we note the dawn of an affectation of simplicity, which gradually led them to imitate the primitives. The best of these disciples, however, Flandrin, put an ardent faith into his somewhat melancholy eloquence. His compositions in Saint-Germain-des-Prés are set side by side with the barbarous sculptures of the Romanesque capitals, the colour of which was restored at this period. Thus the two chronological extremes of Christian art were juxtaposed. When we glance from the elegant correctness of the modern to the awkward and heavy application of the primitive, we see that the expressive power of art is far from increasing in proportion to skill. Flandrin lacked nothing that is essential to the religious painter, not even the faith of Fra Angelico; but his art seems a very fragile calligraphy upon this old Romanesque masonry (Fig. 721).

The pupils of David, and later those of Ingres, had at first sought only the phantoms that wander among the ruins during their sojourn in Italy. It required an unpretentious painter like Hubert Robert to take pleasure in the picturesqueness of actual men and things, or a poet of light like Claude Lorrain to forget the mementoes of the antique. Nevertheless, more than one of the students of the French Academy in Rome, and sometimes even the Director himself, felt the

FIG. 727.—LÉOPOLD ROBERT. ARRIVAL
OF HARVESTERS IN THE PONTINE MARSHES.
(The Louvre, Paris.)

346

fascination of their Italian models so strongly that they forgot to transform them into Madonnas and heroes. Schnetz, Léopold Robert (Fig. 727), and Hébert have given us images of the Roman herdsman and the fisherman of the Adriatic. The most absolute idealists were able to compromise with realities more easily in Italy than elsewhere. In this nature, which is everywhere permeated with history, in the midst of

FIG. 728.—DELAROCHE.
THE PRINCES IN THE TOWER.
(The Louvre, Paris.)

a people whose finest types have sat as models to the masters for centuries, even naturalistic painting seems to be touched with classical poetry; a mythological soul hovers over the Campagna, and the dancing Neapolitan soon appears a faun.

Painting reflected the curiosity with which the minds of men turned to the Middle Ages in the reign of Louis Philippe. The mediæval subject was not the exclusive property of the Romantic

FIG. 729.—DELAROCHE.
BONAPARTE ON MOUNT SAINT-BERNARD.
(Windsor Castle.)

School; the last of the Davidians, Ingres and his pupils, depicted the Middle Ages, no less freely than antiquity. The July Monarchy had turned the palace of Versailles into a museum of French history. All the contemporary painters were called upon to produce in haste vast compositions celebrating the glorious events of that history from the baptism of Clovis to the conquest of Algeria. This series naturally included a number of Napoleonic paintings and works of the School of Le Brun, for Louis XIV and Napoleon had not left the glorification of their exploits to their successors.

FIG. 730.—DELAROCHE. THE MURDER OF THE DUKE
OF GUISE.
(Condé Museum, Chantilly.)

Nearly all the French painters took part in the undertaking, and its pictures are by no means all masterpieces. They are large decorations in which the accessories and the costumes fill the stage, but too often the artist was not enough interested in his subject to put any feeling into it, or not enough of a painter to give it any picturesqueness. Yet it is to this enterprise that we owe two of Delacroix's great works, the *Battle of Taillebourg* and the *Crusaders at Constantinople,* the one seething with fury, the other full of a kind of grandiose melancholy (Figs. 696, 698).

Horace Vernet (1789-1863), a facile painter and skilful illustrator, was among the most gifted of these artistic chroniclers. His innumerable military pictures are like the spirited tale of a trooper, relating heroic actions and camp adventures with the same simplicity and good humour (Fig. 726). But Paul Delaroche (1797-1856) is the most representative of these artists who devoted themselves to the illustration of history. He satisfied the curiosity of the readers and auditors of Augustin Thierry, Guizot or Barante, giving a body, a physiognomy and a plausible costume to various illustrious personages: Elizabeth of England, Charles I, Cromwell, Henry III, Richelieu. He had a talent for theatrical representation, and real skill in awakening curiosity or anxiety by showing, not the catastrophe itself, but the episodes leading up to it, or its epilogue. This dexterous stage-manager greatly interested the *bourgeoisie* of the

FIG. 731.—RAFFET. THE REVEILLE.
(LITHOGRAPH.)
(Bibliothèque Nationale, Print Room.)

time of Louis Philippe, and he never shocked it by any Romantic truculence; his correct technique delighted the lovers of the golden mean, and they admired in him a chastened Delacroix, just as in Delavigne they hailed a more tranquil Victor Hugo. Tony RobertFleury also painted the Middle Ages or the Renaissance, expressing the sentiment of its per-

FIG. 732.—RAFFET. THE MIDNIGHT REVIEW.
(LITHOGRAPH.)
(Bibliothèque Nationale, Print Room.)

sonages with some dramatic force and with stronger colour than Delaroche. Isabey, a less ambitious artist, was content to make the light flicker on the velvet and satin of his pretty puppets, and to concentrate the sumptuous colour of the great Venetian and Flemish decorators in little figures.

It was the educated middle classes who read the eloquent pages of history written by Delaroche; but there was a much larger public for the drawings of Raffet and Daumier. Below the more pompous works flourished a popular imagery, direct, violent and rapid as life itself. Fixed by lithography, it preserves the emotions and the passions of a feverish time. Without Charlet and Raffet, we should not have realised how Orleanist France was haunted by memories of the Revolution and the Empire, how popular the volunteers in wooden shoes of 1793, the grenadiers of the Grande Armée, the conscripts of 1814, and the Emperor on his white horse, in his little cocked hat and his riding coat, continued to be. The theme of the grumbling veteran occurs frequently in the works of the official

FIG. 733.—CHARLET. THE ARMY IN
AFRICA. (LITHOGRAPH.)
(Bibliothèque Nationale, Print Room.)

FIG. 734.—DAUMIER. RUE TRANSNONAIN, APRIL 15, 1834. (LITHOGRAPH.)
(Bibliothèque Nationale, Print Room.)

painter, Horace Vernet; but his lucid and brilliant pictures have less poetry than those murky engravings where Raffet shows us squares of infantry against which the cavalry dash like waves against rocks, or massive, swarming battalions advancing at the double. It was this draughtsman who recorded in his drawings a Napoleonic legend as it was imagined by romantic spirits. In the Revue Nocturne he passes in review before the Emperor cuirassiers, with their horsehair plumes, and fantastic horses risen from the shades and still draped in tattered veils of shadow; and elsewhere in a strange land of skeletons a drummer marches with so fierce a step, beating the reveille with such fury, that he rouses in passing a crowd of phantoms and the tempest of heroism sweeps along these pale apparitions. (Figs. 731, 732.)

Lithography played an active polemical part throughout this period; actual as the newspaper article, it was freely employed in the political battles that were waged under the Monarchy of July. A few years of relative liberty, from 1830 to 1835, sufficed to make Louis Philippe one of the most caricatured figures in history. Decamps and Daumier expressed the general hatred of the fallen king, Charles X, and of Louis Philippe, the improvised king who had emerged from a popular Revolution. Henri Monnier created Joseph Prudhomme. the commercial *bourgeois*, puffed up with his own importance, and stupefied by philosophical pretensions, the expansive imbecile who

FIG. 735.—GAVARNI. (LITHOGRAPH.)
"MR. ÉMILE JOLIBOIS?"
"YES, IT'S I."
(Bibliothèque Nationale, Print Room.)

dies without any inkling that he is nothing but a pompous fool. Gavarni's nervous hand recorded fashionable life, the festivities of carnival time, the Bohemia of the student, and the conjugal misfortunes of the National Guard. Daumier in particular has left us powerful and atrocious images of society, of the king and his rateable *bourgeoisie* busily directing a revolution by which they hoped to live, but which was to destroy them. Daumier treated the human figure with astonishing audacity; his irritable extravagance reveals a temperament still essentially romantic; he deformed, twisted,

FIG. 736.—DAUMIER.
THE DIVORCERS. (LITHOGRAPH.)
(Bibliothèque Nationale, Print Room.)

elongated or inflated bodies and faces, to show character or emphasise a type. These great caricaturists were the precursors of the realists. Orleanist society lives again with Monnier's *Joseph Prudhomme,* Gavarni's *Lorette,* Daumier's *Ventre Legislatif* and *Robert Macaire,*

FIG. 737—DEVÉRIA.
WOMAN IN BALL DRESS.
(LITHOGRAPH.)
(Rouart Collection, Paris.)

the precursors of his later type, the famous *Rataplan,* imperialist agent. The grotesque Romanticist prepared the way for the dull ugliness of realism.

Classicists and Romanticists, in spite of their divergencies, had this in common, that they were one and all painters of the studio, the museum, or the reception-room. Boucher had shown how to decorate a panel for a boudoir, David how to colour an antique hero, Ingres how to draw a living model, Delacroix how to materialise brilliant fictions; no one had, so far, recommended painters to go and set up their easels in the open air, not even Joseph Vernet. Classical idealism had omitted landscape. And yet writers had been

351

FIG. 738.—GAVARNI. GRISETTES.
(LITHOGRAPH.)
(Bibliothèque Nationale, Print Room.)

describing Nature for years; a novel sentimentality was manifesting itself in connection with rural aspects. It is a production of extreme civilization. We never feel the full value of liberty till we are deprived of it. The Parisians, above all, were in love with the trees and fields they had lost. Among these citizens who loved to escape to the outskirts of the capital, there were some painters. Later one of his friends wrote to Rousseau, the great landscape painter: "Do you remember the time when in our garrets in the rue Taitbout, sitting in our narrow windows, with our feet hanging over the edge of the roof, we looked at the corners of the houses and chimney-pots, which you compared, half closing your eyes, to mountains and great trees, scattered over a broken country? Not being able to go to the Alps or into the gay fields, you made for yourself a picturesque landscape from these hideous carcasses."

The first of the men who attempted to paint the country, obscure artists, unnoticed by their contemporaries, did not venture far from the city; they stopped at the first halting-place of the stage-coach, and brought back some view of Meudon or Vincennes; in these Paris is always on the next incline of the horizon; solitary and silent Nature is not suggested as yet. It seemed to be lifeless in a time when no one had yet penetrated the secret soul of inanimate things. But romantic poetry taught men to see a reflection of their own passions in landscape; many

FIG. 730.—DAUMIER. THE ROBBERS
AND THE ASS.
(The Louvre, Paris.)

of those who first painted it, seem concerned to render spiritual states when they represented clouds or trees. At first the difficulties were of a technical order. Foliage, clouds, and distant horizons were novel objects for these painters of history or portraits. How many conventions had to be forgotten, how many new

FIG. 740.—MARILHAT. RUINS OF THE MOSQUE OF CALIPH HAKEM. AT CAIRO.
(The Louvre. Paris.)

terms invented! When at the end of the reign of Louis XVI, perfectly sincere artists had attempted to copy grass and water from Nature, they had found only dull, non-translucent colour on their palettes. The audacity of Delacroix and the fantasies of the Romanticists had at least shown that

FIG. 741.—ISABEY. VIEW OF DIEPPE.
(Museum, Nancy.)

colour could be freely treated. Instead of spreading it like plaster, neatly glazed, Delacroix, when he painted the *Massacre of Scio*, juxtaposed brilliant tints and frank touches, leaving the eye to harmonise these vivid tones. Delacroix had already been inspired by the English landscape painters; the French landscape painters profited by his example. But Dela-

FIG. 742.—G. MICHEL. ENVIRONS OF MONTMARTRE.
(The Louvre, Paris.)

FIG. 743—HUET. INUNDATION AT SAINT-CLOUD.
(The Louvre, Paris.)

croix was essentially a history-painter; and his style, like that of the Classicists, was better fitted for the treatment of figures and draperies than for that of serrated foliage, vaporous clouds or aspects of the soil.

That which we call "Nature" is a thing of extraordinary complexity, and the French painters of this "Nature" would, no doubt, have been more tentative in their researches if the Dutchmen of the seventeenth century had not composed admirable landscapes before their time. The first generation of French landscape painters was of the Dutch family; they were sincere and clearsighted; but distant memories dominate their individual work. Until the time of the Impressionists, we shall recognise the vision of the masters of Amsterdam and Harlem in the manner of choosing and arranging a scene.

The first efforts of landscape were hesitating. A forgotten artist, Georges Michel, shows a powerful sincerity in spite of a somewhat rugged technique. Slate-grey clouds over a russet landscape give the environs of Montmartre the melancholy majesty of a Ruysdael (Fig. 742). A vague sentimentality or romantic dreams troubled the sight of many a painter. They could not yet look frankly at clouds and trees. Paul Huet's nature is as emotional as that of Delacroix. The landscape is observed more conscientiously; but the painter has done his utmost to give it a sentimental tone and a meditative cast. Sometimes he shows it tender and spring-like; but he preferred its more tragic aspects, an inundation in a winter landscape, or the fury of waves in a

FIG. 744.—COROT. VIEW OF THE COLISEUM.
(The Louvre, Paris.)

storm (Fig. 743). Others, like Cabat, suffered from their Poussinesque aspirations. He sought to give an eternal aspect to changing images, and his trees and clouds make the impression of mythological scenes. A De la Berge, on the other hand, painted a tree as it would appear through a magnifying glass, laboriously reproducing its foliage and the accidents of its bark, spelling out, letter by letter, the luxuriant language of nature, looking too attentively at the object to see it, and painting too conscientiously to paint well.

FIG. 745.—COROT. SOUVENIR OF ITALY.
(The Louvre, Paris.)

By the year 1830, however, a young man, Corot (1796–1875), had made great progress in the discovery of Nature and its picturesque qualities, because he was not embarrassed by the thousand difficulties which arrested more than one painter. He did not belong to the group of painters known as the School of Fontainebleau; he outstripped them all, after starting from historical landscape, in the manner of Aligny, and of his master, Bertin. In his long and prolific life, Corot certainly varied his effects, but he always reduced the most complex landscape to the delicate gradations of luminous values. Local colours were subdued or effaced, that they might not disturb his subtle modulations. Always a confused mass of that foliage which the Dutchmen liked to paint in detail; always the stony hardness of the foreground, the hairy covering of dry grass or the acid crudity of the meadow enveloped by a light veil of shadow. Even in the full light, a diaphanous mist veils the

FIG. 746.—COROT. THE PONDS AT VILLE-D'AVRAY.
(Museum of Rouen.)

FIG. 747.—COROT. DIANA'S BATH.
(Museum of Bordeaux.)

verdure of Nature, and though his light is limpid, it caresses objects and never defines them sharply. It is nearly always the light of twilight or dawn, when oblique rays cast large vague shadows, shadows which are never opaque, just as the light is never brilliant. In his latest works, the shadows become even lighter and more subtle; the vaporous haze is shot with silver sparks and satiny gleams, a wet leaf or the smooth white bark of some tree shines through it. Thus the same scale of values—independent of material colours—serves to represent the dry landscape of Umbria, and the rainy district of Picardy. Italian vegetation, the burnt grass, pale olive trees and dusty cypresses, in the same manner as the silver birches, the willows with trembling leaves, the grass sprinkled with dewdrops. And thus Corot was able, in all sincerity, to confound in his memory the Lake of Albano and the pond of Ville d'Avray, the Tuscan chalk and the fogs of the Ile de France. The very nymphs and fauns, which his more majestic landscapes seem to conjure up spontaneously, appear as phantoms, luminous and flickering as shreds of mist torn by the breeze and dancing among moonbeams. The manner of Corot, which was that of Claude Lorrain, and was to be that of Cazin and Pointelin, appeals more strongly to the soul than any other. While some attempt to reproduce Nature faithfully, or seek to give it a sentimental aspect, Corot looks at it frankly, but retains only its immaterial elements, its light and

FIG. 748.—COROT. LANDSCAPE.
(Museum of Lille.)

atmosphere. This reality, simplified, spiritualised, fixed in the memory, and blurred by our faculties of forgetfulness, is already a dream (Figs. 744-750).

Corot, confronted with the most complex scene, at once found a pure and supple melody which expressed its very spirit. Rousseau (1812-1867), on the contrary, dispersed himself, so to

FIG. 749.—COROT. THE ARRAS ROAD.
(The Louvre, Paris.)

speak, in the infinity of Nature; he desired to seize a complete image of it, and applied himself with all his energies to the rendering of its varied aspects, the plains of the Landes, the rocks of Auvergne, and above all, the ancient oaks of the forest of Fontainebleau. His manner is difficult to define, partly because the painter put little of his personality into his work, and partly because it follows reality with its variations. The only characteristic common to all his works is a grave and fervent, almost a religious, application. He allows himself to be enticed by the forest, and he loses his way in it, like Hop o' my Thumb; the perpetual indecision which does honour to his artistic conscience spoilt a great part of his work. His vision seizes too many small details; he hesitates before bushes, moss and foliage. He established himself in the forest of Fontainebleau to paint the old oaks. His pictures do not always tell us the hour, nor even the season, for light sheds a changeful lustre over things, and Rousseau was intent on getting likeness, that is to say, a permanent character. But he hides nothing of the tree which he paints, neither its age nor its character; notice

FIG. 750.—COROT. THE BELFRY AT DOUAI.
(The Louvre, Paris.)

FIG. 751.—ROUSSEAU. THE POOL IN THE MEADOW
(The Louvre, Paris.)

the old twisted trunk which has suffered so much on that rocky soil, its knotted branches which have struggled to reach the light, and the dense, sombre, mysterious foliage through which the sun does not penetrate; small canvases, rough as if covered by lichens, where you feel the humming of countless little insects, while a continual rustling of the wind among the great trees fills the silence of the forest. He does not fail to show that a branch too heavy and too old has broken off and that in some storm a tree was thrown down and only holds up to the sky a yellow stump, a split trunk whose sharp edges remind us of the

FIG. 752.—ROUSSEAU. THE CHARCOAL-
BURNER'S HUT.
(Gould Collection.)

rending of the wood. Rousseau was, of course, inspired by the trees of Ruysdael and Hobbema; but did these Dutchmen bring such fidelity, such a passion of exactitude to bear upon their reproductions of Nature? They have left no such varied gallery, no such powerful portraits of forest personalities (Figs. 751, 754). Not far from Rousseau,

FIG. 753.—ROUSSEAU. THE OUTLET FROM THE FOREST.
(The Louvre, Paris.)

Diaz was also at work in the forest. In the half light that filters through foliage, a ray piercing the dark thicket sometimes kindles a spark on the damp grass, the velvet mosses, the gold of dead leaves or the silver bark of birches; to Diaz this spectacle was full of such mystery and wonder that he was led astray from the path of artistic probity by a kind of

FIG. 754.—ROUSSEAU. THE SUNLIT OAK.
(Mesdag Collection.)

FIG. 755.—DAUBIGNY. THE BANKS OF THE OISE.
(The Louvre, Paris.)

chromatic intoxication. The most austere aspects of Nature are rich enough to kindle the imagination of the colourist. Her copyists of this type are apt to forget her in the delight they get from the variations she inspires; more than once, we shall see the robust trunk of naturalistic art bearing

stray branches which put forth delicious but barren flowers.

Jules Dupré's art, on the other hand, was vigorous. He was not content merely to record an episodic, curious, or amusing effect; he did not scatter his attention by rendering the grass, the moss and the little branches with too great particularity. He composes strongly,

FIG. 756.—DIAZ. LA MARE AUX FÉES.
(THE FAIRIES' POOL.)
(Gould Collection.)

FIG. 757.—DAUBIGNY. THE LOCK AT OPTEVOZ.
(Museum of Rouen.)

and sacrifices a host of details to a robust general effect; his large masses are well placed, the most brilliant lights in the centre, the whole solid and compact. Beside the contrast of light, the plays of colour are pushed to an extreme. In his fat impasto, we divine, as in the works of Decamps, a complicated chemistry, learned combinations by means of which the utmost is won from colour. In this thick colour deep greens merge into russet tones, with a strong yet gentle effect, as in the atuumn woods. The sketch from Nature was transformed in the studio; a tree, a house, a flock of sheep, the simple realistic motive, was amplified and isolated, till it took on an august majesty; an exact study of landscape soon became a romantic scene (Figs. 758, 760, 761).

Younger artists, such as Chintreuil and Daubigny, no longer had to play the part of pioneers; the road was less rugged for them, for others had passed along it. Their work has the smiling charm of painless achievement. Chintreuil is pure, spring-like, and luminous; like the Impressionists who came long after him, his palette consisted solely of high tones (Fig. 759). Daubigny's work is impregnated with the freshness of the fields; a strong sap seems to stir in his opulent technique, which is facile and serene as fertile soil; the general effect is always gentle, though the brush sometimes affected a certain roughness; the handling is free to the verge of extravagance, though the painter approached more and more closely to strict exactitude. Some of these landscapes suggest an instantaneous impression by their elliptical execution. Daubigny is more especially the painter of quiet valleys, rich, flower-spangled pastures, and

FIG. 758.—JULES DUPRE. LOW TIDE.
(*Photo. Giraudon.*)

FIG. 759.—CHINTREUIL. SPACE.
(The Louvre, Paris.)

softly-flowing rivers. Fixed lines, meadows well spread out, a river slow and still which reflects the wide sky, and the poplars on the banks, the landscape which a thoughtful boatman sees as he drifts along. His Nature promises delight, and gives a sense of well-being. In Corot's landscapes, we sometimes see a fluting shepherd; in Daubigny's, we always divine the fisherman and his rod (Figs. 755-757).

Among these landscape painters there were animal painters, as in Holland. Among our Ruysdaels and our Hobbemas there were also some Paul Potters. They were not content to place their flocks in meadow-lands; their sheep and cattle became the principal motive of the composition, Brascassat painted red and white bulls, sleek and lustrous as chestnuts bursting from their shells. Charles Jacques' sheep, on the other hand, are dull and woolly; they are by a master who was thoroughly familiar with the flock, who understood its manner of huddling together and scattering, who knew the true place of shepherd and dog, etc. (Fig. 763). Troyon's animals are

FIG. 760.—J. DUPRÉ. MORNING.
(The Louvre, Paris.

FIG. 761.—J. DUPRÉ. THE OLD OAK.
(The Louvre, Paris.)

more ambitious, and aim at a stronger effect; the bulk of his grazing cattle is set majestically against the horizon, and the landscape, without being altogether insignificant, is skilfully subordinated to them (Figs. 764, 765).

At this point, about the middle of the nineteenth century, we may close this first chapter of the history of French landscape; it was what we may call the Dutch period; in execution, in choice of subject, and in dimensions, these so-called masters of the school of Fontainebleau are closely akin to the masters of Haarlem and the Hague. But the French School was not to remain constant to this first form. Landscape is dear to artists who would rather observe than invent, and too great an aptitude for copying paralyses painting and shortens the life of a school. When they had completed the portrait of their country, the Dutchmen laid aside their brushes. French landscape, on the contrary, continued its evolution; it did

FIG. 762.—DAUBIGNY. SPRING.
The Louvre, Paris.)

not remain a limited *genre.* Inanimate objects had only existed in relation to man; but landscape was to encroach even upon the prerogative of man; his personality was to be dissipated in the mirage of light and the reflection of things. The vocabulary of the picturesque continues to be enriched by sensations hitherto unknown. Land-

FIG. 763.—CHARLES JACQUES.
FLOCK OF SHEEP.
(French Embassy at Berlin.)

scape was to transform all painting, and to renovate our visual habits.

Sculpture is less impressionable than painting; technical and material necessities impose a slow continuity on this art, even in periods of violent revolution. At the close of the eighteenth century, sculptors had not felt the influences of idealism and of arch e-ology to the same degree as painters. Roman heroes had already long taken the place of Boucher's shepherds, when Pajou and Houdon were still modelling their sparkling and voluptuous figures. But sculpture could not continue to express sentiments which no longer existed. Houdon, Pajou and Clodion felt their ardour gradually dying down in the icy atmosphere of Davidian art. When they chiselled the exploits of the Grande Armée in bas-reliefs for the Arc du Carrousel, or raised a statue to the modern Cæsar, they adopted the generalised form and commonplace rotundity which painting had lately accepted as akin to the antique. The architecture of the Empire had brought back into favour the decorative panel in very low, but clearly defined, relief, which had been popular with the decorators of the Renaissance. More than one *Victory* erected in honour of Napoleon is obviously akin to the

FIG. 764.—TROYON. OXEN GOING OUT
TO PLOUGH.
(The Louvre, Paris.)

FIG. 765.—TROYON. THE BOUNDARY.
(The Louvre, Paris.)

allegories of Jean Goujon. But sculpture had no David then to animate the uniform majesty of this style with vigorous sentiments. Chaudet, Bosio, and the Italian Canova, who worked for Napoleon, have left no such image of the heroism of the period as *The Distribution of the Eagles,* or the *Battle Field of Eylau.* Here, again, sculptors were baffled by the difficulties of representing modern costume. They were so much under the spell of antiquity, so confident in their principles, that they accepted the worst consequences of these, and were not shocked by Chaudet's Napoleon in a toga, Canova's Napoleon naked as the Borghese Mars, and generals of the Republic or of the Empire as scantily draped as Apollos. Realistic epochs prefer the ugliness of modern costume to this absurd nudity. There is in sculpture a kind of antinomy which seems difficult to resolve; an inert costume is offered to this art, the function of which is the reproduction of living forms. Sculptors have accordingly carved breast bones and not frock coats, shins and not boots. It is only to be regretted that they did not more perfectly fix the profound palpitation of the life whose external forms they modelled so carefully.

Sculpture, the language of definite forms, lends itself ill to the translation of lyrical reverie. The generation of sculptors educated in the studios of the Empire lived through the Romantic agitation, without any very marked resulting transformation in their classical manner. They could not,

FIG. 766.—TROYON. FEEDING POULTRY.
(The Louvre, Paris.)

like the painters, change their *dramatis personæ*, and abandon Olympus for the misty divinities of Ossian; the antique nudities offered too many plastic resources to be sacrificed to Gothic knights or ladies. Sculptors accordingly often demanded from Greek muscles the expression of Romantic emotion.

Louis XVIII's Government merely commissioned Bosio and Lemot to replace the figures of Henry IV, Louis XIII and Louis XIV, which had been shattered during the Revolution; this work was simply restoration. The Monarchy of July had very different ambitions. The reign of Louis Philippe produced more statues than that of Louis XIV, but the Citizen King glorified the nation, not the monarchy; works which date from this period are the Cities of France seated round the obelisk in the Place de la Concorde, some

FIG. 767.—JOUFFROY.
A YOUNG GIRL TELLING HER
FIRST SECRET TO VENUS.
(The Louvre, Paris.)

of the Heroes in the fore-courts at Versailles, and the Women of France in the Luxembourg, a series of mediocre statues which the charming framework of the garden makes more attractive than many masterpieces.

Until this period sculpture, when not decorative, had been religious, mythological and monarchical; now its function was to be indefinitely extended. This art, reserved at first for the gods, and then for kings, was now to consecrate the immortality of "great men." No worship can subsist without images; hero-worship gave renewed vitality to sculpture. National subscriptions provided for the erection of statues in every town which had given birth

FIG. 768.—CORTOT. THE SOLDIER
OF MARATHON.
(The Louvre, Paris.)

FIG. 769.—DAVID D'ANGERS. PEDIMENT OF THE PANTHÉON, PARIS.

to a victorious general, a scholar, an inventor or an artist; the history of France was exploited by sculptors as it had been by painters in the galleries of Versailles. The Revolution, the Empire, the age of Louis XIV, the Renaissance, and even the Middle Ages, inspired innumerable figures.

The artist who played the most important part in this national work was David d'Angers (1788-1856). A Jacobin and a Classicist, like his namesake, the painter of the Sabine women and Marat, he was passionately devoted to the antique, and violently agitated by the political fury of his day. The tremor of modern life agitates that idealist. His work is in-

FIG. 770.—DAVID D'ANGERS. MEDALLION OF VICTOR HUGO.

FIG. 771.—DAVID D'ANGERS. DROUOT, AT NANCY. (*Photo. Neurdein.*)

FIG. 772.—DAVID D'ANGERS. MEDALLION OF MME. RÉCAMIER.

formed with an energy unparalleled before him, in themes imitated from the *Laocöon* and the Belvedere Apollo. In his pediment of the Panthéon (Fig. 769), France, supported by Liberty and History, distributes crowns of immortality, and on either side, scholars, artists, jurists, generals, Bonaparte and his grenadiers, hold out their hands to receive them. In this triangle David summarised the glorification in which all France was interested. He carved a long series of statues of "great men," and with a few exceptions—Racine at La Ferté Milon, for instance—he clothed them boldly in modern costume. On a pedestal, the carved sides of which tell of glorious achievements or proclaim symbolically the benefits of an invention, there is raised a monumental figure having an enormous head, with agitated features, and the whole silhouette is full of movement. David's numerous busts and medallions reveal a disciple of Gall, intent on showing the marks of genius in the features of the face and the bumps of the skull; but these exercises in phrenology astonish without convincing; such distortions of the face are more appropriate to the art of caricaturists like Dantan or Daumier.

FIG. 773.—FOYATIER. SPARTACUS.
(The Louvre, Paris.)

FIG. 774.—DAVID D'ANGERS. PHILOPŒMON.
(The Louvre, Paris.)

The famous group carved by Rude for the Arc de Triomphe de l'Etoile was finished in 1837, the same year as the Pantheon pediment. Rude (1784-1855) had an extraordinary power of forcing the human body to suggest the frenzy of passion. There is an epic afflatus in his otherwise classical work, exalted still more by the memories of the Revolution and of the Empire; he does not distinguish clearly whether his inspiration comes from Leonidas or Napoleon, from Brutus or from Mirabeau.

Rude continued to use the traditional language; his volunteers are Greek or Roman soldiers; centurions' helmets are mingled with that of Pericles; they are not the moustached vagabonds of Raffet. They march with a confidence one recognises as irresistible; and the artist has given us an audacious revelation of their spirit in the furious *Marseillaise* who yells above their heads. This colossal group is one of the few modern works in which a collective soul is

367

FIG. 775.—RUDE. THE MARSEILLAISE.
ARC DE TRIOMPHE DE L'ÉTOILE.

manifest; before such an image many a Frenchman must have felt a heroic exaltation evoked as by the trumpets of a war march. The humanity which inspired such works was full of the memories of 1793. Louis Philippe's government, which repressed so many insurrections, and demolished so many barricades, could not stifle the explosion of revolutionary art. After the lapse of nearly half a century art immortalised the solemn moment when the Revolution flew to arms, the year of Valmy (Fig. 775).

Louis Philippe contributed to the imperial apotheosis; the Emperor played his part in this glorification of the past. When the ashes of Napoleon were brought back from St. Helena, Visconti built a monumental tomb at the Invalides to receive them. A kind of fatality seemed to combine the names of Napoleon and Louis XIV at every turn; in the Louvre which the Emperor had proposed to finish, at Versailles where his battles were recorded, in the Place Vendôme, where the column of the Grande Armée replaced the statue of the Grand Monarque, and finally, under Mansart's cupola. We feel here how much artistic monuments gain in majesty and beauty from memories and history; Visconti's heavy sarcophagus seems by no means too ponderous for the glory it supports, and the graceful *Victories* which guard it have a solemnity unusual in the works of Pradier (Fig. 783). This accomplished pupil of Bosio pleased both Classicists and Romanticists by his purity of form and refinement of sentiment. His style or his hand is apparent in innumerable

FIG. 776.—RUDE. NAPOLEON AWAKING
TO IMMORTALITY.
(The Louvre, Paris.)

monuments and decorative works of this period, fountains, clocks, etc. (Fig. 782).

There were, however, sculptors who followed more closely the Romantic impulse which inspired the painters of the day; some of them, like Jehan du Seigneur, let loose a sort of muscular tempest to express violent passion (Fig. 781).

Préault believed, with Delacroix, that the fire of improvisation and energy of execution are essential to sincere expression, and that the work would be more living if the artist wrestled with his block of stone. He sometimes succeeded in wringing a cry of passion, as it were, from wood or marble; but the material seems to have suffered from the brutal touch of his agitated genius (Fig. 779).

FIG. 777.—RUDE. STATUE OF MARSHAL NEY AT PARIS.

Barye (1796-1875) alone achieved absolute success in an art untrammelled by classical tradition. He studied animals, their characteristic outlines and their attitudes, at the museum, and afterwards reconstituted their wild life in the desert. This was a whole empire added to the somewhat narrow domain of statuary; for the Egyptian lions are decorative figures, and the Greeks confined their animal studies to the horse. Barye's animals are portraits; whether monumental or decorative, gigantic groups or letter-weights, they are full of a vigorous vitality. The dark, lustrous bronze suggests the play of muscles under the thick fur and the curves and folds are like springs tightened by an irresistible force. His wild beasts are shown in their constant struggle for

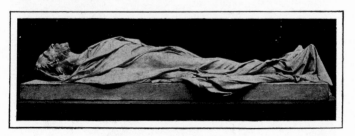

FIG. 778.—RUDE. TOMB OF GENERAL CAVAIGNAC.
(Montmartre Cemetery, Paris.)

369

FIG. 779.—PRÉAULT.
CRUCIFIX.
(Church of Saint-Gervais, Paris.)

food, crawling, bounding, crouching over their prey; we seem to hear the crunching of bones, and the growls of pleasure in this grim battle between the hungry pursuer and the weak fugitive. Barye's work is one of the finest discoveries of modern sculpture; it is marked by the rare artistic quality of a perfect balance between technique and conception. After Barye, Cain, Dalou and Gardet set their haughty lions to guard the doors of palaces, and Frémiet was not unmindful of the sharp, abrupt silhouettes of his horsemen. Since Barye's appearance, the curly, benevolent lions which used to smile at children in the public gardens, with one paw on a ball, have made way for the strange bulk of great wild beasts, and the fury of their mortal encounters.

The Revolution shattered the continuity of French traditional art, monarchical and religious. It destroyed many effigies of saints and kings, and violated many tombs; transformations so vital as the adoption of Christianity, the Reformation, and the Revolution cannot be brought about without some injury to the furniture of the ancient society by the new order. Works of art are not mere inert forms; they are haunted idols. In spite of the decrees of the Convention, the repression of the ancient régime was savagely exercised upon everything it had left behind it. When this wave of fury had spent itself, attempts were made to reconcile the modern world with the remains of the past. There was an artistic, as well as a religious and monarchical restoration. Mutilated statues, violated tombs and empty shrines became mere inoffensive relics, documents for the historian, and treasures for the amateur; museums received

FIG. 780.—PRADIER. SAPPHO.
(The Louvre, Paris.)

this wreckage of the churches; archæological enthusiasm took the place of religious fervour. It is not surprising that the æsthetic sentiment should resemble a kind of lay piety, since works of art are so often the disused accessories of worship.

Two men contributed very prominently to this reconciliation in the name of beauty, between modern and mediæval France; Chateaubriand, who revealed the senti-

FIG. 781.—JEHAN DU SEIGNEUR.
ORLANDO FURIOSO.
(The Louvre, Paris.)

mental power of the Gothic monuments to the Romanticists, and Lenoir, who during the revolutionary turmoil received into his Museum of French Monuments the ancient stones, tombs and statues which had been torn from their places and thrown into the gutter. The *Génie du Christianisme* and the relics accumulated in the Musée des Petits-Augustins kindled French imagination. The Middle Age revealed itself, richly coloured, moving and mysterious, as in the dim light of the cathedral; the purest Classicists, even Ingres himself, dreamt of the Middle Ages. The first ones who studied it brought to their work so much feeling that an echo of their poetry still lightens at times the dull labours of the learned. Chateaubriand and Lenoir gave the first impetus to that extensive and varied work which was to occupy the nineteenth century, the age *par excellence* of careful research among archives, catalogues of works of art, restoration of ruins and foundation of museums.

FIG. 782.—PRADIER. FOUNTAIN AT NÎMES.
(*Photo. Févrot.*)

FIG. 783.—VISCONTI. TOMB OF NAPOLEON I
AT THE INVALIDES, PARIS.
(Photo. Neurdein.)

Architecture was transformed by this interest in the Middle Ages. In the first place, the Gothic ruins made men forget Hubert Robert's Roman ruins; painters preferred the old houses of Rouen to the remains of the Forum. Poets described the *Burgs* of German legend in sombre colours, and lithographers popularised reproductions of moss-grown towers and fretted gables. They never ceased to ridicule the cupolas and columns, and the geometrical regularity of the classical monuments, and this architecture has been persistently decried ever since. Yet it was not enough to criticise it; its assailants should have offered a substitute; but architecture is not so easily transformed as painting or poetry. The literary fame of the Gothic forms naturally affected decoration. Romantic art admired the intricate style of German Gothic; Chateaubriand had declared that the vault of a cathedral imitates the branches of ancient forests. Small objects, and the frontispieces of books were adorned with complicated ribs. Even some Gothic tombs were constructed. The "English garden," always fashionable, became more and more melancholy; sometimes it sheltered the fragments of an abbey or some anonymous recumbent figure, rigid in his armour, with folded hands, one of Charlemagne's knights, or a Merovingian Frank at the least.

Then the archæologists, historians or architects, Mérimée, Lassus, and Viollet-le-Duc, began to study the Gothic buildings in France. Many of these were

FIG. 784.—BARYE. THE CENTAUR.
(The Louvre, Paris.)

in ruins, and thus there came about a vast enterprise of restoration, an endless work, to which a great part of the activity of French architects has been devoted. The France of the nineteenth century, which created so many museums, was also to preserve historical and artistic monuments. First

FIG. 785.—BARYE. TIGER AND CROCODILE.
(The Louvre, Paris.)

Lenoir set to work at Cluny, Baltard at Saint-Germain-des-Prés, Lassus at Saint-Germain-l'Auxerrois, the Sainte-Chapelle, Notre-Dame of Paris, and Chartres; then Ruprich-Robert at Mont Saint-Michel, Abadie at Périgueux, Boeswilwald at Laon, Viollet-le-Duc at Notre-Dame of Paris, at Carcassonne and at Pierrefond.

These architects were not content to restore. When they were thoroughly acquainted with the Gothic organism, they thought themselves capable of resuscitating it. The building of basilicas ceased. Sometimes it was considered enough to give a Gothic façade to some old church, as at Saint Ouen at Rouen. Elsewhere, at Sainte-Clotilde, Paris, and Saint-Epvre, Nancy, etc., architects built an entire new church in the style of the thirteenth or fourteenth century. But it is not sufficient to love a form of architecture, nor even to understand it well, in order to revive it. The most successful Gothic *pasticci* are extremely cold; the modern constructor brings his classical habits to his task, regularity of plan, symmetry and clarity of design, that rigorous regularity which determines the form of the building in all its details, and that division of labour which makes the architect exclusively a draughtsman and the workman a mere stone-cutter. In the old cathedrals, the stone is full of life in every part;

FIG. 786.—BARYE. ELEPHANT.
(The Louvre, Paris.)

FIG. 787.—FAÇADE OF THE CHURCH
OF SAINT OUEN, AT ROUEN.
(*Photo. Neurdein.*)

the work is varied, rich, and unexpected; the modern copies are stunted in their growth; the dry geometry of contemporary architects has been unable to capture the soul of the Gothic cathedral.

The Romantic movement has not been permanent in all respects. French thought has been formed by too long training. The artist never seems to us altogether the master, free to treat his art according to his temperament. In this respect Delacroix has not triumphed over Ingres. We are very far from agreeing upon a dogma of æsthetics and yet if a work appears full of daring originality everyone, both friends and enemies, recalls the great traditions to combat or to defend it. Delacroix had already set the example by invoking in his own favour Poussin. Even the Revolutionaries with us fall back upon tradition. They have never entirely abjured our classic spirit. The Romantic movement may nevertheless be said to have transformed the conditions of French art; ever since this explosion of individualism, the idea that a man of genius imposes his originality on his contemporaries, and forces them to think and feel with him, has held its ground. Art is no longer a result of society; rather does it mould society, and indeed, our painters undoubtedly modify our manners of seeing and feeling; Naturalists and Impressionists discovered unknown aspects for the public. They were daring, because the Romanticists had taught that the work of genius is a stroke of audacity which succeeds. Our greatest artists waged war against the taste of their times. Con-

FIG. 788.—APSE OF THE CHURCH OF
SAINTE-CLOTILDE, PARIS.

374

flict between them, to whom invention is a necessity, and the public, which they have to educate, is inevitable. The strife began in the time of Louis Philippe; this period witnessed the birth of the antagonism between the "artist" and the "bourgeois." A sort of battle raged. With Ingres, Delacroix, and all those who came after them, we constantly find the feelings which are developed by combativeness, the desire to conquer, the rage of defeat, the pride of triumph, and more often doubt as to the final success. Artists no longer enjoyed the peaceful security of the masters of the old régime.

Finally, Romanticism taught us that to understand a work we must enter into communion with the individual or collective soul which it embodies.

FIG. 789.—NAVE OF SAINT-EPVRE, AT NANCY.

(*Photo. Neurdein.*)

Since we have looked for a hidden message in it, and not for the more or less successful realisation of ideal beauty, we have learnt to love even the obsolete forms of art; the Classicist, always ready to despise all that offended his taste, condemned himself to ignore the ages which were ignorant of his canons. By speaking frankly of themselves, the Romanticists have accustomed us to think that artists throughout the ages did the same, even unconsciously. And since we have ceased to judge in the name of taste when we would appreciate the depth and delicacy of inspiration, many works which seemed dead have come to life. The Classicist, metaphysical and dogmatic, was very disdainful; Romanticism has enlarged our æsthetic sympathy by revealing the secret sentiment that underlies beauty.

BIBLIOGRAPHY

L. Bénédite, *Rapport sur l'Exposition de 1900, Beaux-Arts*, Paris, 1904.—In the *Musée d'Art* (XIXth century), Paris, 1907 : Ch. Saunier, *L'Architecture*, P. Vitry, *La Sculpture ;* Ch. Saunier, M. Hamel, M. Tourneux, G. Riat, G. Geffroy, *La Peinture ;* H. Focillon, *La Gravure ;* V. Champier, *L'Art décoratif.*—E. Schmidt, *Französische Plastik und Architektur*, Leipzig, 1904.—E. Guillaume, *La Sculpture au XIXe siècle (G. B. A.*, 1900, II).—H. Jouin, *David d'Angers*, 2 vols., Paris, 1878.—A. Bertrand, *Fr. Rude*, Paris, 1888.—L. de Fourcaud, *Rude*, Paris, 1903.—P. Mantz, *Barye (G. B. A.*, 1867, I).—A. Alexandre, *Barye*, Paris, 1889.—Richard Muther, *Geschichte der Malerei im XIX Jahrhundert*, Munich, 1893, 3 vols.—Richard Muther, *Ein Jahrhundert französischer Malerei*, Berlin, 1901.—A. Michel, *Notes sur l'Art moderne* (*Peinture*), Paris, 1896.—A. Michel, *L'Exposition centennale de Peinture française (G. B. A.*, 1900, II).—J. Meier-Graefe, *Entwickelung der Modernen Kunst*, 3 vols., Stuttgart, 1904, English ed. 1906.—R. Marx, *Etudes sur l'Ecole française*, Paris, 1902.—K. Schmidt, *Französische Malerei*, 1800–1900, Leipzig, 1903.—M. Hamel, *La Peinture française au XIXe siècle (Revue de Paris*, 1900).—H. Marcel, *La Peinture française au XIXe siècle*, Paris, 1905.—E. Chesneau, *Les Chefs d'école*, Paris, 1862.—Ch. Blanc, *Les Artistes de mon temps*, Paris, 1876.—Th. Sylvestre, *Les Artistes français*, Paris, 1877.—A. Robaut, *L'Œuvre complet d'E. Delacroix*, Paris, 1885.—L. Rosenthal, *La Peinture romantique*, 1815–1830, Dijon, 1900.—E. Delacroix, *Journal*, Paris, 1893–1895, 3 vols.—M. Tourneux, *Delacroix*, Paris, 1903.—P. Mantz, *Decamps* (*G. B. A.*, 1862, I).—Th. Gautier, *Les Beaux-Arts en Europe*, 1855.— Ch. Blanc, *Les trois Vernet*, Paris, 1898.—G. Planche, *Portraits d'artistes*, Paris, 1898.—Amaury-Duval, *L. Atelier d'Ingres*, Paris.—Ch. Blanc, *Ingres* (*G. B. A.*, 1867, I).—H. Delaborde, *Ingres*, Paris, 1870.— H. Lapauze, *Portraits dessinés d'Ingres*, Paris, 1903.—J. Mommeja, *Ingres*, Paris, 1903.—L. Mabilleau, *Les Dessins d'Ingres à Montauban* (*G. B. A.*, 1894, II).—L. Flandrin, *H. Flandrin*, Paris, 1903.—P. Mantz, *Raffet* (*G. B. A.*, 1860, II).—F. Lhomme, *Raffet*, Paris, n.d.—H. Beraldi, *Raffet* (*G. B. A.*, 1892, I, p. 353); *Charlet* (*Ibid.*, 1893, II, p. 46).—H. Marcel, *H. Daumier*, Paris, n.d.—J.-L. Vaudoyer and P. Alfassa, *Les Salles de la Monarchie de Juillet au Musée de Versailles* (*R. A. A. M.*), 1910, II).—Th. Thoré, *Salons*, Paris, 1870, 2 vols.—E. Michel, *Les Maîtres du Paysage*, Paris, 1906.—E. Michel, *La Forêt de Fontainebleau*, Paris, 1909.—Moreau-Nélaton, *Corot*, Paris, 1905.—Walther Gensel, *Corot und Troyon*, Bielefeld, 1905.—Fr. Henriet, *Charles Daubigny et son œuvre*, Paris, 1878.

FIG. 790.—PUVIS DE CHAVANNES. LETTERS AND THE SCIENCES. (FRAGMENT.)
(Amphitheatre of the Sorbonne.) (*Photo. Fiorillo.*)

CHAPTER III

NATURALISM

Architecture in Towns: the Transformation of Paris.—The Classical Style modified by Eclectic Taste.—Iron Structures.—Essays in the Modern Style.—Naturalistic Paintings.—Courbet.—Jean François Millet.—History Painting.—Orientalism.—Portraiture.—Decorative Painting from Ingres to Puvis de Chavannes.—From Naturalism to Impressionism.—Impressionism in Landscape, Decoration and Design.—The Reaction against Impressionism.—Contemporary Art.—Classical Sculpture: Florentine Influence.—Naturalism in Sculpture: Carpeaux, Dalou, Rodin, Bartholomé.

DURING the second half of the nineteenth century, scholars gradually supplanted poets in the general governance of minds. The Romanticist, Victor Hugo or Delacroix, like Narcissus bending over his fountain, only looked at Nature to see the reflection of himself. To him, the universe was but a storehouse of images on which he drew to give colour to his poetry. When these exuberant personalities had sobered down, reality appeared to them, and interested them. The landscape painters had set the example; following in their wake, painters and sculptors, as well as writers, began to think that absolute exactitude was the true ambition of art; this submission to the object is a scientist's virtue, and, indeed, Naturalism is the artistic form of the positive spirit.

During this period, the continuity of French life was interrupted by sudden revolutions. Artists were not, of course, unmoved by the agitations which keep us poised, as it were, between revolution and compression; but the convulsions of social fury did not disturb

ART IN FRANCE

FIG. 791.—BIRD'S EYE VIEW OF "ARC DE TRIOMPHE DE L'ÉTOILE."
(Photo. from "Paris vu en ballon," by A. Schoelcher and O. Décugis.)

the radiant summits of art. Architecture, which always expresses the general character of communities clearly, was at once very prolific, and somewhat lacking in originality; this seems to show that the general existence was not so unstable as it seemed to be, and that society had not yet evolved a new form of collective life. These abrupt changes were after all only a question of political régime, a battle of pure theory or of personal interest. Governments, whatever they are, must always have one and the same object, which is to aid in the increase of riches. The conflicting movements which agitated superficial France must not be allowed to hide that deep current, the slow pressure of which nothing can resist. Every day, a rather larger number of men achieve a little ease, or in other words, a relative prosperity and an average intellectual culture. This was the great social event of the nineteenth century, and modern art was to manifest this indefinite enfranchisement of the middle classes after its fashion.

We should be less contemptuous of nineteenth century architecture if we studied it in its collective conceptions and not in its individual buildings. It is true that the past century invented no type of church, *château*, or palace, nor even of town house or theatre. But it realised a new conception of the Town. Under Louis XIV, and more especially under Louis XV, architects had already designed decorative schemes which had embraced much more than the façade of a single

FIG. 792.—DUBAN. COURT OF THE ÉCOLE DES BEAUX-ARTS, PARIS.

building. Certain squares of classic regularity had been introduced into the confused Paris of the Middle Ages. But it was more especially in the nineteenth century that ancient towns were transformed, and innumerable houses were given that unity of style and that symmetry which had hitherto been reserved for a palace, a church, or a public square.

Napoleon had not had time to execute the grandiose transformations he proposed in his capital; nevertheless, his Arc de Triomphe was undertaken, and prepared the way for the wide avenues bearing the names of generals and of battles, which now radiate from the Etoile. At the Tuileries, Percier and Fontaine began the second arm which the palace was to stretch

FIG. 793.—BIRD'S EYE VIEW OF THE LOUVRE.

(Photo. from "Paris vu en ballon," by A. Schoelcher and O. Décugis.)

towards the Louvre, and the remains of the ancient structure were gradually banished from the quadrilateral as the junction neared completion. Pierre Lescot's little pavilions, and Philibert Delorme's Tuileries were finally united after many tentative essays. Since then, the destruction of the Tuileries has opened out the Court of the Carrousel, and the two wings of the Louvre now extend towards the immense avenue which leads to the Arc de Triomphe. Historical vicissitudes have caused this palace no longer to suggest the arrangement of a French town house. But with façades on every side, and traversed by as many passages as an urban quarter, it nevertheless preserves its majestic unity; its architects bore in mind the decoration of the primitive parts, and, above all, they devised a dexterous arrangement to mask the original asymmetry of a building composed of two bodies, the Louvre and the Tuile-

FIG. 794.—DUC. PALAIS DE JUSTICE, PARIS. FAÇADE ON THE PLACE DAUPHINE.

FIG. 795.—VAUDREMER. CHURCH OF
SAINT-PIERRE AT MONTROUGE.

ries, which were not simultaneously conceived.

The Restoration and the July
Monarchy abstained from vast
municipal enterprises. Louis
Philippe's principal commissions
were for fountains in the public
squares and at cross roads. Guillon
designed those of the Place de la
Concorde, Visconti that of the
Place Louvois, of Molière and of
Saint Sulpice; imitating Paris, the
cities of Bordeaux and Nîmes set
up nymphs in the style of Pradier
on their fountains. But it was
more especially under the Second
Empire that Paris was methodically transformed. Political causes
hastened this metamorphosis; the old city of the Cabochiens, of
the League, of the Fronde, of 1792, 1830 and 1848, the Paris of
revolutions, was difficult to hold; Louis XVI, Charles X and
Louis Philippe had felt the irksomeness of being shut up in the
Tuileries, the prisoners of their subjects. Under Louis Philippe,
at the slightest alarm, the network of narrow streets bristled with
barricades: an overturned omni-
bus and a few paving-stones
sufficed to hold up the king's
emissaries, while chairs and
tables rained from every window.
Napoleon III could not think of
abandoning Paris; but, under the
administration of Haussmann,
engineers and architects created a
new city. After the fashion of Le
Nôtre, when he was laying out a
French park, they drove wide
avenues and regular streets boldly
through the tangle of old buildings; even the most ordinary
houses, with no pretensions to
artistic merit, were brought into
the system of decoration, and

FIG. 796.—LEPÈRE AND HITTORF.
CHURCH OF SAINT VINCENT-DE-PAUL, PARIS.

380

made to contribute to the general
effect.

The principle of classic regularity went beyond the limits of a
façade or a square, and extended
to the whole town. The audacity
of these architects lay in their application of this conception to a city
so ancient and so vital as Paris.
They rebuilt the Cité and the two
banks which face it; they pierced
Paris with wide rectilinear avenues, extending from one monument
to another, just as the alleys at
Versailles unite two fountains or
two groups of sculpture. "I have
never," writes Baron Haussmann,

FIG. 797.—BALLU. CHURCH OF
LA TRINITÉ, PARIS.

"traced the line of any sort of street, and, still less, of any principal
artery of Paris, without considering the point of view which could
be given it." In this way, at the end of the avenue which he follows,
the pedestrian sees a dome, a spire or a picturesque silhouette which
arouses his interest and leads him on to a square from which
other avenues radiate. These large arteries, sweeping through the
crowded quarters of old Paris, revealed many an ancient building,
greatly surprised at being thus
brought into the light. Around
those which the modern town left
intact, the houses of the neighbourhood seem to stand away, for we
can no longer tolerate any crowd-
ing round an important structure.
The transformation is not yet complete; a new Paris continues to
replace that of the seventeenth and
eighteenth centuries, just as this
classical Paris had superseded
mediæval Paris.

The majority of the buildings
carried out in the nineteenth century were designed to decorate the
city, both plan and site of palace
and church were chosen with a view

FIG. 798.—BALTARD. INTERIOR
OF THE CHURCH OF SAINT-AUGUSTIN.

FIG. 799.—LABROUSTE. BIBLIOTHÈQUE
SAINTE-GENEVIÈVE, PARIS.

to a general urban effect. Churches like Saint-Pierre at Montrouge and Saint Augustin, palaces like the Trocadéro, the Grand Palais and the Petit Palais of the Champs Elysées (Figs. 804, 805), buildings like the Opera House (Fig. 801), are primarily admirable for their suitability to the plan of the avenues and the configuration of the soil. The palace of Longchamp (Fig. 807) and Notre Dame-de-la-Grande at Marseilles, Notre Dame de Fourvières at Lyons (Fig. 809), and the Sacré Cœur at Montmartre (Fig. 810), show less originality in their architecture than in their intelligent choice of situation.

The most typical work of the nineteenth century was the organisation of a great town, with wide open spaces, straight avenues, and a simple plan which affords large perspectives and facilitates circulation. Though it did not invent a religious style, or create new palaces and *châteaux*, this century transformed the private house, adapting it to the general decoration of the street, and arranging it more conveniently. The semi-uniformity of façades manifests that social discipline which limits individualism. The problem for the architect of our houses is to reconcile general convenience and personal comfort elegantly.

Such transformations as those we have indicated are not always well received; they offended the reverence with which the nineteenth century regarded old stones. The quarters which are disappearing amused the imagination, and the houses which are rising in their

FIG. 800.—BIRD'S EYE VIEW OF THE OPERA HOUSE.

(Photo. from "Paris vu en ballon," by A. Schoelcher and O. Décugis.)

places make no such appeal. In the eighteenth century Cochin the Younger said that Rouen was the ugliest town in France, for the very reason which makes us now consider it the most picturesque. Cochin spoke as a modern, and we are all antiquarians. The beauty of the buildings owes a

FIG. 801.—GARNIER. OPERA HOUSE, PARIS.

good deal to association; we regret the remains of history too much to be able to admire the cold and commodious structures which replace them. This gives rise to vain recriminations. A living city cannot be a museum of relics.

Modern French architecture, though it aims at comfort, remains faithful to classical decoration. If but a few important monuments survived from which to reconstruct the artistic history of the last three centuries—the Louvre, Versailles, the Place de la Concorde, the Bourse, and the Palais des Champs-Elysées—we might pass from summit to summit, from Louis XIV to 1900, without overstepping the boundaries of classical art, or encountering other forms than those accepted since the time of the Greeks by Mediterranean and Western civilisation. French society had undergone many cataclysms, but at the end of the nineteenth century architects were still erecting colonnades, just as Perrault, Mansart and Gabriel had done. Classical taste has been made more flexible, enriched by the eclecticism natural to a century of historians and travellers. Decorative elements are borrowed from all countries and all ages; we are no longer astonished by a Hindoo, an Arab, or an Egyptian motive. In religious architecture more especially, Gothic, Romanesque and Byzantine imitations have persisted. Religion, which

FIG. 802.—GARNIER. GRAND STAIRCASE IN THE OPERA HOUSE, PARIS.

FIG. 803.—BIRD'S EYE VIEW OF THE GRAND PALAIS
AND THE PETIT PALAIS AT PARIS.

(Photo. from " Paris vu en ballon," by A.
Schoelcher and O. Décugis.)

no longer suffices for the guidance of human thought and activity, can not now create a style; life no longer fashions art, and art has to find its forms independently; it has sought them in the storehouse of the past. At Saint-Augustin (Fig. 798), Baltard bent his iron into Byzantine forms; in the Church of La Trinité (Fig. 797), Ballu preferred the style of the Italian Renaissance; both adapted their buildings to the luxury of the fashionable quarters in which they stand; at La Trinité, as at the Opera House, an open corridor enables fair worshippers to step from their carriages without wetting their costumes.

Garnier's Opera House (Figs. 801, 802), one of the most important works of the nineteenth century, shows how decorative eclecticism can adapt itself to modern needs. Garnier repeated the internal arrangement of the great theatre built by Louis at Bordeaux; the façade, with its galleries and colonnades, recalls the architecture of the Venetian Renaissance, that of Sansovino and Palladio; but a great number of details are borrowed from Greece, Asia, and Egypt. The exterior duly suggests the character of the building and its internal design, with the galleries for the foyer, the cupola over the auditorium, and the huge pediment, which not only completes the silhouette, but indicates the division between stage and auditorium. The architect aimed at a richness of effect that should surpass the Versailles of Mansart and Le Brun. He used polychrome marbles, and

FIG. 804.—DEGLANE. LE GRAND PALAIS IN THE
CHAMPS-ÉLYSÉES, PARIS.

resuscitated Byzantine mosaic. But modern dress has none of the splendour of Louis XIV costume, and the austere simplicity of black coats forms a strange contrast to this more than royal setting.

Nénot's Sorbonne must be cited as an example of the skill with which intricate problems have been solved; the architect

FIG. 805.—GIRAULT. LE PETIT PALAIS IN THE CHAMPS-ÉLYSÉES, PARIS.

had to build a Temple of Science, vast and complicated as the travail of modern thought, upon a difficult site in a restricted space, and at the same time, to respect certain aspects of Richelieu's ancient monument. While utilitarian exigencies become more imperious every day in libraries, museums, universities, and countless other public buildings, our architects cannot bring themselves to sacrifice noble classical façades.

Nevertheless, a growing audacity in the application of iron has created a new type of building. A metallic architecture has grown up side by side with the traditional stone architecture. Periodical exhibitions have done much to bring this about. The Central Markets (Halles), built by Baltard, showed that iron is an indispensable material for constructing an immense shelter without

FIG. 806.—SALLE DES ILLUSTRES, IN THE CAPITOLE AT TOULOUSE.

encumbering the ground with supporting walls and pillars. Pointed architecture was surpassed in its own domain; builders in stone could never have thrown ribs of such a span upon such slender abutments; the engineer can easily build a metal cage which would contain a Gothic nave. Iron, a very elastic yet resistant material, capable of free extension,

FIG. 807.—ESPÉRANDIEU. PALAIS DE LONGCHAMP, MARSEILLES.

has replaced stone wherever stone formerly replaced wood in vault and framework. Baltard in the Church of Saint-Augustin, Labrouste in the Bibliothèque Sainte-Geneviève and the Bibliothèque Nationale, Duc in a hall of the Palais de Justice, accordingly utilised iron girders, which play the same part as the ribs in the Gothic vault. Metallic naves are essential in railway stations, which have to be enlarged periodically, and in exhibition buildings, which are always temporary.

But iron has not superseded stone in its decorative function. The majority of these metallic skeletons are faced by walls, which bear the traditional ornament. The latest French railway stations and the most recent exhibition buildings, those of 1900, in the Champs-Elysées are market-halls, masked by classic façades. The intervention of iron has therefore caused no breach of continuity in the style of Mansart and Gabriel. It is used for convenience; but the beauty of stone cannot be sacrificed. Various attempts have, indeed, been made to reject it. The huge Galerie des Machines built by Dutert for the Exhibition of 1889, was acclaimed as the masterpiece of metallic construction. It

FIG. 808.—VAUDOYER. CATHEDRAL OF MARSEILLES.
(*Photo. Neurdein.*)

has recently been demolished to show Gabriel's pavilions again. Iron, in spite of the extraordinary flexibility of its powers, cannot oust the traditional materials of the mason. Without doubt engineers raise vaults and arches which appear prodigious when measured by the scale of stone construction, but power only astonishes us in proportion to human force. When arms were replaced by machines we no longer had any scale by which to measure the vastness shown us. Iron architecture, calculated scientifically on paper, and afterwards realised mechanically, is not susceptible to chance, accident or success. Between conception and achievement, there is no place in it for initiative, effort, or application. True, these metallic halls bear

FIG. 809.—APSE OF NOTRE-DAME-
DE-FOURVIÈRES, LYONS.
(*Photo. Neurdein.*)

the impress of human intelligence, but they show no trace of human labour. Astonished though we may be at the length of bars of metal, cast and welded, and hoisted mechanically into position, we turn from them to look with far greater interest at a wrought iron panel artistically hammered. The hand of man alone can draw a work of art from inert matter. Machinery stamps everything it produces with its own indifference.

FIG. 810.—SACRÉ-CŒUR,
MONTMARTRE, PARIS.
(*Photo. Neurdein.*)

The difficulty of finding a new ornamental style for furniture, jewels, and all the accessories of modern life and luxury, is often ascribed to the stagnation of architecture. From the pseudo-Gothic evolved by the Romantic imagination, to the Empire style, perpetuated and popularised by the July Monarchy, there is no style which has not been revived, and is not still current. That artistic heritage which enriches our museums, has weighed very heavily upon essays in a "new art," ever since the passion for ancient things passed from the world

ART IN FRANCE

FIG. 811.—BIRD'S EYE VIEW OF THE
SEINE IN PARIS.
(Photo. from "Paris vu en ballon," by
A. Schoelcher and O. Décugis.)

of collectors into well-to-do society as a whole.

In the closing years of the nineteenth century, Frenchmen began to recognise that in their admiration for the furniture of Louis XV and Louis XVI, they had forgotten to make any of their own. They began to look about for an original method of decoration suitable to modern life. It was an impossible enterprise, for a decorative system is not a spontaneous creation; one style generates another. The "modern style" itself chose ancestors; its initiators were also imitators; but they sought inspiration outside of classical and national styles. Grasset owed a good deal to the Middle Ages; others admired the Japanese, their light colours, their capricious lines, and the asymmetrical forms of their art, which, unlike our own, had never been dominated by stone architecture. Others again were attracted by English, Belgian, and Austrian models, by the furniture of all the countries which have a decorative style independent of the French.

Finally—and this was the beginning of real and fecund innovation—artists like Gallé of Nancy drew from the plant world delicate fancies which they applied to pottery, jewels, and furniture. But the chasm between a flower and a vase or a chair is so great that vegetable ornaments must either remain a purely extrinsic adornment, or the object must undergo a decorative contortion. In spite of this, the style of Nancy frequently shows a happy boldness in its adventurous caprices. Majorelle's furniture sometimes sacrifices logic

FIG. 812.—THE VIADUCT AT GARABIT.

388

to fancy, but it always shows real beauty of line, and the richness of a regal style. The city of Stanislas, Heré, and Lamour has not degenerated. Since the close of the era of fantastic exaggeration, it is easy to recognise an original and well defined type in certain modern furniture. The innovators have rejected the plaque-decoration of the ancient styles, their applications of metal and marquetry; the beauty of their works lies in the grain of the wood, and the manner in which it is carved. Eugène Gaillard designs elegant curves which expand into carved motives at the angles; Dufrêne, Selmersheim and Plumet manifest a sane and reasonable classic

FIG. 813.—E. NAVARRE AND R. ROUSSELOT, ARCHITECTS. HOUSE AT NEUILLY, 14, BOULEVARD D'INKERMANN. FAÇADE ON THE BOULEVARD.
(*Photo. "l'Architecte."*)

purity. In this beautiful furniture, solid, logical and practical, the parts held together by welded joints which give to the whole a

FIG. 814.—DUPONT, ARCHITECT. MODERN IRON GRILLE OF A HOUSE IN THE RUE SAINT-FERDINAND.

perfect homogeneity, the continuity of the curves recalls the forms of vegetable growth. Although original, their furniture retains the general proportions of Louis XV and Louis XVI works. They do not adopt the square joinery of the English, the cubic forms of the Viennese, the abrupt asymmetrical curves of the Belgians; they are modern in their somewhat bare simplicity, but we feel them to be the products of a race refined by centuries of social culture.

On the other hand, there are objects the forms of which are not so clearly designated by their uses. Jewels and pottery impose no such limitations on invention as furniture. For these little objects, more decorative than useful, artists have found new forms and employ new materials. One of the aspects in

FIG. 815.—A. SAUVAGE AND C. SARAZIN,
ARCHITECTS. VILLA AT COMPIÈGNE.
(*Photo. "l'Architecte."*)

which nineteenth century art had shown the greatest poverty was in its application of the same decorative forms to wooden panels, iron gates and china vases. One of the originalities of the modern style is that it has more respect for the quality of its material and turns it to better account. Carriès, Chaplet, Delaherche and many others have produced robust vases of enamelled pottery, and have overlaid them with rich colour. Lalique has made jewels which rival flowers and insects in grace and splendour. Robert and Brandt have resuscitated iron-work, the one by hammering gate-panels, the other by forging delicate pieces of ornament.

In spite of all the talent lavished on it, this new style is far from finding universal acceptance. This is because the society for which artists produce their work is much more difficult to conquer than in the time when it was limited to the narrow circle of the court and the city. How, indeed, can we expect to see in decorative taste that unity which exists nowhere, either in literature, politics or morals. Moreover, the love of antiquities, far from dying out, has become more general; fashion renews itself without abandoning retrospective styles.

The advocates of a modern art have somewhat abused their argument that a new society requires a new decorative style. Is it so certain that steam-engines and telegraph wires have entirely transformed our ideals of

FIG. 816.—A. BLUYSEN, ARCHITECT. VILLA AT
THE SEASIDE. (*Photo. "l'Architecte."*)

existence? Our civilisation has two aspects, one of which is certainly modified continuously, that which shows workrooms, offices and shops. But man will never look for pleasure in the places where he works; he reserves it for the interior in which he spends his leisure. And although methods of making money have changed a good

FIG. 817.—P. FOLLOT. BEDROOM.
(*Photo. "Art et Décoration."*)

deal, those of enjoying it have varied much less. The factories and machinery which feed contemporaneous luxury have not transformed the habits of social life. A cultivated and prosperous society which becomes more numerous every day, continues the life led in the eighteenth century by the restricted class of the aristocracy and rich citizens. It is very well content with the furniture in which the ancient régime found a perfect combination of elegance and comfort. The use of this furniture is, in fact, no whit more irksome to it than

FIG. 818.—CARRIÈS, BY HIMSELF.
TERRA-COTTA.
(Palais des Beaux-Arts de la Ville de Paris.)

the expression of ideas in the language of the Encyclopædists. Decorative "neologisms" have only been essential in the disposition of railway carriages, steamers and automobiles. Here because they were compulsory the new forms have appeared very naturally. Will the essays of modern art make any change in the general style of architecture and furniture, or will they leave nothing but a few charming trifles behind? The issue seems uncertain at present; the artistic past of France is so admirable and so varied that it is difficult to do justice to the present in this country. Foreign countries, Belgium, England and Germany, accept the experiments of modern decoration with less hesitation. Their luxury escapes more easily from the

FIG. 819.—DELAHERCHE.
VASE. STONEWARE.
(*Photo. "Art et Décoration."*)

domination of the past. Their architecture and furniture do not have to efface the memory of such admirable works as, for instance, a hotel or a sofa of the period of Louis XVI. France of the "Ancien Régime" outlives itself in its art. It imposes its aristocratic furniture on our contemporary bourgeoisie. The past with us is so admirable and so varied that it prevents us from doing justice to the present.

The fine shades of contemporary sensibility are revealed more especially in painting. It is here that the naturalistic tendencies which dominated the second half of the nineteenth century are most apparent. About the year 1850 the third artistic revolution achieved in the name of truth within less than a hundred years took place. David had dethroned Boucher, and was dethroned by Ingres. Now Courbet (1819–1877) rose in revolt against Ingres and Delacroix. His naturalism was a new thing in France. Until then French painters had, after the Florentine manner, made their sketches from the model, but not their pictures. And French painting often lacked the technical vigor and the spirited execution which we admire in the great naturalistic schools, in Caravaggio, as in Ribera and Velasquez, Rubens and Jordaens, Hals and Rembrandt. Among French painters, the work of the brain had always intervened between visual observation and manual reproduction. Géricault had made some attempt to render the aspects of Nature in their integrity by means of colour; but his work was prematurely ended. It was not till the middle of the century that integral Naturalism imposed itself on French painting. Courbet was its initiator.

He attempted to treat the human figure as the Fontainebleau landscape painters had treated nature. He showed us the peasants of Ornans with their

FIG. 820.—LALIQUE. BROOCH.
(*Photo. "Art et Décoration."*)

392

odd costumes and their grotesque heads, just as Rousseau had painted his gnarled old oaks. His figures were quite unlike those of Millet, for by their dimensions—and dimension is an important element in painting —Millet's little personages belonged to so-called genre-painting, and a great many pictures had already represented peasants of 20 centimetres; but figures of 1 metre 80 had always belonged to mythology or history. Further, the moral style of Millet corrected trivial vulgarity. Courbet, on the contrary, painted a man or a woman in the grass or on the soil with no more preparation or embarrassment than if they had been trees or oxen. His breadth of execu-

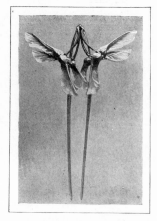

FIG. 821.—GAILLARD. COMB.
(*Photo. "Art et Décoration."*)

tion was very different from the careful, tentative technique of the Fontainebleau landscape painters. He was a robust workman, whose guiding principle was never to invent or to correct. In the midst of the somewhat insipid art of the Neo-Pompeians of the Second Empire, he appeared like a mason before a wall, brandishing his palette-knife and singing at the top of his voice. He needed all his self-confidence to meet the ridicule which assailed him. At a time

FIG. 822.—COURBET. THE FUNERAL AT ORNANS.
(The Louvre, Paris.) (*Photo. Vignais.*)

FIG. 823.—COURBET.
" BONJOUR, MONSIEUR COURBET."
(Museum, Montpellier.)

when Classicists and Romanticists were at one in scorning vulgarity, an artist of better education or of more refined intelligence would have recoiled from the difficulty. It is a constant danger for modern art that it is subject to the taste of a highly cultivated civilisation ; an insidious politeness lays its discipline upon all well-bred people. Courbet was not well-bred ; he talked loudly, in spite of laughter, and his example loosened many tongues. Young painters learned from his pictures that a faithful rendering of Nature need not entail loss of energy in care for accuracy, but that such a rendering may rather awaken energy, and lead to a number of expressive discoveries which remain hidden from the idealist.

Courbet, however, lacked much of the equipment he required for a perfectly novel presentment of Nature. He did not compose a new palette ; he borrowed that of the old Bolognese, of Guercino, Caravaggio, and the Spaniards, all those artists he had studied in the Louvre, and who had taught him to envelop his vigorous figures in opaque shadows and leaden colours ; Géricault and Delacroix had forestalled him in this lavish use of bitumen. For the realist Courbet, this material had very serious drawbacks ; even in the open air, his personages moved in darkness. In the *Funeral at Ornans* (Fig. 822) the sky is veiled in crape. When Courbet went south to Montpellier to see his patron,

FIG. 824.—COURBET. DEER COVERT.
(The Louvre, Paris.)

M. Bruyes, the light still remained poor and yellow (Fig. 823). The painter had not cleaned his palette. The realists of all schools have loved the strong shadows which throw bodies into relief and make the lights more brilliant. Ribot, a robust painter in the manner of Ribera, gives us nocturnal figures, shrouded in the smoky atmosphere proper to the caves of the Bolognese school.

FIG. 825.—COURBET. THE STONE-BREAKERS.
(Dresden Gallery.) (*Photo. Kuhn.*)

Courbet did not carry his principle to its logical conclusion; he wished to paint Nature, but he contemplated it from his studio. In the famous work he called *Allegorie reelle*—a sort of profession of faith in paint—he assembled his favourite models, critics, admirers, *lorettes*, workmen, a nude woman, etc., and in the midst of this studio thronged with Parisians, the artist himself is seen painting a Franche-Comté landscape! His figures, in fact, were painted in his studio and placed in landscapes painted from memory. Courbet realised at last that his "integral naturalism" could not be achieved without open-air effects. But essays in this direction show that he was embarrassed by difficulties which could only be solved by new methods. How indeed was this "Guercino of Franche-Comté" to paint light? When he attempted it, he could only make his colours paler, and they took on a flat, grayish tone. Corot alone could have taught him that to see light, we must look less at objects themselves than at their encompassing atmosphere. The naturalistic revolution was to be accomplished by Courbet's successors.

FIG. 826.—COURBET. THE WAVE.
(The Louvre, Paris.)

Millet (1814–1875) was not a realist in

FIG. 827.—RÉGAMEY. CUIRASSIERS AT AN INN.
(The Luxembourg, Paris.)

Courbet's sense. He did not copy his peasants from models. His images are exact, but they bear the impress of deep thought; his memory furnished the types and gestures he organised. He invented no pictorial novelties, and sought no new effects; like the Classicists, he only saw in painting a language for the translation of ideas and emotions.

Millet and Rousseau were neighbours at Barbizon, near Fontainebleau, on the edge of the forest, and while Rousseau penetrated into the depths of the woodland, Millet sought the plain. The forest, which is left to us from the period of barbarism, is not a natural home of man. He goes thither for refuge or to hide himself. The field, on the contrary, is his perpetual conquest and, whether visible or not, he is present in every part of it. While Rousseau showed the struggle of the tree for life, Millet recorded man's conflict with the earth from which he demands his bread. His peasants do not sing and dance like Corot's shepherds, to whom radiant Nature communicates her joy; they are not the personages of eclogues, but the austere labourers of rude Georgics. The soil he paints has just been shaved by the scythe and is still stiff with the short stubble of the cut grain, or it is the heavy clods thrown out by the ploughshare and crushed beneath the foot of the sower; it is the hard earth which the hoe breaks with difficulty, cutting through brambles and striking upon stones. Even in the absence of man, the earth recalls the peasant who cultivates it. The plough or harrow lies upon it, ready for the

FIG. 828.—RIBOT. SAINT SEBASTIAN.
(The Luxembourg, Paris.)

work of the morrow. This earth he draws and paints like a face with character, and, in fact, to the man who is always bending over her, does she not show a face, either good or bad? The dwelling is never far off, a poor shelter of stones and thatch, where the woman, when she is not in the fields, passes the slow days spinning wool, washing linen, feeding the little

FIG. 829.—BONVIN. THE REFECTORY.
(The Luxembourg, Paris.)

ones, absorbed in some simple task, like Chardin's housewives.

A draughtsman of gestures, Millet saw in them a definite utility, a means to an end; he shows us the whole body tense with effort. And this painter of rugged contours, who saw in the husbandman the machine of necessary labour, admired Michelangelo, the supple creator of athletic gestures. His peasant in coarse wooden shoes presses heavily upon the earth; his body is bent with long stooping over the soil, and he stands erect stiffly, as if this attitude had ceased to be a natural one to him; his silhouette, isolated against the bare sky, takes on a severe majesty. Millet follows this drama between man and the land with a virile emotion; he does not

FIG. 830.—ALPHONSE LEGROS.
THE EX-VOTO.
(Museum, Dijon.)

attempt to relieve it by any picturesque effect; he invokes inanimate nature only to suggest the cycle of the seasons—the August sun which burns the harvester, the frosts which harden the ground, the quiet of the approaching night, the hour when labour ceases, when through the gold of the twilight comes the sound of the angelus.

He did not paint directly from nature, and yet he seized effects of light. The one he loved best often appears behind

397

FIG. 831.—MILLET. THE GLEANERS.
(The Louvre, Paris.)

his figures; the diffused light seems to be biting into their silhouettes. The hatchings of his pastels suggest gleams of light upon objects very admirably. He painted his little figures with a loaded brush and fat colours; his forms are at once clumsy and gentle; the tint envelopes, subdues and extinguishes shimmer and reflections. No one, save perhaps Chardin, had painted little pictures thus before, on coarse canvas, with a dull, dry, porous impasto. We think of Millet himself, of his robust and caressing touch, before the peasant he has shown us grafting a tree, carefully manipulating the tender shoot with his hard, rough fingers. He liked that thick, clotty surface because it has a rustic touch, rough like ruined walls or mossy bark or old roof tiles, bristly like reaped fields, muddy as the farmyard, dusty as the hayloft, woolly as sheep and coarse knitted smock-frocks. The very walls are without sharp edges, the old church at Gréville, settled well into the ground, has a roof irregular and made up of angles and projections.

His little figures are, in their way, as idealistic as those of Poussin, and sometimes they would seem to have been executed with the same technical nonchalance. But, if Millet reminds us so much of the great classical master, it is more especially because there is always a profound thought in his compositions; he insisted on a kind of logic in his pictures, an element of inevitability, "the presence of persons and things for a definite purpose." Seasons succeed each other, the

FIG. 832.—MILLET. THE SHEPHERDESS.
(*Photo. Kuhn.*)

398

earth germinates, blossoms and lies bare, and since man first began to cultivate it, the toiler bending over it has used the same gestures, the same processes. Millet has rendered his attitude so truthfully, the man is so at one with his occupation and surroundings, that he typifies the husbandman of all ages and countries; the poor toiler suddenly fills the universe and eternity, and his piti-

FIG. 833.—MILLET. THE ANGELUS.
(The Louvre, Paris.)

ful silhouette is projected in all its immensity upon these two infinities.

Millet's sensibility was his bond of union with Romanticism. Poussin and the Classicists dwelt in imaginary regions. The ideas which engrossed them were a kind of superior pastime to them; the world they painted had been fashioned by history; an ingenious civilisation reveals itself in every detail of their learned art. But with Millet, as with Rembrandt, art loses its serenity and is nourished by human sentiment, emotional meditation, melancholy, pity, a kind of communion with the obscure souls of animals, and the silent life of things. No art in France had ever shown fewer traces of studio and museum. Only Rembrandt has shown such a power of emotion through pathos and tenderness. This successor of the Classicists was saturated with romantic melancholy; he combined the clear intelligence of Poussin with a virile pathos (Figs. 831–836).

The results of Millet's poetry are by no means exhausted. There is a certain affinity between his thought and that of

FIG. 834.—MILLET. THE HARROW.
(*Photo. Kuhn.*)

FIG. 835.—MILLET. THE MAN WITH THE HOE.
(*Photo. Kuhn.*)

Cazin, who also loved to associate man with nature, and who harmonised the attitudes of his figures with the desolation of twilight among the *dunes* most admirably. The biblical memories he evokes at times are by no means incongruous; his peasants are humble and simple enough to seem as ancient as humanity itself. The silent landscape which enfolds them is full of a gentle, caressing quality. The pallid colour imitates the transparence of a clear night, or the pale light of the moon on sleeping villages (Figs. 837, 838, 841). Jules Breton's peasant girls are, as Millet remarked, too pretty to stay in their villages. They certainly do not lack coquetry, and the sun when it sets throws a becoming light over these young girls, dressed in rags, who take the attitudes of canephoræ. Lhermitte's labourers have a kind of majesty. His sunburnt reapers and robust washerwomen are real rustic workers. Harpignies, an accomplished draughtsman of branch and foliage, suppressed human figures in his landscape, and painted simplified oak-trees with a confidence unknown to Rousseau (Fig. 842).

The realistic spirit, making itself felt in every branch of art, has transformed "history-painting." Planned for the use of a society of humanists, it had never ceased to be a reconstruction of the ancient world. The growth of historical curiosity, the discoveries of archæology, and finally the victories of the naturalistic painters, modified it greatly in the second half of the nineteenth century.

FIG. 836.—MILLET. MOTHER FEEDING HER CHILD.
(Museum, Marseilles.)

Historical colour, which is realism applied to the past, has become more sharply characteristic and better authenticated. In Poussin's works, the archæological data were scanty; here a pyramid, there a temple; a somewhat abstract generalisation of landscape and costume made careful exactitude unnecessary. Now, the Academie des Inscriptions instructs the Académie des Beaux Arts; the resulting picture is sometimes a piece of marquetry; "documents" are adjusted, completed, and fitted into the pattern. Between the conception of history among modern French painters

FIG. 837.—CAZIN. HAGAR AND ISHMAEL.
(The Luxembourg, Paris.)

and that of the Davidians, there is as great a difference as between Flaubert's *Salammbô* and Chateaubriand's *Martyrs*.

During the Second Empire, after Ingres had painted his little *Stratonice*, and Couture his immense *Roman Orgy*, there was a

FIG. 838.—CAZIN. TOBIAS AND THE
ANGEL.
(Museum, Lille.)

revival of archeological painting. These ingenious reconstructions aroused a great deal of public interest. G. Boulanger and Gérôme painted delicate figures in Pompeian surroundings. Gérôme was admirable both in his artistic thoroughness and his amusing intelligence; a draughtsman no less impeccable than Ingres, an illustrator no less ingenious than Delaroche, he treated even tragic themes wittily. Cabanel was an excellent disciple of Ingres, whose languorous, caressing line he sometimes recaptures. Bouguereau has carried the refined elegance of this manner to a point when even the most learned melodies take the

401

FIG. 839.—LÉON BELLY.   POOL IN THE FOREST
OF FONTAINEBLEAU.

(Mme. L. Belly's Collection.)

form of ritournelles. Jules Lefebvre and L. O. Merson must also be reckoned among these pure artists whose works lack passion, but whose conscientious technique becomes more and more salutary an example, as the rebels against syntax and orthography increase in numbers (Figs. 862-865).

Historical accuracy becomes excessive in the work of Tissot and Meissonier. "Documentation" is carried to its extreme limit by James Tissot in the laborious illustrations by which, with the help of actual studies in Palestine, he has attempted to reconstruct the landscape and costumes of the Gospels (Fig. 845). His realistic efforts have revived religious imagery, the demand for which had been ill satisfied by Flandrin's abstract painting. Meissonier (1814-1891) is one of the most important of those artists who have set great store on accuracy in their inventions. He has this paradoxical quality, that while he shows a prodigious minuteness of realism, he never treats any but imaginary episodes. His photographic vision is fixed upon the past; the Dutch manner is often cited in connection with his art, and no doubt he was influenced by the Little Masters of the Hague and Amsterdam; but there is this difference between them, that, whereas they depicted the life of their own times, Meissonier lived altogether outside of his. He has less taste for reality than for peculiarity. He is an explorer and a collector. His painting is as precious and dead as an exposition of bric-a-brac. He loved the

FIG. 840.—POINTELIN.   EVENING IN THE JURA.
(The Luxembourg, Paris.)

eighteenth century and the Napoleonic period for the picturesque elegance of their costume and the beauty of their equipments. He has shown us the Emperor and his army; the army of 1807, rushing upon the enemy under the chieftain's eye; the army of 1814, dragging itself after the Emperor, as yet unconquered, but enveloped in an atmosphere of impending disaster

FIG. 841.—CAZIN. IN PICARDY.
(*Photo. Crevaux.*)

(Fig. 843). He painted in miniature, preserving the effect of large composition. He accomplished such a *tour-de-force* as that of preserving every detail in the figure of a horseman no bigger than his finger. His pictures make admirable illustrations for histories. The little figures are very effective in a page. The good illustrator is revealed in the verve and spirit with which he draws clothes and gestures. Meissonier remains the master of this particular genre. No one had ever rendered the action of a horse or the elaborate details of a uniform so precisely. Not only did he create the little picture of the Musketeer; we owe him a new style of military painting, afterwards brilliantly developed by Edouard Detaille. Protais and Yvon depicted war with an intermixture of heroism or sentiment;

FIG. 842.—HARPIGNIES. MOONRISE.
(The Luxembourg, Paris.)

but it was the battle they were concerned to show us. Meissonier's first preoccupation was picturesque costume, and Edouard Detaille's soldier is often a mere *figurant* in a pageant of costume. Memories of 1870, 1806 and 1793 sometimes transformed these correct troopers into real combatants: mud and powder have

FIG. 843.—MEISSONIER. 1814.
(The Louvre, Paris.) (*Photo. Lecadre.*)

soiled the uniforms, and under the rainy sky the sun just before it sets throws sometimes a heroic purple on the standards. But there is more of the fury of battle in Alphonse de Neuville's pictures(Figs.846-849).

History - painting acquired a new significance in the work of Gustave Moreau, an ideologue and mythologist, like those poets who have enveloped their philosophy in a garb of gorgeous myth. He combined Ingres and Delacroix somewhat in the manner of Chassériau; like the "Parnassiens"[1] he strove to enshrine the imaginative ardour of Romanticism in the chiselled forms of pure Classicism. He set his ivory figures studded with gems in strange landscapes; learned and artificial, chimercial and fascinating, his painting lays the débris of ancient civilisations before our eyes; goldsmith's work, mosaic, the rarest materials of human industry, there is everything in this philosophical jewellery save the direct aspects of life. The art of Gustave Moreau was continued in little sanctuaries where only rare initiates entered; studios secluded like those monasteries where the Byzantine monkish artists had preserved such a rich inheritance from the Greeks and the Orient that they never thought of looking at nature itself (Figs. 858-861).

Archæological excavation, which was so fruitful at the close of the nineteenth century, has

FIG. 844.—MEISSONIER. THE BRAWL.
(Collection of the King of England)
(*Photo. Lecadre.*)

[1] A School of French poets, whose tendency is indicated in the above comparison.

revolutionised our historical imagination, and increased its retrospective grasp prodigiously. At Pompeii the pickaxe of the excavator is daily turning out accessories for the painter. Schliemann's discoveries at Mycenæ and Tiryns have modified the traditional conception of the Homeric warrior. Rochegrosse shows us a strange, primitive, terrific Asia and Greece, with fantastic armour and tattooed barbarians. Prehistoric themes have also entered into the domain of art; Cormon has reconstructed the life of cave-dwellers, lacustrians, and bear hunters armed with weapons of flint (Fig. 853).

But realistic vision and methods have been more especially applied to reconstructions of the past, and sometimes even to allegorical figures. The Davidians were abstract even when they were painting Napoleon and his soldiers; their humanity lacked physical life and the light of the real sun. Now, the personages of history are of flesh and blood. And even the variegated palettes of Orientalists and Impressionists sometimes present the heroes of antiquity in a new aspect.

FIG. 845.—TISSOT. THE MAGI.
(Collection of M. de Brunhoff.)

Leonidas and Romulus could no longer show themselves in the Forum or at Thermopylæ without exposing their marble nudity to the fantasies of "pleinairisme" (open-air effects).

Tattegrain chooses expressive landscapes as a setting for his gaily coloured scenes from the Middle Ages, and no painter has been more successful in vivifying history than Jean Paul Laurens; in his case, documentation has not stifled imagination, and realism has never become accurate and erudite platitude; he is one of those rare painters whose personages are neither actors on a stage nor amateurs in fancy dress. His imagination has been nourished on Michelet's sombre Middle Ages, and his vigorous brush reconstructs mediæval savagery, Merovingian crimes, the cold cruelty of the Inquisition, ecclesiastical vendettas, the devastating fury of revolution and battle. A virile poetry breathes from his works, and informs even his pictures of modern life (Fig. 852).

FIG. 846.—AIMÉ MOROT. REZONVILLE.
(The Luxembourg, Paris.)

Nevertheless, history-painting, which was once to art what epic poetry and tragedy were to poetry, has lost much of its prestige. The best pupils of the Ecole des Beaux Arts have abandoned this lofty style, and return to it only for large decorative compositions. Aimé Morot is content to be an excellent portrait-painter. Machard, Ferrier and Flameng have followed his example. The majority of *prix de Rome* [1] very soon renounce history in order to paint rich worthies in frock coats and fashionable ladies in ball dresses. The excellent portraits which appear in such numbers at the annual Salons, show that the most promising pupils of the Ecole are not the less proficient because they abstain from imaginative efforts.

Oriental landscapes and motives were among the themes dear to French painters of the nineteenth century. Numerous literary and political reasons developed this curiosity about Eastern

FIG. 847.—DE NEUVILLE. THE CEMETERY OF SAINT-PRIVAT.
(The Luxembourg, Paris.)

[1] Students who gain a travelling scholarship, which entitles them to a sojourn at the French School of Art in Rome.

406

FIG. 848.—DETAILLE. ENTRY OF THE GRANDE ARMÉE INTO PARIS, 1800 (FRAGMENT).
(Hôtel de Ville, Paris.)

things. Romanticism naturally loved its brilliant colours. Decamps, Delacroix, Dehodencq and Marilhat painted multicoloured turbans, robes and textiles, architecture with minarets, majestic ruins and burning sands; many, like Ziem, stopped short at Venice, and the dazzling vision of her marble palaces suspended between sky and water has blotted out the rest of the world for them (Fig. 851).

Naturalism did not injure Orientalism; the taste for strange impressions became keener; reality ceases to be vulgar when it is exotic. Before his early death, Henri Regnault had revived Delacroix's Mauresque Ro-manticism, and had found in Spain a spirited and richly coloured style, whereas in Paris he would doubtless have allowed himself to be recalled to a more discreet distinction. Fromentin painted Arabs hunting, and touched the satin coats of their horses with a delicate brush (Fig. 855). He would never have been willing to copy with equal exactness a French poacher rabbit-hunt-ing. Benjamin Constant

FIG. 849.—DE NEUVILLE. CHAMPIGNY.
(Museum, Versailles.)

FIG. 850.—HÉBERT. MALARIA.
(The Luxembourg, Paris.)

affected more theatrical Orientals, and sought to terrify us by depicting the secret butcheries of the Seraglio, while dazzling us by the splendour of the scene. But there is a more familiar and more quietly picturesque East, that of Guillaumet in the last generation, and now of Dinet, and of many other painters, who bring back brilliant impressions of their travels in Asia, Indo-China, and Japan (Figs. 856, 857). Painting became richer adapting itself to differences of climate, as it had to the differences of seasons and hours. Orientalism reconciles tradition and the innovators. It has enabled the Romanticists to become unavowed naturalists; it incites good pupils to seek new impressions, and offers a kind of chartered licence to the prudent artist.

Foreign art is greatly on the increase in France. Artists flock to Paris now to study or to acquaint themselves with the latest European tendencies, just as they flocked to Rome in the sixteenth and seventeenth centuries. Museums have, further, become schools in which painters are formed long after they have finished their apprenticeship. This instruction by the Old Masters is more especially evident in portraiture. Where invention is less essential, artists are more inclined to imitate style. We have seen landscape painters deriving from the Dutch, and Courbet inspired by the Bolognese. Manet owes some of his boldness to the Spaniards and to Hals; admirable masters of technique, such as Bonvin, Vollon, Roybet and Bail, are pupils of Holland. Roybet dif-

FIG. 851.—ZIEM. VENICE.
(The Luxembourg, Paris.)

fuses light on textures and accessories; Bail concentrates the peaceful sunshine that filters into kitchens and linen closets. Ricard discovered some of the secrets of Titian's deep and vital colour, and applied them with the more fragile grace proper to less robust models (Figs. 874, 875). Henner has reduced his art to the caressing pallor

FIG. 852.—J.-P. LAURENS. EXCOMMUNICATION
OF ROBERT LE PIEUX.
(The Luxembourg, Paris.)

which illuminated the nudities of Prud'hon, and sometimes those of Correggio. His white nymphs are merged in warm shadows, or their auburn hair gleams like a sombre flame against the turquoise of the background (Figs. 880, 881).

But the Spaniards of the seventeenth century have been the favourite masters, as was only to be expected at a period of frank naturalism. Manet, and a little later Carolus-Duran, learned in the School of Velasquez the art of bold antitheses and soft tonalities, in which the deep black of a dress, the brilliant carnations of a face, and in that face, the vivid red of the lips and the lustre of the eye, are relieved against a silvery grey background (Fig. 878). Bonnat is another French-Spaniard; we recognise a disciple of Ribera in this robust modeller, who throws his figures into strong relief by means of violent shadows. His austere solidity is appropriate to his favourite models. Modern custom, which has suppressed decorative costume, and reduced individuals to uniformity under identical garments, has tended to emphasise facial character. What is left of the fabrics of ceremony; the stars of the general, the red ribbon of the Legion of Honour, or the green palms of the

FIG. 853.—CORMON. CAIN.
(The Luxembourg, Paris.)

FIG. 854.—REGNAULT. GENERAL PRIM.
(The Louvre, Paris.)

Academician. The wrinkled brow, the furrowed cheek, all that reveals continuity of mental effort, is the more striking for the absence of distracting accessories. Man no longer appears in the trappings of the courtier or the dandy; his face is deeply scored by the travail of the brain. Bonnat hammers out these virile masks with the utmost mastery; he builds up opaque shadows round them, and forces us to concentrate our attention on the white head. The Hyacinthe Rigaud of the third Republic paints distinguished sexagenarians without wigs or ruffles (Figs. 876, 877).

The aristocratic elegance of eighteenth-century England has won disciples in France simultaneously with Spanish naturalism. The portrait-painters who have adopted this manner, Benjamin Constant and more especially Humbert, have reverted to these park-like backgrounds which give a discreet splendour to the setting of elegant female figures. Humbert has a knack of adapting his models to slight landscape sketches, and although the portrait is none the less faithful, the sitter profits by the harmonious charm; in addition, this admirable painter has proved himself an excellent decorator, preserving unity in vast compositions, arranging fine attitudes in well-balanced landscapes, coloured with distinction and sobriety. Jacques Blanche is also a disciple of the English; he has their alert art, their touch, and their technical subtleties; the contrast between his Parisian celebrities and Bonnat's important per-

FIG. 855.—FROMENTIN. HAWKING.
(Condé Museum, Chantilly.)

sonages is no less marked than that of his restless, mobile manner with the confident technique of the painter of officialdom.

Two original portrait-painters, Fantin-Latour and Carrière, sacrificed many pictorial qualities to achieve moral expression, in the intensity of which they greatly sur-

FIG. 856.—GUILLAUMET. LA SEGUIA.
(The Luxembourg, Paris.)

passed the normal limits of the genre. Their figures were not those of indifferent models, chance clients, but those of friends and familiars. Fantin's delicate, subtle painting is no less discreet than his sitters; these have no graces of costume or attitude, and the painter sometimes grouped them as artlessly as if they had placed themselves before a photographer's camera; the colour seems overlaid by the venerable dust which covers things that have been shut up too long untouched; the painter and his sitters lived outside the mutations of fashion and its refinements (Fig. 879).

To make his language more expressive, and to emphasise the moral life, Carriére effaced material phenomena. His colour is subdued, and only light shadows remain to model his sorrowful or laughing faces. Spreading a delicate *grisaille* over the canvas, his caressing brush follows, expands, and amplifies, enveloping gestures, and forms which seek and clasp each other. This veiled reality, which leaves the eye almost unoccupied, induces reverie; no painter has ever succeeded thus in showing the atmosphere of tenderness which envelopes beings who love one another, and the collective soul which unites the countless bodies of a crowd in a common movement. This desire to penetrate to the obscure

FIG. 857.—GUILLAUMET. LAGHOUAT.
(The Luxembourg, Paris.)

depths of psychological life causes our modern artists to overstep the limits of their art perpetually, to produce music without rhythm, poetry without thought, sculpture without form, and painting without colour. Art dies away to rejoin the intangible (Figs. 882, 883).

In contrast to the naturalism which is always in search of greater truth, we must now place the painting which seeks for beauty. The painters of the Restoration and of the July Monarchy did not lack decorative enterprises; the successors of David, Ingres and his pupils, were able to embark on vast compositions for the churches, the Louvre, and Versailles. But these painters were hardly decorators. The reforms of David had been made in the name of severe beauty; painters, returning to a somewhat heavy rigidity of composition, correctness of drawing, and austerity of style, had lost the amenity of Boucher's manner. Their initial difficulty was to adapt these chilly paintings to mural decoration, and to apply figures with rounded contours and polished limbs to panels and ceilings. They found further that their pictorial themes required renovation. Christian iconography was confined to the churches; as to the mythological repertory, it seemed very old fashioned in an age that could no longer treat it brilliantly. Since the Gospels and Olympus had alike failed them, where were the decorators of the nineteenth century to find motives and a style, ideas and forms?

Delacroix's decorations returned to Venetian and Flemish traditions, Veronese and Rubens. He

enframed his tumultuous compositions and his brilliant colours in gold; but such splendour requires the royal galleries of the Louvre or the Luxembourg, and this opulent style could not become general. Although Chassériau owes a good deal to him, it was rather the style of Ingres which finally prevailed. Ingres equalised the reliefs on the surface of the wall, attenuated the colours, and fixed the figures in tranquil attitudes; the equilibrium of the forms was in harmony with the lines of the architecture.

Following his example, Delaroche, in his painting of the so-called Hemicycle in the Ecole des Beaux-Arts, made a strenuous attempt to give decorative breadth to his somewhat tame

FIG. 860.—G. MOREAU. ORPHEUS.
(The Luxembourg, Paris.)

style, like a correct writer of prose who is ambitious to be grandiloquent. His composition was based on the *Apotheosis of Homer;* but Delaroche's great men are listless and inattentive; they seem to be chatting together before the beginning of a sitting. Delaroche once more stops in the anteroom. There is no soul in the assembly; it lacks the religious atmosphere of some sacred grove. Chenavard understood that a huge painting cannot satisfy the modern spirit unless it offers a noble theme for meditation. We are no longer unsophisticated enough to be content with a purely fanciful spectacle, like those of Veronese. Chenavard accordingly proposed to make philosophy play the part in his painting which religious emotion had played in that of Flandrin. Every man who claimed to be a serious thinker under Louis Philippe, was fond of excursions into the past, to determine the causes of the French Revolution.

FIG. 861.—G. MOREAU. VENICE (WATER-COLOUR).
(The Luxembourg, Paris.)

FIG. 862.—LEFEBVRE.
TRUTH.
(The Luxembourg, Paris.)

Every history of the period might have been called: *The Origin of the Revolution.* Chenavard very nearly translated this book into paint in the secularised Pantheon of 1848. His symbolical decoration was never carried out. He philosophised too much to paint well. His ideas could not always find plastic expression. A few of his works have survived, in which dark, muscular forms move uneasily; they are Michelangelo's creations, deprived of their superhuman power. Chenavard's art, austere and abstract as that of Ary Scheffer, makes us realise that ideology will not suffice to produce energy.

Chassériau had not time to fulfil his destiny (1819-1856). As far as we can judge by some few paintings saved from the ruins of the Tuileries, he would have become a magnificent decorator. Like Flandrin, he had learnt the secret of noble attitudes and outlines, the full curves and ample gestures of fair odalisques; but Delacroix's colour, and memories of Morocco gave a certain Romantic fever to the bodies which Flandrin endowed only with a peaceful sentimentality. We even recognise the restless, unhealthy colour of Delacroix, and the nervous, staccato touch of his tentative brush (Figs. 863, 866).

Paul Baudry, in his work at the Opera House, endeavoured to be as sumptuous as the framework he had to fill. Thought would have been out of place in this domain. His allegories of Music and Dancing are merely pretexts for splendid forms and happy grouping. The work which reveals him puts before us a Venus in the manner of Titian, but vivacious, brilliant, roused from the drowsy voluptuousness of the Venetian. He was an

FIG. 863.—CHASSÉRIAU. NUDE WOMAN.
(Museum of Avignon.)

eclectic of great distinction. He had taken from the Italian Renaissance the best of its essence, the pliant forms of Michelangelo, the harmonious grouping of Raphael, and as often as he could the light silver color of Veronese. The only thing that this painter, so finely trained, lacked was a greater power of invention. (Figs. 864, 865, 870.) Delaunay may be classed with him as an excellent painter, capable of setting elegant and robust figures on a ceiling; the alert flexibility of Florence is combined with the rich colour of Venice in his animated compositions (Fig. 868).

The Third Republic has demanded a great deal of decoration from its history-painters. It became apparent that they were losing in decorative

FIG. 8 4 —BAI D RY.
THE TOILET OF VENUS.
(Museum of Bordeaux.)

value what they were gaining in realistic precision. The panels in the Pantheon, the Hôtel de Ville of Paris, and the Capitole of Toulouse are for the most part immense historical pictures. In very richly decorated galleries, they make a good effect, but when the architecture is simple, they look extremely heavy. On the gray stone of the Pantheon, many of the paintings are like pictures waiting for their frames. Elsewhere a pendentive cuts a motive designed for a square into a triangle, or a window, a door, or a pilaster encroaches disastrously upon a figure. The architect hampers the painter at every turn, because the painter has left him too much out of account.

Painters as realistic as Courbet, Gervex and Roll have sometimes

FIG. 865.—CABANEL. THE BIRTH OF VENUS.
(The Luxembourg, Paris.)

enlarged their pictures and made them into decorative panels. Why not, we may ask. The greatest of decorators, Veronese and Rubens, were fervent naturalists; but in these cases, truth was compatible with imagination: when they painted living flesh and elaborate costumes, they did not cease

FIG. 866.—CHASSÉRIAU. THE TEPIDARIUM.
(The Louvre, Paris.)

to invent radiant visions. Our realists lack the resource of such fictions; material truth is a heavy burden for a decorator. In Roll's vast compositions, and those which were painted in French hôtels de ville between 1880 and 1900, the crowds are the actual crowds of the streets, but the painter's skill has not always enabled him to correct the commonplace nature of the spectacle. Roll has, nevertheless, executed some charming panels with landscape effects, brilliant summer or spring sunshine, women, and flowers, in which his robust technique has been modified; but if the impression is agreeable, the thought seems trivial; the over-realistic decorator errs by heaviness when he is serious, by insignificance when he is superficial (Figs. 894, 895).

And yet this very Naturalism has done decorative art a service, in that it has enabled it to declare itself frankly. Ingres, Delaroche, Delacroix and Chassériau had only one style for painting a picture and a wall. Their style, which was neither purely realistic nor purely idealistic, was the same on a vast ceiling and in a little frame. When the vocabulary of painters became overloaded with material sensations, the necessity for a decorative style made itself felt, and the rupture between the art which lives by resemblance and the art which seeks delight was complete. Courbet and Puvis de Chavannes turned away at the same time, but in opposite directions, from the normal style of painting. One seemed possessed by violent, the other by benevolent mania; for the one, painting was purely

FIG. 867.—G. BOULANGER.
PRINCE NAPOLEON'S POMPEIAN HOUSE.
(Museum of Versailles.)

the language of sensation;
for the other, it realised
poetic visions and evoked
serene meditations.

Puvis de Chavannes
(1824-1898) created a
decorative style; he was
more successful than
Flandrin and Chenavard,
Lyonnais like himself, in
translating noble thoughts
into the language of form,
and in emancipating him-
self from the prosaic ex-
actitude of the Naturalists.

FIG. 868.—DELAUNAY. THE PLAGUE AT ROME.
(The Luxembourg, Paris.)

His painting is as tranquil as the architecture it clothes; his figures
are fixed in truthful and majestic attitudes, attitudes of repose, or
at least of bodies in perfect equilibrium; with their simplified
silhouettes and a certain stiffness of the joints, they have that
perfect solidity, that candid air which marked Giotto's figures,
and is lacking in Ingres and Flandrin's calligraphic elegance.
His favourite colours repeat the pale tones and the soft charm of
Florentine fresco, as if the chalk on the wall had melted into the
blues and reds. They require no gold frame to enhance their effect;
surrounded by the cold, bare stone, they retain their luminous
delicacy. Puvis de Chavannes did not achieve this colour at once;
it was only by degrees that his men and things began to veil themselves in a transparent whiteness, by means of which they lose their

materiality to become
harmonious patches upon
the wall, very soft to the
eye, in spite of their solid
construction.

But the creation of a
vocabulary is no great
thing; Puvis abandoned
the traditional motives,
Christian and pagan, and
imagined a new world, a
world at once real and
ideal, which is not that of
Olympus or the Gospels,

FIG. 869.—CABANEL. PHÆDRA.
(Museum of Montpellier.)

417

FIG. 870.—BAUDRY.   THE RAPE OF PSYCHE.
(Château of Chantilly.)

of history or of reality.   The idea is always so simple that it seems commonplace when it is expressed in words: Peace, War, Work, Play, Art.   Puvis adapted this large symbolism, rich in noble attitudes, to a variety of sites, for his decoration, always subordinated to the exigencies of architecture, is also brought into moral harmony with its surroundings.   It is true that the initial works, *Peace* and *War,* were not destined for the city of Amiens, where circumstances have placed them, but the paintings which completed the decoration of the Museum of Picardy illustrate Picard landscape, and the life of the province. In the Museum of Rouen, we have Nature inspiring the Arts; in that of Lyons, the serenity of the pagan dream in the radiant sunlight, and the mystic ardour of the painter-monk in his Tuscan monastery.   In the Marseilles Museum, two compositions indicate the functions of this "Greek Colony" which has remained "the Gate of the East."   Puvis de Chavannes may be said to have created a genre, the decoration of the peristyles of museums, of those monuments so characteristic of our nineteenth century, where we come into contact with the historical and geographical spirit of our provinces.   The great decorator emphasises the local features of their districts, and offers us a noble theme for meditation on the threshold.   His compositions, which are neither pure allegory nor history, owe their vital charm to the landscape.   By the truth of the illumination and of the character of the ground, Puvis has given plausibility

FIG. 871.—GAILLARD.
DOM PROSPER GUÉRANGER.
(ENGRAVED PORTRAIT.)
("Gazette des Beaux-Arts.")

FIG. 872.—CHAPLIN. PORTRAIT
OF A YOUNG GIRL.
(The Luxembourg, Paris.)

FIG. 873.—BASTIEN-LEPAGE.
SARAH BERNHARDT.
(Collection of M. W. Blumenthal.)

to his visions, without giving them exactitude; the poetic physiognomy
of the seasons and regions, Summer and Winter, Rouen and Marseilles, is realised. He has put into living nature pure fictions; he has
modernized and revised the mythological soul of historical landscape.

FIG. 874.—RICARD.
PORTRAIT OF HEILBUTH.

FIG. 875.—RICARD.
PORTRAIT OF A WOMAN.

At the Sorbonne, such poetry breathes from the Sacred Grove in which Letters and Science converse that these allegories lose their scholastic coldness, and participate in divine life and Elysian serenity (Fig. 790). Other landscapes exhale the poetry of past ages. At Lyons, the radiant paganism of Greece, and the Franciscan soul of Umbria. In the Pantheon, Puvis illumines Saint Geneviève's childhood with the white radiance of dawn, and shows us her old age in twilight and gathering night. The artless sweetness of the tone resuscitates the idyllic soul of the legend. This work, entirely modern, seemed as old and as penetrated with humanity as those relics which for generations have received the prayers of pilgrims. It perpetuates the presence of the saint. From the top of the sacred hill the guardian of Paris still watches over the city. (Figs. 884–887.)

Puvis de Chavannes, by no means an impeccable artist, has created a universe, like the great poets of painting. Very often, he recalls Poussin by the power of his thought, the predominance of the conception, the tranquil assurance of the technique, and the plastic rhythm of the composition. In the greatest geniuses of French art, Poussin, Chardin, Millet, and Puvis, manual dexterity has counted for little; they spiritualise their material, obtain the adhesion of thought, and evoke the faculty of reverie without astonishing the eye.

While Puvis was dreaming his dream, Courbet's painting was working out its conclusions. We must now follow the history of

naturalistic painting in its technical discoveries. In his first works, Manet (1832-1883) had been guilty of the same absurdity as Courbet. He placed studio figures in his landscapes. His picture of an *al fresco* meal (*Déjeuner sur l'Herbe*) represents a naked woman on a background of dark green, side by side with men in dark clothes. The sun filters through the foliage, but with very little enthusiasm or gaiety. The true illumination for this young woman would have been the fitful reflections of light under trees. Manet, however, inserted in his landscape a figure the colour of old ivory, a product of Rembrandt's studio, the silhouette of which is

FIG. 878.—CAROLUS-DURAN. THE LADY WITH THE GLOVE.
(The Luxembourg, Paris.)

sharply defined against the aggressive green of the meadow (Fig. 891). Obviously, Manet intended to illuminate his pictures by this method of surrounding large planes of light with opaque shadows. But such a method, unfortunately, fixes the contours heavily; the object has more solidity, more body thus treated, than those of the abstract academic paintings; but it is far from bathing in the radiant illumination of broad daylight. At this period Manet was an admirer and pupil of the Spaniards with their dark shadows, and of Hals with his staccato touch. He had extraordinary visual delicacy, which was as yet but imperfectly seconded by his technical skill; his colour was dirty, and could not render the freshness of his impression. Certain notes of his brush sum up subtle and vivid sensations; they are charming inventions among a great

FIG. 879.—FANTIN-LATOUR. MANET'S STUDIO AT LES BATIGNOLLES.
(The Luxembourg, Paris.)

FIG. 880.—HENNER.   READING GIRL.
(Collection of Mme. Porgès.)

number of less happily inspired expressions. His vivacity of touch redeems the heaviness of his material; Manet excels less in his scale of colour than in his nervous, elliptical handling; the Impressionists who succeeded him rendered the luminous transparence of the open air more perfectly, but their brushing is quiet and monotonous (Figs. 890, 891).

Other painters, such as Bastien-Lepage, tried to suggest the open air by an equal diffusion of light on the landscape and the figures set in it. The painter tried to atone by precision of drawing for the loss of solidity entailed by this monotonous equality. But Bastien-Lepage's delicate gradations fade away in the distance like a well modulated voice which is too weak to make itself heard save at close quarters. Frank oppositions of light and colour are necessary to illuminate a large picture. This refined painter applied the delicate execution hitherto reserved for aristocratic portraits or mythological divinities to the rendering of a peasant picking up potatoes (Fig. 889). Dagnan-Bouveret has gone even further, bringing the physiognomical research of a Leonardo to bear upon his rustic models (Fig. 897). Bastien-Lepage's *plein-airisme* is to be recognised in a large number of painters, Gervex, Duez, Albert Maignan, and Roll, who have illuminated large compositions by relieving Ribot's and Manet's sombre tonality with silvery tones. Roll is a vigorous painter who throws rays of sunlight

FIG. 881.—HENNER.   IDYL.
(The Luxembourg, Paris.)

into his unctuous colour. But in his painting light produced by oppositions of black and white is replaced by a vivid polychromy.

About the year 1875, while Manet was still living, certain painters invented a new process. Claude Monet and his disciples, Sisley, Pissarro, Renoir, and even Manet himself, form a well defined group, because they had a common aim, and attained it by similar means; a polemical incident gave them the name of "Impressionists." Courbet and Manet had failed to render the brilliance and delicacy of light, because their only method had been the opposition of light and dark, black and white. But although the painter has no real light on his palette, he has colours as vivid as

FIG. 882.—CARRIÈRE. CHILDREN'S KISSES.
(Moreau-Nélaton Collection.)
(Musée des Arts Décoratifs.)

those of reality. Now certain masters, Rubens, Turner and Delacroix, had already shown that the play of light and shade may be adequately translated by a play of colours. Physicists have taught us that a ray of sunshine, passing through a prism, is decomposed into three pure colours, yellow, red, and blue, which mingle at their confines and form three composite colours, violet, green and orange. The more or less conscious method of the Impressionists consists in replacing that light, the splendour of which the painter cannot directly reproduce, by its constituent colours, the equivalents of which he has on his palette. He uses pure colour as far as possible, that he may lose nothing of his means; for colours become dirty and neutral by intermixture.

FIG. 883.—CARRIÈRE. MATERNITY.
(The Luxembourg, Paris.)

FIG. 884.—PUVIS
DE CHAVANNES.
SAINT GENEVIÈVE
WATCHING OVER PARIS.
(Panthéon, Paris.)

But these colours cannot reproduce light, unless they are combined, like the colours of the prism. The Impressionist painter leaves this process to the spectator; the eye reverses the process of the prism; it recomposes what the painter has decomposed. The painters of light rekindle the reflections which the painters of pure form had extinguished; but in the effort to fix the intangible specks which float in the atmosphere, they are often obliged to sacrifice the material colour of things, the local tint. The Impressionists gave severe shocks to our prejudices as to local colour; they frankly coloured a face with blue or orange reflections, and experimented on the human figure with those luminous fantasies which had hitherto been reserved for clouds and water, because these bodies have only borrowed colours. Finally, as the painter does not represent objects in their materiality, but only in their luminous appearance, the Impressionist brush does not define forms; the reflections in which the light is dispersed must not appear to imitate the actual colour of things; it must float, as it were, in the atmosphere, and vibrate like luminous atoms. Design, in the ordinary sense of the term, is volatilised. A good Impressionist landscape extinguishes everything near it; its light is so subtle and so brilliant that it has been accounted a sufficient motive for the picture. The Impressionist does not represent a tree, a lake, or a house, but the shade of the tree, pierced by a few rays of light, or the appearance of a wall at different times of the day. A stack of corn, a mist, the carved façade

FIG. 885.—PUVIS DE CHAVANNES.
CHILDHOOD OF SAINT GENEVIÈVE.
(Panthéon, Paris.)

424

of a church, a pool with water-lilies, sufficed Claude Monet for the thread on which he strung his glittering gems (Figs. 899-901).

The reflections of Impressionism are to be found in the greater part of contemporary painting; its sparks kindled a blaze of fireworks in decorative art. Landscape painters have so far profited by it that

FIG. 886.—PUVIS DE CHAVANNES. THE SACRED GROVE. (Museum of Lyons.)

they have learnt to differentiate the light of special hours and regions. Théodore Rousseau made but a slight distinction between southern sunshine and that of the Ile-de-France; Corot confounded that of Italy with that of Picardy. They obliterated the too characteristic brilliancy of each particular hour and of every individual sky. A new world has been discovered and explored which no painter can now ignore.

The Impressionists have formed a decorative style; the brilliant polychromy of their palettes incites these subtle observers continually to new fantasies of colour. Claude Monet fell into the hallucination of dazzling visions even when he was merely endeavouring to get a true effect, and Lebourg sometimes recalls Turner.

FIG. 887.—PUVIS DE CHAVANNES. MARSEILLES, PORT OF THE ORIENT.

(Museum of Marseilles.)

But the Impressionist method is solvent for design, and soon betrays its insufficiency outside the realm of landscape. Certain painters, such as Renoir and Besnard, have bathed their large figures in fitful light; they note its iridescence on a pearly skin, and mingle the reflections of sun and water in the liquid suppleness of their bathing women. Besnard's deco-

FIG. 888.—CAROLUS-DURAN. THE MURDERED MAN.
(Museum of Lille.)

rations have a lyric lightness and movement; they amuse the eye by their unexpected arrangement, their audacious perspective, their spiritual freedom. They suggest Fragonard's lively ardour, Tiepolo's boldness, his balanced masses, his sudden rays of light. But the inspiration is purely modern; the atmosphere is that of the laboratory; the colours are as crude as those of pharmaceutical jars, the light dazzling and explosive, the figures restless and electrical as flames. That brilliant method sometimes even falsifies the ideology of the painter. Certain ideas lose a little of their serene gravity through this vibrating style. Besnard preserves form admirably amidst his reflections; the jets of light follow the modelling; the supple hatchings of the brush continue to design even when the fantasies of the colour die out. He has painted some excellent portraits, in which the personality of the model is not too much dispersed in the capricious play of reflections amongst flowers and stuffs (Figs. 906, 907). Gaston La Touche, Louis Picard, Mlle. Dufan, and Chéret also practice this explosive decoration. Invented by fervid Naturalists, the Impressionist language now serves for the expression of pictorial fantasy. Poetic fiction has emerged from sensation; a flame has burst from matter.

Henri Martin has attempted and succeeded in a decorative style in which he combines the realism of Roll, the flickering sunlight of the Impressionists, the breadth and calm rhythm of Puvis de Chavannes. Men of our own day, peasants or city folk, take attitudes which seem sometimes pretentious

FIG. 889.—BASTIEN-LEPAGE. HAYMAKING.
(The Luxembourg, Paris.)

for people who are not draped in togas, with their eyes toward heaven and their feet dragging wearily, like the poets of early legend; but the vulgarity of the figures is redeemed by the extraordinary beauty of the landscape and the moving poetry of the light. Henri Martin has not adopted Puvis de Chavannes' flat colour; he paints with independent touches which

FIG. 890.—MANET.
THE BAR OF THE FOLIES-BERGÈRE.

make the atmosphere vibrate, without destroying the solid structure of his vast compositions; this mosaic he doubtless learnt in his native Toulouse, that "Pointillist" city, built of little bricks, and paved with little stones (Figs. 910, 911). This "Pointillisme"[1] is modified and attenuated till it dies away altogether in Le Sidaner's quiet landscapes and Ernest Laurent's tender and mysterious portraits.

Drawing as practised by French artists since the Renaissance has been an abstract modelling, a kind of design for sculpture. There is an Impressionism of line, analogous to that of light and colour. Like the technique of colour division this drawing is implicit in the art of Delacroix; it suggests not only form but movement; it does not seek solid reality behind changeful appearance; it accepts disorder and inexactitude, and sacrifices literal accuracy to characterisation. Japanese albums taught it the dislocation of line, undulating perspective, dissymmetrical composition, and all the curiosities of arrangement which figures passing in our field of vision can

FIG. 891.—MANET. BREAKFAST ON THE GRASS.
(Moreau-Nélaton Collection.)

[1] The method of painting by juxtaposing small particles of pure colour.

assume. Degas is one of the masters of this art. He chose all the most unexpected aspects of reality, and all the most artificial elements of our society, the world of theatres and races, jockeys perched on slender thoroughbreds, or the pirouettes of ballet dancers (Fig. 905). Forain is of the same school; he describes the world of the Stock Exchange, of politics and of the theatre, and loves to show these modern powers, the financier, the deputy, and the dancer, in juxtaposition. He will be accounted the Daumier of our age; but Daumier was always a Romanticist, burning with generous rage; Forain's drawing, abrupt and decisive, carries a cold, insulting irony in its brutal lines. Raffaelli, the draughtsman of bare suburbs and swarming streets, of wretched tatterdemalions and small tradespeople, should also perhaps be classed with these students of characteristic traits (Fig. 898). Steinlen is not a draughtsman of this group. He is rather a descendant of Millet, who could express a lifetime of misery in a heavy silhouette (Fig. 892).

Impressionism was the invention of a new language rather than of a new mode of thought. It is the result of a visual analysis; painters took notes and registered curious effects; and now a great many of them, returning to their studios, are projecting works more significant in content. Amongst these pioneer groups, two tendencies are clearly apparent. Certain artists are faithful to the light colours, but are less exclusively preoccupied with the truth of luminous effects than their prototypes; painters like Cézanne, Gauguin and Maurice Denis seem to aim more at decorative or expressive effects. They have a horror of the Naturalism from which

428

they have emerged. They accept the brilliant palette of their predecessors, but merely for decorative purposes; some of them, Maurice Denis, for instance, have recognised that these pure colours recall the azure, the flame-like red and the lily-white of Fra Angelico, and they lay on their rainbow tints in broad unbroken tones like those of a

FIG. 894.—ROLL.   THE CENTENARY OF 1789.
(Museum of Versailles.)

tapestry or of a fresco by Giotto. Objects no longer melt into the atmosphere; emphatic lines encircle forms, and these lines are delirious. Monet saw his forms bathed in light, but he allowed us to discern correct modelling amidst his flickering reflections. The heavy profiles which enclose the forms of the Cézanne-Gauguin School do not help us to a mental reconstruction of their tottering houses and crippled figures. It is scarcely probable that these artists will persuade us to renounce the grammar of design which has been accepted since the Renaissance. Design bears a relation to the laws of vision analogous to that of syntax to the laws of thought. Such a discipline can only disappear as a result of complete intellectual disintegration, such as that which marked the downfall of the antique world. This affected barbarism might prove fertile in countries where culture is still elementary; in France it can only be noted as the passing diversion of decadents.

FIG. 895.—ROLL.
THE NURSE.
(Museum of Amiens.)

We must look in another direction for indications of future developments. At the heyday of Impressionist sun-studies, a group of young painters began to be distinguished by the dark tonality of their pictures. Cottet, Simon, Ménard, Dauchez and others after them, deserted the open air for the studio, and returned to what may be called museum-

FIG. 896.—PISSARRO. LA PLACE
DU THÉÂTRE FRANÇAIS.
(Durand-Ruel Collection.)

painting, with strong shadows and subtleties of execution which do not aim exclusively at truth. They are not really impressionists at all, neither are they realists after the manner of Courbet. They do not paint any object they happen to see. Their pictures are not studies enlarged and carried out, but compositions carefully planned to express individuality. Their technique sometimes recalls Courbet; but it is the spirit of Millet which informs their art. They have extinguished the Impressionist fireworks, because their magic iridescence prevents one from seeing the solidity of things; very vivid polychromy dazzles the eye and holds it captive; that loud confused music disturbs our thoughts; dark colour is less distracting to meditation, and we can recognise a thought more easily in its tranquillity. These painters seek the perennial physiognomy that underlies the variations of hours and seasons. They strip the soil of its vesture of light and verdure; they love to show the skeleton of the earth. They have a strong predilection for Brittany, a district in which the variations of time and season transform the aspects of Nature but slightly. Among the innumerable portraits of the French provinces which appear annually at the Salon, none leave a deeper impression upon the memory than Ménard's Mediterranean scenes, and the Brittany of Simon, Dauchez and Cottet. Here is that colourless land, with hard outlines, where it is believed that traces

FIG. 897.—DAGNAN-BOUVERET.
THE CONSCRIPTS.
(Palais Bourbon.)

430

can still be found of geological upheavals. Occasionally a steely ocean eats away the land and a bay of green water penetrates between the rocks. As one approaches the Pointe du Raz, vegetation grows scarcer and the ground appears bare. The gray houses, pale, painted white, have the faded tints of a washed-out dawn, the colour of storm and rain; the

FIG. 898.—RAFFAELLI. GUESTS AWAITING A
WEDDING PARTY.
(The Luxembourg, Paris.)

"Bigoudins" in stiff attitudes and black dresses, with reddened faces, as sad in joy as in sorrow, belong to the landscape like the lines of white and slaty clouds which weigh on the horizon, like the walls of dry stones which outline the irregularities of the land and shut in the uncultivated fields. In Ménard and Dauchez we note a desire to generalise the character of the landscape; they grasp the aspect of gulf, lake, forest, and ruin as a whole. The image they give us has not the episodic character of a motive painted from Nature; they have seized it in its essence by an effort of the mind rather than of the eye. Often an antique monument gives that idea of eternity. So our Classicists of the seventeenth century, Poussin and Lorrain, composed Arcadias and seaports under the setting sun. To produce such landscapes, it is not enough to see well and copy well; it is necessary to feel the inherent logic which has given objects their form. Claude Lorrain and Joseph Vernet were guilty of geological absurdities in their landscapes. Their modern heirs commit no such blunders, they know how the strata slide, how the rocks break, how clouds form and beaches are made,

FIG. 899.—CLAUDE MONET.
PORTRAIT OF A WOMAN.
(Museum of Berlin.)

431

FIG. 900.—CLAUDE MONET. LONDON BRIDGE.
(Durand-Ruel Collection.)

Their drawing defines the personality of rock or cloud unerringly, and reveals the soul of the landscape (Figs. 912-915).

Impressionism confined itself to the mobile surface of things, to phenomena which make little appeal to emotion or intelligence. It was, in painting, that phase of pure observation through which all forms of intellectual labour have passed. The Impressionist collects from nature true effects, as the scholar notes facts of which he only demands exactness. But even in painting, the French mind cannot long resign itself to the function of a recording apparatus. There are many signs that it is turning once more to the classical attitude. Does not the nobility of art lie in the fact that human thought is everywhere present in it? But this new Classicism has not rejected its romantic and naturalistic heritage. Since the time of romantic thought things themselves are penetrated by sentimentality, and the picturesque resources acquired by the naturalists remain a permanent acquisition. Whereas the Classicists confined their observation to the face and the attitude of the body, modern research extends to the inanimate regions, and painters now look for the relations of thought and matter in the physiognomy of land and sky. In this chastened naturalism we may recognise an ancient French tradition, transmitted by Millet and by Puvis de Chavannes; the classical intellect of the Frenchman will only absorb so much of fact as it can assimilate without loss of lucidity. A system, even if limited, is more satisfactory to it than a mass of ill-organ-

FIG. 901.—CLAUDE MONET. LA GARE SAINT-LAZARE.
(The Luxembourg, Paris.)

ised truths. The spirit of system dwells in art and science. Searching for truth and beauty it only submits to facts in order to dominate them.

Of the pictorial manners we have now passed in review, none can be said to have become absolutely out-of-date; the representatives of these various styles appear side by side in the annual Salons.

FIG. 902.—SISLEY. SNOW EFFECT.
(Durand-Ruel Collection.)

Thus the difficulty of defining the contemporary school is not only due to the fact that we, who are living among the individuals, cannot readily discern groups. The word School has no longer its old significance. It meant formerly families of painters, related by a common ideal and similar methods, just as the State implied uniformity of religious and political sentiments. Individualism, which has shattered this uniformity, has destroyed both State and School in the early sense. The solidarity which now unites the men of a group and the artists of a school is of a different kind. None of the successive kinds of beauty have disappeared from the city of the arts, and all the parties which in turn held sway are still represented. A general toleration weakens the rivalry of these former enemies; there is no longer either victor or vanquished. The complexity of society corresponds to that of styles; there are admirers for all. The unity of the French School, if it exists, is not to be found in community of character; the eclecticism of taste, and the violent competition which emphasises

FIG. 903.—SISLEY. BANKS OF A RIVER.
(The Luxembourg, Paris.)

433

FIG. 904.—RENOIR. THE DÉJEUNER.
(Durand-Ruel Collection.)

originality, disperse talents and oppose them, instead of making them converge to a common ideal.

But among all these different forms of art, there is a kind of solidarity born of contrast and a division of artistic labour. The realism of a Thierry Bouts and the idealism of a Memling, the realism of a Filippo Lippi and the idealism of a Fra Angelico, were distinguished only by very subtle gradations. Individual deviations did not divert Flemish or Florentine painting from its general tendency. But what a gulf lies between the brutal naturalism of a Courbet and the world of Puvis de Chavannes' dreams! They separate with equal decisiveness to the two sides of the common way. The art of a period responds to a constant demand; extreme characteristics cannot develop without exciting antitheses. If there were only one style, it could not be that of Degas, nor even that of Millet, of Puvis or of Rodin. Monet's fairyland made Carrière's colourless nocturnes acceptable; the extraordinary dexterity of some artists makes us turn with pleasure to the ingenuous awkwardness of others; the sculpture that suggests moulded forms prepares us to acclaim Rodin's expressive violence. We find scattered among violently contrasting works those dissimilar qualities which the men of the past liked to find united in the same work. The energies of art no longer develop in compact fasces; they ramify in a thou-

FIG. 905.—DEGAS. THE DANCER.
(The Luxembourg, Paris.)

sand divergent branches; but the organism would not be properly balanced if they did not spread about the parent trunk with a certain symmetry. This is no longer the regularity of the French park, but the denser growth of the forest, where each shoot struggles towards the light.

In this confused struggle, two forces are opposed, and the balance is obtained by this opposition of the regulating force

FIG. 906.—BESNARD.   THE EVENING OF LIFE.
(Mairie du 1er arrondissement, Paris.)

of resistance, and the force of movement.   The conservative element is represented more especially by those who fear above all things the sacrifice of traditional virtues, the patrimony of the School; technical perfection, elegance, all the qualities acquired by the work of generations, and transmitted by teaching.   The innovators, or at least the bolder spirits among these, have no respect for this venerable heritage.   They speak boldly the artistic language they have themselves created.   But nothing shows the necessity of a strong tradition more clearly than an over aggressive individualism. The conservative break is no less salutary than the revolutionary impulse; art would stagnate or go astray if it lacked one or the other.   The true innovator is he who, bearing all the weight of tradition, yet has the courage to lead the way.

In sculpture, tradition has more power against individualism; the naturalistic tendency showed itself here in the second half of the nineteenth century; but sculpture

FIG. 907.—BESNARD.   THE FORTUNATE ISLAND.
(Musée des Arts décoratifs, Paris.)

evolves slowly. The language of stone and bronze is less docile than that of colour. Material conditions never vary and tradition imposes itself here with clearer authority. Painting had achieved and abandoned several aspects of " integral realism," while sculpture was still making the same effort to bring modelling into closer contact with the forms of life, and adapt it to the movements of passion.

Towards the middle of the century, sculpture had recovered from the Romantic emotion. Jehan du Seigneur and Préault had not succeeded in subduing their material. Rude, indeed, had convulsed his figures with modern passion, but for the most part he had preserved the attitudes of antique heroism. Barye alone had adopted freer methods, because he had modelled the muscles of the larger wild beasts. But from Cortot to Pradier, and from Pradier to Guillaume, sculpture had retained the Graeco-Roman rounded modelling and proportions. Eugène Guillaume's figures (1822-1905) seem to demonstrate that living forms are merely those of a somewhat imperfect geometry; he reduced the most irregular forms to simple planes, and deduced a generalised model from the living model. He cast beautiful Roman types in bronze and liked to carve in marble curling beards and the pliant folds of the toga. His works, which are marked by a pure and somewhat cold distinction, are those of a pupil of the ancients. But his intelligence was

FIG. 910.—HENRI MARTIN. THE MOWERS.
(Capitole of Toulouse.) (*Photo. Crevaux.*)

mainly critical; he drew taste, elegance and correctness from the antique sources, but not the secret of vitality.

Meanwhile, Florentine influence intervened to modify that of the ancients. Many French artists stopped at Florence on their way to Rome, and there discovered the sculpture of the fifteenth century. Before these dry and nervous works they found out that there was a good deal of insipidity in Græco-Roman facility. The deeply artistic realism of Ghiberti, Donatello and Verrocchio inspired a whole generation of French artists very happily. We see appear figures of bronze with slender outlines, with pointed extremities; after the soft contours of the Venuses here is the incisive delicacy and the slenderness of the Florentine Davids and St. Johns; after the heroic muscularity, the leanness of the adolescent; after the broad

FIG. 911.—HENRI MARTIN. THE OLD SHEPHERD.
(Sorbonne.) (*Photo. Crevaux.*)

FIG. 912.—COTTET. LOW MASS
IN BRITTANY.
(Petit-Palais, Paris.)

modelling of the nude, the meticulous chiselling of details. Falguière, Frémiet, Paul Dubois, Eugène Barrias, Gérôme and Antonin Mercié, resuscitated this style in their respective manners. This Florentine influence was more propitious to sculptors than to painters; the works of the fifteenth century really lent new expression to statuary, whereas imitation of the Pre-Raphaelites failed to give birth to a visible school of painting. Michelangelo's athletic forms and daring attitudes also inspired a number of lively and expressive works. Carpeaux sometimes recalls the great Florentine, and Paul Dubois has placed four bronze figures at the angles of General Lamoricière's tomb in Nantes Cathedral (Fig. 916) grave and meditative as those of the Medici Chapel. René de Saint-Marceaux, again, has more than once translated the proud beauty and the vigour of the Sistine nudities into marble.

Florence also played a part in the work of those admirable artists, Chaplain and Roty, who gave so much prestige to the art of the medallist. Florentine carving showed them how to put the nerve of life into the metal lines. Chaplain has struck some energetic effigies in which the solid relief of great sculpture is enclosed in contours as pure as those of a drawing by Ingres (Fig. 918). In Roty's medals, the delicate refinement of the forms gives his allegories a charm of youth and a freshness hardly to be

FIG. 913.—R. MÉNARD. THE LAKE.
(The Luxembourg, Paris.)

looked for in these little metal pictures (Fig. 920). The Florentine style, which combined so learnedly the sense of life and the refinement of art, helps in this way our own sculpture to free itself from majestic banality and lifeless nobility.

The images of contemporary life, no less than the example of the past, have given sculptors

the courage to innovate. The same generation witnessed the appearance of naturalism among sculptors and among painters. While Courbet's aggressive art was raising an uproar, Carpeaux (1827-1875) was throwing the ardour of his temperament into living forms. The world in which he lived chastened his impetuosity without sapping his vigour. The lively and sensual society of the Second Empire, the haughty elegance of princesses, and the charm of opera-dancers were portrayed by this robust kneader of clay. Even to his mythological figures he gave a carnal life, and not the generalised and somewhat abstract modelling of classical sculpture. His *Ugolino* makes us think of Michelangelo's tormented giants, and his laughing nymphs of Clodion's plump female fauns. His impressions are preserved still warm in the bronze or in the stone because he limited himself to interpreting physical sensations, the shiver of pleasure, the fire of a look, gay laughter or the muscular excitement of the dance. His *Four Quarters of the World* are agile dancers. His true Muse was Terpsichore, or rather the fair women he saw waltzing

FIG. 916.—P. DUBOIS.   TOMB OF LAMORICIÈRE.
(Cathedral of Nantes.)

in the ball-rooms of the Tuileries (Figs. 921–924, 927).

Carpeaux redis-covered the warmth and movement of life; his work contains a lesson that was quickly under-stood. A Flemish sap runs through the crea-tions of this Valenciennes sculptor. That of his successors seems to have been set in motion by the vivacity of Toulouse. Falguière spoke at first in the sharp and nervous language of the Florentines. But he gradually revealed his predilection for the robust feminine nudities to which his chisel gave even the quivering life of the epidermis. His models, short-nosed with low foreheads, firm breasts and active limbs, lend their robust vitality and their physical joyousness to the haughty figures of Juno or the huntress Diana (Figs. 931, 933). Antonin Mercié's talent has great flexibility, whether he exercises it on intelligence, on melan-choly, or on tenderness (Figs. 925, 932). Injalbert is carried away by an impetuosity akin to that of Rubens; more than one Southern sculptor has indeed translated the brilliant touch and even something of the colour of the Flemish master into stone. None of these sacrificed classic purity of form; but all gave breath and life to their material.

If French sculpture is making its way towards new develop-ments, this is due in great part to the initiative of Dalou (1838–1902). His work is a résumé of an important evolution of French sculpture. He began as an elegant decorator in the Ren-aissance style dear to the Second Empire. But a powerful vitality was seething in him; he threw

FIG. 917.—GÉRÔME.   BONAPARTE.
(The Luxembourg, Paris.)

aside the affected subtleties of the style, and his impetuous vigour occasionally betrayed him into vulgarity. He had something of Rude's afflatus; but since Rude, marble had borrowed the warmth and softness of flesh, and Dalou's modelling no longer shows the muscular system of antique heroes with its clearly defined planes, but the swelling outline and agitated contours of Rubens' figures. Dalou was further one of the artists who did most to win plastic expression from

FIG. 918.—CHAPLAIN.
MEDAL OF V. HUGO.
(*Photo. Giraudon.*)

modern costume. He never finished the monument to workmen which he contemplated; but his numerous preparations for it were not in vain.

Since the Renaissance, sculptors had seen in the human body a magnificent but useless machine; the ideal divinities take elegant attitudes; they sometimes make use of passionate gestures to show their strength or flexibility; but they never make any effort with an instrument or a tool. Millet showed how moving and majestic the gesture of the sower, the reaper and the water-carrier, or the bending attitude of the gleaner may be. After the painter, the sculptor discovered

FIG. 919.—DANIEL-DUPUIS.
THE SPRING.

in his turn that there is nothing more logical, better balanced and consequently more harmonious than a navvy wielding his pick or a blacksmith at the forge. Dalou was one of those who taught young sculptors the expressive beauty of a body straining every nerve in some useful effort. Young artists such as Henry Bouchard and Roger Bloche show every day how much vigour and emotional charm

FIG. 920.—ROTY.
MARRIAGE.

441

FIG. 921.—CARPEAUX.
MARQUIS DE LA BORDE.
(The Louvre, Paris.)

may be expressed by sculpture which deals with the man of the factory and the man of the fields (Figs. 938, 939).

In the last quarter of the nineteenth century, the language of sculpture has gained considerably in richness and flexibility. The innovators have sometimes disconcerted the public by their audacities; but many of these have gradually compelled acceptance. The most original and powerful of these sculptors was Rodin; many young artists have taken him for their guide, and his work is characteristic of the latest evolution of French sculpture. He practises a kind of plastic poetry, which sometimes offends our conception of objective forms. The colouristic fantasies of the Impressionists were perhaps less amazing, because they were not out of harmony with the caprices of light. But in sculpture, even more than in painting, it is difficult for us to lay aside the sense of objective truth. Now Rodin very often makes his modelling subserve the will of his genius audaciously enough; he is no more a realist than was Delacroix; he has proved himself a perfect master of anatomical science, but this science is not his guide; he adapts the forms of life to his conceptions, and sacrifices what we call elegance or correctness without scruple. The planes which he carves, the lines he accentuates, cannot be seen in a photograph or in a cast. Often he leaves his forms unfinished, hardly disengaged from the marble, because they suffice for the expression of his idea in this incomplete state. Well defined contours would emphasize

FIG. 922.—CARPEAUX. DANCE.
(Façade of the Opera House, Paris.)

the individualities without adding to the latent force which one divines beneath the swellings and depressions of the marble. Michelangelo's giants contain as much fiery energy as Rodin's figures, but they never lose their supreme elegance. Their gestures show the languor of lassitude or the tension of effort. Rodin's figures overstep these limits. It is because they express the paroxysms of human passion, from delight to torture, that they seem unable to control the twitching of their rebellious muscles. The rugged, contorted, interlaced masses,

which he twists and bends at will, suggest wills and sufferings stronger than themselves. It is not absurd thus to submerge human personality in a world of forms and lines which exceeds it; the physical and moral harmony of an individual may be overwhelmed by the stress of passion. The bronze limbs of the "Citizens of Calais" seem rude and inert; their hands hang heavy as paving-stones at

FIG. 924.—CARPEAUX. UGOLINO.
(The Louvre, Paris.)

the end of over-long arms; the feet that press the ground seem almost incapable of movement; and the "Thinker," a giant rugged as a menhir, concentrates all his troglodyte strength and contracts his mighty muscles over some poor glimmer of thought. On the other hand, the marble becomes mellow, warm and fluid, to render the tenderness of an embrace, and suggest a lingering and caressing contact (Figs. 935–937).

This art, which realised ambitions dear to the Romanticists, is frankly hostile to the ideals of classical sculpture. All the post-Renaissance sculptors, even the most daring, such as

443

FIG. 925.—A. MERCIÉ.
DAVID.
(The Luxembourg, Paris.)

Michelangelo and Puget, were governed by ideas of beauty and correctness. If Rodin has ancestors, we must look for them in the fourteenth and fifteenth centuries, at the time when Gothic idealism had died out and classic idealism was not yet born. It was then that vigorous artists like Claus Sluter and Donatello let loose the indomitable violence of their genius in rugged figures. The danger in an art so unfettered by any restraints is that it may not always be intelligible. In the artistic as in the social order, even the most gifted individuals must accept a little of the common discipline. The artist does violence to the language of form when he forces it to express a certain character, even at the price of incorrectness. The sculptor who proposes to make his modelling dramatic or tender in itself runs the risk of being misunderstood, like the writer who sets out to make music with words. There is no inevitable harmony between the means and the end. If the thought is inadequate, the work remains amorphous; and we see only an inert mass of material. Such an art is inexorable to the lapses of genius; if his inspiration falters, the artist has neither the resources of realism nor the rules of taste which govern normal sculpture to support him. Rodin's poetry becomes intolerable in some of his disciples; it is only the artist of genius who can set aside the rules of science and of traditional correctness with impunity; average mortals must respect syntax, or their speech becomes delirium.

Art such as Rodin's is so well attuned to modern individualism that it has naturally had a strong influence on the young generation of artists. There is now a style in sculpture which deliberately preserves all the evidences of impatience, awkwardness, and nervousness in execution. The modeller in clay has added his style to that of the worker in metal or

FIG. 926.—DUBOIS.
THE FLORENTINE SINGER.
(The Luxembourg, Paris.)

444

marble. The bronze is allowed to fix, and occasionally to give, a brutal emphasis to the fortuitous prints of thumb or trowel. Contemporary sculpture tends more and more to lose the smooth elegance and quiet amenity of the earlier art. In the work of several sculptors of original talent, Pierre Roche, Bareau, Bouchard, Landowski, Ségoffin, and Roger Bloche, we see that this attempt to render the aspect and

FIG. 927.—CARPEAUX. MODEL FOR THE GROUP OF FLORA.

emotions of modern man has by no means failed; we discern sensibility and passion in many somewhat unattractive groups. Some clever pupils of this school have attempted a compromise between elegant correctness and insistence on expressive contours. This Impressionism of sculpture, like that of painting, has transformed the technique even of those who least approve it.

In spite of its fertility, modern sculpture shows a certain indecision of vocation. What becomes of the population of statues which appears annually at our exhibitions? Some go into our museums; but even though the museums are among the most living institutions of our civilization we may ask if statuary might not play a more useful part, and one more closely related to the social order? Those who cite the wealth of sculpture which adorns the porches of our Gothic cathedrals wish that sculptors would collaborate more closely with architects, and apply themselves more especially to decoration. But

FIG. 928.—FRÉMIET. ORANG-OUTANG AND SAVAGE IN BORNEO.

they have now been practising an independent and expressive art too long to be able to accept architecture as their *raison d'être*. The best of modern sculptors, Puget and Carpeaux, decorated classical façades with very undisciplined figures. Our modern statuary will continue to be scattered along the avenues and to penetrate into our houses under the diminutive form of bric-a-brac.

Commemorative monuments are now the principal resource of sculptors. Since sculpture has provided public images for that religion of hero-worship, glorious memories, and abstract principles which has replaced popular saints and the mythology of the Humanists, statuary has recovered a certain social utility which it lacked at the end of the eighteenth century. These stone documents record the faith of France in the nineteenth century, and the forms of her ideal. The art of David d'Angers dealt with celebrities approved by the verdict of centuries, but now innumerable statues glorify names which have not undergone the test of time. Sculptors show their ingenuity by variations of arrangement, combining the portrait of the great man and allegories of his virtues more or less happily. But art cannot give a soul when the memorial is the expression of an impossible worship. A public monument ought to give utterance to a really national idea; its beauty demands the admiration of the crowd; if it lacks this sympathetic atmosphere, it is merely a museum exhibit which looks out of place in the open air.

On the other hand, when a modern work has been the translation of a grand and moving idea, it has rarely been mediocre. After 1871, certain figures expressed heroic fury or despairing pertinacity. Bartholdi's *Roaring Lion*,

FIG. 930.—FRÉMIET.
JEANNE D'ARC.
(Place des Pyramides, Paris.)

446

Chapu's *Youth* presenting the palm of the hero to Henri Regnault, Antonin Mercié's *Gloria Victis* and other works offered their pride and grace as a salve to national pride. Happy the sculptor who can thus fix the emotion of a whole people in a beautiful form! Even the somewhat trivial charm of Pradier's statue in the Place de la Concorde has taken on a sort of mournful beauty. Several sculptors have been happily inspired by Jeanne d'Arc, because a great wealth of sentiment is inherent in such a figure. Chapu's Jeanne is a humble peasant girl ennobled by her communion with the supernatural. Paul Dubois', with sword uplifted and eyes fixed on a celestial vision, urges her horse against the enemy. Frémiet's grasps her oriflamme, graceful and triumphant as a Saint George (Fig. 930).

FIG. 931.—FALGUIÈRE. SAINT VINCENT DE PAUL.
(Panthéon, Paris.)

There is no danger of lack of ideas for expression in a country where the general consciousness is vibrating with life, full of memories, ready to feel in common. It is the duty of sculpture to catch and fix these profound struggles of the human or national soul. Sculpture can best give visible form to these great feelings. They appear more definite when the genius of an artist has given them body. The gods of paganism and the saints of the Middle Ages are for this reason to a great extent the creation of art. In modern thought there is an entire confused religion, from which sculpture can sometimes disentangle the divinities.

Among the many modern works in which individual emotion is expressed, there are also certain monuments which bring us into communion with the collective soul of France. Sculpture has not

FIG. 932.—MERCIÉ
REMEMBRANCE.
(The Luxembourg, Paris.)

447

FIG. 933.—FALGUIÈRE.
DIANA DRAWING HER BOW.

failed to fill its part. Dalou and Bartholomé will have left records as moving and sincere as Rude's *Marseillaise*, the divinities of Versailles, or the saints of the thirteenth century.

In 1900, Dalou completed his *Monument of the Republic*, in the Place de la Nation, in Paris. Sculpture, which once gave human shape to the gods, and then deified royalty, has made several attempts to glorify Democracy. In 1793 and 1848, it figured as a cold Minerva, and that abstract allegory was not less suitable to the style of our artists than to the austerity of those Spartan republics. Dalou created a popular type of vigorous beauty, the Phrygian cap on her head, and a coarse robe veiling her muscular limbs, akin to her who sings the Marseillaise in Rude's group, and climbs upon the barricade in Delacroix's picture. Now she is calm and triumphant, and with her hand she makes a conciliatory gesture. The procession advances slowly, pushing the car, a huge mass round which the sculptor has grouped majestic beasts, plump children, women of the people who are types of Fecundity, workmen of Herculean vigour, a tumultuous force, disciplined by an irresistible progression. Hideous alligators distorted by rage were to have hurled water on the triumphal cortège; Gardet replaced them by less aggressive animals. All this movement, splendour, and colour recalls Rubens and also the sumptuous style used by Le Brun to glorify Louis XIV. Dalou, the sincere democrat, has reverted to monarchical allegory for the apotheosis of the Republic (Fig. 941). These modern sentiments are at home in the traditional and classical forms; that descendant of the Faubourg of the Barricades would not be out of place in the avenues of Versailles.

FIG. 934.—DALOU. MONUMENT
TO DELACROIX.
(Luxembourg Gardens, Paris.)

NATURALISM

Bartholomé's *Monument to the Dead* has lately proved that sculpture has not ceased to be the eloquent language of deep emotion. The imperishable stone is a fit material for the eternal theme of Death. The sculptor has grouped his figures on the façade of an Egyptian tomb. On each side, figures which are so many types of human lamentation, drag themselves towards the door of the hypogea. Old men

FIG. 935.—RODIN. MONUMENT TO THE SIX CITIZENS, CALAIS.

with twisted limbs come staggering, young bodies writhe and rebel, drag themselves with a sort of feverish languor, some wild with terror hide their eyes. But a sudden, strange courage takes hold of these dying ones as they reach the threshold and it is with a gentle serenity that they glide into the night. In the tomb below lie a man and woman, guarded by a genius with outstretched arms. What is the function of this genius of immortality ? The sculptor does not show us these corpses rising from the grave. They will

FIG. 936.—RODIN. BUST OF A WOMAN.

(The Luxembourg, Paris.)

not wake again; the work does not presage the resurrection. The Last Judgments of the Middle Ages showed a new life coming out of death. The dead bodies of the fifteenth century, the skeletons of Gothic charnel houses evoked only contempt for the life of the body and no one misunderstood the idea of those figures. There is nothing of that kind here. The living creatures carved by Bartholomé at the threshold of the tomb lament, because they cannot consent to the universal law stoically, and because they have not the confidence given by faith.

FIG. 937.—RODIN. THE KISS.
(The Luxembourg, Paris.)

These are poor humans attached to life and whom nothing consoles for death. The consoling hope of a thirteenth-century believer finds no place here, and the artist has not ventured to give an image of the resurrection. We are conscious of that same indecision which weighs upon venerable ceremonies, the old rites of which have been corrected by the philosophical spirit, that emptiness which rationalism has created in a sensibility that has remained religious. How is it that a monument which concentrates so much despair under an indifferent heaven does not disgust us with life? It is because the artist has modelled his weeping figures with a kind of caressing gentleness. A young girl turns to kiss her hand in farewell, and the sadness of her fate is irradiated as it were by the incomparable grace of her gesture. The prestige of art takes the place of the absent consolation. The tender sorrow of Christianity breathes from these figures of pagan beauty and the very simplicity of the sculpture recalls the beautiful Gothic technique.

The men of to-day like to commingle in this way sorrow and death with the profound joy of beauty. Since Chateaubriand, our century has liked these transpositions of noble sentiments and hidden its lack of faith under the magnificence of art. A wonderful monument, it is as direct as the work of a primitive and yet quivering with modern sensuousness. It oversteps our epoch and speaks to humanity. The power of its emotion will grow in measure as the centuries meet before it in the communion of the suffering of all generations.

How should we fittingly conclude a book which follows history to the present day, and to which every successive year will add its page? Let us end it before

FIG. 938.—ROGER BLOCHE.
COLD.
(The Luxembourg, Paris.)

450

these works which combine a lofty idea, great talents, and a significance far-reaching enough to unite the France of to-day with that of the past, works which illustrate the continuity of French art, showing how it reconciles forms of government and effaces, not only revolutions, but even the vicissitudes of religious belief.

Each French style has been a reflection of French institutions, and French art remains a faithful chronicle of French history. The varied and delightful aspects of the country appear in the buildings of its cities, the old stones of its soil, and the relics in the museums. If we visit its ancient towns, we shall find great local variations; some will always remain Gothic, because they reached their apogee in the Middle Ages; others are still irradiated by the smile of the Renaissance; others again still bear the impress of Roman majesty. But the same history may

FIG. 939.—DALOU.
PEASANT.
(The Luxembourg, Paris.)

be read in every city. In the majority of these, the nineteenth century placed Doric peristyles on the town halls and translated administrative centralisation by a uniform classicism. The eighteenth century is to be recognised by the brilliant elegance with which it adorned French reason, like the graceful episcopal palaces which are found nestling in the shadow of old cathedrals. The seventeenth century was not entirely absorbed by Versailles; we come now and again upon austere mansions of the time of Louis XIV, which seem to embody the somewhat morose loyalty of old parliamentarians. The joyousness of the Renaissance is revealed in its exuberant and spontaneous architecture, its stone fantasies, its gay turrets and sunny gardens. But the eye always returns to the Gothic cathedral, buttressed by the houses that cluster round its feet that it may raise its vault the higher and point heavenwards with its spire, an evidence

FIG. 940.—TH. RIVIÈRE.
PHRYNE. (SÈVRES CHINA.
(Arts décoratifs.)

FIG. 941.—DALOU. THE TRIUMPH
OF THE REPUBLIC.
(Place de la Nation, Paris.)

of what French or human genius can do when, in the shelter of a firmly constituted society, all its efforts are concentrated in a common purpose. As distance makes the ages more obscure, their monuments emerge more clearly: feudal fortresses, once impregnable on their rocks, then shattered by the royal cannon, and gradually dispersed in the neighbouring villages, which used its stones to build their houses; forsaken monasteries, where the little flame the monks kept alive with pious hands after the twilight of the antique world has died out slowly in the strong light of modern day; Roman ruins, with their imperishable masonry, where men sometimes sought shelter during the tempests of barbarism, relics the imperial majesty of which has dominated national history. Rome indeed still persists in our encumbered civilisation. Often the modern engineer, as he turns over the soil, brings to light a carved altar or some mutilated head of a Gaul shaved in the Roman fashion. These old stones go to the local museum to join the pictures Paris sends annually to the provinces. Thus we may traverse some twenty centuries in the quiet streets of a French country town; twenty centuries of fine culture and active civilisation, of life during which a society has been made and remade continuously, and has decked its changing manifestations with new forms of beauty.

NATURALISM

FIG. 942.—BARTHOLOMÉ. MONUMENT TO THE DEAD.
(Cemetery of Pére-Lachaise, Paris.)

BIBLIOGRAPHY

Baron Haussmann, *Mémoires du Baron Haussmann*, Paris, 1890–1893, 3 vols.; the third volume deals with the great works carried out in Paris.—Felix Narjoux, *Monuments élevés par la Ville*, 1850–1880, Paris, 1881–1882, 5 vols.—Th. Ballu, *Monographie de l'Église de la Sainte-Trinité*, Paris, 1868; *Monographie de l'Église Saint-Ambroise*, Paris, 1874.—Ch. Garnier, *Le Nouvel Opéra de Paris*, Paris, 1880, 2 vols. of illustrations.—C. Sédille, *Charles Garnier* (*G. B. A.*, 1898, II).—L. Magne, *L'Architecture française du Siècle*, Paris, 1889.—H. Fiérens-Gevaert, *Nouveaux Essais sur l'Art contemporain*, Paris, 1903.—A. de Baudot, *L'Architecture et le Ciment armé*, Paris, 1905.—De Laborde, *Rapport...sur l'Exposition Universelle de Londres en 1852*.—Lucien Lambeau, *L'Hôtel de Ville de Paris*, Paris, 1909.—A. Alphand, *Les Promenades de Paris*, Paris, n.d.—L. Riotor, *Carpeaux*, Paris, n.d.—M. Dreyfous, *Dalou*, Paris, 1903.—L. Bénédite, *Al. Falguière*, Paris, 1902.—F. Mazerolle, *Catalogue des Médailleurs; Gazette numismatique française*, 1897–1904.—E. Babelon, *J.-C. Chaplain et l'Art de la Médaille au XIXᵉ siècle* (*R. A. A. M.*, 1909, II).—E. Rod, *Rodin* (*G. B. A.*, 1898, I).—F. Lawton, *The Life and Work of Auguste Rodin*, New York, 1906.—Judith Cladel, *Auguste Rodin, l'Œuvre et l'Homme*, Paris, 1908.—Castagnary, *Salons*, 2 vols., 1892.—G. Riat, *Courbet*, Paris, 1906.—Sensier, *La Vie et l'Œuvre de Fr. Millet*, Paris.—D. C. Thomson, *Millet and the Barbizon School*, London, 1903.—W. Gensel, *Millet und Rousseau*, Bielefeld, 1902.—H. Marcel, *Millet*, Paris, 1903.—R. Rolland, *Millet*, London, 1903.—P. Desjardins, *En mémoire de J.-C. Cazin* (*G. B. A.*, 1901, II).—G. Lafenestre, *La Peinture française du XIXᵉ siècle*, Paris, 1898.—On the representatives of classical tradition: Baudry, Cabanel, Delaunay, Hébert.—C. Mauclair, *The great French Painters, 1830 to the present Day*, London, 1903.—O. Gréard, *Meissonier*, Paris, 1897.—M. Vachon, *Detaille*, Paris, 1896.—L. Gonse, *E. Fromentin*, Paris, 1881.—A. Renan, *La Peinture orientaliste* (*G. B. A.*, 1894, I).—G. Larroumet, *H. Regnault*, Paris, 1890.—Ch. Ephrussi, *P. Baudry*, Paris, 1887.—Ary Renan, *Gustave Moreau* (*G. B. A.*, 1886, I).—L. Bénédite, *Gustave Moreau et Burne Jones* (*R. A. A. M.*, 1899, I).—M. Vachon, *Puvis de Chavannes*, Paris, 1896.—L. de Fourcaud, *Jules Bastien-Lepage* (*G. B. A.*, 1885, I).—Jacques Blanche, *Fantin-Latour* (*Revue de Paris*, 1906).—Lorquet, *La Peinture française contemporaine*,

453

ART IN FRANCE

Paris, 1900.—G. Geffroy, *La Vie Artistique*, Paris, 6 vols.—Th. Duret, *Manet et son œuvre*, Paris, 1902.—G. Lecomte, *L'Art impressionniste*, Paris, 1892.—A. Mellerio, *L'Exposition de 1900 et l'Impressionnisme*, Paris, 1900.—P. Signac, *D'Eugène Delacroix au Néo impressionnisme*, Paris, 1900. — C. Mauclair, *L'Impressionnisme*, Paris, 1903. — H. von Tschudi, *Ed. Manet*, Berlin, 1902.—J. Meier-Graefe, *Manet und sein Kreis*, Berlin, 1903.—G. Séailles, *Manet (Revue de Paris,* 1910).—J. Meier-Graefe, *Der Moderne Impressionismus*, Berlin, 1903.—R. de la Sizeranne, *Questions esthétiques*, 1904.—Paul Mantz, *La Caricature moderne* (*G. B. A.,* 1888, I).—G. Lecomte, *Albert Besnard* (*G. B. A.,* 1905, I).—G. Séailles, *Eug. Carrière*, Paris, 1901.—G. Geffroy, *L'Œuvre de Carrière*, Paris, 1902.—For the Cézanne-Gauguin group, cf. the articles on the *Salon d'Automne* in the *G. B. A.*, and by Charles Morice in the *Mercure de France.*—On the "modern style," cf. the reviews: *Art et Décoration, l'Art décoratif, The Studio,* and R. Marx, *Les Arts à l'Exposition de* 1900, *La Décoration et les Industries d'Art* (*G. B. A.,* 1900–1901).—L. de Fourcaud, *E. Gallé, R. A. A. M.,* 1902, I.

FIG. 943.—GARDET. MICE AND SNAIL.
(SÈVRES CHINA.)

INDEX

References to Illustrations are indicated by an *. Buildings and public places are entered under the heading of the towns in which they exist.

456

INDEX

458

INDEX

INDEX

INDEX

461

INDEX

462

INDEX

INDEX

466

INDEX

INDEX

COLOURED PLATES